U0624638

A Brief Introduction to American Literature

美国文学

（修订版）

主　编　左金梅
副主编　（按姓氏笔画排序）
乔国强　李旭奎
张德玉　赵德玉

中国海洋大学出版社
·青岛·

图书在版编目(CIP)数据

美国文学/左金梅主编. —修订版. —青岛:中国海洋大学出版社,2006.8
ISBN978－7－81067－832－2　　(2022.1重印)
Ⅰ.美…　Ⅱ.左…　Ⅲ.①英语－高等学校－教学参考资料②文学史－美国－英文　Ⅳ.①H31②I712.09

中国版本图书馆CIP数据核字(2006)第048664号

美国文学(修订版)
左金梅　**主编**

出版发行　中国海洋大学出版社
社　　址　青岛市香港东路23号　　**邮政编码**　266071
网　　址　http://pub.ouc.edu.cn
订购电话　0532－82032573　82032644(传真)
责任编辑　李夕聪　邵成军　　**电　　话**　0532－82032122
电子信箱　xicongli@yahoo.com.cn
印　　制　日照报业印刷有限公司
版　　次　2006年8月第1版
印　　次　2022年1月第7次印刷
开　　本　850 mm×1 168 mm　1/32
印　　张　14.375
字　　数　420千字
定　　价　42.00元

版权所有　　侵权必究

前　言

《美国文学》(修订版)是以2000年出版的《美国文学》为基础，根据作者这些年在美国文学教学中的实践经验和同行专家的一些建议，就美国文学的当代部分补充了大量的新内容，以适应学生的需要。

本书分五部分：殖民地时期、美国革命时期、浪漫主义时期、现实主义时期及现代主义时期。19世纪以前的美国文学只是一些信息的报道和宗教的或政治的宣传，算不上真正意义上的文学，19世纪和20世纪才是美国文学作为独立的民族文学形成和发展的鼎盛阶段。所以，本书简略介绍了前两个时期的文学，用较大篇幅论述了后三个时期的文学。每个时期分为历史背景、文学和流派特点、作者简介及重要作品的文体风格和主题思想、重点选文等若干章节，选文后附有注释和思考题。

在编写本书过程中，力求达到：章节条理、层次分明、文字通俗易懂，重点突出，以便于读者在较短的时间内掌握有关的知识。

《美国文学》与本人主编的《西方文学》、《英国文学》和《当代西方文论》已成为有关西方文学方面的比较完整的系列教材，在我校英语专业已使用过数届，并被指定为我校英语专业外国语言学和英语语言文学研究生入学考试的参考书，也有其他兄弟院校开始陆续使用。书中若有疏误之处，敬请有关同行和广大读者批评指正。

左金梅

2006年6月6日

Contents

Part One Colonial America

Chapter Ⅰ American Puritanism

1. The New World

America was isolated from the other continents until Christopher Columbus discovered it in 1492. The discovery stimulated the Europeans into this fascinating and strange continent in rapid succession. These Europeans—the Spanish, the Dutch, the Swedes, the French, and the English—pushed the aboriginal inhabitants (American Indians) westward and established their own colonies respectively. Thus arose the New World.

2. Puritan Fathers

The English made their first successful settlement at Jamestown, Virginia in 1607, and then other English colonies emerged one after another, especially after the arrival of the "Mayflower" in Plymouth in 1620. The early British settlers were quite a few of them Puritans. Puritans were members of the Church of England , who had been dismayed by Elizabeth's compromise church of 1563 (a mixture of Catholic structure and Protestant doctrine), sought the complete removal of all church rituals that had overtones of Catholicism, aimed at reforms in its doctrines and great strictness in religious disciplines, and thus were directed against by state persecution. To avoid the religious persecution, some of them managed to escape to the New World and became known as Puritan Fathers or Pilgrim Fathers of the American nation.

3. *The Puritan Principles*

The principles and practices of puritans were popularly known as puritanism. Puritanism accepted the doctrines of Calvinism: the sovereignty of God, the supreme authority of the Bible, and the irresistibility of God's will for man in every act of his life from cradle to grave. These doctrines led the Puritans to examine their souls to find whether they were of the elect and to search the Bible to determine God's will. Thus piety, austerity of taste, diligence, thrift and introspection were common puritan traits.

4. *Characteristics of American Puritans*

On the one hand, the American Puritans, like their brothers back in England, were religious idealists who came to the wildness of this new land with the belief that they would restore the church to the purity of the first century church as established by Jesus Christ himself and the hope that they would build a new Garden of Eden in America enjoying God's blessings. On the other hand, the American Puritans became more practical, that is, they became more and more preoccupied with business and profits, as they had to be, for when they arrived in the wild land they had to struggle for survival. The very severity of the frontier conditions taught them to be tougher, to be ever ready for any misfortune and tragic failures that might lie in wait for them. On the whole, in Perry Misler's words, the American Puritan was "a doctrinaire and an opportunist".

5. *The Puritan Heritage*

Early Puritanism has had continuous strong influence upon American thought and culture. Martins Day has summarized some of the most important elements of this puritan legacy as follows: ① rigid sense of morality; ② emphasis upon material success; ③ self-reliance; ④ feeling for democracy; ⑤ enthusiasm for education; ⑥ fervor for social reform; ⑦ conflict of conscience arising from an awareness that material success is not adequate as a major goal in life.

With regard to American literature, puritanism exerted its influence in three ways. ① Early Puritans dreamed of building a new Garden of Eden in America, (a perfect land) where they would live a free life. Fired with such a sense of mission, the Puritans looked even the worst of life in the face with a tremendous amount of optimism. Thus optimism characterised early American literature. ② The American Puritans tended to observe things in a metaphorical mode. To them the physical, phenomenal world was nothing but a symbol of God and physical life was simultaneously spiritual. Such a perception left symbolism as one chief feature of American literature. ③ As far as technique is concerned, the puritan style of writing is characterised by simplicity, which left an indelible imprint on American writing.

Chapter Ⅱ The Colonial Literature

1. Characteristics of the Colonial Literature

American literature grew out of humble origins. There were no literal works in a real sense in the early colonial period. The early myths were personal literature in the forms of diaries, travel books, letters, journals, sermons, histories and prose. In content, they wrote about the voyage to the new land, about adapting themselves to unfamiliar climates and crops, about dealing with Indians, and especially about religion. In form, English literary traditions were imitated. The first American writer was Captain John Smith whose reports of exploration and settlement have been described as the first American literature written in English.

2. William Bradford (1590—1657)

William Bradford was one of the Puritan Fathers who came to America in 1620 and then the first governor of Plymouth. He has left us a priceless gift: *The History of Plymouth Plantation*. Bradford started the book of history in 1630, ten years after the Mayflower voyage. He covered the experiences of the small group of Puritans who were persecuted in England, migrated to Holland in 1608 and then to the New world in 1620. The plight of the Pilgrim Fathers, landing at Plymouth Rock, was outlined in the book:

Being thus passed the vast ocean, and a sea of troubles before in their preparation..., they had now no friends to welcome them, no inns to entertain or refresh their weather-beaten bodies, no houses or much less towns to repair or to seek for succour.... Besides, what could they see but a hideous and desolate wildness, full of wild beasts and wild men?...

3. Anne Bradstreet (1612—1672)

Anne Bradstreet was the first notable poet in America literature with an authentic puritan voice. Her poetry, together with that of Edward Taylor's, rose to professional level and are now regarded as the true poetry of 17th century New England. In her life, she wrote many poems of religious experience and domestic intimacy, some of which were collected by her brother-in-law under the title of "*The Tenth Muse Lately Sprung up in America*." Thus she was later known as the Tenth Muse. The poem for which Anne Bradstreet has been best known is her "Contemplations". This poem is her most independent and integral work which compares the life of mankind with that of nonhuman nature and offers the reader an insight into the symbolic mode of perception and the piety of the early puritans. In the ninth stanza, the poet wrote:

I heard the merry grasshopper then sing,
The black-clad cricket bear a second part;
They kept one tune and played on the same string,
seeming to glory in their little art.
Shall creatures abject thus their voices raise.
And in their kind resound their Maker's praise.
Whilst, I as mute, can warble forth no higher lays?

4. *Edward Taylor (1642—1729)*

Edward Taylor is popularly regarded as the best puritan poet of colonial America. He wrote metaphysical poems, in the tradition of Donne and Herbert, treating religious themes and burning with an intense love for God. In his poem "Huswifery", he saw religious significance in a simple daily incident like a housewife spinning:

Make me, O Lord, thy spinning wheel complete
　　The holy word my distaff make for me
Make mine affections thy swift flyers neat,
　　And make my soul thy holy spool to be.
My conversation make to be thy reel,
And reel the yarn thereon spun of thy wheel.

5. *Jonathan Edwards (1703—1758)*

Edwards was the country's greatest theologian and probably the last great voice that was ever been heard in America to reassert the Calvinist doctrines during the "Great Awakening". However, his faith was logical as well as mystical. On the one hand, he preached the power and mysterious God and the depravity of man. On the other hand, he accepted the new rationalism of Locke and Newton, who thought that man could be made good and that he could even understand the mysteries of the universe. That is probably why he is at once known as the first modern American and the country's last medieval man.

In his life time Edwards had published nine major works and numerous sermons. His greatest and most complete philosophical works include *Freedom of the Will* (1754), *The Doctrine of Original Sin Defended* (1758), and *The Nature of True Virtue* (1765). These works were strenuous efforts to show the relations between religious emotions and virtues and they attempted to solve the question of the existence of free will in a predestined universe. With regard to technique, they were characterised by closeness of texture and preciseness. This qualifies him as the most sensitive stylist in American puritanism. And he became, aside from Benjamin Franklin, the most influential of all colonial American writers.

Part Two American Independence

Chapter Ⅰ American Revolution and Enlightenment

1. American Revolution

With the quick expansion of European colonies in North America, European colonists soon came into collision and wars with each other. As the result of a series of wars, the British colonies defeated the other European colonies and established its dominant position in America, with respect to the Great Britain. However as time went on, the British colonies came into revolt against the British government who had taken a series of measures to hamper the development of native colonial economy and to insure the colonies' dependence on it. In the seventies of the 18th century the British colonies rose in arms against their mother country and the war for independence began. The war lasted for eight years (1776—1783) and ended in the formation of a Federal bourgeois democratic republic—the United States of America.

2. Enlightenment

Enlightenment, also called the Age of Reason, was an intellectual movement that originated in Europe in the 17th century and finally came to the English colonies in America in the 18th century. It stressed the powers of human reason, the importance of scientific methods and discoveries instead of the omnipresence and omnipotence of God. Inspired and enlightened by Isaac Newton's new scientific idea that the universe is not a mystery moving at the whim of an inscrutable god but a mechanism operating by a rational formula that can be understood by any intelligent men and woman, the Enlighteners believed that human society must operate by natural laws and, that by discovering and approaching laws, mankind could achieve almost infinite progress. So the idea of progress became one of the dominant concepts of the age. In America, the Enlightenment contributed to freeing the Americans from the limitations of puritanism and stimulating them to strive for the establishment of their independent and democratic nation.

Chapter Ⅱ The Literature of Revolution and Enlightenment

1. *The Literary Features*

The great historical events and the intellectual movement of the 17th century exerted influence upon and found expression in its literature. Theology that dominated the Puritan phase of American writing gave way to politics and common sense. Generally speaking, the 18th century American literature had the following principal features: ① The men of letters of the age were preoccupied with rationality and showed a profound love for the order and beauty of classical art. ② In form, American literature throughout the century was largely patterned on the writing of the 18th century English classical writers. It was derived from and dependent on the English literal style which was characterised by clarity, precision and order. Benjamin Franklin shaped his writing after *the Spectator Papers* (1711—1712) of the English essayists of Addison and Steele. Philip Freneau, the most important poet of that time, derived his regular couplets from the English poet Alexander Pope. (The 18th century America did not produce great novelists or playwrights.) ③ In content, the 18th century America literature was characterised by its utilitarian tendency. The writings of the revolutionary writers such as Franklin, Paine and Jefferson were intended to serve this philosophical or political purpose, that is, to "polish the manners and habits of society" for the revolutionary independence.

2. Thomas Paine (1737—1809)

Thomas Paine ranks among the most important American prose writers of the 18th century. He wrote a number of political pamphlets which helped to spur and inspire the two greatest revolutions of his age. In January, 1776, he published his most famous *Common Sense*, declaring that the crisis with which the north American colonies were then faced could only be solved by an appeal to man's instincts and common sense. The booklet was warmly received in the colonies both as a justification for their cause of independence and as an encouragement to the painfully fighting people. Paine became forthwith the most articulate spokesman of the American Revolution. In December, 1776, at one of the darkest moments of the revolution, after Washington's defeat in New York and his desperate retreat toward Philadelphia, Paine brought out the first of the series of pamphlets under the title of *American Crisis*. It roused the colonists with the famous words, "These are the times that try men's souls." and "The harder the conflict, the more glorious the triumph." When Washington had *Crisis* I read aloud to his soldiers it proved a heartening stimulus to further action with hope and confidence. After the Revolution he went to Europe and wrote *The Rights of Man* and *The Age of Reason*, attacking the irrationality of religion and preaching the doctrines of natural rights and the equality of men.

3. *Thomas Jefferson* (*1743—1826*)

Thomas Jefferson, a great liberal leader in politics and the third president of the United States, has been taken as one of the most versatile and enlightened men of his generation. He was a member of the Continental Congress, Governor of Virginia, American Minister to France, the first Secretary of State, Vice President, and President of the United States. Besides an outstanding political leader who was devoted to the ideal of individual freedom, Jefferson was also a very successful literary man. As a writer, Jefferson is famous for his simple, clear, powerful and graceful prose style, which is manifest in *Declaration of Independence*. In addition to his neoclassical prose style that has gained him a position in the history of American literature, Jefferson has been admired particularly for his social philosophy oriented toward the equal rights of man and the rational happiness of the individual, as he stated in *Declaration*: "We hold these truths to be self-evident, that all men are created equal, that they are endowed by their creator with certain unalienable Rights, that among these are life, liberty and the pursuit of Happiness."

4. *Philip Freneau* (*1752—1832*)

Philip Freneau was the most significant poet of the 18th Century America. He was important in a number of ways. First, he was "poet of the American Revolution." He used his poetic talents in the service of a nation struggling for independence, writing ardent patriotic verse for the righteous cause of his people and scathing satire of the British. Secondly, Freneau was the "father of American poetry." Alone of his generation, he managed to evade the prevailing atmosphere of imitativeness, to see life around directly, to appreciate the natural scenes on the new continent and the native Indian civilization, downing nationalism in American literature. The national spirit of his poetry pointed forward to the intellectual and literary independence which achieved its maturity first in the writings of men like Emerson and Whitman. Thirdly, Freneau played the transitional role between neoclassicism and romanticism. On the one hand, Freneau used the diction, poetic forms, landscapes, mythologies, and deistic thought of the 18th century. On the other hand, his poetry exhibited the lyric qualities, the serious images, and the adulations of American romanticism in the next century. His first poem "The House of Night," is one of the first distinctly romantic poems in American literature. Freneau's celebration of nature, in such poems as "The Wild Honey Suckle" anticipated the 19th century use of simple nature imagery. And his poem "The Indian Burying Ground" anticipated romantic primitivism and the celebration of the "Noble Savage".

THE WILD HONEY SUCKLE[1]

Fair flower, that dost so comely grow,
Hid in this silent, dull retreat,
Untouched thy honeyed blossoms blow,
Unseen thy little branches greet;
    No roving foot shall crush thee here,
    No busy hand provoke a tear.

By Nature's self in white arrayed,
She bade thee shun the vulgar eye,
And planted here the guardian shade,
And sent soft waters murmuring by;
    Thus quietly thy summer goes,
    Thy days declining to repose.

Smit with those charms, that must decay,
I grieve to see your future doom;
They died—nor were those flowers more gay.
The flowers that did in Eden bloom:
    Unpitying frosts, and Autumn's power
    Shall leave no vestige of this flower

From morning suns and evening dews
At first thy little being came:
If nothing once, you nothing lose,
For when you die you are the same;
    The space between, is but an hour,
    The frail duration of a flower.

THE INDIAN BURYING GROUND[2]

In spite of all the learned have said,
I still my old opinion keep;
The posture, that we give the dead,
Points out the soul's eternal sleep.

Not so the ancients of these lands—
The Indian, when from life released,
Again is seated with his friends,
And shares again the joyous feast.

His imaged birds, and painted bowl,
And venison, for a journey dressed,
Bespeak the nature of the soul,
Activity, that knows no rest.

His bow, for action ready bent,
And arrows, with a head of stone,
Can only mean that life is spent,
And not the old ideas gone.

Thou, stranger, that shalt come this way,
No fraud upon the dead commit—
Observe the swelling turf, and say
They do not lie, but here they sit.

Here still a lofty rock remains,
On which the curious eye may trace
(Now wasted, half, by wearing rains)
The fancies of a race.

Here still an aged elm aspires,
Beneath whose far-projecting shade

(And which the shepherd still admires)
        The children of the forest played!

There oft a restless Indian queen
        (Pale Shebqn[3] with her braided hair)
And many a barbarous form is seen
        To chide the man that lingers there.

By midnight moons, o'er moistening dews;
        In habit for the chase arrayed,
The hunter still the deer pursues,
        The hunter and the deer, a shade!

And long shall timorous fancy see
        The painted chief, and pointed spear,
And Reason's self shall bow the knee
        To shadows and delusions here.

Notes:

1. Then the popular name for a familiar shrub, *azalea viscosa*, sometimes "swamp honeysuckle."
2. "The North American Indians bury their dead in a sitting posture; decorating the corpse with wampum, the images of birds, quadrupeds, etc.; and (If that of a warrior) with bows, arrows, tomhawks, and other millitary weapons" [Freneau's note].
3. The queen of a Sheba, a powerful Arabian country, paid a visit in homage to Solomon and became legendary in literature for her beauty and wisdom.

Chapter Ⅲ Benjamin Franklin (1706—1790)

① *Benjamin Franklin—Jack of All Trades*

Bejamin Franklin is fixed in the American mind in a series of images—a tradesman, a statesman, a scientist and a literary man. He is the model of the self-made man, a culture-hero whose life exemplifies the American dream of the poor boy who makes good.

A business man: Franklin was born in a poor candlemaker's family. He had little formal education. At twelve he was apprenticed to his elder brother, a printer, and began at 16 to publish essays under pseudonym Silence Dogood commenting on the social life in Boston. At 17, he ran off to Philadelphia, where he became a thriving printer, publishing his *Poor Richard's Almanac*.

A scientist: At 42 when he was wealthy and famous, Franklin retired from business to devote himself to science and public service. As a scientist he studied the Gulf Stream, fossils, and earthquakes; invented bifocal spectacles and the lightning rod (Franklin Rod), and made fundamental discoveries about the character of electricity.

A statesman: Franklin helped organise the American Philosophical Society, the University of Pennsylvania, and the first charity hospital in the colonies. During American Revolution, he was made ambassador to Europe who spoke out against British imperialism and beguiled France into joining the American War of Independence; was named delegates of the Continental Congress and the constitutional convention; and was the only American to sign the four documents that created the republic: *Declaration of Indepen-*

dence, *the Treaty of Alliance with France*, *the Treaty of Peace with England*, *and the Constitution*. At the time of his death, his countrymen considered him, more than Washington, to be the father of his country.

A writer: Franklin was the greatest literary artist in America in the Age of Enlightenment. He was a master of the periodical essay, of satire, and of political journalism. He helped establish a tradition in American writing of the simple, utilitarian style, and with his *Autobiography* he set the form for autobiography as a genre. He created America's first great book. And he remains today the most widely read and influential of all American writers.

The prototype of the American dream: From the settlement of the New continent, the American dreamed to build their own paradise in the wilderness, believing they could make individual success by self-reliance. Franklin's success set them an example and fulfilled their dream, which was characterised by self-reliance, faith in the progress of society and the ideals of future, practical and optimistic attitude toward life, and final success. Franklin's life and writings became instruments of instruction used by parents to teach their offspring that public virtue and courage are keys to the worldly success, and the model he set has been inspiring generations of Americans.

② *Franklin's Literary Works*

Franklin's reputation as a great man of letters rests chiefly upon his two masterpieces: *Poor Richard's Almanac* and *The Autobiography*.

Almanac: It was modeled on the sort of farmer's annual calendar widely sold at the time. These annuals originally included dates of the full moon, notes of local high and low tides, suggestions as to the best time for planting various crops, prognostications about the weather in the coming year. As he kept publishing the *Almanac* year after year, Franklin expanded its literary part to the intense delight of its readers. Apart from poems and essays, he managed to put in many proverbs and common-sense witticisms, which taught as much as amused. The *Almanac* includes such proverbs as:

- Early to bed and early to rise
  Makes a man healthy, wealthy and wise.
- He rises late must trot all day.
- A penny saved is a penny earned.
- For age and want, save while you may; no morning sun lasts a whole day.
- Women and wine, game and deceit make the wealth small, and the wants great.
- He that would thrive must ask his wife.
- Keep the shop and the shop will keep you.
- God help them that help themselves.
- Diligence is the mother of good luck.
- Lost time is never found again.

The Autobiography: *The Autobiography of Benjamin Franklin* was the first of its kind in American literature. It is the simple yet very fascinating record of a man rising to wealth and fame from a state of poverty and obscurity into which he was born, the faithful account of the colorful career of America's first self-made man. The book has four parts, written at different times. The first part was written in 1771 covering his early years to 1730. It is the most engrossing in its anecdotes, personalities, and self-revelation. The later parts summarize the mounting triumphs in his many fields of interest. *The Autobiography*, besides a story of a shrewd and industrious businessman, whose rags-riches experience became the prototype of many Americans' dream of success, was a typical embodiment of Puritanism and the Enlightenment. The Enlightener's emphasis on rationalism, order, and education, along with the puritan's emphasis on self-improvement, self-analysis, and moral and ethical values all found expression in it.

③ Franklin's Style

Franklin's mastery of a prose style is characterized by simplicity, clarity, directness, concision, flexibility and order, as he said: "... the words used should be the most expression that the language affords... Nothing should be expressed in two words that can as well be expressed in one." His diction and expression are plain and precise. His syntax is short, smooth, well-balanced, and graceful. His style has had great influence on later American writings.

From THE AUTOBIOGRAPHY[1]

TWYFORD[2], at the Bishop of St. Asaph's. 1771.

Dear Son:

I have ever had a pleasure in obtaining any little anecdotes of my ancestors. You may remember the inquiries I make among the remains of my relations when you were with me in England[3], and the journey I undertook for that purpose. Now imagining it may be equally agreeable to you to know the circumstances of my life, many of which you are yet unacquainted with, and expecting a week's uninterrupted leisure in present country retirement, I sit down to write them for you. Besides, there are some other inducements that excite me to this undertaking. Having emerged from the poverty and obscurity in which I was born and bred to a state of affluence and some degree of reputation in the world, and having gone so far through life with a considerable share of felicity, the conducing means I make use of, which with the blessing of God so well succeeded, my posterity may like to know, as they may find some of them suitable to their own situations, and therefore fit to be imitated. That felicity, when I reflected on it, has induced me sometimes to say that were it offered to my choice I should have no objection to a repetition of the same life from its beginning, only asking the advantages authors have in a second edition to correct some faults of the first. So would I, if I might, besides correcting the faults, change some sinister accidents and events of it for others more favorable, but though this was denied, I should still accept the offer. However, since such a repetition is not to be expected, the next thing most like having one's life over again seems to be a *recollection* of that life, and to make that recollection as durable as possible by putting it down in writing. . .

The notes one of my uncles (who had the same kind of curiosity in collecting family anecdotes) once put into my hands furnished me with several particulars relating to our ancestors. From these notes I learned that the family had lived in the same village, Ecton, in Northamptonshire, for three hundred years, and how much longer he knew not (perhaps from the time when the name Franklin, that before was the name of an order of people, was assumed by them for a surname when others took surnames all over the kingdom)[4], on a freehold of about thirty acres, aided by the smith's business, which had continued in the family till his time, the eldest son being always bred to that business—a custom which he and my father both followed as to eldest sons. When I searched the register at Ecton, I found an account of their births, marriages, and burials from the year 1555 only, there being no register kept in that parish at any time preceding. By that register I perceived that I was the youngest son of the youngest son for five generations back. My grandfather Thomas, who was born in 1598, lived at Ecton till he grew too old to follow business longer, when he went to live with his son John, a dyer at Banbury in Oxfordshire, with whom my father served an apprenticeship. There my grandfather died and lies buried. We saw his gravestone in 1758. His eldest son, Thomas, lived in the house of Ecton, and left it with the land to his only child, a daughter, who with her husband, one Fisher of Wellingboough, sold it to Mr. Isted, now lord of the manor there. My grandfather had four sons that grew up, viz: Thomas, John, Benjamin, and Josiah...

Josiah, my father, married young, and carried his wife with three children into New England about 1682. The conventicle[5] having been forbidden by law and frequently disturbed induced some considerable men of his acquaintance to remove to that country and he was prevailed with to accompany them thither, where they expected to enjoy their mode of religion with freedom. By the same wife he had four children more born there, and by a second wife ten more, in all seventeen; of which I remember thirteen sitting at one time at his table, who all grew up to be men and was born in Boston, New England. My mother, the second wife, was Abiah Folger, a daughter of Pete Folger[6], one of the first settlers of New England, of whom honorable mention is made by Cotton Mather, in his church history of that country, entitled *Magnalia Christi Americana*, as "a godly, learned Englishman," if I remember the words rightly. I have heard that he wrote sundry small occasional pieces, but only one of them was printed, which I saw now many years since...

My elder brother were all put apprentices to different trades.

I was put to the grammar school at eight years of age, my father intending to devote me, as the tithe of his sons, to the service of the church. My early readiness in learning to read (which must have been early, as I do not remember when I could not read) and the opinion of all his friends that I should certainly make a good scholar encouraged him in this purpose of his. My uncle Benjamin, too, approved of it, and proposed to give me all his shorthand volumes of sermons, I suppose as a stock to set up with, if I would learn his character[7]. I continued, however, at the grammar school not quite one year, though in that time I had risen gradually from the middle of the class of that year to be the head of it, and farther was removed into the next class above it, in order to go with that into the third at the end of the year. But my father, in the meantime, from a view of the expense of a college education, which having so large a family he could not well afford, and the mean living many so educated were afterwards able to obtain—reasons that he gave to his friends in my hearing—altered his first intention, took me from the grammar school, and sent me to a school for writing and arithmetic, kept by a then famous man, Mr. George Brownell, very successful in his profession generally, and that by mild, encouraging methods. Under him I acquired fair writing pretty soon, but I failed in the arithmetic, and made no progress in it. At ten years old I was taken home to assist my father in his business, which was that of a tallow-chandler and soap-boiler; a business he was not bred to, but had assumed on his arrival in New England, and on finding his dying trade would not maintain his family, being in little request. Accordingly, I was employed in cutting wick for the candles, filling the dipping mold and the molds for cast candles, attending the shop, going of errands, etc. . . .

From a child I was fond of reading, and all the little money that came into my hands was ever laid out in books. Pleased with the *Pilgrim's Progress*, my first collection was of John Bunyan's works in separate little volumes. I afterwards sold them to enable me to buy R. Burton's *Historical Collections*; they were small chapman's books, and cheap, forty or fifty in all. My father's little library consisted chiefly of books in polemic divinity, most of which I read and have since often regretted that at a time when I had such a thirst for knowledge, more proper books had not fallen in my way, since it was now resolved I should not be a clergyman. *Plutarch's Lives* there was, in which I read abundantly, and I still think that time spent to great advantage. There was also a book of Defoe's[8], called *an Essay on Projects*, and another of Dr. Mather's[9], called *Essay to Do Good*, which perhaps gave me a turn of thinking that had an influence on some of the principal future events in my life.

This bookish inclination at length determined my father to make me a printer, though he had already one son (James) of that profession. In 1717 my brother James returned from England with a press and letters to set up his business in Boston. I liked it much better than that of my father, but still had a hankering for the sea. To prevent the apprehended effect of such an inclination, my father was impatient to have me bound to my brother. I stood out some time, but at last was persuaded, and signed the indentures when I was yet but twelve years old. I was to serve as an apprentice till I was twenty-one years of age, only I was to be allowed journeyman's wages during the last year. In a little time I made great proficiency in the business and became a useful hand to my brother. I now had access to better books. An acquaintance with the apprentices of booksellers enabled me sometimes to borrow a small one, which I was careful to return soon and clean. Often I sat up in my room reading the greatest part of the night, when the book was borrowed in the evening and to be returned early in the morning, lest it should be missed or wanted.

And after some time an ingenious tradesman, Mr. Matthew Adams, who had a pretty collection of books, and who frequented our printing-house, took notice of me, invite me to his library, and very kindly lent me such books as I chose to read. I now took a fancy to poetry, and made some little pieces; my brother, thinking it might turn to account, encouraged me, and put me on composing two occasionalballads. One was called *The Lighthouse Tragedy*, and contained an account of the drowning of Captain Worthilake with his two daughters; the other was a sailor's song, on the taking of Teach (or Blackbeard), the pirate[10]. They were wretched stuff, in the Grub-street-ballad style; and when they were printed he sent me about the town to sell them. The first sold wonderfully, the event being recent, having made a great noise. This flattered my vanity; but my father discouraged me by ridiculing my performances and telling me verse-makers were generally beggars. So I escaped being a poet, most probably a very bad one; but as prose writing has been of great use to me in the course of my life, and was a principal means of my advancement, I shall tell you how, in such a situation, I acquired what little ability I have in that way...

About this time I met with an odd volume of the *Spectator*[11]. It was the third. I had never before seen any of them. I bought it, read it over and over, and was much delighted with it. I thought the writing excellent, and wished, if possible, to imitate it. With that view I took some of the papers, and making short hints of the sentiment in each sentence, laid them by a few days, and then, without looking at the book, tried to complete the papers again by expressing each hinted sentiment at length, and as fully as it had been expressed before, in any suitable words that should come to hand. Then I compared my *Spectator* with the original, discovered some of my faults, and corrected them. But I found I wanted a stock of words, or a readiness in recollecting and using them, which I thought I should I have acquired before that time if I had gone on making verses; since the continual occasion for words of the same import, but of different length to suit the measure, or of different sound for the rhyme, would have laid me under a constant necessity of searching for variety and also have tended to fix that variety in my mind and make me master of it. Therefore, I took some of the tales and turned them into verse, and, after a time, when I had pretty well forgotten the prose, turned them back again. I also sometimes jumbled my collections of hints into confusion, and after some weeks endeavored to reduce them into the best order, before I began to form the full sentences and complete the paper. This was to teach me method in the arrangement of thoughts. By comparing my work afterwards with the original, I discovered many faults and amended them...

While I was intent on improving my language, I met with an English grammar (I think it was Greenwood's), at the end of which there two little sketches of the arts of rhetoric and logic, the latter finishing with a specimen of a dispute in the Socratic method; and soon after I procured Xenophon's *Memorable Things of Socrates*[12], wherein there are many instances of the same method. I was charmed with it, adopted it, dropped my abrupt contradiction and positive argumentation and put on the humble inquirer and doubter. And being then, from reading Shaftesbury and Collins, become a real doubter in many points of our religious doctrine, I found this method safest for myself and very embarrassing to those against whom I used it; therefore I took a delight in it, practiced it continually, and grew very artful and expert in drawing people, even of superior knowledge, into concessions, the consequences of which they did not foresee, entangling them in difficulties out of which they could not extricate themselves, and so obtaining victories that neither myself nor my cause always deserved. I continued this method some few years, but gradually left it, retaining only the habit of expressing myself in terms of modest diffidence, never using, when I advanced anything that may possibly be disputed, the words *certainly*, *undoubtedly*, or any others that give the air of positiveness to an opinion; but rather say, I conceive or apprehend a thing to be so or so; it appears to me, or I should think it so or so, for such and such reasons; or I imagine it to be so; or it is so, if I am not mistaken. This habit, I believe, has been of great advantage to me when I have had occasion to inculcate my opinions and persuade men into measures that I have been from time to time engaged in promoting; and, as the chief ends of conversation are to *inform* or to be *informed*, to *please* or to *persuade*, I wish well-meaning, sensible men would not lessen their power of doing good by a positive, assuming manner that seldom fails to disgust, tends to create opposition and to defeat every one of those purposes for which speech was given to us, to wit, giving or receiving information or pleasure...

Notes:

1. At sixty-five, Franklin wrote an account of his first twenty-four years, intended for his son, William, then colonial governor of New Jersey. Years later he was persuaded by friends to continue it. Additions in 1783, 1784, and 1788 more than doubled the size of the original manuscript, but brought the account only to the years 1757—1759, before the great period of Franklin's public service and international influence. He did not publish this work. The selections here are based on the collation of Bigelow with Farrand's original manuscript readings in *Benjamin Franklin's Memoirs*. The language of the present text is not "modernized," but mechanical conventions have been regu-

larized.

2. In England, near Winchester. Franklin had become intimate with Jonathan Shipley, bishop of St. Asaph's, who approved a more liberal policy for the colonies.

3. His son, William Franklin, went to England as his father's secretary in 1757, studied law there, and later served as royal governor of New Jersey.

4. Yale notes a memorandum, written perhaps by Benjamin Franklin, in Temple Franklin's edition, quoting on this subject a fifteenth-century English legal authority. Benjamin's father wrote him, May 26, 1739, discussing the origin of the name and giving some account of the English Franklins. Franklin properly associated the name with "an order of people"; the "freehold" tenant had tax privileges.

5. Religious assemblies of dissenters, made illegal by the Act of Uniformity, 1662.

6. Peter Folger (1617—1690), pioneer of Nantucket, a schoolmaster, published a volume of ballads condemning the Puritans for lack of religions.

7. His shorthand.

8. Daniel Defoe's *Essay upon Projects* (1679) advanced such liberal social proposals as insurance and popular education.

9. Cotton Mather's essays, originally entitled *Bonifacius* (1710), emphasized practical virtues, and influenced Franklin's early *Dogood Papers* (1722).

10. During 1717—1718, George Worthilake, keeper of the Boston Light, was drowned with family while rowing to Boston; and "Blackbeard," or Edward Teach, famed pirate of the southern coast, was killed by a British naval expedition.

11. Famous British periodical (1711—1712) largely the work of Joseph Addison and Sir Richard Steele.

12. Title of Edward Bysshe's translation (1712) of Xenophon's *Memorabilia*. Note that Franklin was already familiar with the "Socratic method" of argument from reading James Greenwood's *Grammar* (1711), which emphasized, in the fashion of the day, the logical bases of grammar and rhetoric.

Part Three The Age of Romanticism

Chapter Ⅰ The Rise of American Romanticism

1. *Historical Background*

After the establishment of the Federal Government of 1789, American entered a new age. Its population was considerably added to by the influx of immigration. The American pioneers pushed the frontier further west beyond the Mississippi. Before 1860, the United States began to change into an industrial and urban society. The rapid growth of population, the westward expansion and the spread of industrialism produced something of an economic boom and, with it, a tremendous sense of optimism and hope among the people. The buoyant mood of the nation, along with the European Romantic movement which had flourished in early 19th century, shaped the attitudes of America's writers and brought the American Romanticism into being.

2. *Characteristics of Romanticism*

Romanticism as a literary movement swept through western Europe, culminated in England from 1748 to 1832, and came to America early in the 19th century. It was pluralistic: its manifestations were as varied, as individualistic, and as conflicting as the cultures and the intellects from which it sprang. Yet romantics shared certain general characteristics:

Standing in reaction against the neoclassical who stressed formality, order, and authority, the romantic emphasized freedom and individualism, believing that imagination and emotion were formally superior to rules and reason.

The romantic was full of moral enthusiasm, believing ideality and elevation was a reality that was more lofting and realistic than the evidence of the substantial things (material reality).

The romantic assumed that the natural world is a source of goodness and man's societies a source of corruption. Thus he showed a profound admiration and love for nature, believing the beauty and perfection of nature could produce in him an unspeakable joy and exaltation.

The romantic had a persistent interest in the medieval literature, such as epics, ballads, and other forms of folk literature, in which he formed inspiration of various kinds.

The romantic also laid emphasis on mystery and the supernatural as opposed to common sense.

3. *Features of American Romanticism*

Influenced by European Romanticism, American Romanticism was in a way imitative: American romantic writing was some of them modelled on English and European works and shared the general characteristics of European Romanticism. In spite of the strong foreign influence, American Romanticism exhibited from the very outset distinct features of its own. First, American romantic authors were quite responsive to the stimulus which American experience offered. Their subjects were often the national ideals of individualism and democracy, history, and frontier life of the new nation. Henry Wadswoth Longfellow's tentative treatment of the frontier and the Indians, Washington Irving's portrayal of the scenes from the Hudson Valley, William Cullen Bryant's sketches of the wild west prairie where no human beings had ever set foot, James Fenimore Copper's five leather stocking tales with their vivid description of American limitless forests, together with other works by writers like Emerson, Thoreau, Hawthorne, Melville and Whitman, manifested that American writers were creating an indigenous American literature. Secondly puritan influence over American romantics was conspicuously noticeable. One of its manifestations is the fact that American romantic authors tended more to moralise than their European brothers. For instance, Hawthorne's *The Scarlet Letter* was intended to edify more than to entertain.

Chapter Ⅱ Early Romanticism

1. Characteristics of Early Romanticism

As a result of the foreign and native factors at work, American Romanticism was both imitative and independent. Early romantic writers like Irving, Cooper, and the group of New England poets such as Byrant, Longfellow, Whittier, Holmes and Lowell tended to model their works upon English and European masters. These people cast a nostalgic glance across the Atlantic, and took their culture from the English authors like John Dryden, Alexander Pope,

Joseph Addison, Robert Burns, Byron and Wordsworth. In their works, they emphasized such subjects as home, family and children, nature, and idealized love, and most of them showed apparent indifference to the major problems of America life like the westward expansion and democracy and equality. In technique they used traditional meters and stanza forms. In language their English was usually British. In a word, the early American romantic writers were largely imitators of British writers. Yet, they contributed a lot to "The Flowering of New England".

2. Early Romantic Novelists

Washington Irving (1783—1859)

① *Biographical Introduction*

Irving was born in the year the United States won its independence from Britain, and he was named after the new nation's greatest revolutionary general and first president. As the youngest of eleven children of a prosperous New York merchant, Irving became a precocious reader and wrote numerous juvenile poems, plays and essays. At sixteen he began the study of the law, but he had little relish for it. He preferred instead to pass his time in reading. In 1809, his first literary triumph, *A History of New York*, appeared. In 1815 he went to England to take care of his family business there, and when it failed, he had to write to support himself. With the publication of *The Sketch Book* (1820), he began to receive international acclaim. In 1826, his literary fame earned him appointment as an American diplomatic attache in Spain. Three years later, he was an American diplomat in London. When he was nearing fifty, he returned to the Hudson river where he lived as a country squire, writing a series of histories and biographies. He died in 1859 without being married.

② *Irving's Point of View*

Irving's writing revealed a sense of contrast between continental Europe and America. Irving tended to find value in the past and in the traditions of the Old World. He did not share the hopeful American vision of the New World as an Eden, free of the corrupt traditions of Europe. Amid the rising materialism and commercialism of the time, he stood for the comforting values of an older civilization, for the well-established principles and customs of the old world, as he says in his essay "The Author's Account of Himself", "we are a young people... and must take our examples and models in a great degree, from the existing nations of Eruope." Thus Irving is most clearly seen today as a nice old gentleman speaking English not American.

③ *Irving's Contribution to American Literature*

Irving's contribution to American literature is unique in more ways than one. He was the first American writer of imaginative fame; he introduced the familiar essay from Europe to America; he ranked among the first of the modern men of letters to write history and biography as literary entertainment; his strong sense of humor that characterised some of his best works gave an impetus to the growth and popularity of American indigenous humor of which Mark Twain became the classic; *The Sketch Book* initiated the short story as a genre in American literature and marked the beginning of American Romanticism with such romantic subjects as the Gothic, the supernatural, and the longing for the good old days.

④ ***Irving's Style***

Irving's style is imitative. He wrote in the neoclassical tradition of Joseph Addison and Oliver Goldsmith, but he was a highly skillful writer. His style can only be described as beautiful, like Irving the man who was gentle and pleasant and refined. It gives the reader sensuous beauty. When you read Irving, you can see, smell, taste and touch, and enjoy his lucid style as much as the stories. So he is regarded nowadays as the first great stylist of American Romanticism. There are quite a few striking features which characterise Irving's writings. First, Irving avoided moralising as much as possible. He wrote to amuse and entertain, which departs from the basic principles of his puritan forebears. Secondly, he was good at enveloping his stories in a Gothic and supernatural atmosphere. Thirdly, his characters are vivid and true so that they tend to linger in the mind of the reader. Fourthly, the humor which filled the very texture of his writings is so effective that the reader can not help laughing, while reading him. Lastly, Irving's language is so refined and musical that some people read Irving just for the music of his language.

⑤ ***Irving's Major Works***

Although Irving was a prolific and versatile writer in his own day, he is now best remembered as the author of *Rip Van Winkle* and *The Legend of Sleepy Hollow*.

Rip Van Winkle is a fantasy tale about a man who somehow stepped outside the main stream of life. The hero, Rip Van Winkle, is a simple, good-natured, and hen-pecked man. He does everything except take care of his own farm and family. He helps everyone except his wife and his own folks. His wife keeps nagging in his ears about his carelessness and idleness. To escape his nagging wife, he often goes hunting in the mountains near his home with his gun and dog as his companions. One autumn day he chances upon a group of little men in early Dutch costumes bowling at ninepins. Driven by his curiosity and thirst, Rip joins them and drinks their wine, which soon leads to his sound sleep. Awaking, he finds twenty years lapsed and his wife dead. He lives with his daughter, now a happy mother, in easy circumstances without worrying about the harsh treatment of his wife. But he prefers to live the way he did before.

The Legend of Sleepy Hollow tells another miraculous story about an unsuccessful love affair. Ichabod Crane, a Connecticut schoolteacher, covets the hand of Katrina Van Tassel and covets even more the rich New York farmland that she will inherit. His rival, Brom Bones, rides up to Crane at midnight in the Hollow disguised as a headless horseman, and scares the Yankee completely out of the courtship and out of the country.

The two stories share legendary elements, which reveals, to some extent, the conservative attitude of the author toward the American Revolution and his nostalgia for the life before the Revolution. Rip goes to sleep before the War of Independence and wakes up after it. The change that has occurred in the twenty years is not always for the better. Whereas, before the war, there was peace and harmony, there comes now the scramble for power between parties. The tempo of life has quickened. Pre-war leisurely existence has acquired a busy, bustling, disputatious tone. Instead of feeling happy about the country finally independent from the yoke of British colonial rule, Rip is pleased with his new life chiefly because he has got his neck out of the yoke of matrimony. Ichobad Crane is a greedy, superstitious New Englander, shrewd, commercial, a city-slicker, who is rather an interloper, a somewhat destructive force, and who comes along to swindle the villagers. His book learning turns on him, and he is driven away from where he does not belong, so that the serene village remains permanently good and happy. Brom Bones, on the other hand, is of a Huck Finn-type of country bumpkin, rough, vigorous but inwardly very good, a frontier type put out there to shift for himself. At last, the old-fashioned savage men defeats the now civilised man.

THE LEGEND OF SLEEPY HOLLOW

(*Excerpt*)

All the stories of ghosts and goblins that he had heard in the afternoon, now came crowding upon his recollection. The night grew darker and darker; the stars seemed to sink deeper in the sky, and driving clouds occasionally hid them from his sight. He had never felt so lonely and dismal. He was, moreover, approaching the very place where many of the scenes of the ghost stories had been laid. In the centre of the road stood an enormous tulip-tree, which towered like a giant above all the other trees of the neighborhood, and formed a kind of landmark. Its limbs were gnarled, and fantastic, large enough to form trunks for ordinary trees, twisting down almost to the earth, and rising again into the air. It was connected with the tragical story of the unfortunate André, who had been taken prisoner hard by; and was universally known by the name of Major André's tree. The common people regarded it with a mixture of respect and superstition, partly out of sympathy for the fate of its ill-starred namesake, and partly from the tales of strange sights and doleful lamentations told concerning it.

As Ichabod approached this fearful tree, he began to whistle: he thought his whistle was answered—it was but a blast sweeping sharply through the dry branches. As he approached a little nearer, he thought he saw something white, hanging in the midst of the tree—he paused and ceased whistling; but on looking more narrowly, perceived that it was a place where the tree had been scathed by lightning, and the white wood laid bare. Suddenly he heard a groan—his teeth chattered and his knees smote against the saddle: it was but the rubbing of one huge bough upon another, as they were swayed about by the breeze. He passed the tree in safety, but new perils lay before him.

About two hundred yards from the tree a small brook crossed the road, and ran into a marshy and thickly-wooded glen, known by the name of Wiley's swamp. A few rough logs, laid side by side, served for a bridge over this stream. On that side of the road where the brook entered the wood, a group of oaks and chestnuts, matted thick with wild grapevines, threw a cavernous gloom over it. To pass this bridge was the severest trial. It was at this identical spot that the unfortunate Andreé was captured, and under the covert of those chestnuts and vines were the sturdy yeomen concealed who surprised him. This has ever since been considered a haunted stream, and fearful are the feelings of the schoolboy who has to pass it alone after dark.

As he approached the stream his heart began to thump; he summoned up, however, all his resolution, gave his horse half a score of kicks in the ribs, and attempted to dash briskly across the bridge; but instead of starting forward, the perverse old animal make a lateral movement, and ran broadside against the fence. Ichabod, whose fears increased with the delay, jerked the reins on the other side, and kicked lustily with the contrary foot; it was all in vain; his steed started, it is true, but it was only to lounge to the opposite side of the road into a thicket of brambles and alder bushes. The schoolmaster now bestowed both whip and heel upon the starveling ribs of old Gunpowder, who dashed forward, snuffling and snorting, but came to a stand just by the bridge, with a suddenness that had nearly sent his rider sprawling over his head. Just at his moment a plashy tramp by the side of the bridge caught the sensitive ears of Ichabod. In the dark shadow of the grove, on the margin of the brook, he beheld something huge, misshapen, black and towering. It stirred not, but seemed gathered up in the gloom, like some gigantic monster ready to spring upon the traveller.

The hair of the affrighted pedagogue rose upon his head with terror. What was to be done? To turn and fly was now too late; and besides, what chance was there of escaping ghost or goblin, of such it was, which could ride upon the wings of the wind? Summoning up, therefore, a show of courage, he demanded in stammering accents—"Who are you?" He received no reply. He repeated his demand in a still more agitated voice. Still there was no answer. Once more he cudgelled the sides of the inflexible Gunpowder, and, shutting his eye, broke forth with involuntary fervor into a psalm tune. Just then the shadowy object of alarm put itself in motion, and, with a scramble and a bound, stood at once in the middle of the road. Though the night was dark and dismal, yet the form of the unknown might now in some degree be ascertained. He appeared to be a horseman of large dimensions, and mounted on a black horse of powerful frame. He made no offer of molestation or sociability, but kept aloof on one side of the road, jogging along on the blind side of old Gunpowder, who had now got over his fright and waywardness.

Ichabod, who had no relish for this strange midnight companion, and bethought himself of the adventure of Brom Bones with the Galloping Hessian, now quickened his steed, in hopes of leaving him behind. The stranger, however, quickened his horse to an equal pace. Ichabod pulled up and fell into a walk, thinking to lag behind—the other did the same. His heart began to sink within him; he endeavored to resume his psalm tune, but his parched tongue clove to the roof of his mouth, and he could not utter a stave. There was something in the moody and dogged silence of this pertinacious companion, that was mysterious and appalling. It was soon fearfully accounted for. On mounting a rising ground, which brought the figure of his fellow-traveller in relief against the sky, gigantic in height, and muffled in a cloak, Ichabod was horror-struck, on perceiving that he was headless! —but his horror was still more increased, on observing that the head, which should have rested on his shoulders, was carried before him on the pommel of the saddle: his terror rose to desperation; he rained a shower of kicks and blows upon Gunpowder, hoping, by a sudden movement, to give his companion the slip — but the spectre started full jump with him. Away then they dashed, through thick and thin; stones flying, and sparks flashing at every bound. Ichabod's flimsy garments fluttered in the air, as he stretched his long lank body away over his horse's head, in the eagerness of his flight.

They had now reached the road which turns off to Sleepy Hollow; but Gunpowder, who seemed possessed with a demon, instead of keeping up it, made an opposite turn, and plunged headlong down hill to the left. This road leads through a sandy hollow, shaded by trees for about a quarter of a mile, where it crosses the bridge famous in goblin story, and just beyond swells the green knoll on which stands the whitewashed church.

As yet the panic of the steed had given his unskillful rider an apparent advantage in the chase; but just as he had got half way through the hollow, the girths of the saddle gave way, and he felt it slipping from under him. He seized it by the pommel, and endeavored to hold it firm, but in vain; and had just time to save himself by clasping old Gunpowder round the neck, when the saddle fell to the earth, and he heard it trampled under foot by his pursuer. For a moment the terror of Hans Van Ripper's wrath passed across his mind—for it was his Sunday saddle, but this was no time for petty fears; the goblin was hard on his haunches; and (unskillful rider that he was!) he had much ado to maintain his seat; something slipping on one side, sometimes on another, and sometimes jolted on the high ridge of his horse's back-bone, with a violence that he verily feared would cleave him asunder.

An opening in the trees now cheered him with the hopes that the church bridge was at hand. The wavering reflection of a silver star in the bosom of the brook told him that he was not mistaken. He saw the walls of the church dimly glaring under the tree beyond. He recollected the place where Brom Bones's ghostly competitor had disappeared. "If I can but reach that bridge," thought Ichabod, "I am safe." Just then he heard the black steed panting and blowing close behind him; he even fancied that he felt his hot breath. Another convulsive kick in the ribs, and old Gunpowder sprang upon the bridge, he thundered over the resounding planks, he gained the opposite side; and now Ichabod cast a look behind to see if his pursuer should vanish, according to rule, in a flash of fire and brimstone. Just then he saw the goblin rising in his stirups, and in the very act of hurling his head at him. Ichabod endeavored to dodge the horrible missile, but too late. It encountered his cranium with a tremendous crash—he was tumbled headlong into the dust, and Gunpowder, the black steed, and the goblin rider, passed by like a whirlwind.

The next morning the old horse was found without his saddle, and with the bridle under his feet, soberly cropping the grass at his master's gate. Ichabod did not make his appearance at breakfast. Dinner-hour came, but no Ichabod. The boys assembled at the school-house, and strolled idly about the banks of the brooks; but no schoolmaster. Hans Van Ripper now began to feel some uneasiness about the fate of poor Ichabod, and his saddle. An inquiry was set on foot, and after diligent investigation they came upon his traces. In one part of the road leading to the church was found the saddle trampled in the dirt; the tracks of horses' hoofs deeply dented in the road, and evidently at furious speed, were traced to the bridge, beyond which, on the bank of a broad part of the brook, where the water ran deep and black, was found the hat of the unfortunate Ichabod, and close beside it a shattered pumpkin.

The brook was searched, but the body of the school-master was not to be discovered. Hans Van Ripper, as executor of his estate, examined the bundle which contained all his worldly effects. They consisted of two shirts and a half; two stocks for the neck; a pair or two of worsted stockings; an old pair of corduroy small-clothes; a rusty razor; a book of psalm tunes, full of dogs' ears; and a broken pitchpipe. As to the books and furniture of the school-house, they belonged to the community, excepting Cotton Mather's *History of Witchcraft*, a New England Almanac, and a book of dreams and fortune-telling; in which last was a sheet of foolscap much scribbled and blotted in several fruitless attempts to make a copy of verses in honor of the heiress of Van Tassel. These magic books and the poetic scrawl were forthwith consigned to the flames by Hans Van Ripper; who from that time forward determined to send his children no more to school; observing, that he never knew any good come of this same reading and writing. Whatever money the school-master possessed, and he had received his quarter's pay but a day or two before, he must have had about his person at the time of his disappearance.

The mysterious event caused much speculation at the church on the following Sunday. Knots of gazers and gossips were collected in the churchyard, at the bridge; and at the spot where the hat and pumpkin had been found. The stories of Brouwer, of Bones, and a whole budget of others, were called to mind; and when they had diligently considered them all, and compared them with the symptoms of the present case, they shook their heads, and came to the conclusion that Ichabod had been carried off by the galloping Hessian. As he was a bachelor, and in nobody's debt, nobody troubled his head any more about him. The school was removed to a different quarter of the hollow, and another pedagogue reigned in his stead.

It is true, an old farmer, who had been down to New York on a visit several years after, and from whom this account of the ghostly adventure was received, brought home the intelligence that Ichabod Crane was still alive; that he had left the neighborhood, partly through fear of the goblin and Hans Van Ripper, and partly in mortification at having been suddenly dismissed by the heiress; that he had changed his quarters to a distant part of the country; had kept school and studied law at the same time, had been admitted to the bar, turned politician, electioneered, written for the newspapers, and finally had been made a justice of the Ten Pound Court. Brom Bones too, who shortly after his rival's disappearance conducted the blooming Katrina in triumph to the altar, was observed to look exceedingly knowing whenever the story of Ichabod was related, and always burst into a hearty laugh at the mention of the pumpkin; which led some to suspect that he knew more about the matter than he chose to tell.

The old country wives, however, who are the best judges of these matters, maintain to this day that Ichabod was spirited away by supernatural means, and it is a favorite story often told about the neighborhood round the winter evening fire. The bridge became more than ever an object of superstitious awe, and that may be the reason why the road has been altered of late years, so as to approach the church by the border of the millpond. The schoolhouse being deserted, soon fell to decay, and was reported to be haunted by the ghost of the unfortunated pedagogue; and the ploughboy, loitering homeward of a still summer evening, has often fancied his voice at a distance chanting a melancholy psalm tune among the tranquil solitudes of Sleepy Hollow.

Questions for Consideration:

1. How does the writer's description of the surroundings establish the atmosphere of the story?
2. What do you think of the writer's language?

James Fenimore Cooper (1789—1851)

James Fenimore Cooper was born into a rich land-holding family of New Jersey, educated at the local school in his childhood, and then sent to Yale. After three year's study at Yale, he went and spent five years at sea. In the years 1826 to 1833, he travelled widely in Europe, inspired not only by the beauty of nature, historical romances, urban development but also by the great achievements of European romanticism. He seized upon the romantic novel of the

Scott type in his model and began his literary career when he was thirty years of age. His first successful work was *The Spy* (1821), a historical romance about the American Revolution, which established Cooper as the first distinguished American novel writer. In the three decades that followed, Cooper wrote thirty-three novels, and numerous volumes of history, social comment, and travels, introducing four major themes—America history, the frontiers, the sea, and the European scene.

Cooper's enduring fame rests on his frontier stories, especially the series of the five novels that comprise the *Leatherstocking Tales* (1823 to 1841). In their order of events, the novels are *The Deerslayer*, *The Last of the Mohicans*, *The Pathfinder*, *The Pioneers* and *The prairie*. The five novels depict the frontier life of American settlers who search for enduring moral values amidst incessant change, and creates a myth of the formative period of the American nation. The central figure in the novels, Natty Bumppo in his various names such as Hawk Eye, the Pathfinder, the Deerslayer or Leatherstocking, is a pioneer who effectively approximates the American national experience of adventures in the west, and the *Leatherstocking Tales* is the history of modern civilization advancing on the spreading wilderness, and of the juxtapostition of the works of man and the reign of nature. The majestic theme of the irresistible force of civilization that destroyed the American wilderness and all its noble simplicities is where Cooper's greatest achievement lies.

THE LAST OF THE MOHICANS, XXXII[1]

The Hawk-eye of the Indian Wars

During the time Uncas[2] was making this disposition of his forces, the woods were as still, and, with the exception of those who had met in council, apparently, as much untenanted, as when they came fresh from the hands of their Almighty Creator. The eye could range, in every direction, through the long and shadowed vistas of the trees; but nowhere was any object to be seen, that did not properly belong to the peaceful and slumbering scenery. Here and there a bird was heard fluttering among the branches of the beeches, and occasionally a squirrel dropped a nut, drawing the startled looks of the party, for a moment to the place; but the instant the casual interruption ceased, the passing air was heard murmuring above their heads, along that verdant and undulating surface of forest, which spread itself unbroken, unless by stream or lake, over such a vast region of country. Across the tract of wilderness, which lay between the Delawares and the village of their enemies, it seemed as of the foot of man had never trodden, so breathing and deep was the silence in which it lay. But Hawk-eye, whose duty led him foremost in the adventure, knew the character of those with whom he was about to contend, too well, to trust the treacherous quiet.

When he saw his little band again collected, the scout threw "kill-deer"[3] into the hollow of his arm, and making a silent signal that he would be followed, . . . turned, and perceived that his party had been followed thus far by the singingmaster.

"Do you know, friend," asked the scout gravely, and perhaps with a little of the pride of conscious deserving in his manner, "that this is a band of rangers, chosen for the most desperate service, and put under the command of one, who, though another might say it with a better face, will not be apt to leave them idle. It may not be five, it cannot be thirty, minutes before we tread on the body of a Huron, living or dead."

"Though not admonished of your intentions in words," returned David, whose face was a little flushed, and whose ordinarily quiet and unmeaning eyes glimmered with an expression of unusual fire, "your men have reminded me of the children of Jacob going out to battle against the Shechemites, for wickedly aspiring to wedlock with a woman of a race that was favoured of the lord.[4] Now, I have journeyed far, and sojourned much, in good and evil, with the maiden ye seek; and, though not a man of war, with my loins girded and my sword sharpened, yet would I gladly strike a blow in her behalf."

The scout hesitated, as if weighing the chances of such a strange enlistment in his mind before he answered—

"You know not the use of any we'pon. You carry no rifle; and believe me, what the Mingoes take they will freely give again."

"Though not a vaunting and bloodily disposed Goliath," returned David, drawing a sling from beneath his parti-coloured and uncouth attire, "I have not forgotten the example of the Jewish boy.[5] With this ancient instrument of war have I practised much in my youth, and peradventure the skill has not entirely departed from me."

"Ah!" said Hawk-eye, considering the deer-skin thong and apron, with a cold and discouraging eye; "the thing might do its work."... Pointing in the direction he wished to proceed, Hawk-eye advanced, the band breaking off in single files, and following so accurately in his footsteps, as to leave, if we except Heyward and David, the trail of but a single man.

The party was, however, scarcely uncovered, before a volley from a dozen rifles was heard in their rear, and a Delaware leaping high into the air, like a wounded deer, fell at his whole length, perfectly dead. . .

Animating his followers by his voice, and his own example, Hawk-eye then gave the word to bear down upon their foes. The charge, in that rude species of warfare, consisted merely in pushing from cover to cover, nigher to the enemy, and in this manoeuvre he was instantly and successfully obeyed. The Hurons were compelled to withdraw, and the scene of the contest rapidly changed form the more open ground on which it had commenced, to a spot where the assailed found a thicket to rest upon. Here the struggle was protracted, arduous, and, seemingly, of doubtful issue. The Delawares, though none of them fell, were beginning to bleed freely, in consequence of the disadvantage at which they were held. . .

Then, turning, with a prompt and decided air, . . . he called about to his Indians, in their own language. His words were answered by a shout, and at a given signal, each warrior made a swift movement around his particular tree. The sight of so many dark bodies, glancing before their eyes at the same instant, drew a hasty, and, consequently, an ineffectual fire from the Hurons. Then, without stopping to breathe, the Delawares leaped, in long bounds, towards the wood, like so many panthers springing upon their prey. Hawk-eye was in front, brandishing his terrible rifle, and animating his followers by his example. A few of the older and more cunning Hurons, who had not been deceived by the artifice which had been practised to draw their fire, now made a close and deadly discharge of their pieces, and justified the apprehensions of the scout, by felling three of his foremost warriors. But the shock was insufficient ot repel their impetus of the charge. The

Delawares broke into the cover, with the ferocity of their natures, and swept away every trace of resistance by the fury of the onset.

The combat endured only for an instant, hand to hand, and then the assailed yielded ground rapidly, until they reached the opposite margin of the thicket, where they clung to their cover, with the sort of obstinacy that is so often witnessed in bunted brutes. At this critical moment, when the success of the struggle was again becoming doubtful, the crack of a rifle was heard behind the Hurons, and a bullet came whizzing from among some beaver lodges, which were situated in the cleaning, in their rear, and was followed by the fierce and appalling yell of the war-whoop.

"There speaks the Sagamore!"[6] shouted Hawk-eye, answering the cry with his own stentorian voice; "we have them now in face and back!"

The effect on the Hurons was instantaneous. Discouraged by so unexpected an assault, from a quarter that left them no opportunity for cover, their warriors uttered a common yell of disappointment and despair, and breaking off in a body, they spread themselves across the opening, heedless of every other consideration but flight. Many fell, in making the experiment, under the bullets and the blows of the pursuing Delawares.

We shall not pause to detail the meeting between the scout and Chingachgook...

At the instant the whoop was given, and a dozen Hurons fell by a discharge from Chingachgook and his band. The shout that followed, was answered by a single war-cry from the forest, and a yell passed through the air, that sounded as though a thousand throats were united in a common effort. The Hurons staggered, deserting the centre of their line, and Uncas issued through the opening they left, from the forest, at the head of a hundred warriors.

Waving his hands right and left, the young chief pointed out the enemy to his followers, who instantly separated in the pursuit. The war now divided, both wings of the broken Hurons seeking protection in the woods again, hotly pressed by the victorious warriors of the Lenape.[7] A minute might have passed, but the sounds were already receding in different directions, and gradually losing their distinctness beneath the echoing arches of the woods. One little knot of Hurons, however, had disdained to seek a cover, and were retiring, like lions at bay, slowly and sullenly up the acclivity... Magua was conspicuous in this party, both by his fierce and savage mien, and by the air of haughty authority he yet maintained.

In his eagerness to expedite the pursuit, Uncas had left himself nearly alone; but the moment his eye caught the figure of le Subtil,[8] every other consideration was forgotten. Raising his cry of battle, which recalled some six or seven warriors, and reckless of the disparity of their numbers, he rushed upon his enemy. Le Renard, who watched the movement, paused to receive him with secret joy. But at the moment when he thought the rashness of his impetuous young assailant had left him at his mercy, another shout was given, and la Longue Carabine[9] was seen rushing to the rescue, attended by all his white associates. The Huron instantly turned, and commenced a rapid retreat up the ascent.

There was no time for greetings or congratulations, for Uncas, though unconscious of the presence of his friends, continued the pursuit with the velocity of the wind... Still Magua, though daring and much exposed, escaped from every effort against his life, with that sort of fabled protection, that was made to overlook the fortunes of favoured heroes in the legends of ancient poetry. Raising a yell that spoke volumes of anger and disappointment, the subtle chief, when he saw his comrades fallen, darted away from the place, attended by his two only surviving friends, leaving the Delawares engaged in stripping the dead of the bloody trophies of their victory.

But Uncas, who had vainly sought him in the mélée, bounded forward in pursuit; Hawk-eye, Heyward, and David, still pressing on his footsteps. The utmost that the scout could effect, was to keep the muzzle of his rifled a little in advance of his friend, to whom, however, it answered every purpose of a charmed shield. Once Magua appeared disposed to make another and a final effort to revenge his losses; but abandoning his intentions so soon as demonstrated, he leaped into a thicket of bushes, through which he was followed by his enemies, and suddenly entered the mouth of the cave already known to the reader. Hawk-eye, who had only forborne to fire in tenderness to Uncas, raised a shout of success, and proclaimed aloud, that now they were certain of their game. The pursuers dashed into the long and narrow entrance, in time to catch a glimpse of the retreating forms of the Hurons. Their passage through the natural galleries and subterraneous apartments of the cavern was preceded by the shrieks adn cried of hundreds of women and children. The place, seen by its dim and uncertain light, appeared like the shades of the infernal regions, across which unhappy ghosts and savage demons were flitting in multitudes.

Still Uncas kept his eye on Magua, as if life to him possessed but a single object. Heyward and the scout still pressed on his rear, actuated, though, possibly, in a less degree, by a common feeling. But their way was becoming intricate, in those dark and gloomy passages, and the glimpses of the retiring warriors less distinct and frequent; and for a moment the trace was believed to be lost, when a white robe was seen fluttering in the further extremity of a passage that seemed to lead up the mountain.

"'Tis Cora," exclaimed Heyward, in a voice in which horror and delight were wildly mingled.

"Cora! Cora!" echoed Uncas, bounding forward like a deer.

"'Tis the maiden!" shouted the scout. "Courage, lady; we come—we come."...

"We must close!" said the scout, passing his friends by a desperate leap; "the knaves will pick us all off at this distance; and see; they hole the maiden so as to shield themselves!"

Though his words were unheeded, or rather unheard, his example was followed by his companions, who, by incredible exertions, got near enough to the fugitives to perceive that Cora was borne along between the two warroirs, while Magua prescribed the direction and manner of their flight. At this moment the forms of all four were strongly drawn against an opening in the sky, and then they disappeared. Nearly frantic with disappointment, Uncas and Heyward increased efforts that already seemed superhuman, and they issued from the cavern on the side of the mountain, in time to note the route of the pursued. The course lay up the ascent, and still continued hazardous and laborious... But the impetuous young men were rewarded, by finding that, encumbered with Cora, the Hurons were rapidly losing ground in the race.

"Stay; dog of the Wyandots!" exclaimed Uncas, shaking his bright tomahawk at Magua; "a Delaware girl calls stay!"

"I will go no farther," cried Cora, stopping unexpectedly on a ledge of rocks, that overhung a deep precipice, at no great distance from the summit of the mountain. "Kill me if thou wilt, detestable Huron, I will go no farther."

The supporters of the maiden raised their ready tomahawks with the impious joy that friends are thought to take in mischief, but Magua suddenly stayed the uplifted arms. The Huron chief, after casting the weapons he had wrested from his companions over the rock, drew his knife, and turned to his captive, with a look in which conflicting passions fiercely contended.

"Woman," he said, "choose; the wigwam or the knife of Subtil!"

Cora regarded him not; but dropping on her knees, with a rich glow suffusing itself over her features, she raised her eyes and stretched her arms towards Heaven, saying, in a meek and yet confiding voice—

"I am thine! do with me as thou seest best!"

"Woman," repeated Magua hoarsely, and endeavouring in vain to catch a glance from her serene and beaming eye, "choose."

But Cora neither heard nor heeded his demand. The form of the Huron trembled in every fibre, and he raised arm on high, but dropped it again, with a bewildered air, like one who doubted. Once more he struggled with himself, and lifted the keen weapon again—but just then a piercing cry was heard above them, and Uncas appeared, leaping frantically, from a fearful height, upon the ledge. Magua recoiled a step, and one of his assistants, profiting by the chance, sheathed his own knife in the bosom of the maiden.

The Huron sprang like a tiger on his offending and already retreating countryman, but the falling form of Uncas separated the unnatural combatants. Diverted from his object by this interruption, and maddened by the murder he had just witnessed, Magua buried his weapon in the back of the prostrate Delaware, uttering an unearthly shout, as he committed the dastardly deed. But Uncas arose from the blow, as the wounded panther turns upon his foe, and struck the murderer of Cora to his feet, by an effort in which the last of his failing strength was expended. Then , with a stern and steady look, he turned to le Subtil, and indicated, by the expression of his eyes, all that he would do, had not the power deserted him. The latter seized the nerveless arm of the unresisting Delaware, and passed his knife into his bosom three several times, before his victim, still keeping his gaze riveted on his enemy with a look of inextinguishable scorn, fell dead at his feet.

"Mercy! mercy! Huron," cried Heyward, from above, in tones nearly choked by horror: "give mercy, and thou shalt receive it!"

Whirling the bloody knife up at the imploring youth, the victorious Magua uttered a cry so fierce, so wild, and yet so joyous, that it conveyed the sounds of savage triumph to the ears of those who fought in the valley, a thousand feet below. He was answered by an appalling burst from the lips of the scout, whose tall person was just then seen moving swiftly towards him, along those dangerous crags, with steps as bold and reckless, as if he possessed the power to move in middle air. But when the hunter reached the scene of the ruthless massacre, the ledge was tenanted only by the dead.

His keen eye took a single look at the victims, and then shot its fierce glances over the difficulties of the ascent in his front. A form stood at the brow of the mountain, on the very ledge of the giddy height, with uplifted arms, in an awful attitude of menace. Without stopping to consider his person, the rifle of Haw-eye was raised, but a rock, which fell on the head of one of the fugitives below, exposed the indignant and glowing countenance of the honest Gamut. Then Magua issued from a crevice, and stepping with calm indifference over the body of the last of his associates, he leaped a wide fissure, and ascended the rocks at a point where the arm of David could not reach him. A single bound would carry him to the brow of the precipice, and assure his safety. Before taking the leap, however, the Huron paused, and shaking his hand at the scout, he shouted—

"The pale-faces are dogs! the Delawares women! Magua leaves them on the rocks, for the crows!"

Laughing hoarsely, he made a desperate leap, and fell short of his mark: though his hands grasped a shrub on the verge of the height. The form of Hawk-eye had crouched like a beast about to take its spring, and his frame trembled so violently with eagerness, that the muzzle of the half raised rifle played like a leaf fluttering in the wind. Without exhausting himself with fruitless efforts, the cunning Magua suffered his body to drop to the length of his arms, and found a fragment for his feet to rest on. Then summoning all his powers, he renewed the attempt, and so far succeeded, as to draw his knees on the edge of the mountain. It was now, when the body of his enemy was most collected together, that the agitated weapon of the scout was drawn to his shoulder. The surrounding rocks, themselves, were not steadier than the piece became for the single instant that it poured out its contents. The arms of the Huron relaxed, and his body fell back a little, while his knees still kept their position. Turning a relentless look on his enemy, he shook his hand at him, in grim defiance. But his hold loosened, and his dark person was seen cutting the air with its head downwards, for a fleeting instant, until it glided past the fringe of shrubbery which clung to the mountain, in its rapid flight to destruction.[10]

Notes:

1. In this novel, Natty Bumppo, a mature and seasoned scout, is known as Hawk-eye. The central event is the capture of the British Fort William Henry by the French and their Huron allies in 1757. The English commander's daughters, Cora and Alice Munro, have been guided through the forest by Magua, an Indian secret agent of the French, who hopes to gain possession of

Cora by betraying the party to the French. Hawk-eye has foiled this plot, assisted by his faithful friends, the Delaware chieftain Chingachgook and his warrior son Uncas, and by David Gamut, a wandering music master.

In the present chapter this party has left the fallen fort under safe conduct from the French, accompanied by Munro and by Major Duncan Heyward, the fiancé of Alice Munro. But Magua provokes an Indian attack, in which the girls are captured. Alice is gallantly rescued by her fiancé; but under tribal law the Delawares are obliged to permit Magua to depart with Cora, since she is his own captive. However, under the leadership of Uncas, they at once pursue the Hurons, among whom Magua has taken refuge.

2. The "Last of the Mohicans," who is killed in this chapter.
3. His rifle, which had become legendary; *cf*. the swords of famous knights of romance.
4. *cf*. Genesis xxxiv; Jacob slew the Shechemite for this violation.
5. The boy David killed Goliath with a stone from a sling; *cf*. I Samuel xvii.
6. The chief, Chingachgock.
7. The Lenni Lenape, another name for the Delawares.
8. "Le Renard Subtil" ("Crafty Fox") is the nickname given to Magua by the French.
9. "The Long Rifle," as the French have nicknamed Hawk-eye.
10. After this adventure Hawk-eye returns to the forest, to become the Pathfinder of a later novel.

3. *Early Romantic Poets*

William Cullen Bryant (1794—1878)

Bryant was the first native American lyric poet to gain world-wide fame. Although his early poetry reflected some features of imitation of European poetry, his best poetry was written not of European nightingales and Roman or Greek landscapes but of American sparrows, and of American prairies, and of the trees and flowers and grass of New England. Famous as a poet of nature, Bryant wrote of his own experience in nature. To him, nature was the symbol of the Maker and the infinite source; and the purpose of nature was to keep man's mind directed to the Supreme Craftsman. Bryant held that nature should impart moralization, and it should elevate man. Byrant's best poems are "Thanatopsis" and "To a Waterfowl".

"Thanatopsis" is Bryant's best-known poem. It was written in blank verse with the theme of death. In this poem of death, both God and immortality are notably absent. Nature eventually claims all it has created and sustained. Man should conduct his life virtuously by nature's dictates so that courageously he may face reabsorption into nature.

"To a Waterfawl" describes the poet's observation of a bird escaping from a fowler on the horizon at sunset, and expresses the poet's sense of a divine power that guides and protects life and should be obeyed by man as well as bird.

TO A WATERFOWL

Whither, midst falling dew,
While glow the heavens with the last steps of day,
Far through their rosy depths dost thou pursue
Thy solitary way?

Vainly the fowler's eye
Might mark thy distant flight to do the wrong,
As, darkly seen against the crimson sky,
Thy figure floats along.

Seek'st thou the plashy brink
Of weedy lake or marge of river wide,
Or where the rocking billows rise and sink
On the chafed ocean-side?

There is a Power whose care
Teaches thy way along that pathless coast—
The desert[2] and illimitable air, —
Lone wandering, but not lost.

All day thy wings have fanned,
At that far height, the cold, thin atmosphere,
Yet stoop not, weary, to the welcome land,
Though the dark night is near.

And soon that toil shall end;
Soon shalt thou find a summer home, and rest,
And scream among thy fellows; reeds shall bend,
Soon, o'er thy sheltered nest.

Thou'rt[3] gone, the abyss of heaven
Hath swallowed up thy form; yet, on my heart
Deeply has sunk the lesson thou hast given,
And shall not soon depart.

He who, from zone to zone,
Guides through the boundless sky thy certain flight,
In the long way that I must tread alone
Will lead my steps aright.

Notes:

1. hunter's
2. deserted, lonely
3. you are

Henry Wadsworth Longfellow(1807—1882)

Longfellow was one of the most serious and most popular writers of his age. He stayed in Europe for a long time and gained a broader knowledge of European literature, which enabled him to embody in his poetry chief romantic tendencies, like humanitarian attitude, love for nature and for the past, especially the picturesque old world of medieval legend and piety. However, the romanticism of his poetry was counter balanced by classical and Christian ethics. Generally speaking, the characteristics and appeal of his poetry lie in spiritual aspiration, simple piety, homely affection, love of beauty, refinement of thought and manners. As a popular poet, Longfellow's fame rests chiefly on his search for new forms and the arresting didacticism in his poetry. He was the master of the sonnet, the lyric and the narrative. His poetry strongly embodied the optimistic sentiment and the love of a good lesson, which urges the reader to practice the simple obvious virtues, as exemplified by "A Psalm of Life".

"A Psalm of Life" remains Longfellow's most famous poem. It urges the sentimentalist to action and vigorous achievement. In this poem, moral aphorisms are so melodiously and lucidly expressed that all could understand and repeat them.

Longfellow's other famous works include *Poems on Slavery*, *Ballads and Other Poems*, and the three long narrative poems—"Evangeline,""The Courtship of Miles Standish", and "Song of Hiawatha", the last of which is the first famous epic of American Indians in American literature.

A Psalm of Life
WHAT THE HEART OF THE YOUNG MAN SAID TO THE PSALMIST

Tell me not, in mournful numbers,
Life is but an empty dream! —
For the soul is dead that slumbers,
And things are not what they seem.

Life is real! Life is earnest!
And the grave is not its goal;
Dust thou art, to dust returnest,
Was not spoken of the soul.

Not enjoyment, and not sorrow,
Is our destined end or way;
But to act, that each tomorrow
Find us farther than today.

Art is long, and Time is fleeting,
And our hearts, though stout and brave,
Still, like muffled drums, are beating
Funeral marches to the grave.

In the world's broad field of battle,
In the bivouac of Life,
Be not like dumb, driven cattle!
Be a hero in the strife!

Trust no Future, howe'er pleasant!
Let the dead past bury its dead!
Act, —act in the living Present!

Heart within, and God o'erhead!

Lives of great men all remind us
We can make our lives sublime,
And, departing, leave behind us
Footprints on the sand of time;

Footprints, that perhaps another,
Sailing o'er life's solemn main,
A forlorn and shipwrecked brother,
Seeing, shall take heart again.

Let us; then be up and doing,
With a heart for any fate;
Still achieving, still pursuing,
Learn to labor and to wait.

Chapter Ⅲ Late Romanticism

1. *Characteristics of Late Romanticism and the Flowering of American Literature*

Unlike the early-romantic writers whose writings were imitative, the late romantic writers such as Emerson, Thoreau, Hawthorne, Melville and Whitman were instrumental, in one way or another, in creating an indigenous American literature. These writers wrote about the new experiences of their new nation in their peculiarly American ways instead of imitating and importing from other lands, and brought the flowering of American literature in the nineteenth century. Such a flowering of literature was most impressively seen in a period of six years from 1850 to 1856, when a number of monumental masterpieces almost unbelievably poured into the stream of American literature. These achievements included Hawthorne's *The Scarlet Letter* (1850) and *The House of the Seven Gables* (1851), Thoreau's *Walden* (1854), Emerson's *Representative Men* (1850) and *English Traits* (1856), Melville's *Moby-Dick* (1851), and Whitman's *Leaves of Grass* (1855). With these great works, the historians and critics hold almost by common consent that American literature has grown into maturity.

2. *Late Romantic Poets—Whitman, Dickinson, Poe*

Walt Whitman (1819—1892)

① ***Biographical Introduction***

Whitman was brought up in a working-class background on Long Island, New York. He had five years of schooling and a good deal of "loafing" and reading. Thirsting for experience and gregariousness in habit, Whitman tried at a variety of jobs and picked up a first-hand knowledge of life and people in the new world. He worked as an office boy, a printer's apprentice, schoolmaster, printer, editor of eight successive newspapers, journalist. In 1844, Whitman traveled to New Orleans and saw very much the Mississippi heartlands. This experience with the people and country furnished both material and guiding spirit for his epic, *Leaves of Grass*, on which Whitman's popularity rests.

② ***The Development of Leaves of Grass***

Leaves of Grass is the title under which virtually all of Whitman's poetry was published. Between 1855 and 1897 it passed through ten editions, which grew steadily to accommodate both new material and revisions of the old. The first edition, published by Whitman himself, was largely given over to the long poetic manifesto later titled "Song of Myself". It did not sell well, but it made a stir on the American literary scene. It broke with the poetic convention, and its sexuality and exotic and vulgar language brought harsh criticism on it. The Leaves were called "noxious weeds", its poetry "poetry of barbarism," and "a mass of stupid filth." But it received a favorable reaction from Emerson. The second edition of 1856 and the third edition of 1860 were fruit of considerable growth in output and technique. The fifth edition were added to by Whitman's poems of the Civil War and of Lincoln such as "O Captain! My Captain!" By 1881, the year of the seventh edition, *Leaves of Grass* had taken on what was essentially its final form and later works would appear as annexes to the main trunk.

③ ***Whitman's View and Theme***

Whitman embraces idealism. He relies on insight and intuition. His poetry becomes a happy medium for communicating his views on the cosmos and on man. The future union of the nations and the world and the cosmos; the equal potential divinity of everything from grass to mankind; the ideals of equality and democracy; the dignity, the self-reliant spirit and the joy of the common man; the immanence of God; the multiplicity of nature and the need for a poetry commensurate with it—all these find adequate expression in his poems. In his "Song of Myself", Whitman revealed a world of equality without rank and hierarchy. Whitman combined the ideal of the democratic common man and that of the rugged individual. He envisioned the poet a hero, that savior and a prophet, one who leads the community. In later years Whitman came to see the failure of democracy and the social and moral corruption in American, as was revealed in his *Democratic Vista*, but he thought these could be cured by the self-reform of the individual.

④ **Whitman's Style**

Whitman was a daring experimentalist. His early poems are in conventional rime and metre, but apparently he found the restriction disappointing. He began to experiment in about 1847, then he broke free from the traditional iambic pentameter and wrote free verse. One of the major principles of Whitman's technique is parallelism or a rhythm of thought in which the line, not the conventional foot, as the rhythmical unit. Another principle is phonetic recurrence, i.e., the systematic repetition of words and phrases at the beginning, in the middle or at the end of the line. These two principles coordinate with and reinforce each other, giving free rein to the poet's imagination in his life-long attempt to celebrate life in the new world. Besides, Whitman's poetry suggests rather than tells. His whole leaves are rather a dramatization of the idea. This is perhaps why Whitman is not easy to read.

⑤ **Whitman's Influence**

Whitman's influence over modern poetry is great in the world as well as in America. Many poets in England, France, Italy and Latin America were in his debt. In America, modern American poets like T.S. Eliot and Ezra Pound would not have been what they were without Whitman. Pound recognised him as the father figure who led the break from the past. Carl Sandburg carried, in his *Chicago poems*, the Whitmanesque tradition into the twentieth century. Whitman has been compared to a mountain in American literary history. Although his excessive optimism led to a decline of his reputation, the last few decades have seen an immense change in critical attitude toward him and his poetry. Contemporary American poetry, whatever school or form, bears witness to his great influence. His innovations in diction and versification, his frankness about sex, his inclusion of the common place and the ugly and his censure of the weaknesses of the American democratic practice have paved his way to a share of immortality in American literature:

SONG OF MYSELF

(*Excerpt*)

I celebrate myself, and sing myself,
And what I assume you shall assume,
For every atom belonging to me as good belongs to you.
I loafe and invite my soul,
I lean and loafe at my ease observing a spear of summer grass.
My tongue, every atom of my blood, form'd from this soil, this air,
Born here of parents born here from parent the same, and their parents the same,
I, now thirty-seven years old in perfect health begin,
Hoping to cease not till death.
Creeds and schools in abeyance,
Retiring back a while sufficed at what they are, but never forgotten,
I harbor for good or bad, I permit to speak at every hazard,
Nature without check with original energy.

I HEAR AMERICA SINGING

I hear America singing, the varied carols I hear,
Those of mechanics, each one singing his[1] as it[2] should be blithe and strong,
The carpenter singing his as he measures his plank or beam,
The mason singing his as he makes ready for work, or leaves off work,
The boatman singing what belongs to him in his boat, the deckhand singing on the steamboat deck,
The shoemaker singing as he sits on his bench, the hatter singing as he stands,
The wood-cutter's song, the ploughboy's on his way in the morning, or at noon intermission or at sundown,
The delicious singing of the mother, or of the young wife at work, or of the girl sewing or washing,
Each singing what belongs to him or her and to none else[3],
The day what belongs to the day[4], at night the party of young fellows, robust, friendly,
Singing with open mouths their strong melodious songs.

Question for Consideration:

What implication do you think "I" and "myself" give?

Emily Dickinson(1830—1886)

① ***Biographical Introduction***

Dickinson was born in 1830 into a Calvinist family of Amberst. Massachusetts, where she lived for almost all her life, except a few years when she was educated at Mount Holyoke Female Seminary.

She lived a life that was outwardly almost eventless and remained single to the end of her life. With exception of a few brief early visits to Washington, Philadelphia, and Boston, she spent all her time at home and in her large garden, reading and writing and baking bread for the family. She wrote altogether about 2000 poems of which only seven appeared in print in her life time. After her death, her sister, emptying Emily's desk to burn all her correspondence as Emily had specially directed, was amazed to find many poems neatly copied on small pieces of paper stitched together to form little booklets. She requested Thomas Wentworth Higginson, editor of the Atlantic to edit it. In 1890 a group of one hundred appeared in print. They attracted much attention from a public by then ready to welcome a new poetry, and several other volumes followed at intervals until, in 1955, a complete edition was issued.

② ***Dickinson's View and Theme***

By far the largest portion of Dickinson's poetry concerns death and immortality, themes which lie at the centre of Dickinson's world. Dickinson's many friends died before her and the fact that death seemed to occur often in the Amberst of the time added to her gloomy meditation. "My life closed twice before its close" portrays the poet as ever-ready for the assault of death as she experienced death twice when she lost two of her best friends, Benjamin Newton and Charles Wadsworth. For Dickinson death leads to immortality as is illustrated in "Because I could not stop for death," and "As imperceptibly as grief". Death comes as a gentleman taking a lady for a drive in a carriage, which holds "immortality". Death comes imperceptibly as grief and marks the beginning of a higher life. Dickinson's preoccupation with the subject of death amounted to an obsession so that she began to conceive of the process of dying in poems such as "I heard a fly buzz when I died". However, in this poem, she was skeptical and ambivalent about the possibility of achieving immortality.

Dickinson's nature poems are also great in number and rich in matter. Natural phenomena, changes of seasons, heavenly bodies, animals, birds and insects, flowers of various kinds, and many other subjects related to nature find their way into her poetry. Dickinson observed nature closely and described it vividly but never with the feeling of being lost in it, or altogether part of it, nor was she surprised when its creatures also kept their distance. To Dickinson, nature is both gaily benevolent and cruel. The grandeur of a sunrise ("I'll tell you how the sun rose."), the sense of momentary transitoriness ("A Route of Evanescence") and the power and majesty of a summer storm are among the themes Dickinson handled in her own original way. In the meantime the cold indifference of nature is also revealed in his poems. "A bird came down the walk" may serve as a symbol of nature itself with which the poet tries to establish a form of connection and understanding, but all in vain: alienation exists between.

Dickinson also wrote some poems about love. Like his death and nature poems, her love poems were original. "Mine—by the Right of the White Election" expresses a passionate and eternal love in an elegiac tone. "Wild Nights—Wild Nights" presents the boat and the sea as symbols of male and female lovers which combine into wild consummated love, expressing love in an objective, easy manner.

Besides death and immortality, nature, and love, Dickinson's poems are concerned about ethics, with respect to which, she emphasizes free will and human responsibility. Her poems, "*To fight aloud*" and "*A triumph may be* " view the cause and cure of evil as mainly within the individual, whose highest duty is "Renunciation" of anything low or hostile to man's spiritual heritage and self-respect.

③ *Features of Dickinson's Poems*

Although Dickinson lived in the flood of the romantic revolution, she seems to have nothing in common with the leading writers of the time. She imitates nobody and seems to be wholly original, taking the stuff of her poetry merely from her personal experiences in order to express what she felt about love, nature, death and immortality, and developing her own poetic form with many peculiar features. In addition to such characteristics as the abundant use of dashes, and irregular and often idiosyncratic punctuation and capitalization, her mode of expression is characterized by clear-cut and delicately original imagery, precise diction, and fragmentary and enigmatic metrical pattern. All these characteristics of her poetry were to become popular through Stephen Crane and with the Imagists such as Ezra Pound in the present century. She became, with Stephen Crane, the precursor of the Imagist movement. One more thing that characterises Dickinson's poetry is that her basic tone is tragic. This is because of the influence of the predestination and pessimism of Calvinism on her childhood and adolescence.

④ *Similarities and Differences Between Whitman and Dickinson*

Walt Whitman and Emily Dickinson are considered by many to

be the greatest and most original poets, in whom modern American poetry is to find its sources. Both Whitman and Dickinson were independent American poets in theme and technique. Thematically, both extolled an emergent America, its expansion, its individualism and its Americanness, but in their different ways. Whitman seemed to keep his eye on society at large while Dickinson explored the inner life of the individual. In technical terms, both added to the literary independence of the new nation by breaking free of the convention of the iambic pentameter and exhibiting a freedom in form unknown before, also in different ways. Whitman's form is noted for its endless, all-inclusive catalogs, whereas Dickinson's is characterized by its concise, direct and simple diction and syntax.

A NARROW FELLOW IN THE GRASS

A narrow Fellow in the Grass
Occasionally rides—
You may have met Him—did you not
His notice[1] sudden is—

The Grass divides as with a Comb—
A spotted shaft is seen—
And then it closes at your feet
And opens further on—

He likes a Boggy Acre
A Floor too cool for Corn—
Yet when a Boy, and Barefoot—
I more than once at Noon

Have passed, I thought, a Whip lash
Unbraiding in the Sun

When stooping to secure it
It wrinkled, and was gone—

Several of Nature's People
I know, and they know me—
I feel for them a transport
Of cordiality—

But never met this Fellow
Attended, or alone
Without a tighter breathing
And Zero at the Bone—

BECAUSE I COULD NOT STOP FOR DEATH

Because I could not stop for Death—
He kindly stopped for me—
The Carriage held but just Ourselves—
And Immortality.

We slowly drove—He knew no haste
And I had put away
My labor and my leisure too,
For His Civility—

We passed the School, where Children strove
At Recess—in the Ring—
We passed the Fields of Gazing Grain—
We passed the Setting Sun—

Or rather—He passed Us—
The Dew drew quivering and chill—
For only Gossamer, my Gown—
My Tippet—only Tulle—

We paused before a House that seemed
The Swelling of the Ground—
The Roof was scarcely visible—
The Cornice—in the Ground—

Since then this Centuries—and yet
Feels shorter than the Day
I first surmised the Horses' Heads
Were toward Eternity

Questions for consideration:

1. What sort of character is Death? In what mood did she accompany him?
2. What is the implication of the description of school children at play?

Edgar Allan Poe (1809—1849)

① *Biographical Introduction*

Edgar Allan Poe had a short life of poverty, anxiety, and fantastic tragedy. Poe was born in Boston, the child of struggling traveling actors. He lost both of his parents at the age of two and was taken care of by John Allan a wealthy merchant of Virginia. The Allans failed to offer the Orphan a normal home and Poe enjoyed nothing but an unhappy relationship together. Most of Poe's education was in England from 1815 to 1820. In 1826 he entered the University of Virginia and left after one year because of gambling debts. In 1827, Poe had a quarrel with the Allans and ran away to Boston, where he enlisted in the Army for two years and served at

West Point for about eight months. Having been dismissed from these posts, Poe had to be dependent upon his pen for a living. From 1830 onward Poe was editor of a number of periodicals and wrote critical articles, short stories and poems, which brought him increasing reputation in literary circles. But his literary success never made him wealthy. In 1847, his wife's death shattered him. He took to drink and drugs and died in loneliness, poverty, intoxication and illness in 1849. Though poor all his life, Poe was a man of literary genius. Now he has been universally recognised as a poet of the first rank, a great writer of fiction, and a critic of acumen and insight.

② ***Literary Criticism***

Poe was the first important literary critic in American literature. His most noted critical works include *Twice-Told Tales*, *Philosophy of Composition*, and *The Poetic Principle*, in which he formulated his theories for the short story and poetry.

The short story in Poe's view must be of such length as to be read at one sitting so as to give the reader the totality of impression; the very first sentence ought to help to bring out the "single effect" of the story; no word should be used which does not contribute to the "preestablished" design of the work; a tale should reveal some logical truth with "the fullest satisfaction," and should end with the last sentence, leaving a sense of finality.

The poem, he says, should be short, readable at one sitting. Its chief aim is beauty, namely, to produce a feeling of beauty in the reader. The aim of beauty is to elevate the soul, and the highest development of it is melancholy, that is, to excite the soul to tears. Thus the death of a beautiful woman is, unquestionably, the most poetical topic in the world—and equally it is beyond doubt that the lips best suited "for such a topic are those of a bereaved lover." Poe is opposed to "the heresy of the didactic" and calls for pure poetry with no social or moral function. Poe also stresses the musical quality of verse and defines true poetry as "the rhythmical creation of beauty" Thus, in his poetry, all poetic devices such as alliteration, assonance, and consonance are brought into full play. Poe's critical theories are more or less satisfied by his own creations of imagination.

③ ***Poetry***

As a literary man, Poe is, first of all, known for his poetry. Throughout his career, Poe wrote all together fifty poems or more, which are of a uniformly high caliber and enbody his conviction that the function of poetry is not to summarize and interpret earthly experience, but to create a mood in which the soul soars toward supernatural beauty. In the following, we will discuss about some of his best poems.

"Sonnet To Science", is an English or Shakespearean sonnet. It attacks the factual picture of the world presented by the eighteenth century science. Science as against art and imagination is treated as a villain. It has wickedly dissipated the illusionary, poetic vision. But the universe actually contains wonders and truths incomprehensible to the mere materialist.

"To Helen" is generally considered a tribute to Mrs Jane Stanard, a Rickmond matron considerate of the youthful Poe. This piece celebrates an idealized woman as the incarnation of the pure, unattainable, romanticized beauty of antiquity. It is the abstract yearning of the youthful male for the perfect woman. The symbol of

Helen of Troy permits the mind to comprehend a long-departed civilization.

"The Raven" is the best known of Poe's verse. It exemplifies Poe's poetic theories in every way. It is about 100 lines, perfectly readable at one sitting. A sense of melancholy over the death of a beloved beautiful young woman pervades the whole poem. In a stormy night, a young man was grieving for his lost Lenore when he was visited by a raven which croaks "Nevermore" to every question of the young man and turns his grief to madness. The poem is also a marvel of regularity with beautiful rhythm.

"Annabel Lee" is commonly thought to refer to Poe's deceased wife. Its mood is that of serene acceptance. Love here is associated not with the usual emblems of rose or music, but with the elemental and eternal rhythms of the moon and stars. In it Poe strives to create a vision of beauty and a melodious sound strong enough to block out the ugly real world he hates and fears.

④ *Short Stories*

As a short story writer, Poe was simultaneously a romantic dreamer and a rationalist, a fantast and a realist. On the one hand he was much given to the world of imagination and fancy and on the other hand, he was logical to a fault with an intuitive faculty. In theme Poe anticipated twentieth-century literature in his treatment of disintegration of the self in a world of T. S. Eliot's "nothingness", a world where there is neither joy, nor love, nor light, nor peace, nor help from pain. To describe the disintegrating process of the soul, Poe was particularly interested in the deep abyss of the unconscious and subconscious mental activity of the people and sometimes Poe revealed this area of human experience with alarming accuracy.

Poe's fictional characters are mostly neurotics, who are either like Melville's "isolators," with no sense of their identity, no name, no place nor parentage, dislocated, alienated from society, or a criminal who attempts to establish his sense of identity by the crime that he commits, or a bereaved lover. Poe's most enduring tales are those of suspense and horror, including *The Pit and the Pendulum*, *The Fall of the House of Usher*, *The Cask of Amontillado*, and *The Masque of the Red Death*. Distinct from these are tales of mystery or detective stories, which include *The Murders in the Rue Morgue* and *The Gold Bug*.

Ligeia was one of Poe's favorites. The narrator deeply loves his first wife, Ligeia of the passionate eyes. After her death he marries lady Rowena, who is interested solely in his money, and lives in a gothic abbey in England. Rowena dies and then miraculously rises. Her reopened eyes are those of the passionate Ligeia. The tale of reincarnation might be interpreted as a hallucination of the narrator, whose opium-induced fancy transforms Rowena into Ligeia. Here Poe is concerned with a struggle to retain physical and mental identity after death. The will of Ligeia is so powerful that it resists extinction and successfully contends in the spirit world with the soul of Rowena.

The Fall of the House of Usher is remarkable for its vivid graphic effects. On a stormy night, the narrator visits his old friend Roderik Usher in the weakened Gothic castle Madeline. Roderink's twin sister apparently dies and is buried alive in one secluded part of the house. She emerges from her coffin to clasp Roderick in her arms, bearing both to the floor in death. The narrator flees in terror to witness the collapse of the house into a gloomy lake. Roderick is the totally isolated and alienated psyche given over to the forces of madness and death. The collapse of the house is symbolic of the ultimate annihilation of Roderick.

⑤ *Poe's Unique Position in American Literature*

Poe was the first major American critic who offered a set of formulated principles in relation to the criticism of literature as well as to the creation of the work of art. Different from almost all his contemporary romantic critics, who tended to manifest in their criticism excessive appreciative sympathy, moralism, and a narrow provincialism, Poe made effort to "limit criticism to comment upon Art." This emphasis upon the value of art, form, and unity played an active role in the development of the analytical approach, a method typical of modern criticism. As a creative writer, Poe is different from his contemporaries in that Poe insists on the primary importance of the work of art itself, while others follow the romantic stress on the expression of the personality of the artist. Poe is the first American author who formalized the technique of the short story, in pursuit of the totality of effect through compression, immediacy, verisimilitude, and finality. He also invented the detective story and developed a new fiction of psychological analysis. As a great poet, Poe's aesthetics and conscious craftsmanship, his attack on "the heresy of the didactic" and his call for "the rhythmical creation of beauty" have influenced French symbolists and the devotees of "art for art's sake". All these mentioned above enable Poe to stand as one of the really great creative writers in American literature. However, Poe's conception of the form of a literary work is classical. His classical traditional style is sometimes too rational and too ordinary to reflect the peculiarity of his central theme.

THE RAVEN[1]

Once upon a midnight dreary, while I pondered weak and weary,
Over many a quaint and curious volume of forgotten lore,
While I nodded, nearly napping, suddenly there came a tapping,
As of some one gently rapping, rapping at my chamber door.
"It is some visitor," I muttered, "tapping at my chamber door—"
Only this and nothing more.

Ah, distinctly I remember it was in the bleak December,
And each separate dying ember wrought its ghost upon the floor.
Eagerly I wished the morrow;—vainly I had sought to borrow
From my books surcease of sorrow—sorrow for the lost Lenore—
For the rare and radiant maiden whom the angels name Lenore—
Nameless here for evermore.

And the silken sad uncertain rustling of each purple curtain
Thrilled me—filled me with fantastic terrors never felt before;
So that now, to still the beating of my heart, I stood repeating,
"'Tis some visitor entreating entrance at my chamber door—
Some late visitor entreating entrance at my chamber door;—
Darkness there, and nothing more."

Deep into that darkness peering, long I stood there wondering, fearing,
Doubting, dreaming dreams no mortals ever dared to dream before;
But the silence was unbroken, and the stillness gave no token,
And the only word there spoken was the whispered word, "Lenore!"
This I whispered, and an echo murmured back the word, "Lenore!"—
Merely this and nothing more.

Back into the chamber turning, all my soul within me burning,

Soon again I heard a tapping somewhat louder than before.
"Surely," said I, "surely that is something at my window lattice;
Let me see, then, what thereat is, and this mystery explore—
Let my heart be still a moment and this mystery explore;—
'Tis the wind and nothing more!"
Open here I flung the shutter, when, with many a flirt and flutter,
In there stepped a stately raven of the saintly days of yore;
Not the least obeisance made he; not a minute stopped or stayed he;
But, with mien of lord or lady, perched above my chamber door—
Perched upon a bust of Pallas[2] just above my chamber door—
Perched, and sat, and nothing more.
Then this ebony bird beguiling my sad fancy into smiling,
By the grave and stern decorum of the countenance it wore,
"Though thy crest be shorn and shaven, thou," I said, "art sure no craven,
Ghastly grim and ancient raven wandering from the Nightly shore—
Tell me what thy lordly name is on the Night's Plutonian shore!"[3]
Quoth the raven, "Nevermore."
Much I marvelled this ungainly fowl to hear discourse so plainly,
Though its answer little meaning—little relevancy bore;
For we cannot help agreeing that no living human being
Ever yet was blessed with seeing bird above his chamber door—
Bird or beast upon the sculptured bust above his chamber door,
With such name as "Nevermore."
But the raven, sitting lonely on the placid bust, spoke only
That one word, as if his soul in that one word did he outpour.
Nothing farther then he uttered—not a feather then he fluttered—
Till I scarcely more than muttered, "Other friends have flown before—
On the morrow he will leave me as my hopes have flown before."
Then the bird said, "Nevermore."

Startled at the stillness broken by reply so aptly spoken,
"Doubtless," said I, "what it utters is its only stock and store,
Caught from some unhappy master whom unmerciful Disaster
Followed fast and followed faster till his songs one burden bore—
Till the dirges of his Hope that melancholy burden bore
Of 'Never-nevermore.'"
But the raven still beguiling all my sad soul into smiling,
Straight I wheeled a cushioned seat in front of bird and bust and door;
There, upon the velvet sinking, I betook myself to linking
Fancy unto fancy, thinking what this ominous bird of yore—
What this grim, ungainly, ghastly, gaunt, and ominous bird of yore
Meant in croaking "Nevermore."
This I sat engaged in guessing, but no syllable expressing,
To the fowl whose fiery eyes now burned into my bosom's core;
This and more I sat divining, with my head at ease reclining
On the cushion's velvet lining that the lamplight gloated[4] o'er,
But whose velvet violet lining with the lamplight gloating o'er,
She shall press, ah, nevermore!
Then, methought, the air grew denser, perfumed from an unseen censer
Swung by angels whose faint foot-falls tinkled on the tufted floor.
"Wretch," I cried, "thy God hath lent thee—by these angels he hath sent thee
Respite—respite and nepenthe[5] from thy memories of Lenore!
Quaff, oh quaff this kind nepenthe and forget this lost Lenore!"
Quoth the raven, "Nevermore."
"Prophet!" said I, "thing of evil! —prophet still, if bird or devil! —
Whether Tempter sent, or whether tempest tossed thee here ashore,
Desolate, yet all undaunted, on this desert land enchanted—

Oh this home by Horror haunted, —tell me truly, I implore—
Is there—is there balm in Gilead?[6]—tell me—tell me, I implore!"
Quoth the raven, "Nevermore."
"Prophet!"said I, "thing of evil! —prophet still, if bird or devil!
By that heaven that bends above us—by that God we both adore—
Tell this soul with sorrow laden if, within the distant Aidenn?
It shall clasp a sainted maiden whom the angels name Lenore—
Clasp a rare and radiant maiden whom the angels name Lenore."
Quoth the raven, "Nevermore."
"Be that word our sign of parting, bird or fiend!" I shrieked, upstarting—
"Get thee back into the tempest and the Night's Plutonian shore!
Leave no black plume as a token of that lie thy soul hath spoken!
Leave my loneliness unbroken! —quit the bust above my door!
Take thy beak from out my heart, and take thy form from off my door!"
Quoth the raven, "Nevermore."
And the raven, never flitting, still is sitting, still is sitting
Oh the pallid bust of Pallas just above my chamber door;
And his eyes have all the seeming of a demon's that is dreaming,
And the lamp-light o'er him streaming throws his shadow on the floor;
And my soul from out that shadow that lies floating on the floor
Shall be lifted—nevermore!

Notes:

1. One complete autograph MS. survives, and variant readings appeared in the numerous magazine publications of "The Raven" before Poe's death. The 1845 *Poems* version is followed here. His recapitulation of its creation (see *The Philosophy of Composition*) is an excellent example of analytical criticism, substantiating his assertion that he had carefully calculated this poem for popular appeal. Yet the "lost Lenore" is a central experience in Poe's life; the

power of the poem depends in considerable degree upon the tension between calculated effect and genuine emotional experience. Lenore is variously identified as Miss Royster, a youthful sweetheart, and as Virginia, his wife, whose long and hopeless illness was ended by death in 1847.

2. Poe's conscious selection of Pallas Athena, goddess of wisdom, for the raven's perch, recalls his reported attempt, in an early draft, to have the bitter truth revealed by an owl, Athena's traditional bird of wisdom.
3. The infernal regions were ruled by Pluto.
4. A double meaning is inherent in the rare usage of the word "gloated" in the sense of "to refrast light from."
5. In classical mythology, a potion banishing sorrow, as in the Odyssey, IV, 419—430.
6. Cf. Jeremiah viii. 22: "Is there no balm in Gilead?"—a reference to an esteemed medicinal herb from that region.
7. variant spelling and pronunciation for "Eden."

3. Late Romantic Essayists—Emerson and Thoreau

① Emerson—the Leader of New England Transcendentalism

Ralph Waldo Emerson (1830—1883) was widely known and admired as a poet, philosopher, public lecturer, and essayist of his day, whose essays were the most important work in English prose produced in the nineteenth century. Emerson was born in Boston, graduated from Harvard, taught school for a short time, then became a minister of the second church of Boston in 1829. He resigned his position two years later and went to Europe. He made friends with Coleridge, Carlyle and Wordsworth and brought back with him the influence of European Romanticism. With people of like minds such as Thoreau he formed the Transcendentalist club to discuss matters of interest to the life of the nation as a whole and found the Transcendentalist journal, *The Dial*, to explain their ideas. In 1831

Emerson published his epoch-making book *Nature*, which is generally regarded as the Bible of New England Transcendentalism. Two years later two of his famous Transcendentalist speeches, "The American Scholar" and "The Divinity School Address" appeared. Then Emerson embarked on a series of lecture tours in England and America, teaching and spreading his transcendentalist doctrine. Many of his lectures were later distilled into his famous *Essays* and other works.

NATURE[1]

A subtle chain of countless rings
The nest unto the farthest brings;
The eye reads omens where it goes,
And speaks ail languages the rose;
And, striving to be man, the worm
Mounts through all the spires of form.

Introduction

Our age is retrospective. It builds the sepulchres of the fathers. It writes biographies, histories, and criticism. The foregoing generations beheld God and nature face to face; we, through their eyes. Why should not we also enjoy an original relation to the universe? Why should not we have a poetry and philosophy of insight and not of tradition, and a religion by revelation to us, and not the history of theirs? Embosomed for a season in nature, whose floods of life stream around and through us, and invite us by the powers they supply, to action proportioned to nature, why should we grope among the dry bones of the past, or put the living generation into masquerade out of its faded wardrobe? The sun shines to-day also. There is more wool and flax in the fields. There are new lands, new men, new thoughts. Let us demand our own works and laws and worship.

Undoubtedly we have no questions to ask which are unanswerable. We must trust the perfection of the creation so far, as to believe that whatever curiosity the order of things has awakened in our minds, the order of things can satisfy. Every man's condition is a solution in hieroglyphic to those inquiries he would put. He acts it as life, before he apprehends it as truth. In like manner, nature is already, in its forms and tendencies, describing its own design. Let us interrogate the great apparition, that shines so peacefully around us. Let us inquire, to what end is nature?

All science has one aim, namely, to find a theory of nature. We have theories of races and of functions, but scarcely yet a remote approach to an idea of creation. We are now so far from the road to truth, that religious teachers dispute and hate each other, and speculative men are esteemed unsound and frivolous. But to a sound judgment, the most abstract truth is the most practical. Whenever a true theory appears, it will be its own evidence. Its test is, that it will explain all phenomena. Now many are thought not only unexplained but inexplicable; as language, sleep, madness, dreams, beasts, sex.

Philosophically considered, the universe is composed of Nature and the Soul. Strictly speaking, therefore, all that is separate from us, all which Philosophy distinguishes as the NOT ME, that is, both nature and art, all other men and my own body, must be ranked under this name, NATURE. In enumerating the values of nature and casting up their sum, I shall use the word in both senses; —in its common and in its philosophical import. In inquiries so general as our present one, the inaccuracy is not material; no confusion of thought will occur. Nature, in the common sense, refers to essences unchanged by man, space, the air, the river, the leaf. Art is applied to the mixture of his will with the same things, as in a house, a canal, a statue, a picture. But his operations taken together are so insignificant, a little chipping, baking, patching, and washing, that in an impression so grand as that of the world on the human mind, they do not vary the result.

Chapter 1　Nature

To go into solitude, a man needs to retire as much from his chamber as from society. I am not solitary whilst I read and write, though nobody is with me. But if a man would be alone, let him look at the stars. The rays that come from those heavenly worlds, will separate between him and vulgar things. One might think the atmosphere was made transparent with this design, to give man, in the heavenly bodies, the perpetual presence of the sublime. Seen in the streets of cities, how great they are! If the stars should appear one night in a thousand years, how would men believe and adore; and preserve for many generations the remembrance of the city of God which had been shown! But every night come out these envoys of beauty, and light the universe with their admonishing smile.

The stars awaken a certain reverence, because though always present, they are always inaccessible; but all natural objects make a kindred impression, when the mind is open to their influence. Nature never wears a mean appearance. Neither does the wisest man extort all her secret, and lose his curiosity by finding out all her perfection. Nature never became a toy to a wise spirit. The flowers, the animals, the mountains, reflected all the wisdom of his best hour, as much as they had delighted the simplicity of his childhood.

When we speak of nature in this manner, we have a distinct but most poetical sense in the mind. We mean the integrity of impression made by manifold natural objects. It is this which distinguishes the stick of timber of the wood-cutter, from the tree of the poet. The charming landscape which I saw this morning, is indubitably made up of some twenty or thirty farms. Miller owns this field, Locke that, and Manning the woodland beyond. But none of them owns the landscape. There is a property in the horizon which no man has but he whose eye can integrate all the parts, that is, the poet. This is best part of these men's farms, yet to this their warranty-deeds give no title.

To speak truly, few adult persons can see nature. Most persons do not see the sun. At least they have a very superficial seeing. The sun illuminates only the eye of the man, but shines into the eye and the heart of the child. The lover of nature is he whose inward and outward senses are still truly adjusted to each other; who has retained the spirit of infancy even into the era of manhood. His intercourse with heaven and earth, becomes part of his daily food. In the presence of nature, a wild delight runs through the man, in spite of real sorrows. Nature says, —he is my creature, and maugre[2] all his impertinent griefs, he shall be glad with me. Not the sun or the summer alone, but every hour and season yields its tribute of delight; for every hour and change corresponds to and authorizes a different state of the mind, from breathless moon to grimmest midnight. Nature is a setting that fits equally well a comic or a mourning piece. In good health, the air is a cordial of incredible virtue. Crossing a bare common, in snow puddles, at twilight, under a clouded sky, without having in my thoughts any occurrence of special good fortune, I have enjoyed a perfect exhilaration. Almost I fear to think how glad I am. In the woods too, a man casts off his years, as the snake his slough, and at what period soever of life, is always a child. In the woods, is perpetual youth. Within these plantations of God, a decorum and sanctity reign, a perennial festival is dressed, and the guest sees not how he should tire of them in a thousand years. In the woods, we return to reason and faith. There I feel that nothing can befall me in life, —no disgrace, no calamity, (leaving me my eyes,) which nature cannot repair. Standing on the bare ground, —my head bathed by the blithe air, and uplifted into infinite space, —all mean egotism vanishes. I become a transparent eye-ball. I am nothing. I see all. The currents of the Universal Being circulate through me; I am part or particle[3] of God. The name of the nearest friend sounds then foreign and accidental. To be brothers, to be acquaintances, —master or servant, is then a trifle and a disturbance. I am the lover of uncontained and immortal beauty. In the wilderness. I find something more dear and connate than in streets or villages. In the tranquil landscape, and especially in the distant line of the horizon, man beholds somewhat as beautiful as his own nature.

The greatest delight which the fields and woods minister, is the suggestion of an occult relation between man and the vegetable. I am not alone and unacknowledged. They nod to me and I to them. The waving of the boughs in the storm, is new to me and old. It takes me by surprise, and yet is not unknown. Its effect is like that of a higher thought or a better emotion coming over me, when I deemed I was thinking justly or doing right.

Yet it is certain that the power to produce this delight, does not reside in nature, but in man, or in a harmony of both. It is necessary to use these pleasures with great temperance. For, nature is not always tricked in holiday attire, but the same scene which yesterday breathed perfume and glittered as for the frolic of the nymphs, is overspread with melancholy today. Nature always wears the colors of the spirit. To a man laboring under calamity, the heat of his own fire hath sadness in it. Then, there is a kind of contempt of the landscape felt by him who has just lost by death a dear friend. [4]The sky less grand as it shuts down over less worth in the population.

Chapter 2 Commodity[5]

Whoever considers the final cause of the world, will discern a multitude of uses that enter as parts into that result. They all admit of being thrown into one of the following classes. Commodity; Beauty; Language; and Discipline.

Under the general name of Commodity, I rank all those advantages which our senses owe to nature. This, of course, is a benefit which is temporary and mediate, not ultimate, like its service to the soul. Yet although low, it is perfect in its kind, and is the only use of nature which all men apprehend. The misery of man appears like childish petulance, when we explore the steady and prodigal provision that has been made for his support and delight on this green ball which floats him through the heavens. What angels invented these splendid ornaments, these rich conveniences, this ocean of air above, this tent of dropping clouds, this striped coat of climates, this fourfold year? Beasts, fire, water, stones, and corn serve him. The field is at once his floor, his work-yard, his play-ground, his garden, and his bed.

"More servants wait on man
Than he'll take notice of."—[6]

Nature, in its ministry to man, is not only the material, but is also the process and the result. All the parts incessantly work into each other's hands for the profit of man. The wind sows the seed; the sun evaporates the sea; the wind blows the vapor to the field; the ice, on the other side of the planet, condenses rain on this, the rain feeds the plant; the plant the animal; and thus the endless circulations of the divine charity nourish man.

The useful arts are but reproductions or new combinations by the wit of man, of the same natural benefactors. He no longer waits for favoring gales, but by means of steam, he realizes the fable of Eolus's bag,[7] and carries the two and thirty winds in the boiler of his boat. To diminish friction, he paves the road with iron bars, and, mounting a coach with a ship-load of men, animals, and merchandise behind him, he darts through the country, from town to town, like an eagle of a swallow through the air. By the aggregate of these aids, how is the face of the world changed, from the era Noah to that of Napoleon! The private poor man hath cities, ships, canals, bridges, built for him. He goes to the post-office, and the human race run on his errands; to the court-house, and nations repair his wrongs. He sets his house upon the road, and the human race go forth every morning, and shovel out the snow, and cut a path for him.

But there is no need of specifying particulars in this class of uses. The catalogue is endless, and the examples so obvious, that I shall leave them to the reader's reflection, with the general remark, that this mercenary benefit is one which has respect to a farther good. A man is fed, not that he may be fed but that he may work.

Notes:

1. Emerson's first major work, *Nature*, was also the first comprehensive expression of American transcendentalism. For the student it provides a fresh and lyrical intimation of many of the leading ideas that Emerson developed in vari-

ous later essays and poems. The author first mentioned this book in a diary entry made in 1833, on his return voyage from the first European visit, during which he had met a number of European writers, especially Carlyle. In 1834, when he settled in the Old Manse, his grandfather's home in Concord, he had already written five chapters. He completed the first draft of the volume there, in the very room in which Hawthorne later wrote his *Mosses from an Old Manse*. The small first edition of *Nature*, published anonymously in 1836, gained critical attention, but few general readers. It was not reprinted until 1849, when it was collected in *Nature, Addresses, and Lectures*. At that time Emerson substituted, as epigraph, the present poem, instead of the quotation from Plotinus which had introduced the first edition: "Nature is but an image or imitation of wisdom, the last thing of the soul; Nature being a thing which doth only do, but not know." The new epigraph supported the concept of evolution presented in *Nature*. Darwin's *Origin of Species* did not appear until 1859, but Emerson had seen the classification of species in 1833 at the Paris Jardin des Plantes, while Lamarck was anticipating Darwin, and Lyell's popular *Geology* emphasized fossil remains. The transcendentalists, and Emerson in particular, regarded theories of evolution as supporting a concept of progress and unity as ancient as the early Greek nature philosophy. These ideas persist throughout *Nature*.

2. Despite.
3. The Centenary Edition (1903) bases its reading, "parcel," on a manuscript variant.
4. Writing this at the age of thirty-two, Emerson already had "lost by death" his first wife, a bride of eighteen months; within the last two years, two brothers.
5. In a sense now unfamiliar, commodity is a physical good.
6. From "Man," by George Hetbert (1539—1633).
7. In the *Odyssey*, Book X, Eolus gave Odysseus "a mighty bag, bottling storm winds," which his envious sailors opened, producing a tempest.
8. *Kosmos* (cosmos). By this Greek word, meaning essentially "a universal order or harmony of parts," Emerson suggests his own conception of beauty.

② *The Features of New England Transcendentalism*

New England Transcendentalism was the summit phase of American Romanticism. As the most eloquent spokesman of New England Transcendentalism, Emerson gave an elaborate account of the Transcendentalist views in his works, which can be summarized as follows: First, the Transcendentalists placed emphasis on spirit, or the Oversoul, as the most important thing in the universe. The Oversoul was an all-pervading power for goodness omnipresent and omnipotent, from which all things came and of which all were a part. It existed in nature and man alike. The individual soul of man could go beyond the physical limits of the body, emerge himself with nature, and share the omniscience of the Oversoul. God is operative in the soul of man and thus man is divine. Secondly, Transcendentalists stressed the importance of the individual. To them the individual was the most important element of society. The regeneration of society could only come about through the regeneration of the individual. The ideal type of the individual should be the self-reliant man who depends upon himself, cultivates himself and brings out the divine in himself to get himself perfect and improved. The possibilities for man to develop and improve himself are infinite. This is what Emerson means by "the infinitude of man". Thirdly, the Transcendentalists offered a fresh perception of nature as symbolic of the spirit. To them, nature was not purely matter. It was alive, filled with God's overwhelming presence, on the human mind. The physical world was a symbol of the spiritual and all things in nature tended to be symbolic. This added to the tradition of literary symbolism in American literature.

③ ***Henry David Thoreau*** (1817—1862)

Thoreau was another renowned New England Transcendentalist. His great Transcendentalist work is *Walden*, which is a faithful record of his reflections when he was in solitary communion with nature, an eloquent indication that Thoreau embraced Emerson's Transcendentalist philosophy that nature was a symbol of God and could exerted a restorative, health influence on man's spiritual well-being. The book showed that the author was in perfect harmony with nature, which helped man to achieve personal spiritual perfection.

WALDEN[1]

I do not propose to write an ode to dejection, but to brag as lustily as chanticleer in the morning, standing on his roost, if only to wake my neighbors up.

Economy

When I wrote the following pages, or rather the bulk of them, I lived alone, in the woods, a mile from any neighbor, in a house which I had built myself, on the shore of Walden Pond, in Concord, Massachusetts, and earned my living by the labor of my hands only. I lived there two years and two months. At present I am a sojourner in civilized life again.

I should not obtrude my affairs so much on the notice of my readers if very particular inquiries had not been made by my townsmen concerning my mode of life, which some would call impertinent, though they do not appear to me at all impertinent, but, considering the circumstances, very natural and pertinent. Some have asked what I got to eat; if I did not feel lonesome; if I was not afraid; and the like. Others have been curious to learn what portion of my income I devoted to charitable purposes; and some, who have large families, how many poor children I maintained. I will therefore ask those of my readers who feel no particular interest in me to pardon me if I undertake to answer some of these questions in this book. In most books, the *I*, or first person, is omitted; in this it will be retained; that, in respect to egotism, is the main difference. We commonly do not remember that it is, after all, always the first person that is speaking. I should not talk so much about myself if there were any body else whom I knew as well. Unfortunately, I am confined to this theme by the narrowness of my experience. Moreover, I, on my side, require of every writer, first or last, a simple and sincere account of his own life, and not merely what he has heard of other men's lives; some such account as he would send to his kindred from a distant land; for if he has lived sincerely, it must have been in a distant land to me. Perhaps these pages are more particularly addressed to poor students. As for the rest of my readers, they will accept such portions as apply to them. I trust that none will stretch the seams in putting on the coat, for it may do good service to him whom it fits.

I would fain say something, not so much concerning the Chinese and Sandwich Islanders as you who read these pages, who are said to live in New England, something about your condition, especially your outward condition or circumstances in this world, in this town, what it is, whether it is necessary that it be as bad as it is, whether it cannot be improved as well as not. I have travelled a good deal in Concord; and every where, in shops, and offices, and fields, the inhabitants have appeared to me to be doing penance in a thousand remarkable ways. What I have heard of

Bramins[2] sitting exposed to four fires and looking in the face of the sun; or hanging suspended, with their heads downward, over flames; or looking at the heavens over their shoulders "until it becomes impossible for them to resume their natural position, while from the twist of the neck nothing but liquids can pass into the stomach;" or dwelling, chained for life, at the foot of a tree; or measuring with their bodies, like caterpillars, the breadth of vast empires; or standing on one leg on the tops of pillars,—even these forms of conscious penance are hardly more incredible and astonishing than the scenes which I daily witness. The twelve labors of Hercules[3] were trifling in comparison with those which my neighbors have undertaken; for they were only twelve, and had an end; but I could never see that these men slew or captured any monster or finished any labor. They have no friend to burn with a hot iron the root of the hydra's head, but as soon as one head is crushed, two spring up.

I see young men, my townsmen, whose misfortune it is to have inherited farms, houses, barns, cattle, and farming tools; for these are more easily acquired than got rid of Better if they had been born in the open pasture and suckled by a wolf, that they might have seen with clearer eyes what field they were called to labor in. Who made them serfs of the soil? Why should they eat their sixty acres, when man is condemned to eat only his peck of dirt? Why should they begin digging their graves as soon as they are born? They have got to live a man's life, pushing all these things before them, and get on as well as they can. How many a poor immortal soul have I met well nigh crushed and smothered under its load, creeping down the road of life, pushing before it a barn seventy-five feet by forty, its Augean stables[4] never cleansed, and one hundred acres of land, tillage, mowing, pasture, and woodlot! The portionless, who struggle with no such unnecessary inherited encumbrances, find it labor enough to subdue and cultivate a few cubic feet of flesh.

But men labor under a mistake. The better part of the man is soon ploughing the soil for compost. By a seeming fate, commonly called necessity, they are employed, as it says in an old book, laying up treasures which moth and rust will corrupt and thieves break through and steal.[5] It is a fool's life, as they will find when they get to the end of it, if not before. It is said that Deucalion and Pyrrha[6] created men by throwing stones over their heads behind them:—

> Inde genus durum sumus, experiensque laborum,
> Et documenta damus quâ simus origine nati.

Or, as Raleigh rhymes it in his sonorous way,—

> "From thence our kind hard-hearted is, enduring pain and care,
> Approving that our bodies of a stony nature are."

So much for a blind obedience to a blundering oracle, throwing the stones over their heads behind them, and not seeing where they fell.

Most men, even in this comparatively free country, through mere ignorance and mistake, are so occupied with the factitious cares and superfluously coarse labors of life that its finer fruits cannot be plucked by them. Their fingers, firm excessive toil, are too clumsy and tremble too much for that. Actually, the laboring man has not leisure for a true integrity day by day; he cannot afford to sustain relations to men; his labor would be depreciated in the market; he has no time to be any thing but a machine. How can he remember well his ignorance—which his growth requires—who has so often to use his knowledge? We should feed and clothe him gratuitously sometimes, and recruit him with our cordials, before judge of him. The finest qualities of our nature, like the bloom on fruits can be preserved only by the most delicate handling. Yet we do not treat ourselves nor one another thus tenderly.

Some of you, we all know, are poor, find it hard to live, are sometimes, as it were, gasping for breath. I have no doubt that some of you who read this book are unable to pay for all the dinners which you have actually eaten, or for the coats and shoes which are fast wearing or are already worn out, and have come to this page to spend borrowed or stolen time, robbing your creditors of an hour. It is very evident what mean and sneaking lives many of you live, for my sight has been whetted by experience; always on the limits, trying to get into business and trying to get out of debt, a very ancient slough, called by the Latins *aes alienum*, another's brass, for some of their coins were made of brass; still living, and dying, and buried by this other's brass; always promising to pay, promising to pay, to-morrow, and dying to-day, insolvent; seeking to curry favor, to get custom, by how many modes, only not state-prison offences; lying, flattering, voting, contracting yourselves into a nutshell of civility, or dilating into an atmosphere of thin and vaporous generosity, that you may persuade your neighbor to let you make his shoes, or his hat, or his coat, or his carriage, or import his groceries for him; making yourselves sick, then you may lay up something against a sick day, something to be backed away old chest, or in a stocking behind the plastering, or more safely, in the brick bank; no matter where, no matter how much or how little.

I sometimes wonder that we can be so frivolous, I may almost say, as to attend to the gross but somewhat foreign form of servitude called Negro Slavery, there are so many keen and subtle masters that enslave both north and south. It is hard to have a southern overseer; it is worse to have a northern one; but worst of all when you are the slave-driver of yourself. Talk of a divinity in man! Look at the teamster on the highway, wending to market by day or night; does any divinity stir within him? His highest duty to fodder and water his horses! What is his destiny to him compared with the shipping interests? Does not he drive for Squire Make-a-stir? How godlike, how immortal, is he? See how he cowers and smeaks, how vaguely all the day he fears, not being immortal nor divine, but the slave and prisoner of his own opinion of himself, a fame won by his own deeds. Public opinion is a weak tyrant compared with our own private opinion. What a man thinks of himself, that it is which determines, or rather indicates, his fate. Self-emancipation even in the West Indian provinces of the fancy and imagination, —what Wilberforce[7] is there to bring that about? Think, also, of the ladies of the land weaving toilet cushions against the last day, not to betray too green an interest in their fates! As if you could kill time without injuring eternity.

The mass of men lead lives of quiet desperation. What is called resignation is confirmed desperation. From the desperate city you go into the desperate country, and have to console yourself with the bravery of minks and muskrats. A sterotyped but unconscious despair is concealed even under what are called the games and amusements of mankind. There is no play in them, for this comes after work. But it is a characteristic of wisdom not to do desperate things.

When we consider what, to use the words of the catechism, it the chief end of man,[8] and what are the true necessaries and means of life, it appears as if men had deliberately chosen the common mode of living because they preferred it to any other. Yet they honestly think there is no choice left. But alert and healthy natures remember that the sun rose clear. It is never too late to give up our prejudices. No way of thinking or doing, however ancient, can be trusted without proof. What everybody echoes or in silence passes by as true to-day may turn out to be falsehood tomorrow, mere smoke of opinion, which some had trusted for a cloud that would sprinkle fertilizing rain on their fields. What old people say you cannot do you try and find that you can. Old deeds for old people, and new deeds for new. Old people did not know enough once, perchance, to fetch fresh fuel to keep the fire a-going; new people put a little dry wood under a pot, and are whirled round the globe with the speed of birds, in a way to kill old people, as the phrase is. Age is no better, hardly so well, qualified for an instructor as youth, for it has not profited so much as it has lost. One may almost doubt if the wisest man has learned anything of absolute value by living. Practically, the old have no very important advice to give the young, their own experience has been so partial, and their lives have been such miserable failures, for private reasons, as they must believe; and it may be that they have some faith left which belies that experience, and they are only less young than they were. I have lived some thirty years on this planet, and I have yet to hear the first syllable of valuable or even earnest advice from my seniors. They have told me nothing, and probably cannot tell me any thing, to the purpose. Here is life, an experment to a great extent untried by me; but it does not avail me that they have tried it. If I have any experience which I think valuable, I am sure to reflect that this my Mentors[9] said nothing about...

Notes:

1. The earliest manuscript of this world-famous book, entitled *Walden, or Life in the Woods*, was prepared, as Thoreau states, "about 1846." It was later revised in the preparation of readings for meetings of the Concord Lyceum and

again for publication as a volume in 1854, the source of the present text. Thoreau's knowledge was a constant fact of his intellect, not the result of the mere memory of information. Consequently, *Walden* is a complex organization of themes related to the central concept of individualism: such as the economy of individualism (the experiment at Walden Pond); the spiritual and temporal values of individualism in society or in solitude; the survival of self-reliance amid depersonalizing social organizations; the related observation of animal and plant life; and the transcendental concept of the accomplished human personality, simultaneously aware of relations both with Time and the Timeless.

2. Usually Brahmin; of the highest Hindu caste. The unexpected propriety of the absurd comparison is vintage Thoreau.
3. Son of the Greek god Zeus, but born of a mortal; his twelve superhuman feats included one with human help—that of Iolas. At death, deified as an incarnation of manly strength, he married Hebe, goddess of youth.
4. The stables of Augeus housed 3,000 oxen and had not been cleaned for thirty years, but Hercules accomplished this task in one day by making the Pencus and the Alpheus rivers flow through the stalls.
5. Matthew vi: 19—20.
6. The survivors of the flood by which Zeus destroyed mankind. The Latin quotation is from Ovid's, *Metamorphoses*, Ⅰ.414-415, the translation from Sir Walter Raleigh's *History of the World*.
7. William Wilberforce (1759—1833), leader of the anti-slavery forces in England.
8. See response—"To glorify God, and to enjoy Him forever." Westminster Shorter Catechism.
9. Engaged in siege of Troy, Odysseus chose Mentor as guardian for his son Telemachus; hence, "mentor" signifies a wise teacher. See Homer's *Odyssey*.

4. Late Romantic Novelists—Hawthorne and Melville

Nathaniel Hawthorne(1804—1864)

① *Biographical Introduction*

Hawthorne has been considered to be the first great American writer of fiction to work in the moralistic tradition. Hawthorne was born into a puritan family in Salem. His father died when he was only four, leaving the widow and the child to shift for themselves. In 1821, he went to Bowdoin College where he made friends with Longfellow and Franklin Pierce. After graduation, he returned to his hometown and lived in seclusion for 12 years, reading widely and preparing for his literary career. The year of the 1837 saw the publication of his *Twice-Told Tales*, a collection of short stories, which was successful. He worked in the customhouse in Boston and Salem. Another collection of short stories, *Mosses from an Old Manse* came out in 1846. The appearance of *The Scarlet Letter* marked the maturity of Hawthorne as a novelist, and soon he composed three important novels: *The House of the seven Gables*, *The Blithedale Romance* and *The Marble Faun*.

② *Hawthorne's Theme and View*

Different from his contemporaries, in relation to themes, Hawthorne showed a great interest in the problems of sin and evil. To Hawthorne evil existed in the human heart and everyone possessed some evil secret. Most of his works dealt with evil such as poisoning, murder, adultery, and crime. In dealing with evil, Hawtborne penetrated into the human soul to explore the result of sin, the moral and psychological effect on the human conscience. It is in such an exploration that Hawthorne revealed his criticism of life. Hawthorne's black vision illustrates to some extent the influence that the Calvinist doctrine of "original sin" and "total depravity" had upon his mind, and also explains Hawthorne's aloofness from Emersonian Transcendental optimism and his skepticism about it.

Hawthorne also took a great interest in history and antiquity, To him the industralised world had nothing but a common place prosperity, which offered no genial atmosphere for literary creation. A man with any literary ambition would have to resort to the help of his imagination and to recall what was valuable in the past. Antiquity and history could enable him to dream strange things and make them look like truth. Therefore, besides sin and evil, Hawthorne was also at his best in dealing with the supernatural and New England past.

③ *Hawthorne's Style*

Hawthorne was a great literary artist. His craftsmanship can be summed up as follows. (1) Most of his stories are allegorical. They are full of vivid and symbolic images that embody great moral questions. The black veil in *The Minister's Black Veil* is symbolic of the minister inner evil. (2) Another feature of Hawthorne's art is his ambiguity, of which the technique of multiple view employed in the last part of *The Scarlet Letter* offers a good illustration. Here in the *Conclusion* people are heard to offer different views concerning the sign of the letter on the dead minister's chest. The author's refusal to commit himself gives his work a richness which could otherwise have been impossible to achieve. (3) Hawthorne probed into the human mind. His characters tend to have complex psychologies. There are a semblance of interior monologues which reveal their states of mind. (4)Hawthorne was good at the use of the supernatural. The symbol *A* which appeared in the sky in a twilight atmosphere offers the reader a mystic impression.

④ *Hawthorne's Major Works*

Twice-Told Tales is his first major work. It is a collection of short stories, among which the best known one is "The Minister's Black Veil". Parson Hooper is a minister who dons a black veil on the eve of his marriage. Parishioners disapprove, and his fiancèe leaves him. On his deathbed Hooper perceives a "black veil" upon every face about him, and he is buried with the veil. The story never reveals Hooper's precise motives, but the veil is obviously the visible portrayal of secret or imagined sin. Hooper's obsess severs him from all men and all normal life.

Mosses from an Old Manse is his second volume of short stories, in which there is "Young Goodman Brown". The story is set in early colonial times. Brown leaves his wife, walks in the dark forest, and meets a group of witches. Brown's adventures in the dark forest implies that every human being has some secret evil existing inside.

The Scarlet Letter is Hawthorne's masterpiece. The story is set in the Puritan past of the 17th century. An ageing English scholar sends his beautiful wife Hester Prynne to make their new home in New England. When he comes over two years later he is surprised to see his wife in pillory, wearing a scarlet letter *A* on her breast holding her illicit child in her arms. Determined to find out who her lover is, the old scholar disguises himself as a physician and changes his name to Roger Chillingworth. Gradually he discovers that the vallain is the much admired young clergyman, Arthur Dimmesdale. He keeps preying upon the conscience of Dimmesdale, who cuts himself off from society and suffers secretly for his sin. Dimmesdale withers spiritually as well as physically. Chillingworth withers too. Hester responds to her sin positively. Though she is outlawed by community, she manages to reestablish a meaningful relationship with her fellowmen by trying her best to help them. Her life eventually acquires a real singificance. Through the analysis of the moral and psychological effect of the sin on different people, Hawthorne sang the praise of the moral growth of the woman who had even been sinned.

The House of the Seven Gables is a great novel of family decadence. It exemplifies Hawthorne's belief that sin will get punished. Colonel Ryncheen takes by force the land of Mathew Maule, and condemns him as a wizard. He builds a house on the land while Maule is sent to the scaffold. Before he dies, Maule curses the colonel, saying" God will give him blood to drink". Retribution does come. The house seems to be haunted. The colonel withers and dies. Eventually it is the descendant of the persecuted Maule who gets the upper hand.

Hawthorne's last two major works are *The Blithedale Romance* and *The Marble Faun*. The former is a novel describing the transcendental experiment, and the latter is a novel of moral allegory with Italian setting.

THE MINISTER'S BLACK VEIL

A Parable[1]

The sexton stood in the porch of Millford meeting -house, pulling busily at the bell-rope. The old people of the village came stooping along the street. Children with bright faces, tripped merrily beside their parents, or mimicked a graver gait, in the conscious dignity of their Sunday clothes. Spruce bachelors looked sidelong at the pretty maidens, and fancied that the Sabbath sunshine made them prettier than on week days. When the throng had mostly streamed into the porch, the sexton began to toll the bell, keeping his eye on the Reverend Mr. Hooper's door. The first glimpse of the clergyman's figure was the signal for the bell to cease its summons. "But what has good Parson Hooper got upon his face?" cried the sexton in astonishment.

All within hearing immediately turned about, and beheld the semblance of Mr. Hooper, pacing slowly his meditative way towards the meeting-house. With one accord they started, expressing more wonder than if some strange minister were coming to dust the cushions of Mr. Hooper's pulpit.

"Are you sure it is our parson?" inquired Goodman Gray of the sexton.

"Of a certainty it is good Mr. Hooper," replied the sexton. "He was to have exchanged pulpits with Parson Shute, of Westbury; but Parson Shute sent to excuse himself yesterday, being to preach a funeral sermon."

The cause of so much amazement may appear sufficiently slight. Mr. Hooper, a gentlemanly person, of about thirty, though still a bachelor, was dressed with due clerical neatness, as if a careful wife had starched his band, and brushed the weekly dust from his Sunday's garb. There was but one thing remarkable in his appearance. Swathed about his forehead, and hanging down over his face, so low as to be shaken by his breath, Mr. Hopper had on a black veil. On a nearer view it seemed to consist of two folds of crape, which entirely concealed his features, except the mouth and chin, but probably did not intercept his sight, further than to give a darkened aspect to all living and inanimate things. With this gloomy shade before him, good Mr. Hooper walked onward, at a slow and quiet pace, stooping somewhat, and looking on the ground, as is customary with abstracted men, yet nodding kindly to those of his parishioners who still waited on the meeting-house steps. But so wonder-struck were they that his greeting hardly met with a return.

"I can't really feel as if good Mr. Hooper's face was behind that piece of crape," said the sexton.

"I don't like it," muttered an old woman, as she hobbled into the meeting-house. "He has changed himself into something awful, only by hiding his face."

"Our parson has gone mad!" cried Goodman Gray, following him across the threshold.

A rumor of some unaccountable phenomenon had preceded Mr. Hooper into the meeting-house, and set all the congregation astir. Few could refrain from twisting their heads towards the door; many stood upright, and turned directly about; while several little boys clambered upon the seats, and came down again with a terrible racket. There was a general bustle, a rustling of the women's gowns and shuffling of the men's feet, greatly at variance with that hushed repose which should attend the entrance of the minister. But Mr. Hooper appeared not to notice the perturbation of his people. He entered with an almost noiseless step, bent his head mildly to the pews on each side, and bowed as he passed his oldest parishioner, a whitehaired great-grandsire, who occupied an arm-chair in the centre of the aisle. It was strange to observe how slowly this venerable man became conscious of something singular in the appearance of his pastor. He seemed not fully to partake of the prevailing wonder, till Mr. Hooper had ascended the stairs, and showed himself in the pulpit, face to face with his congregation, except for the black veil. That mysterious emblem was never once withdrawn. It shook with his measured breath, as he gave out the psalm; it threw its obscurity between him and the holy page, as he read the Scriptures; and while he prayed, the veil lay heavily on his uplifted countenance. Did he seek to hide it from the dread Being whom he was addressing?

Such was the effect of this simple piece of crape, that more than one woman of delicate nerves was forced to leave the meeting-house. Yet perhaps the pale-faced congregation was almost as fearful a sight to the minister, as his black veil to them.

Mr. Hopper had the reputation of a good preacher, but not an energetic one: he strove to win his people heavenward by mild, persuasive influences, rather than to drive them thither by the thunders of the Word. The sermon which he now delivered was marked by the same characteristics of style and manner as the general series of his pulpit oratory. But there was something, either in the sentiment of the discourse itself, or in the imagination of the auditors, which made it greatly the most powerful effort that they had ever heard from their pastor's lips. It was tinged, rather more darkly than usual, with the gentle gloom of Mr. Hooper's temperament. The subject had reference to secret sin, and those sad mysteries which we hide from our nearest and dearest, and would fain conceal from our own consciousness, even forgetting that the Omniscient can detect them. A subtle power was breathed into his words. Each member of the congregation, the most innocent girl, and the man of hardened breast, felt as if the preacher had crept upon them, behind his awful veil and discovered their hoarded iniquity of deed or thought. Many spread their clasped hands on their bosoms. There was nothing terrible in what Mr. Hooper said, at least, no violence; and yet, with every tremor of his melancholy voice, the hearers quaked. An unsought pathos came hand in hand with awe. So sensible were the audience of some unwonted attribute in their minister, that they longed for a breath of wind to blow aside the veil, almost believing that a stranger's visage would be discovered, though the form, gesture, and voice were those of Mr. Hooper.

At the close of the services, the people hurried out with indecorous confusion, eager to communicate their pent-up amazement, and conscious of lighter spirits the moment they lost sight of the black veil. Some gathered in little circles, huddled closely together, with their mouths all whispering in the centre; some went homeward alone, wrapt in silent meditation; some talked loudly and profaned the Sabbath day with ostentatious laughter. A few shook their sagacious heads, intimating that they could penetrate the mystery; while one or two affirmed that there was no mystery at all, but only that Mr. Hooper's eyes were so weakened by the midnight lamp, as to require a shade. After a brief interval, forth came good Mr. Hooper also, in the rear of his flock. Turning his veiled face from one group to another, he paid due reverence to the hoary heads, saluted the middle aged with kind dignity as their friend and spiritual guide, greeted the young with mingled authority and love, and laid his hands on the little children's heads to bless them. Such was always his custom on the Sabbath day. Strange and bewildered looks repaid him for his courtesy. None, as on former occasions, aspired to the honor of walking by their pastor's side. Old Squire Saunders, doubtless by an accidental lapse of memory, neglected to invite Mr. Hooper to his table, where the good clergyman had been wont to bless the food, almost every Sunday since his settlement. He returned, therefore, to the parsonage, and , at the moment of closing the door, was observed to look back upon the people, all of whom had their eyes fixed upon the minister. A sad smile gleamed faintly from beneath the black veil, and flickered about his mouth. glimmering as he disappeared.

"How strange," said a lady, "that a simple black veil, such as any woman might wear on her bonnet, should become such a terrible thing on Mr. Hooper's face!"

"Something must surely be amiss with Mr. Hooper's intellects," observed her husband, the physician of the village. "But the strangest part of the affair is the effect of this vagary, even on a sober-minded man like myself. The black veil, though it covers only our pastor's face, throws its influence over his whole person, and makes him ghostlike from head to foot. Do you not feel it so?"

"Truly do I," replied the lady; "and I would not be alone with him for the world. I wonder he is not afraid to be alone with himself!"

"Men sometimes are so," said her husband.

The afternoon service was attended with similar circumstances. At its conclusion, the bell tolled for the funeral of a young lady. The relatives and friends were assembled in the house, and the more distant acquaintances stood about the door, speaking of the good qualities of the deceased, when their talk was interrupted by the appearance of Mr. Hooper, still covered with his black veil. It was now an appropriate emblem. The clergyman stepped into the room where the corpse was laid, and bent over the coffin, to take a last farewell of his deceased parishioner. As he stooped, the veil hung straight down from his forehead, so that, if her eyelids had not been closed forever, the dead maiden might have seen his face. Could Mr. Hooper be fearful of her glance, that he so hastily caught back the black veil? A person who watched the interview between the dead and living, scrupled not to affirm, that, at the instant when the clergyman's features were disclosed, the corpse had slightly shuddered, rustling the shroud and muslin cap, though the countenance retained the composure of death. A superstitious old woman was the only witness of this prodigy. From the coffin Mr. Hooper passed into the chamber of the mourners, and thence to the head of the staircase, to make the funeral prayer. It was a tender and heart-dissolving prayer, full of sorrow, yet so imbued with celestial hopes, that the music of a heavenly harp, swept by the fingers of the dead, seemed faintly to be heard among the saddest accents of the minister. The people trembled, though they but darkly understood him when he prayed that they, and himself, and all of mortal race, might be readily, as he trusted this young maiden had been, for the dreadful hour that should snatch the veil from their faces. The bearers went heavily forth, and the mourners followed, saddening all the street, with the dead before them, and Mr. Hooper in his black veil behind.

"Why do you look back?" said one in the procession to his partner.

"I had a fancy," replied she, "that the minister and the maiden's spirit were walking hand in hand."

"And so had I, at the same moment," said the other.

That night, the handsomest couple in Milford village were to be joined in wedlock. Though reckoned a melancholy man, Mr. Hooper had a placid cheerfulness for such occasions, which often excited a sympathetic smile where livelier merriment would have been thrown away. There was no quality of his disposition which made him more beloved than this. The company at the wedding awaited his arrival with impatience, trusting that the strange awe, which had gathered over him throughout the day, would now be dispelled. But such was not the result. When Mr. Hooper came, the first thing that their eyes rested on was the same horrible black veil, which had added deeper gloom to the funeral, and could portend nothing but evil to the wedding. Such was its immediate effect on the guests that a cloud seemed to have rolled duskily from beneath the black crape and dimmed the light of the candles. The bridal pair stood up before the minister. But the bride's cold fingers quivered in the tremulous hand of the bridegroom, and her deathlike paleness caused a whisper that the maiden who had been buried a few hours before was come from her grave to be married. If ever another wedding were so dismal, it was that famous one where they tolled the wedding knell. After performing the ceremony, Mr. Hooper raised a glass of wine to his lips, wishing happiness to the new-married couple in a strain of mild pleasantry that ought to have brightened the features of the guests, like a cheerful gleam from the hearth. At that instant, catching a glimpse of his figure in the looking-glass, the black veil involved his own spirit in the horror with which it overwhelmed all others. His frame shuddered, his lips grew white, he spilt the untasted wine upon the carpet, and rushed forth into the darkness. For the Earth, too, had on her Black Veil.

The next day, the whole village of Milford talked of little else than Parson Hooper's black veil. That, and the mystery concealed behind it, supplied a topic for discussion between acquaintances meeting in the street, and good women gossiping at their open windows. It was the first item of news that the tavern-keeper told to his guests. The children babbled of it on their way to school. One imitative little imp covered his face with an old black handkerchief, thereby so affrighting his playmates that the panic seized himself, and he well-nigh lost his wits by his own waggery.

It was remarkable that of all the busybodies and impertinent people in the parish, not one ventured to put the plain question to Mr. Hooper, wherefore he did this thing. Hitherto, whenever there appeared the slightest call for such interference, he had never lacked advisers, nor shown himself averse to be guided by their judgment. If he erred at all, it was by so painful a degree of self-distrust, that even the mildest censure would lead him to consider an indifferent action as a crime. Yet, though so well acquainted with this amiable weakness, no individual among his parishioners chose to make the black veil a subject of friendly remonstrance. There was a feeling of dread, neither plainly confessed nor carefully concealed, which caused each to shift the responsibility upon another, till at length it was found expedient to send a deputation to the church, in order to deal with Mr. Hooper about the mystery, before it should grow into a scandal. Never did an embassy so ill discharge its duties. The minister received them with friendly courtesy, but became silent, after they were seated, leaving to his visitors, the whole burden of introducing their important business. The topic, it might be supposed, was obvious enough. There was the black veil swathed round Mr. Hooper's forehead, and concealing every feature above his placid mouth, on which, at times, they could perceive the glimmering of a melancholy smile. But that piece of crape, to their imagination, seemed to hang down before his heart, the symbol of a fearful secret between him and them. Were the veil but cast aside, they might speak freely of it, but not till then. Thus they sat a considerable time, speechless, confused, and shrinking uneasily from Mr. Hooper's eye, which they felt to be fixed upon them with an invisible glance. Finally, the deputies returned abashed to their constituents, pronouncing the matter too weighty to be handled, except by a council of the churches, if, indeed, it might not require a general synod.

But there was one person in the village unappalled by the awe with which the black veil had impressed all beside herself. When the deputies returned without an explanation, or even venturing to demand one, she, with the calm energy of her character, determined to chase away the strange cloud that appeared to be settling round Mr. Hooper, every moment more darkly than before. As his plighted wife, it should be her privilege to know what the black veil concealed. At the minister's first visit, therefore, she entered upon the subject with a direct simplicity, which made the task easier both for him and her. After he had seated himself, she fixed her eyes steadfastly upon the veil, but could discern nothing of the dreadful gloom that had so overawed the multitude: it was but a double fold of crape, hanging down from his forehead to his mouth, and slightly stirring with his breath.

"No," she said aloud, and smiling, "there is nothing terrible in this piece of crape, except that it hides a face which I am always glad to look upon. Come, good sir, let the sun shine from behind the cloud. First lay aside your black veil: then tell me why you put it on."

Mr. Hooper's smile glimmered faintly.

"There is an hour to come," said he, "when all of us shall cast aside our veils. Take it not amiss, beloved friend, if I wear this piece of crape till then."

"Your words are a mystery, too," returned the young lady. "Take away the veil from them, at least."

"Elizabeth, I will," said he, "so far as my vow may suffer me. Know, then, this veil is a type and a symbol, and I am bound to wear it ever, both in light and darkness, in solitude and before the gaze of multitudes, and as with strangers, so with my way.

The impertinence of the latter class compelled him to give up his customary walk at sunset to the burial ground; for when he leaned pensively over the gate, there would always be faces behind the gravestones, peeping at his black veil. A fable went the rounds that the stare of the dead people drove him thence. It grieved him, to the very depth of his kind heart, to observe how the children fled from his approach, breaking up their merriest sports, while his melancholy figure was yet afar off. Their instinctive dread caused him to feel more strongly than aught else, that a preternatural horror was interwoven with the threads of the black crape. In truth, his own antipathy to the veil was known to be so great, that he never willingly passed before a mirror, nor stooped to drink at a still fountain, lest, in its peaceful bosom, he should be affrighted by himself. This was what gave plausibility to the whispers, that Mr. Hooper's conscience tortured him for some great crime too horrible to be entirely concealed, or otherwise than so obscurely intimated. Thus, from beneath the black veil, there rolled a cloud into the sunshine, an ambiguity of sin or sorrow, which enveloped the poor minister, so that love or sympathy could never reach him. It was said that ghost and fiend consorted with him there. With self-shudderings and outward terrors, he walked continually in its shadow, groping darkly within his own soul, or gazing through a medium that saddened the whole world. Even the lawless wind, it was believed, respected his dreadful secret, and never blew aside the veil. But still good Mr. Hooper sadly smiled at the pale visages of the worldly throng as he passed by.

Among all its bad influences, the black veil had one desirable effect, of making its wearer a very efficient clergyman. By the aid of his mysterious emblem—for there was no other apparent cause—he became a man of awful power over souls that were in agony for sin. His converts always regarded him with a dread peculiar to themselves, affirming, though but figuratively, that, before he brought them to celestial light, they had been with him behind the black veil. Its gloom, indeed, enabled him to sympathize with all dark affections. Dying sinners cried aloud for Mr. Hooper, and would not yield their breath till he appeared; though ever, as he stooped to whisper consolation, they shuddered at the veiled face so near their own. Such were the terrors of the black veil, even when Death had bared his visage! Strangers came long distances to attend service at his church, with the mere idle purpose of gazing at his figure, because it was forbidden them to behold his face. But many were made to quake ere they departed! Once, during Governor Belcher's[2] administration, Mr. Hooper was appointed to preach the election sermon. Covered with his black veil, he stood before the chief magistrate, the council, and the representatives, and wrought so deep an impression, that the legislative measures of that year were characterized by all the gloom and piety of our earliest ancestral sway.

In this manner Mr. Hooper spent a long life, irreproachable in outward act, yet shrouded in dismal suspicions; kind and loving, though unloved, and dimly feared; a man apart from men, shunned in their health and joy, but ever summoned to their aid in mortal anguish. As years wore on, shedding their snows above his sable veil, he acquired a name throughout the New England churches, and they called him Father Hooper. Nearly all his parishioners, who were of mature age when he was settled, had been borne away by many a funeral: he had one congregation in the church, and a more crowded one in the churchyard; and having wrought so late into the evening, and done his work so well, it was now good Father Hooper's turn to rest.

Several persons were visible by the shaded candle-light, in the death chamber of the old clergyman. Natural connections he had none. But there was the decorously grave, though unmoved physician, seeking only to mitigate the last pangs of the patient whom he could not save. There were the deacons, and other eminently pious members of his church. There, also, was the Reverend Mr. Clark, of Westbury, a young and zealous divine, who had ridden in haste to pray by the bedside of the expiring minister. There was the nurse, no hired handmaiden of death, but one whose calm affection had endured thus long in secrecy, in solitude, amid the chill of age, and would not perish, even at the dying hour. Who, but Elizabeth! And there lay the hoary head of good Father Hooper upon the death pillow, with the black veil still swathed about his brow, and reaching down over his face, so that each more difficult gasp of his faint breath caused it to stir. All through life that piece of crape had hung between him and the world: it had separated him from cheerful brotherhood and woman's love, and kept him in that saddest of all prisons, his own heart; and still it lay upon his face, as if to deepen the gloom of his darksome chamber, and shade him from the sunshine of eternity.

For some time previous, his mind had been confused, wavering doubtfully between the past and the present, and hovering forward, as it were, at intervals, into the indistinctness of the world to come. There had been feverish turns, which tossed him from side to side, and wore away what little strength he had. But in his most convulsive struggles, and in the wildest vagaries of his intellect, when no other thought retained its sober influence, he still showed an awful solicitude lest the black veil should slip aside. Even if his bewildered soul could have forgotten, there was a faithful woman at his pillow, who, with averted eyes, would have covered that aged face, which she had last beheld in the comeliness of manhood. At length the death-stricken old man lay quietly in the torpor of mental and bodily exhaustion, with an imperceptible pulse, and breath that grew fainter and fainter, except when a long, deep, and irregular inspiration seemed to prelude the flight of his spirit.

The minister of Westbury approached the bedside.

"Venerable Father Hooper," said he, "the moment of your release is at hand. Are you ready for the lifting of the veil that shuts in time from eternity?"

Father Hooper at first replied merely by a feeble motion of his head; then, apprehensive, perhaps, that his meaning might be doubtful, he exerted himself to speak.

"Yea," said he, in faint accents, "my soul hath a patient weariness until that veil be lifted."

"And is it fitting," resumed the Reverend Mr. Clark, "that a man so given to prayer, of such a blameless example, holy in deed and thought, so far as mortal judgment may pronounce; is it fitting that a father in the church should leave a shadow on his memory, that may seem to blacken a life so pure? I pray you my venerable brother, let not this thing be! Suffer us to be gladdened by your triumphant aspect as you go to your reward. Before the veil of eternity be lifted, let me cast aside this black veil from your face!"

And thus speaking, the Reverend Mr. Clark bent forward to reveal the mystery of so many years. But, exerting a sudden energy, that made all the beholders stand aghast, Father Hooper snatched both his hands from beneath the bedclothes, and pressed them strongly on the black veil, resolute to struggle, if the minister of Westbury would contend with a dying man.

"Never!" cried the veiled clergyman. "On earth never!"

"Dark old man!" exclaimed the affrighted minister, "with what horrible crime upon your soul are you now passing to the judgment?"

Father Hooper's breath heaved; it rattled in his throat; but, with a mighty effort, grasping forward with his hands, he caught hold of life, and held it back till he should speak. He even raised himself in bed; and there he sat, shivering with the arms of death around him, while the black veil hung down, awful, at that last moment, in the gathered terrors of a lifetime. And yet the faint, sad smile, so often there, now seemed to glimmer from its obscurity, and linger on Father Hooper's lips.

"Why do you tremble at me alone?" cried he, turning his veiled face round the circle of pale spectators. "Tremble also at each other! Have men avoided me, and women shown no pity, and children screamed and fled, only for my black veil? What, but the mystery which it obscurely typifies, has made this piece of crape so awful? When the friend shows his inmost heart to his friend; the lover to his best beloved; when man does not vainly shrink from the eve of his Creator loathsomely treasuring up the secret of his sin; then deem me a monster, for the symbol beneath which I have lived, and die! I look around me, and lo! on every visage a Black Veil!"

While his auditors shrank from one another, in mutual affright, Father Hooper fell back upon his pillow, a veiled corpse, with a faint smile lingering on his lips. Still veiled, they laid him in his coffin, and a veiled corpse they bore him to the grave. The grass of many years has sprung up and withered on that grave; the bruial stone is moss-grown, and good Mr. Hooper's face is dust; but awful is still the thought that it mouldered beneath the Black Veil!

Notes:

1. The interpretation of this parable has intrigued generations of readers. The dying speech of Parson Hooper connects the symbol of his black veil wth the hypocritical secret sins of mankind. But see also Poe's interpretation in his review of Hawthorne's *Twice-Told Tales*. In this interpretation, the story is associated with *The Scarlet Letter* as much as with "Young Goodman Brown." A clue has also been sought in Hawthorne's footnote to the title of the story, which reads as follows: "Another clergyman in New England, Mr. Joseph Moody, of York, Maine, who died about eighty years since, made himself remarkable by the same eccentricity that is here related of the Reverend Mr. Hooper. In this case, however, the symbol had a different import. In early he had accidentally killed a beloved friend; and from that day till the hour of his own death, he hid his face from man".
2. Jonathan Belcher was governor of Massachusetts and New Hampshire from 1730 to 1741.

Question for consideration:

"The Minister's Black Veil" can be considered a tale in which the action centers upon the hero's refusal to make a commitment and his subsequent isolation and alienation from his fellow humans. How would you discuss this theme?

Herman Melville(1819—1891)

① *Biographical Introduction*

Melville was born into a poor family in New York. He had little education and began to work early. He was a bank clerk, a salesman, a farm-hand, and a schoolteacher. When these all failed to offer him a decent livelihood, he went to sea at the age of twenty. His sea experiences and adventures furnished him with abundant material, and resulted in five novels that brought him wide fame as a writer of sea stories. In 1850 he met Hawthorne and they became good friends. He read Hawthorne's books and was deeply impressed by Hawthorne's black vision. He changed the original scheme of *Moby Dick*. Melville and Hawthorne represented a position of tragic humanism in their time. In 1866, he became a customs official in New York, holding this post until the end of his death.

② *Melville's Theme and View*

Like Hawthorne, Melville held a black view of the world. To him, the world is at once Godless and purposeless. Man in this universe lives a meaningless and futile life. In his works he expressed profoundly the loss of faith and the sense of futility and meaninglessness which characterize modern life of the west. This explains why Melville's fame is going up in the present century.

In relation to his black view is Melville's theme of alienation. To him, alienation exists in life on different levels, between man and man, man and society, and man and nature. Captain Ahab cuts himself from his wife and kid, stays away most of the time from his crew, and he hates Moby Dick, an embodiment of nature. Another theme Melville employed and shared with Cooper and Hawthorne is "rejection and quest". Melville's heroes were forever trying to escape from their corrupt societies and into a better place to live.

③ *Melville's Style*

Like Hawthorne, Melville managed to achieve the effect of ambiguity through employing the technique of multiple view in his narratives. In *Moby Dick*, the whale is portrayed by different characters from different angles. The author does not commit himself and the reader is thrown upon himself for judgement. The author's unwillingness to commit himself helps to create a symbolic effect.

④ *Melville's Major Works*

Melville is known for his sea stories which include *Typee*, *Omoo*, *Mardi*, and his masterpiece *Moby Dick*.

Moby Dick is regarded as one of the world classic. It gives a detailed account of the operations of the whaling industry and illustrates the tragedy of man fighting against overwhelming odds in an indifferent and even hostile universe. The story goes roughly as follows. Ishmael, feeling depressed, seeks escape by going out to sea on the ship, Pequod. The captain is Ahab, the man with one leg. Moby Dick, the white whale, had sheared off his leg on a previous voyage, and Ahab resolves to kill him. The Pequod makes a good catch of whales but Ahab refuses to turn back until he has killed his enemy. Eventually the white whale appears, and the Pequod begins its doomed fight with it. On the first day the whale overturns a boat, and on the second it swamps another. When the third day comes, Ahab and his crew manage to plunge a harpoon into it, but the whale carries the Pequod along with it to its doom. All on board the whaler get drowned, except Ishmael, who survives to tell the tale. The story illustrates Melville's black view that the world is Godless and purposeless. Man lives a meaningless and futile life. Man must place himself at the mercy of nature. He cannot try to seek power over nature. If he does so as Ahab does, he is doomed.

From PIERRE[1]

Book XIV

The Journey and The Pamphlet

All profound things, and emotions of things are preceded and attended by Silence. What a silence is that with which the pale bride precedes the responsive *I will*, to the priest's solemn question, *Wilt thou have this man for thy husband*? In silence, too, the wedded hands are clasped. Yea, in silence the child Christ was born into the world. Silence is the general consecration of the universe. Silence is the invisible laying on of the Divine Pontiff's hands upon the world. Silence is at once the most harmless and the most awful thing in all nature. It speaks of the Reserved Forces of Fate: Silence is the only Voice of our God.

Nor is this so august Silence confined to things simply touching or grand. Like the air, Silence permeates all things, and produces its magical power, as well during that peculiar mood which prevails at a solitary travelers first setting forth on a journey, as at the unimaginable time when before the world was, Silence brooded on the face of the waters.

No word was spoken by its inmates, as the coach bearing our young Enthusiast,[2] Pierre, and his mournful party, sped forth through the dim dawn into the deep midnight, which still occupied, unrepulsed, the hearts of the old woods through which the road wound, very shortly after quitting the village.

When, first entering the coach, Pierre had pressed his hand upon the cushioned seat to steady his way some crumpled leaves of paper had met his fingers. He had instinctively clutched them;

and the same strange clutching mood of his soul which had prompted that instinctive act, did also prevail in causing him now to retain the crumpled paper in his hand for an hour or more of that wonderful intense silence, which the rapid coach bore through the heart of the general stirless morning silence of the fields and the woods.

His thoughts were very dark and wild; for a space there was rebellion and horrid anarchy and infidelity in his soul. This temporary mood may best be likened to that, which—according to a singular story once told in the pulpit by a reverend man of God—invaded the heart of an excellent priest. In the midst of a solemn cathedral, upon a cloudy Sunday afternoon, this priest was in the act of publicly administering the bread at the Holy Sacrament of the Supper, when the Evil One suddenly propounded to him the possibility of the mere moonshine of the Christian Religion. Just such now was the mood of Pierre; to him the Evil One propounded the possibility of the mere moonshine of all his self-renouncing Enthusiasm. The Evil One hooted at him and called him a fool. But by instant and earnest prayer—closing his two eyes, with his two hands still holding the sacramental bread—the devout priest had vanquished the impious Devil. Not so with Pierre. The imperishable monument of his holy Catholic Church; the imperishable record of his Holy Bible; the imperishable intuition of the innate truth of Christianity;—these were the indestructible anchors which still held the priest to his firm Faith's rock, when the sudden storm raised by the Evil One assailed him. But Pierre—where could *he* find the Church, the monument, the Bible, which unequivocally said to him—"Go on; thou art in the Right; I endorse thee all over; go on"—So the difference between the Priest and Pierre was herein:—with the priest it was a matter, whether certain bodiless thoughts of his were true or not true; but with Pierre it was a question whether certain vital acts of his were right or wrong. In this little nut lie germ—like the possible solution of some puzzling problems; and also the discovery of additional, and still more profound problems ensuing upon the solution of the former. For so true is this last, that some men refuse to solve any present problem, for fear of making still more work for themselves in that way.

Now, Pierre thought of the magical, mournful letter of Isabel, he recalled the divine inspiration of that hour when the heroic words burst from his heart—"Comfort thee, and stand by thee, and fight for thee, will thy leapingly acknowledging brother!" These remembrances unfurled themselves in proud exultations in his soul; and from before such glorious banners of Virtue, the club-footed Evil One limped away in dismay. But now the dread fateful parting look of his mother came over him; anew he heard the heart-prescribing words, "Beneath my roof and at my table, he who was once Pierre Glendinning no more puts himself;"—swooning in her snow-white bed, the lifeless Lucy lay before him, wrapt as in the reverberating echoings of her own agonizing shriek: "My heart! my heart!" Then how swift the recurrence to Isabel, and the nameless awfulness of his still imperfectly conscious, incipient, new-mingled emotion toward this mysterious being. "Lo! I leave corpses wherever I go!" groaned Pierre to himself—"Can then my conduct be right? Lo! by my conduct I seem threatened by the possibility of a sin anomalous and accursed, so anomalous, it may well be the one for which Scripture says, there is never forgiveness. Corpses behind me, and the last sin before, how then can my conduct be right?"

In this mood, the silence accompanied him, and the first visible rays of the morning sun in this same mood found him and saluted him. The excitement and the sleepless night just passed, and the strange narcotic of a quiet steady anguish and the sweet quiescence of the air, and the monotonous cradle-like motion of the coach over a road made firm and smooth by a refreshing shower over night; these had wrought their wonted effect upon Isable and Delly; with hidden faces they leaned fast asleep in Pierre's sight. Fast asleep—thus unconscious, oh sweet Isable, oh forlorn Delly, your swift destinies I bear in my own!

Suddenly, as his sad eye fell lower and lower from scanning their magically quiescent persons, his glance lit upon his own clutched hand, which rested on his knee. Some paper protruded from that clutch. He knew not how it had got there, or whence it had come, though himself had closed his own gripe upon it. He lifted his hand and slowly unfingered and unbolted the paper, and unrolled it, and carefully smoothed it, to see what it might be.

It was a thin, tattered, dried-fish-like thing; printed with blurred ink upon mean, sleazy paper. It seemed the opening pages of some ruinous old pamphlet—a pamphlet containing a chapter or so of some very voluminous disquisition. The conclusion was gone. It must have been accidentally left there by some previous traveler, who perhaps in drawing out his handkerchief, had ignorantly extracted his waste paper.

There is a singular infatuation in most men, which leads them in odd moments, intermitting between their regular occupations, and when they find themselves all alone in some quiet corner or nook, to fasten with unaccountable fondness upon the merest rag of old printed paper—some shred of a long-exploded advertisement perhaps—and read it, and study it, and re-read it, and pore over it, and fairly agonize themselves over this miserable, sleazy paper-rag, which at any other time, or in any other place, they would hardly touch with St. Dunstan's long tongs[3]. So now, in a degree, with Pierre. But notwithstanding that he, with most other human beings, shared in the strange hallucination above mentioned, yet the first glimpse of the title of the dried-fish-like, pamphlet-shaped rag, did almost tempt him to pitch it out of the window. For, be a man's mood what it may, what sensible and ordinary mortal could have patience for any considerable period, to knowingly hold in his conscious hand a printed document (and that too a very blurred one as to ink, and a very sleazy one as to paper), so metaphysically and insufferably entitled as this:—"Chronometricals & Horologicals?"

Doubtless, it was something vastly profound; but it is to be observed, that when a man is in a really profound mood, then all merely verbal or written profundites are unspeakably repulsive, and seem downright childish to him. Nevertheless, the silence still continued; the road ran through an almost unplowed and uninhabited region; the slumberers still slumbered before him; the evil mood was becoming well nigh insupportable to him; so, more to force his mind away from the dark realities of things than from any other motive, Pierre finally tried his best to plunge himself into the pamphlet.

Notes:

1. In *Pierre* the title character, heir to great rural estates, has become convinced that a mysterious girl, Isabel, is his half sister, illegitimate child of his dead father. In attempting to protect Isabel without ruining his father's good name, Pierre has announced to his mother and his fiancee that he is married. In this "book" Pierre and Isabel, supposedly married, are fleeing to the city, accompanied by Delly Ulver, an unmarried farmgirl who recently bore a stillborn child.
2. In Swift's time an enthusiast was a religious madman. Melville's usage is about halfway between that meaning and today's, something like "dedicated idealist."
3. In the legend Donstan was an Archbishop to whom the Devil appeared in the form of a seductive woman; Dunstan pinched his nose with tongs that had been in a fire.

Part Four The Age of Realism

Chapter Ⅰ The Rise of Realism

1. Realism

In literature, the term realism is used to identify a literary movement in Europe and the United States in the last half of the 19th century and the early years of the 20th century. But the practice of realism has a long history and can be traced back to ancient times. As Aristotle pointed out in his *On Poetics*, "Sophocles depicts what he thinks man should be like, while Euripides describes people as what they really are". This is the fundamental difference between romanticism and realism.

Realism, as a literary movement, is usually called critical realism, for it rose as a reaction to the social reality round about the 1830s, when the capitalist system was established successively in European countries after the bourgeois revolution. With the development of capitalism, the class contradictions, especially that between the workers and capitalists, were becoming increasingly intense. The ruthless exploitation and suppression of the capital left the working class living in overwhelming poverty, which resulted in a series of proletarian revolutions against capitalism. The revolutions started in France in 1848 and swept over the other European countries later on. But they all failed because of lack of strong leading nuclear powers. The failure brought about a time of disillusionment and loss of hope and a literary revulsion against the false imagination and sentimentality of Romanticism. The need was felt for a return to what was plain and real. Therefore the name realism was given to the new movement in literature.

2. *Features of Critical Realism*

Critical realism is mainly featured in the following ways. ① Critical realism succeeded the literary method of traditional realism, which is characterised by the verisimilitude of detail derived from observation and objective description of the typical character in the typical circumstances. ② By depicting the typical character in the typical circumstances, critical realists exposed the social contradictions of capitalism, criticized the corruption and ugliness of the bourgeois world, and provided a vivid picture of the capitalist society. ③ Critical realists had their own limitations. They criticized capitalism from a democratic and humanistic viewpoint. They regarded the evils of capitalism just as the ugly practice against human nature. Thus their works pointed toward moral evolution and reform rather than revolution. They showed profound sympathy for the common people, but did not find them a way out. ④ The language used by critical realists was usually simple, clear and direct, and their tone was often satiric.

3. *Historical Background of American Realism*

American Realism rose with the Civil War. In 1861, the war between the industrialized North and the agrarian south began. After four years of fighting, the factory defeated the farm and the united states headed toward capitalism.

In post-war America, commerce took the lead in the national economy. Railroads tripled in 15 years and was multiplied five times in 25 years. Petroleum was discovered in sizeable quantities. By 1880 half the population in the east lived in towns and more and more people were leaving farms for cities. Increasing industrialization and mechanization, which was in full swing after the war, soon produced extremes of wealth and poverty. The rich prospered mightily, and immense wealth and power came to such industrial and barking magnates as John D. Rockefeller, Andrew Carnegie, and J. P. Morgan. These barons made fantastic profits and dominated the social and economic life of the nation. A lust for money and power took the place of Emerson's self-reliance. Yet the growth of business and industry worsened the conditions of the poor, and gave rise to reform movements and labor unions that voiced the grievances of debt-ridden farmers and workers living in city slums and laboring in giant, impersonal factories. It was a time of radiant prospects. Beneath the glittering surface of prosperity lay suffering and unhapiness. Disillusionment and frustration were widely felt. What had been expected to be a "Golden Age" turned out to be Mark Twain's "Gilded" one.

Added to this was the fact that the frontier was closing. The frontier had been a factor of great importance in American life. As long as the frontier was there, people could always hope to escape troubles over the next hill and have a better life ahead. Now that the frontier was about to close and people had no shelter to find but to reexamine life. The war and the post-war dazzling wealth and poverty taught people that life, man, and God were not so good as assumed by the transcendentalists. Against the daydream of romanticism appeared a good number of realistic writers like William Dean Howells, Henry James, and Mark Twain, who exposed life to broad daylight.

4. *Features of American Realism*

American realism first appeared in local colourism, which stressed the realistic presentation of the local characters with their regional qualities such as dialects and customs. Bred Harte in the 1860s was the first American colorist to achieve wide popularity, presenting stories of western mining towns with colorful gamblers, outlaws, and scandalous women. The other major writers of local color include Harriet Beecher Stowe, Kate Chopin, Joel Chandler Harris, and Mark Twain, who provided regional stories and tales of the life of America's Westerners, Southerners, and Easterners.

Most American realists found their subject matter in the experiences of the American middle class, describing their houses, families, and jobs, their social customs, achievements, and failures. They tended to limit themselves to optimistic treatment of the surface of life like William Dean Howells, the champion of nineteenth-century realism, who called for the treatment of the "smiling aspects of life", insisting that America was truly a land of hope. Yet the greatest of America's realists, Henry James and Mark Twain, moved well beyond a superficial portrayal of nineteenth-century America. James probed deeply at the individual psychology of his characters, writing in a rich and intricate style that supported his intense scrutiny of complex human experience. Mark Twain, breaking out of the narrow limits of local color fiction, described the breadth of American experience as no one had ever done before, or since.

American realism developed into naturalism at the end of the century. Naturalism, like realism, is a literary movement that began in France in the middle of the 19th century. Naturalists attempted to achieve extreme objectivity and frankness and emphasized the helpless brutal struggle of the low social and economic classes for survival in a cold world full of crushing forces of environment and heredity. American naturalism, shaped by the war, the social upheavals, and the disturbing teachings of Charles Darwin, stressed animality of man, his insignificance in a cold world, and his lack of dignity in face of the blind forces of nature. The pessimism and deterministic ideas of naturalism pervaded the works of such writers as Stephen Crane, Frank Norris, Jack london, Henry Adams, and Theodore Dreiser.

Chapter Ⅱ Three Major Novelists of Realism

——Mark Twain, Howells, and Henry James

Samuel Langhorne Clemens (1835—1910)

Mark Twain

① ***Biographical Introduction***

Samuel Langhorne Clemens is best known by his pseudonym, Mark Twain. Born in Florida, Missouri, he moved with his family to the Mississippi River town of Hannibal when he was four. At the age of 12, his father died and he had to leave school. There after, he traveled throughout the East and Midwest as a journeyman printer. After four years' wandering, he became a river boat pilot on the Mississippi. Then at the outbreak of the Civil War after serving briefly in the Confederate Army, he went to Nevada with his brother, where he learned the tricks of the western newspaper humorist and platform lecturer and adopted his pen-name, "Mark Twain", a cry on the river boat to indicate two fathoms' depth of navigable water. In 1870, he courted and married socialite Olivia Langdon, with whom he settled in Hartford, Connecticut. In 1884, his heavy investment in a badly managed publishing firm and an inefficient typesetting invention drove him into bankruptcy. This, together with the death of his wife and two daughters, darkened his later years. This is why his later literary works became increasingly alienated from the good-humored wit of his earlier ones and reflect a deep pessimism.

② ***Mark Twain's View and Theme***

Mark Twain stated in a letter of 1890 that "the most valuable capital, or culture or education usable in the building of novels is personal experience." Thus his nostalgic account of his past personal experiences, especially his reminiscence of boyhood freedom and independence, which were mostly related to the Mississippi and the West, became his major theme. *Life on the Mississippi* was such a truthful description that the reader could feel the mud of it; *Tom Sawyer* walked out of Twain's pages directly from his fresh memory of his boyhood in the West. By quoting from his own experience, Mark Twain managed to transform into art the finest elements of Western culture.

Mark Twain was a social critic. In all his life, he loved life and people and freedom and justice, felt a pride in human dignity and advocated brotherhood of man. He hated tyranny and iniquity, despised meanness and cruelty, and fought corruption, privilege and abuse whenever he found them with a fierce humor. *Innocent Abroad* (1869) lashed at the pretensions of the American elite. *Roughing It* (1872) offered a carefree picture of the silver fever and the rush to Nevada to stake claims. *The Gilded Age* (1873) satirized the world of luxury, self-deception, hypocrisy and greed. In some of his works such as *Puddnhead Wilson* (1894), Mark Twain made his stance on anti-slavery and anti-lynching clear; and in others like the *Prince and Pauper* (1882) and *A Connecticut Yankee* (1889), he attacked monarchy, feudual caste and inhumanity.

With his financial downfall and the series of misfortunes in his latter days, Mark Twain sought refuge in determinism. To Twain, all is fated, and mankind and the individual human being are without purpose or prospect. In *What Is Man*? (1906) free will is utterly denied. Man is an involuntary machine reacting to stimuli only as his physical equipment and environmental influences dictate. *The Mysterious Stranger* (1916) is an unrelenting indictment of the quality of human existence. The hero's attitude toward mankind is cynical in the extreme. A pawn of deterministic forces, man lacks the power to control his own destiny, the knowledge to decide what is in his own best interest, and the character to act virtuously when the virtuous path is apparent.

③ *Mark Twain's Form and Style*

Mark Twain is a great literary artist. His contribution to the development of realism and the American literature as a whole was through his humor, his theories of localism in American fiction, and his use of colloquial speech.

Mark Twain is America's greatest humorist not only because he offered an uninhibited and peculiarly American humor of gross exaggeration and wild incongruity, fresh and unsubtle, but because his humor served to point up errors in America life—its gaucheries, pretenses, and political debilities—and at the same time expressed a faith in the American dream, optimistic and unquenchable. In some way, it is the discrepancy between the American expectation and the disturbing reality that provoked Mark Twain to adopt the critical weapons of the humorist.

Mark Twain started off as a teller of tall tales and local colorist. He preferred to represent social life through portraits of local places which he knew best. He said, "the novelist lays before you the ways and speech and life of a few people grouped in a certain place—his own place—and that is one book. In time, he and his brethren will report to you the life and the people of the whole nation." Here he clearly defined the place and function of local colorism. Hence, most of Twain's works are concerned with the presentation and interpretation of the local character of the Mississippi and the West.

Mark Twain was filled with loathing of the wordy, flowery eloquence and sentimentality of romanticism. Instead, he developed a clear, vigorous colloquial style, the essence of which lies in the will to fuse form and function. Aiming at expression, not decoration, the new style conforms to the nature of a subject, as is best exemplified in *Huck Finn*, in which the nostalgia for the lost boyhood freedom finds expression in the actual speech habit of an uneducated boy from the American south of the mid-nineteenth century. The style has swept American literature and its influence on the twentieth-century American writers such as Ernest Hemingway, Robert

Frost, Carl Sandburg, and T.S. Eliot is clearly visible.

④ ***Mark Twain's Major Works***

The Celebrated Jumping Frog of Calaveras County (1864) was the title piece of Mark Twain's first book. In this vivid frontier tale of local color, Dan'l Webster, prodigious pet of the gambler Jim Smiley, outjumps all other frogs until a stranger stuffs the frog's gullet with heavy quail shot. This folktale of the gambler outwitted is narrated by garrulous Simon Wheeler in the liveliest American idiom. It brought Mark Twain national attention.

The Gilded Age is Twain's first novel, written in collaboration with Warner. It is a tale of life in Missouri and in Washington and other Eastern cities, covering boyhood experiences and satiric portrayal of political corruption, land speculation, a murder trial, and several tepid love stories. The book is remembered chiefly for its title, which has been accepted as a designation of the years immediately following the Civil War, when the contradictory elements of decline and progress, of poverty and dazzling wealth, of gloom and buoyant hope, coexist.

The Adventures of Tom Sawyer (1876), like all the other best works of Mark Twain's, drew upon his boyhood recollections. Mischievous, imaginative Tom Sawyer and his priggish half brother, Sid, live with their Aunt Polly in the remote town of St. Petersburg on the Mississippi. When Sid "preaches" on Tom for playing Hookey, Tom must whitewash a fence. But Tom, pretending the task is a privilege, inveigles his friends into doing it. When his overtures to the fair Becky Thatcher are repulsed, Tom runs off with his friend Huck Finn. They see Injun Joe murder Dr. Robinson, a crime of which Muff Potter is falsely accused. The two boys and their companion, Joe Harper, decide to become pirates and hide themselves on Jackson's island in the river, whence they return unobserved to attend their own funeral as they are supposed to be drowned. Then followed Muff's acquital, Injun Joe's escape, the boy's discovery of hidden treasure, Tom and Becky's adventure in the cave. All these are sheer melodrama overlaid with psychological realism. Tom's adventures are youthful romantic assaults upon the adult world of the drab commonplace. His triumphs are the wish fulfillments of childhood that yearns for adulation from those who deem themselves wiser and better.

Life on the Mississippi (1883) is Mark Twain's another masterpiece, which is divided into two parts. The first part deals with that great river in the days of its glory when, before the railroads, it was the major thoroughfare from north to south and the centre of both business and pleasure in the huge fertile Mississippi valley. The second part, based on Twain's visit to the river more than twenty years later, tells of changed condition of the post-civil war region with its deserted towns and decaying idle wharves.

The Adventures of Huckleberry Finn (1885) is a sequel to *Tom Sawyer* and Mark Twain's best work. The narrator of this picaresque tale of a voyage by raft on the Mississippi is Huck Finn, who uses the unliterary speech of Mark Twain's youth. When Huck's drunken father tried to get possession of his son's share of the buried treasure, the boy escaped to Jackson's Island, where he found Jim, Miss Watson's escaped Negro slave. The two headed downstream on a raft, Huck torn between his legal duty to return the runaway and his loyalty to his friend and companion. After numerous escapades involving the Grainger-Sheperdson fend and the tricks of two imposters, the "Duke" and the "King", Jim was captured. But after the timely appearance of Tom Sawyer and much surprising good luck, the slave gained his freedom and the boys lost theirs by a return to school. Huck's river journey is the odyssey of youth and life, and his initiation into the adult is an ordeal that deepens his understanding and confirms his powers of judgement as an individual.

The Man That Corrupted Hadleyburg is a famous example of Twain pessimism. Once offended by the townsfolk of the community of Hadleyburg famed for its honesty, Stephenson returns after two years to leave a bag of gold for a citizen who has supposedly assisted him in time of need. The benefactor need only claim the money. There actually never is such a benefactor, but every townsman is willing to perjure himself to get the gold. All are shown up as frauds, and the supposed gold is only lead. Lust for money has corrupted America.

LIFE ON THE MISSISSIPPI

THE BOYS' AMBITION[1]

When I was a boy, there was but one permanent ambition among my comrades in our village[2] on the west bank of the Mississippi River. That was, to be a steamboatman. We had transient ambitions of other sorts, but they were only transient. When a circus came and went, it left us all burning to become clowns; the first negro minstrel show that ever came to our section left us all suffering to try that kind of life; now and then we had a hope that, if we lived and were good, God would permit us to be pirates. These ambitions faded out, each in its turn; but the ambition to be a steamboatman always remained.

Once a day a cheap, gaudy packet arrived upward from St. Louis, and another downward from Keokuk[3]. Before these events, the day was glorious with expectancy; after them, the day was a dead and empty thing. Not only the boys, but the whole village, felt this. After all these years I can picture that old time to myself now, just as it was then: the white town drowsing in the sunshine of a summer's morning; the streets empty, or pretty nearly so; one or two clerks sitting in front of the Water Street stores, with their splint-bottomed chairs tilted back against the walls, chins on breasts, hats slouched over their faces, asleep—with shingle-shavings enough around to show what broke them down; a sow and a litter of pigs loafing along the sidewalk, doing a good business in watermelon rinds and seeds; two or three lonely little freight piles scattered about the "levee"; a pile of "skids" on the slope of the stone-paved wharf, and the fragrant town drunkard asleep in the shadow of them; two or three wood flats at the head of the wharf, but nobody to listen to the peaceful lapping of the wavelets against them; the great Mississippi, the majestic, the magnificent Mississippi, rolling its mile-wide tide along, shining in the sun; the dense forest away on the other side; the "point" above the town, and the "point" below, bounding the river-glimpse and turning it into a sort of sea, and withal a very still and brilliant and lonely one. Presently a film of dark smoke appear above one of those remote "points"; instantly a negro drayman, famous for his quick eye and prodigious voice, lifts up the cry, "S-t-e-a-m-boat-a-comin'!" and the scene changes! The town drunkard stirs, the clerks wake up, a furious clatter of drays follows, every house and store pours out a human contribution, and all in a twinkling the dead town is alive and moving. Drays, carts, men, boys, all go hurrying from many quarters to a common center, the wharf. Assembled there, the people fasten their eyes upon the coming boat as upon a wonder they are seeing for the first time. And the boat is rather a handsome sight, too. She is long and sharp and trim and pretty; she has two tall, fancy-topped chimneys, with a gilded device of some kind swung between them; a fanciful pilot-house, all glass and "gingerbread," perched on top of the "texas" deck[4] behind them; the paddle-boxes are gorgeous with a picture or with gilded rays above the boat's name; the boiler-deck, the hurricane-deck, and the texas deck are fenced and ornamented with clean white railings; there is a flag gallantly flying from the jack-staff; the furnace doors are open and the fires glaring bravely; the upper decks are black with passengers; the captain stands by the big bell, calm, imposing, the envy of all; great volumes of the blackest smoke are rolling and tumbling out of the chimneys—a husbanded grandeur created with a bit of pitch pine just before arriving at a town; the crew are grouped on the forecastle; the broad stage is run far out over the port bow, and an envied deck-hand stands picturesquely on the end of it with a coil of rope in his hand; the pent steam is screaming through the gauge-cocks; the captain lifts his hand, a bell rings, the wheels stop; then they turn back, churning the water to foam, and the steamer is at rest. Then such a scramble as there is to get aboard, and to get ashore, and to take in freight and to discharge freight, all at one and the same time; and such a yelling and cursing as the mates facilitate it all with! Ten minutes later the steamer is under way again, with no flag on the jack-staff and no black smoke issuing from the chimneys. After ten more minutes the town is dead again, and the town drunkard asleep by the skids once more.

My father was justice of the peace, and I supposed he possessed the power of life and death over all men, and could hand anybody that offended him. This was distinction enough for means a general thing; but the desire to be a steamboatman kept intruding, nevertheless. I first wanted to be a cabin-boy, so that I could come out with a white apron on and shake a table-cloth over the side, where all my old comrades could see me later I thought I would rather be the deck-hand who stood on the end of the stage—plank with the coil of rope in his hand, because he was particularly conspicuous. But these were only day-dreams—they were too heavenly to be contemplated as real possibilities. By and by one of our boys went away. He was not heard of for a long time. At last he turned up as apprentice engineer or "striker" on a steamboat. This thing shook the bottom out of all my Sunday-school teachings. That boy had been notoriously worldly, and I just the reverse; yet he was exalted to this eminence, and I left in obscurity and misery. There was nothing generous about this fellow in his greatness. He would always manage to have a rusty bolt to scrub while his boat tarried at our town, and he would sit on the inside guard and scrub it, where we all could see him and envy him and loathe him. And whenever his boat was laid up he would come home and swell around the town in his blackest and greasiest clothes, so that nobody could help remembering that he was a steamboatman; and he used all sorts of steamboat technicalities in his talk, as if he were so used to them that he forgot common people could not understand them. He would speak of the "labboard" side of a horse in an easy, natural way that would make one wish he was dead. And he was always talking about "St. Looy" like an old citizen; he would refer casually to occasions when he was "coming down Fourth Street," or when he as "passing by the Planter's House," or when there was a fire and he took a turn on the brakes of "the old Big Missouri"; and then he would go on and lie about how many towns the size of ours were burned down there that day. Two or three of the boys had long been persons of consideration among us because they had been to St. Louis once and had a vague general knowledge of its wonders, but the day of their glory was over now. They lapsed into a humble silence, and learned to disappear when the ruthless "cub"-engineer approached. This fellow had money, too, and hair-oil. Also an ignorant silver watch and a showy brass watch chain. He wore a leather belt and used no suspenders. If ever a youth was cordially admired and hated by his comrades, this one was. No girl could withstand his charms. He "cut out" every boy in the village. When his boat blew up at last, it diffused a tranquil contentment among us such as we had not known for months. But when he came home the next week, alive, renowned, and appeared in church all battered up and bandaged, a shining hero, stared at and wondered over by everybody, it seemed to us that the partiality of Providence for an undeserving reptile had reached a point where it was open to criticism.

This creature's career could produce but one result, and it speedily followed. Boy after boy managed to get on the river. The minister's son became an engineer. The doctor's and the postmaster's sons became "mud clerks"; the wholesale liquor dealer's son became a barkeeper on a boat; four sons of the chief merchant, and two sons of the county judge, became pilots. Pilot was the grandest position of all. The pilot, even in those days of trivial wages, had a princely salary—from a hundred and fifty to two hundred and fifty dollars a month, and no board to pay. Two months of his wages would pay a preacher's salary for a year. Now some of us were left disconsolate. We could not get on the river—at least our parents would not let us.

So, by and by, I ran away. I said I would never come home again till I was a pilot and could come in glory. But somehow I could not manage it. I went meekly aboard a few of the boats that lay packed together like sardines at the long St. Louis wharf, and humbly inquired for the pilots, but got only a cold shoulder and short words from mates and clerks. I had to make the best of this sort of treatment for the time being, but I had comforting day—dreams of a future when I should be a great and honored pilot, with plenty of money, and could kill some of these mates and clerks and pay for them.

Notes:

1. This is Chapter Ⅳ of *Life on the Mississippi*, and the first chapter of "Old Times on the Mississippi," published in the Atlantic Monthly in 1875.
2. "Hannibal, Missouri" [Twain's note].
3. In southeastern Iowa.
4. The officers' quarters, largest on the boat, were called the "texas," and the deck just over them the "texas deck."

William Dean Howells (1837—1920)

① *Biographical Introduction*

Born in a small town in Ohio, Howells was setting type in his father's printing office by the age of nine. He had little formal education but was schooled by life and wide reading. From 1856 to 1861, Howells worked for the Ohio State Journal. He wrote a campaign biography of Abraham Lincoln, for which he was rewarded with an appointment as U.S. consul in Venice (1861—65). Back in America, he became assistant editor of the Atlantic Monthly in 1866 and editor-in-chief from 1871 to 1881. Resigning as editor of the Atlantic, he traveled in Europe and wrote novels, finally settling in New York in 1891.

Howells was a prolific, versatile and influential author during half a century of American literary life. He not only wrote forty-three novels and story collections, of which a handful have won a permanent place in American literature, but he was also an important editor and critic. Besides, he wrote a large number of plays, about ten travel books, several collections of poetry, several volumes of literary reminiscence, sketches, and collected essays. Howell's chief importance today lies in his leading role as theoretician and practitioner in the movement toward literary realism.

② ***The Champion of Realism***

Early in his career Howells committed himself to the cause of realism and throughout his career he practiced and preached this doctrine.

Howells' literary credo of realism is chiefly elucidated in his most famous critical work *Criticism and Fiction*. Fiction, he asserts, must truthfully delineate the actual emotions, ideas, and impulses that govern real people in the present world. The sources of realism he finds in science and in democracy, where the realist "feels in every nerve the equality of things and the unity of men." He further insists that art should intend primarily to teach rather than to amuse; that art should inculcate morality; and that to be truthful to American life the realist should on the whole depict the more smiling aspects of life, which are the most prevalent and the most typical of it.

Howells's best novels such as *A Modern Instance*, *The Rise of Silas Lapham*, *Indian Summer*, and *A Hazard of New Fortunes* exemplify his principles of realism and achieve remarkable verisimilitude in their depiction of character and setting. From reading Howells one gets a real sense of what people thought, felt, and did in the late nineteen century, for his effects are achieved by a careful attention to ample, accurate detail and reasonable motivations. At the same time, one feels Howells' emphasis on the need for sympathy and moral integrity, and the need for different social classes to harmoniously adapt to their environment and to one another. In *The Rise of Silas Lapham*, we see Lapham keep his morality against bankruptcy and the Laphams and the Coreys trying to overcome their prejudice and come together.

③ *Howells's Major Works*

A Modern Instance (1882) is Howells's earliest success to hold interest for present-day readers. The story is the first significant treatment of divorce in American literature. By tracing the course of a deteriorating marriage in the years following the Civil War, it depicts a society in which traditional religious and family values are disintegrating in the face of commercial influences.

The story begins in a small town of Equity, Maine, where Bartley Hubbard, editor of the village newspaper, falls in love with Maricia Caylord, daughter of a local lawyer. Tired of the obscurity of his job, Bartley goes to Boston with wife to attempt greater things. In his first years in Boston, he prospers in the field of journalism and enjoys domestic happiness with his wife. But then his easygoing, egocentric and hedonistic nature asserts itself. He begins drinking, loses his job, deserts his wife and child, and comes to an Indian divorce court many months later. The story ends with Maricia returning to a lonely life in Equity, and Bartley drifting off to Arizona where he is killed in a quarrel.

The Rise of Silas Lapham (1885) is Howells' best-known

work, distinguished by its able organization and direct style. In this novel Howells combines a study of business and a study of society in a skillful interlocking narrative.

Writing a pioneering novel of business, Howells creates Silas Lapham, a self-made paint manufacturer who has returned from the Civil War, discovered a paint mine on the family farm in Vermont, gone into business, and prospered. Then his business is threatened by stiff competition and a final loss is incurred through the accidental burning of his new house into which he has poured a fortune. After his fall in material things, his rise in morality takes place when he refuses to save his business through unethical means, and in the end he is back in Vermont starting over.

Coupled with the business story is a social plot in which the Laphams attempt to get into Boston society. The house is the symbol of their striving, and its burning ends their hopes. To bring the two plot threads together Howells invents the cultivated Corey family of Boston gentry. Young Tom Corey, in spite of the social differences, gets a job in Silas's office and then falls in love with Penelope, Silas's elder daughter. Tom and Penelope are married and goes away to escape the pressures that would arise from the differences in their families. The union of the second generation of the two families is the symbol of the writer's hope of welding the finest characteristics of different social classes.

A Hazard of New Fortunes (1889) is the major novel of Howells's later career. It is a novel of class struggle, showing Howells's increasing concern with social problems. Basil March, a Boston editor, moves to New York and accepts the editorship of a new magazine financed by Tacob Dryfoos, a hard-fisted newly rich millionaire. Dryfoos is willing to spend the money just for the sake of his son Conrad, a Christian socialist, who is to be the publisher. To his father's dismay, Conrad pursues his philanthropic bent into the slums to assist the poor and press for social reform. Another progressive, Lindau, is invited by March to join the staff of the magazine. A serious alteration arises between Dryfoos' capitalist and Lindau's socialist principles. March is caught in the middle until Lindau voluntarily resigns, later to die of injuries sustained in a streetcar strike in which Conrad is also killed. Dryfoos is muted and repentant at his son's death, but he is merely a tiny cog in the system that perpetuates class inequality. March cannot endorse the violence to which Lindau has recourse, however. His sense of rightousness obliges him to endure the anguish of the present while hoping for more moderate, legitimate mechanisms of redress.

CRITICISM AND FICTION[1]

Chapter 2　The True Standard of the Arts

Mr. Burke's Essay on the Sublime and the Beautiful [is] a singularly modern book, considering how long ago it was wrote (as the great Mr. Steele[2] would have written the participle a little longer ago), and full of a certain well—mannered and agreeable instruction. "As for those called critics," the author says, "they have generally sought the rule of the arts in the wrong place; they have sought among poems, pictures, engravings, statues, and buildings; but art can never give the rules that make an art. This is, I believe, the reason why artists in general, and poets principally, have been confined in so narrow a circle; they have been rather imitators of one another than of nature, Critics follow them, and therefore can do little as guides. I can judge but poorly of anything while I measure it by no other standard than itself. The true standard of the arts is in every man's power; and an easy observation of the most common, sometimes of the meanest things, in nature will give the truest lights, where the greatest sagacity and industry that slights such observation must leave us in the dark, or, what is worse, amuse and mislead us by false lights."

The time is coming, I hope, when each new author, each new artist, will be considered, not in his proportion to any other author or artist, but in his relation to the human nature, known to us all, which it is his privilege, his high duty, to interpret. "The true standard of the artist is in every man's power" already, as Burke says; Michelangelo's "light of the piazza," the glance of the common eye, is and always was the best light on a statue; Goethe's "boy and blackbirds" have in all ages been the real connoisseurs of berries; but hitherto the mass of common men have been afraid to apply their own simplicity, naturalness, and honesty to the appreciation of the beautiful. They have always cast about for the instruction of some one who professed to know better, and who browbeat wholesome common-sense into the self-distrust that ends in sophistication. They have fallen generally to the worst of this bad species, and have been "amused and misled" (how pretty that quaint old use of amuse is!) "by the false lights" of critical vanity and self-righteousness. They have been taught to compare what they see and what they read, not with the things that they have observed and known, but with the things that some other artist or writer has done. Especially if they have themselves the artistic impulse in any direction they are taught to form themselves, not upon life, but upon the masters who became masters only by forming themselves upon life. The seeds of death are planted in them, and they can produce only the still-born, the academic. They are not told to take their work into the public square and see if it seems true to be chance passer, but to test it by the work of the very men who refused and decried any other test of their own work. The young writer who attempts to report the phrase and carriage of every-day life, who tries to tell just how he has heard men talk and seen them look, is made to feel guilty of something low and unworthy by the stupid people who would like to have him show how Shakespeare's men talked and looked, or Scot's, or Thackeray's, or Hawthorne's, or Dickens's; he is instructed to idealize his personages, that is, to take the life-likeness out of them, and put the book-likeness into them. He is approached in the spirit of the wretched pedantry into which learning, much or little, always decays when it withdraws itself and stands apart from experience in an attitude of imagined superiority, and which would say with the same confidence to the scientist: "I see that you are looking at a grasshopper there which you have found in the grass, and I suppose you intend to describe it. Now don't waste your time and sin against culture in that way. I've got a grasshopper here, which has been evolved at considerable pains and expense out of the grasshopper in general; in fact, it's a type. It's made up of wire and cardboard, very prettily painted in a conventional tint, and it's perfectly indestructible. It isn't very much like a real grasshopper, but it's a great deal nicer, and it's served to represent the notion of a grasshopper ever since man emerged from barbarism. You may say that it's artificial. Well, it is artificial; but then it's ideal too; and what you want to do is to cultivate the idea. You'll find the books full of my kind of grasshopper, and scarcely a trace of yours in any of them. The thing that you are proposing to do is commonplace; but if you say that it isn't commonplace, for the very reason that it hasn't been done before, you'll have to admit that it's photographic."

As I said, I hope the time is coming when not only the artist, but the common, average man, who always "has the standard of the arts in his power," will have also the courage to apply it, and will reject the ideal grasshopper wherever he finds it, in science, in literature, in art, because it is not "simple, natural, and honest," because it is not like a real grasshopper. But I will own that I think the time is yet far off, and that the people who have been brought up on the ideal grasshopper, the heroic grasshopper, the impassioned grasshopper, the self-devoted, adventureful, good old romantic cardboard grasshopper must die out before the simple, honest, and natural grasshopper can have a fair field. I am in no haste to compass the end of these good people, whom I find in the meantime very amusing. It is delightful to meet one of them, either in print or out of it—some sweet elderly lady or excellent gentleman whose youth was pastured on the literature of thirty or forty years ago—and to witness the confidence with which they preach their favorite authors as all the law and the prophets. They have commonly read little or nothing since or, if they have, they have judged it by a standard taken from these authors, and never dreamed of judging it by nature; they are destitute of the documents in the case of the later writers; they suppose that Balzac was the beginning of realism, and that Zola is its wicked end; they are quite ignorant, but they are ready to talk you down, if you differ from them, with an assumption of knowledge sufficient for any occasion. The horror, the resentment, with which they receive any question of their literary saints is genuine; you descend at once very far in the moral and social scale, and anything short of offensive personality is too good for you; it is expressed to you that you are one to be avoided, and put down even a little lower than you have naturany fallen.

Those good people, those curious and interesting if somewhat musty back-numbers, must always have a hero, an idol of some sort, and it is droll to find Balzac, who suffered from their sort such bitter scorn and hate for his realism while he was alive, now become a fetich in his turn, to be shaken in the faces of those who will not blindly worship him. But it is no new thing in the history of literature: whatever is established is sacred with those who do not think. At the beginning of the century, when romance was making the same fight against effete classicism which realism is making to-day against effete romanticism, the Italian poet Monti[3] declared that "the romantic was the cold grave of the Beautiful," just as the realistic is now supposed to be. The romantic of that day and the real of this are in certain degree the same. Romanticism then sought, as realism seeks now, to widen the bounds of sympathy, to level every barrier against aesthetic freedom, to escape from the paralysis of tradition. It exhausted itself in this impulse; and it remained for realism to assert that fidelity to experience and probability of motive are essential conditions of a great imaginative literature. It is not a new theory, but it has never before universally characterized literary endeavor. When realism becomes false to itself, when it heaps up facts merely, and maps life instead of picturing it, realism will perish too. Every true realist instinctively knows this, and it is perhaps the reason why he is careful of every fact, and feels himself bound to express or to indicate its meaning at the risk of over-moralizing. In life he finds nothing insignificant; all tells for destiny and character; nothing that God has made is contemptible. He cannot look upon human life and declare this thing or that thing unworthy of notice, any more than the scientist can declare a fact of the material world beneath the dignity of his inquiry. He feels in every nerve the equality of things and the unity of men; his soul is exalted, not by vain shows and shadows and ideals, but by realities, in which alone the truth lives.

Chapter 8 How Can Art Decay?

In fine, I would beseech the literary critics of our country to disabuse themselves of the mischievous notion that they are essential to the progress of literature in the way critics have vainly imagined. Canon Farrar[4] confesses that with the best will in the world to profit by the many criticisms of his books, he has never profited in the least by any of them; and this is almost the universal experience of authors. It is not always the fault of the critics. They sometimes deal honestly and fairly by a book, and not so often they deal adequately. But in making a book, if it is at all a good book, the author has learned all that is knowable about it, and every strong point and every weak point in it, far more accurately than any one else can possibly learn them. He has learned to do better than well for the future; but if his book is bad, he cannot be taught anything about it from the outside. It will perish; and if he has not the root of literature in him, he will perish as an author with it.

But what is it that gives tendency in art, then? What is it makes people like this at one time, and that at another? Above all, what makes a better fashion change for a worse; how can the ugly come to be preferred to the beautiful; in other words, how can an art decay?

This question came up in my mind lately with regard to English fiction and its form, or rather its formlessness. How, for instance, could people who had once known the simple verity, the refined perfection of Miss Austen, enjoy anything less refined and less perfect?

With her example before them, why should not English novelists have gone on writing simply, honestly, artistically, ever after? One would think it must have been impossible for them to do otherwise, if one did not remember, say, the lamentable behavior of the actors who support Mr. Jefferson[5], and their theatricality in the very presence of his beautiful naturalness. It is very difficult, that simplicity, and nothing is so hard as to be honest, as the reader, if he has ever happened to try it, must know. "The big bow wow I can do myself, like any one going," said Scott, but he owned that the exquisite touch of Miss Austen was denied him; and it seems certainly to have been denied in greater or less measure to all her successors. But though reading and writing come by nature, as Dogberry[6] justly said, taste in them may be cultivated, or once cultivated, it may be preserved; and why was it not so among those poor islanders?

Senor Valdes[7] is a realist, but a realist according to his own conception of realism; and he has some words of just censure for the French naturalists, whom he finds unnecessarily, and suspects of being sometimes even mercenarily, nasty. He sees the wide difference that passes between this naturalism and the realism of the English and Spanish; and he goes somewhat further than I should go in condemning it. "The French naturalism represents only a moment, and an insignificant part of life... It is characterized by sadness and narrowness. The prototype of this literature is the Madame Bovary of Flaubert. I am an admirer of this novelist, and especially of this novel; but often in thinking of it I have said, How dreary would literature be if it were no more than this! There is something antipathetic and gloomy and limited in it, as there is in modern French life;" but this seems to me exactly the best possible reason for its being. I believe with Senor Valdes that "no literature can live long without joy," not because of its mistaken aesthetics, however, but because no civilization can live long without

joy. The expression of French life will change when French life changes; and French naturalism is better at its worst than French unnaturalism at its best.

Notes:

1. *Criticism and Fiction* (1891) was the author's formulation, in one volume, of essays that first appeared from 1886 to 1891 in his influential column "The Editor's Study," a regular feature of *Harper's Magazine*. The locations in the volume are shown by the chapter numbers. These selections represent Howells's definition of the new realism that he practiced, "classic" in the sense that its object was a balanced interpretation of the common life of man in the United States; with this he contrasts the emergent naturalism, flourishing particularly in France and Russia, in which he detected a preference, or indeed a necessity, for specialized situations and characters pessimistically predetermined. Among the qualities that made these essays memorable, besides their literary merits, is Howells's concept that the reality of fiction bears a direct relationship to its cultural environment; secondly, that cultural change in the United States has since caused both the classic and the naturalistic fiction to survive.
2. Sir Richard Steele, dramatist, creative stylist of the eighteenth-century periodicals *The Tatler* and *The Spectator*, died in 1729, the year of the birth of Edmund Burke, the Irish statesman.
3. Vincenzo Monti (1754—1828), neoclassical poet.
4. Frederick W. Farrar (1831—1903), British clergyman and writer.
5. Joseph Jefferson (1829—1905), American actor.
6. Dogberry, a smug constable and misuser of words in Shakespeare's *Much Ado About Nothing*.
7. Armando Palacio Valdes (1853—1938), Spanish critic and realistic novelist. His introduction to the English translation of his novel *Sister St. Supice* (1889) is the source of Howells's quotations. The novel was very popular in the United States.

Henry James (1843—1916)

① *Biographical Introduction*

Henry James was born in a wealthy family in New York. His father was a philosopher and his brother, a philosopher and a psychologist. Henry was educated by tutors until 1855, when his family took him to Europe for a cosmopolitan education in Switzerland and Germany. In 1862, Henry briefly attended Harvard Law School, but left it for a writing career. Henry remained a bachelor throughout his life. In 1875, he went abroad to live, setting permanently in England the next year. In 1915, when the United States hesitated to enter World War I, he became a British subject.

Henry James was a prolific writer. His whole life was a long career of continual productivity. The quantity of work he produced filled up a good many volumes—novels, travel papers, critical essays, plays, autobiographies and a series of critical prefaces on the art of fiction.

James' creative life can be divided into three periods. In the first period (1865—1882) he produced a number of novels, among which the most important are *The American*, *Daisy Miller*, and *The Portrait of a Lady*. These novels reveal James's fascination with the international theme, that is, American innocence in contrast with European sophistication. In the second period (1882—1895), James wrote tales of subtle studies of interpersonal relationship. As these novels were poorly received, he turned to play writing, which also proved to be a failure. Then he returned to novel writing and began his final phase of creativity. In this period, James revived his international theme and wrote, among others, the three great novels— *The Ambassadors*, *The Wings of the Dove* and *The Golden Bowl*.

② *James's Themes*

Henry James wrote on a limited range of themes but with subtlety and charm. He frequently depicts the clash of American inexperience and European sophistication. Often the American is an innocent person of wealth and inexperience, travelling in Europe and seeking to penetrate its cultural, social, and ethical mysteries. James sometimes complicates his conflicts by making his representatives of European culture Americans living abroad—hence at times trying to be more European than their native friends and neighbors. James's European Americans fail to achieve personal and social happiness and success, but they gain in moral esteem, in their eyes and those of their friendly readers. James always combines the international theme with other themes. He may have the clash of personalities from different countries and social milieus effectuate in an exposure of such false values as social ambition, patriotism, exertion for fame, and pride in one's pedigree, appearance, social renown, or connections.

③ *James's Form and Style*

Henry James is a psychological realist. His fiction is like life. In his famous essay "The Art of Fiction", he stated that "The only reason for the existence of a novel is that it does attempt to represent life." To correspond to life, James avoided the author's omniscience and used the trick of making his characters reveal themselves with minimal intervention of the author. James termed this method of telling the story, that is, the illumination of the situation and characters through one or several minds, "point of view". The use of the restricted point of view makes his plots hard to follow but exciting because the reader shares the same delusions, limited perceptions, and dawning awareness as the character through whose consciousness the story is filtered. In *The Portrait of a Lady* James places the centre of the subject in the consciousness of the heroine, lsabel Archer whose vigil and meditation is presented as a very elaborate internalmonologue, so that the reader is within her mind and has her inner vision.

James's emphasis on the inner awareness and inward movement of characters is in part responsible for his difficult and complicated style, which is added to by his exploitation of subtle diction and delicate symbolism. Therefore, his work is very demanding to the reader. That's why he was not widely read at his death.

④ ***James's Literary Criticism***

Besides a great psychological novelist, Henry James is a great critic. His immense contribution to literary criticism is that he developed gradually from early evaluation in terms of stiff moral standards to inductive inquiry, flexibility, and a subtle perception of aesthetic nuances. Distrustful of abstract standards, he thought of criticism as a creative art in itself and sought to understand fully the genesis of works of literature.

James's maior pronouncement in the field of criticism was his "The Art of Fiction", a retort to a lecture by Watter Besant, advocating popular and realistic standards for fiction. To James the novel is "the most magnificent form of art", and the chief requirement of novelists is deeply perceptive intelligence and sincerity to their own highest standards. The essential of art is personal vision and the novel should depict life as it is.

⑤ *James's Major Works*

Roderick Hudson (1876), James's first important novel, deals with Americans abroad, like many of his later works. Wealthy Rowland Mallet, dedicated to serving the arts, discovers talent in the young Massachusetts sculptor Roderick Hudson, and offers to send him to Rome to study. In Italy, after briefly justifying his artistic promise, Hudson falls in dissipation and becomes fascinated by Christina Light, an ambitious expatriate American. He deserts his fiancèe, Mary Garland. He persists even when Christina weds the Italian Prince Casamassia, and follows her to the Swiss Alps and there dies in a fall from a mountain. The themes of this story are the impact of Europe upon the innocent American and the plight of an artist who cannot summon the dedication necessary to supreme creative achievement.

The American (1877) is James' second novel, also with the theme of the contrast of American innocence and Old World experience. The hero, Christopher Newman, is a Civil War veteran and a rich former businessman, who brashly comes to Paris to buy the best wife on the market. Through an expatriated American matchmaker Newman meets a young widow, Claire de Cintre, whose proud French family, the Bellegardes, accept his suit but soon afterwards withdraw their promise. Newman protests and lashes back, but Claire's widowed mother and older brother remain inflexible. Newman, from an old family servant, gets proof that Claire's mother has murdered her late husband, and threatens her and her son with exposure as accomplices in Claire's father's death. But they remain obstinate. Claire enters a convent, and Newman, too noble to carry out his revenge, burns the evidence and returns to America.

Daisy Miller (1879) is James's greatest popular success with the novelette. The events and characters are seen through the eyes of Frederick Winterbourne, an American expatriate. The heroine, Daisy Miller, is a wealthy American girl, who is travelling in Europe with her mother and younger brother. Daisy, unaware that she is violating the accepted Continental standards of propriety, behaves with the freedom to which she has been accustomed in Schenectady, New York, and appears unchaperoned in public, especially with a handsome young Italian, Giovanelli. Romantically desirous of seeing Rome's miasmal colosseum by moonlight, Daisy goes there with Giovanelli and accidentally encounters Winterbourne, whom she met and attracted earlier in Switzerland. Winterbourne reproaches Giovanelli for permitting her thus to risk her health and her last shreds of her reputation. After she dies of malarial fever, Winterbourne realises her complete innocence and regrets his doubts about her virtue, admitting that he has "lived too long in foreign parts."

The Portrait of a Lady (1881) is James's most attractive novel. The heroine, Isabel Archer, is taken to Europe by her aunt, Mrs. Lydia Touchett, the eccentric wife of a wealthy American, long resident in England. At Gardencourt, the Touchett country house, Isabel rejects a most eligible suitor, Lord Warburton, and shortly afterwards a wealthy American, Caspar Goodwood, who has followed her to England. Her cousin, Ralph Touchett, because of delicate health remains an undeclared lover. They are joined by Mrs. Touchett's friend, Madame Merle, through whom Isabel becomes acquainted with, and then captivated by Glbert Osmond, an art connoisseur, who lives near Florence with his convent-bred daughter, Pansy. Against the advice of her friends, who recognize that Osmond is interested only in her money (She has inherited a part of Mr. Touchett's fortune), Isabel marries him and is unhappy. A few years later she learns that Pansy is the illegitimate daughter of Osmond and Madame Merle. Isabel visits England just before her cousin Ralph's death, rejects a last appeal by Goodwood, and goes back to her husband in Italy.

The Wing of the Dove (1902) is one of James's three masterworks in his late period. Milly Theale, a wealthy young orphan from New York, suffers from an unspecified terminal disease. To make the best of what time remains to her she goes to Europe, where she encounters and is influenced by Kate Cory, who is engaged to Merton Densher, a minor journalist as poor as herself. Kate plans to have her lover marry Milly, who evidently likes him, so that after Milly's death he may come into her fortune and return to his original love, herself. Ignorant of this plot, Milly comes to care for Densher deeply. Then she learns from Lord Mark, her rejected suitor, the secret engagement between Densher and Kate. After breaking off with Densher, she abandons her will to live. Yet her final act is to overlook the way she has been abused and to settle a large sum upon Densher in her will. Thus Kate's plot fulfills its intended purpose, but Milly's character and behavior have awakened Densher's love which has survived after her death. Having realized this, Densher and Kate decide not to marry. At the same time Kate perceives that Milly, whom she has called a dove, has at the end stretched out her covering wings, hence defeating her rival.

The Ambassadors, though written before *The Wings of the*

Dove, was not published until 1903. Lambert Strether, editor of a magazine in Woollett, Massachusetts, undertakes an ambassadorial mission to Paris for his domineering, widowed fiancèe. He is to learn why her son Chad is dallying abroad and to bring him home to the family business. After he comes under the spell of Paris and meets Mme. de Vionnet, a French countess with whom Chad is entangled, Strether encourages Chad not to return to America. Thereupon Mrs. Newsome sends a squad of new "ambassadors" to recover Strether as well as Chad. At the end of the story, Chad remains in Paris. Strecher's embassy has educated the ambassador. He returns to Woolett with the refined satisfaction with the graceful old world steps. In this novel, James stresses mutual understanding and sympathy between the old world of tradition and the New World of individualism.

The Gold Bowl (1904) is the subtlest and most difficult and also the most poetic of James's novels. A rich American widower named Adam Verver is travelling with his adult daughter Maggie, who marries suave Prince Amerigo of Rome, formerly the lover of Charlotte Stant, a school friend of Maggie's. Sensing her father's loneliness, Maggie urges Charlotte to avail herself of the Verver-Amerigo hospitality, and the result is the marriage of Charlotte and Adam. But father and daughter are so attached to each other that Amerigo and Charlotte resume their sexual liaison. Earlier, Amerigo and Charlotte, while shopping for a wedding present for Maggie, rejected a beautiful gold bowl because it has a tiny crack. Later, Maggie happens upon the bowl and buys it for her father. Through the shopkeeper Maggie learns the intimacy of her husband and Charlotte and realizes the flaw in her and her father's marriages. With great caution, she labors to manipulate all parties into their proper configuration. At length, Adam Verver leaves Maggie with the prince in Europe and returns to America with his wife.

DAISY MILLER[1]

I

At a little town of Vevey, in Switzerland, there is a particularly comfortable hotel; there are indeed many hotels, since the entertainment of tourists is the business of the place, which, as many travellers will remember, is seated upon the edge of a remarkably blue lake[2]—a lake that it behoves every tourist to visit. The shore of the lake presents an unbroken array of establishments of this order, of every category, from the "grand hotel" of the newest fashion, with a chalk-white front, a hundred balconies, and a dozen flags flying from its roof, to the small Swiss pension of an elder day, with its name inscribed in German-looking lettering upon a pink or yellow wall and an awkward summer-house in the angle of the garden. One of the hotels at Vevery, however, is famous, even classical, being distingusihed from many of its upstart neighbours by an air both of luxury and of maturity. In this region, through the month of June, American travellers are extremely numerous; it may be said indeed that Vevey assumes at that time some of the characteristics of an American watering-place. There are sights and sounds that evoke a vision, an echo, of Newport and Saratoga[3]. There is a flitting hither and thither of "stylish" young girls, a rustling of muslin flounces, a rattle of dance-music in the morning hours, a sound of high-pitched voices at all times. You receive an impression of these things at the excellent inn of the "Trois Couronnes"[4], and are transported in fancy to the Ocean House or to Congress Hall. But at the "Trois Couronnes", it must be added, there are other features much at variance with these suggestions; neat German waiters who look like secretaries of legation; Russian princesses sitting in the garden; little Polish boys walking about, held by the hand, with their governors; a view of the snowy crest of the Dent du Midi[5] and the picturesque towers of the Castle of Chillon.

I hardly know whether it was the analogies or the differences that were uppermost in the mind of a young American, who, two or three years ago, sat in the garden of the "Trois Couronnes", looking about him rather idly at some of the graceful objects I have mentioned. It was a beautiful summer morning, and in whatever fashion the young American looked at things they must have seemed to him charming. He had come from Geneva the day before, by the little steamer, to see his aunt, who was staying at the hotel—Geneva having been for a long time his place of residence. But his aunt had a headache—his aunt had almost always a headache—and she was now shut up in her room smelling camphor so that he was at liberty to wander about. He was some seven-and-twenty years of age; when his friends spoke of him they usually said that he was at Geneva "studying." When his enemies spoke of him they said—but after all he had no enemies: he was extremely amiable and generally liked. What I should say is simply that when certain persons spoke of him they conveyed that the reason of his spending so much time at Geneva was that he was extremely devoted to a lady who lived there—a foreign lady, a person older than himself. Very few Americans—truly I think none—had ever seen this lady, about whom there were some singular stories. But Winterbourne had an old attachment for the little capital of Calvinism[6]; he had been put to school there as a boy and had afterwards even gone, on trial—trial of the grey old "Academy"[7] on the steep and stony hillside to college there; friendships. Many of these he had kept, and they were a source of great satisfaction to him.

After knocking at his aunt's door and learning that she was indisposed he had taken a walk about the town and then he had come in to his breakfast. He had now finished that repast, but was enjoying a small cup of coffee which had been served him on a little table in the garden by one of the waiters who looked like *attache's*[8] At last he finished his coffee and lit a cigarette. Presently a small boy came walking along the path—an urchin of nine or ten. The child, who was diminutive for his years, had an aged expression of countenance, a pale complexion and sharp little features. He was dressed in knickerbockers and had red stockings that displayed his poor little spindle-shanks; he also wore a brilliant red cravat. He carried in his hand a long alpenstock, the sharp point of which he thrust into everything he approached—the flower-beds, the garden-benches, the trains of the ladies' dresses. In front of Winterbourne he paused, looking at him with a pair of bright and penetrating little eyes.

"Will you give me a lump of sugar?" he asked in a small sharp hard voice—a voice immature and yet somehow not young.

Winterbourne glanced at the light table near him, on which his coffee-service rested, and saw that several morsels of sugar remained. "Yes, you may take one," he answered; "but I don't think too much sugar good for little boys."

This little boy stepped forward and carefully selected three of the coveted fragments, two of which he buried in the pocket of his knickerbockers, depositing the other as promptly in another place. He poked his alpenstock, lance-fashion, into Winterbourne's bench and tried to crack the lump of sugar with his teeth.

"Oh blazes; it's har-r-d!" he exclaimed, divesting vowel and consonants, pertinently enough, of any taint of softness.

Winterbourne had immediately gathered that he might have the honour of claiming him as a countryman. "Take care you don't hurt your teeth," he said paternally.

"I haven't got any teeth to hurt. They're all come out. I've only got seven teeth. Mother counted them last night, and one came out right afterwards. She said she'd slap me if any more came out. I can't help it. It's this old Europe. It's the climate that makes them come out. In America they didn't come out. It's these hotels."

Winterbourne was much amused. "If you eat three lumps of sugar your mother will certainly slap you", he ventured.

"She's got to give me some candy then", rejoined his young interlocutor. "I can't get any candy here—any American candy. American candy's the best candy."

"And are American little boys the best little boys?" Winterbourne asked.

"I don't know. I'm an American boy," said the child.

"I see you're one of the best!" the young man laughed.

"Are you an American man?" pursued this vivacious infant. And then on his friend's affirmative reply, "American men are the best," he declared with assurance.

His companion thanked him for the compliment, and the child, who had now got astride of his alpenstock, stood looking about him while he attacked another lump of sugar. Winterbourne wondered if he himself had been like this in his infancy, for he had been brought to Europe at about the same age.

"Here comes my sister!" cried his young compatriot. "She's an American girl, you bet!"

Winterbourne looked along the path and saw a beautiful young lady advancing. "American girls are the best girls," he thereupon cheerfully remarked to his visitor.

"My sister ain't the best!" the child promptly returned. "She's always blowing at me."

"I imagine that's your fault, not hers," said Winterbourne. The young lady meanwhile had drawn near. She was dressed in white muslin, with a hundred frills and flounces and knots of pale-coloured ribbon. Bareheaded, she balanced in her hand a large parasol with a deep border of embroidery; and she was strikingly, admirably pretty. "How pretty they are!" thought our friend, who straightened himself in his seat as if he were ready to rise.

The young lady paused in front of his bench, near the parapet of the garden, which overlooked the lake. The small boy had now converted his alpenstock into a vaulting-pole, by the aid of which he was springing about in the gravel and kicking it up not a little. "Why Randolph", she freely began, "what are you doing?"

"I'm going up the Alps!" cried Randolph. "This is the way!" And he gave another extravagant jump, scattering the pebbles about Winterbourne's ears.

"That's the way they come down," said Winterbourne.

"He's an American man!" proclaimed Randolph in his harsh little voice.

The young lady gave no heed to this circumstance, but looked straight at her brother. "Well, I guess you'd better be quiet," she simply observed.

It seemed to Winterbourne that he had been in a manner presented. He got up and stepped slowly toward the charming creature, throwing away his cigarette. "This little boy and I have made acquaintance," he said with great civility. In Geneva, as he had been perfectly aware, a young man wasn't at liberty to speak to a young unmarried lady save under certain rarely-occurring conditions: but here at Vevey what conditions could be better than these? —a pretty American girl coming to stand in front of you in a garden with all the confidence in life. This pretty American girl, whatever that might prove, on hearing Winterbourne's observation simply glanced at him; she turned her head and looked over the parapet, at the lake and the opposite mountains. He wondered whether he had gone too far, but decided that he must gallantly advance rather than retreat. While he was thinking of something else to say the young lady turned again to the little boy, whom she addressed quite as if they were alone together. "I should like to know where you got that pole."

"I bought it!" Randolph shouted.

"You don't mean to say you're going to take it to Italy!"

"Yes, I'm going to take is to Italy!" the child rang out.

She glanced over the front of her dress and smoothed out a knot or two of ribbon. Then she gave her sweet eyes to the prospect again. "Well, I guess you'd better leave it somewhere," she dropped after a moment.

"Are you going to Italy?" Winterbourne now decided very respectfully to enquire.

She glanced at him with lovely remoteness. "Yes, sir," she then replied. And she said nothing more.

"And are you-a-thinking of the Simplon?"[9] he pursued with a slight drop of assurance.

"I don't know," she said. "I suppose it's some mountain. Randolph, what mountain are we thinking of?"

"Thinking of?"—the boy stared.

"Why going right over."

"Going to where?" he demanded.

"Why right down to Italy"—Winerbourne felt vague emulations.

"I don't know," said Randolph. "I don't want to go t' Italy. I want to go to American."

"Oh Italy's a beautiful place!" the young man laughed.

"Can you get candy there?" Randolph asked of all the echoes.

"I hope not," said his sister. "I guess you've had enough candy, and mother thinks so too."

"I haven't had any for ever so long—for a hundred weeks!" cried the boy, still jumping about.

The young lady inspected her flounces and smoothed her ribbons again; and Winterbourne presently risked an observation on the beauty of the view. He was ceasing to be in doubt, for he had begun to perceive that she was really not in the least embarrassed. She might be cold, she might be austere, she might even be prim; for that was apparently—he had already so generalised—what the most "distant" American girls did: they came and planted themselves straight in front of you to show how rigidly unapproachable they were. There hadn't been the slightest flush in her fresh fairness however; so that she was clearly neither offended nor fluttered. Only she was composed—he had seen that before too—of charming little parts that didn't match and that made no *ensemble*;[10] and if she looked another way when he spoke to her, and seemed not particularly to hear him, this was simply her habit, her manner, the result of her having no idea whatever of "form" (with such a tell-tale appendage as Randolph where in the world would she have got it?) in any such connexion. As he talked a little more and pointed out some of the objects of interest in the view, with which she appeared wholly unacquainted, she gradually, none the less, gave him more of the benefit of her attention; and then he saw that act unqualified by the faintest shadow of reserve. It wasn't however what would have been called a "bold" front that she presented, for her expression was as decently limpid as the very cleanest water. Her eyes were the very prettiest conceivable, and indeed Winterbourne hadn't for a long time seen anything prettier than his fair country-woman's various features—her complexion, her nose, her ears, her teeth. He took a great interest generally in that range of effects and was addicted to noting and, as it were, recording them; so that in regard to this young lady's face he made several observations. I wasn't at all insipid, yet at the same time wasn't pointedly—what point, on earth, could she ever make? —expressive; and though it offered such a collection of small finenesses and neatnesses he mentally accused it—very forgivingly—of a want of finish. He thought nothing more likely than that its wearer would have had her own experience of the action of her charms, as she would certainly have acquired a resulting confidence; but even should she depend on this for her main amusement her bright sweet superficial little visage gave out neither mockery nor irony. Before long it became clear that, however these things might be, she was much disposed to conversation. She remarked to Winterbourne that they were going to Rome for the winter—she and her mother and Randolph. She asked him if he was a "real American"; she wouldn't have taken him for one: he seemed more like a German—this flower was gathered as from a large field of comparison—especially when he spoke. Winterbourne, laughing, answered that he had met Germans who spoke like Americans, but not, so far as he remembered, any American with the resemblance she noted. Then he asked her if she mightn't be more at ease should she occupy the bench he had just quitted. She answered that she liked hanging round, but she none the less resignedly, after a little, dropped to the bench. She told him she was from New York State—"if you know where that is"; but our friend really quickened this current by catching hold of her small slippery brother and making him stand a few minutes by his side.

"Tell me your honest name, my boy." So he artfully proceeded.

In response to which the child was indeed unvarnished truth. "Randolph C. Miller. And I'll tell you hers." With which he levelled his alpenstock at his sister.

"You had better wait till you're asked!" said this young lady quite at her leisure.

"I should like very much to know your name," Winterbourne made free to reply.

"Her name's Daisy Miller!" cried the urchin. "But that ain't her real name; that ain't her name on her cards."

"It's a pity you haven't got one of my cards!" Miss Miller quite as naturally remarked.

"Her real name's Annie P. Miller," the boy went on.

It seemed, all amazingly, to do her good. "Ask him his now"—and she indicated their friend.

But to this point Randolph seemed perfectly indifferent; he continued to supply information with regard to his own family. "My father's name is Ezra B. Miller. My father ain't in Europe—he's in a better place than Europe." Winterbourne for a moment supposed this the manner in which the child had been taught to intimate that Mr. Miller had been removed to the sphere of celestial rewards. But Randolph immediately added: "My father's in Schenectady. He's got a big business. My father's rich, you bet."

"Well!" ejaculated Miss Miller, lowering her parasol and looking at the embroidered border. Winterbourne presently released the child, who departed, dragging his alpenstock along the path. "He don't like Europe," said the girl as with an artless instinct for historic truth. "He wants to go back."

"To Schenectady, you mean?"

"Yes, he wants to go right home. He hasn't got any boys

here. There's one boy here, but he always goes round with a teacher. They won't let him play."

"And your brother hasn't any teacher?" Winterbourne enquired

It tapped, at a touch, the spring of confidence. "Mother thought of getting him one—to travel round with as. There was a lady told her of a very good teacher; an American lady—perhaps you know her—Mrs. Sanders. I think she came from Boston. She told her of this teacher, and we thought of getting him to travel round with us. But Randolph said he didn't want a teacher traveling round with us. He said he wouldn't have lessons when he was in the cars.[11] And we are in the cars about half the time. There was an English lady we met in the cars—I think her name was Miss Featherstone; perhaps you know her. She wanted to know why I didn't give Randolph lessons—give him 'instruction,' she called it. I guess he could gave me more instruction than I could give him. He's very smart.

"Yes," said, Winterbourne; "he seems very smart."

"Mother's going to get a teacher for him as soon as we get t'Italy. Can you get good teachers in Italy?"

"Very good, I should think," Winterbourne hastened to reply.

"Or else she's going to find some school. He ought to learn some more. He's only nine. He's going to college." And in this way Miss Miller continued to converse upon the affairs of her family and upon other topics. She sat there with her extremely pretty hands, ornamented with very brilliant rings, folded in her lap, and with her pretty eyes now resting upon those of Winterbourne, now wandering over the garden, the people who passed before her and the beautiful view. She addressed her new acquaintance as if she had known him a long time. He found it very pleasant. It was many years since he had heard a young girl talk so much. It might have been said of this wandering maiden who had come and sat down beside him upon a bench that she chattered. She was very quiet, she sat in a charming tranquil attitude; but her lips and her eyes were constantly moving. She had a soft slender agreeable voice, and her tone was distinctly sociable. She gave Winterbourne a report of her movements and intentions, and those of her mother and brother, in Europe, and enumerated in particular the various hotels at which they had stopped. "That English lady in the cars," she said—"Miss Featherstone—asked me if we didn't all live in hotels in America. I told her I had never been in so many hotels in my life as since I came to Europe. I've never seen so many—it's nothing but hotels." But Miss Miller made this remark with no querulous accent: she appeared to be in the best humour with everything. She declared that the hotels were very good when once you got used to their ways and that Europe was perfectly entrancing. She wasn't disappointed—not a bit. Perhaps it was because she had heard so much about it before. She had ever so many intimate friends who had been there ever so many times, and that way she had got thoroughly posted. And then she had ever so many dresses and things from Paris. Whenever she put on a Paris dress she felt as if she were in Europe.

"It was a kind of a wishing-cap," Winterbourne smiled.

"Yes," said Miss Miller at once and without examining this analogy; "it always made me wish I was here. But I needn't have done that for dresses. I'm sure they send all the pretty ones to America; you see the most frightful things here. The only thing I don't like," she proceeded, "is the society. There ain't any society—or if there is I don't know where it keeps itself. Do you? I suppose there's some society somewhere, but I haven't seen anything of it. I'm very fond of society and I've always had plenty of it. I don't mean only in Schenectady, but in New York. I used to go to New York every winter. In New York I had lots of society. Last winter I had seventeen dinners given me, and three of them were by gentlemen," added Daisy Miller. "I've more friends in New York than in Schenectady—more gentlemen friends; and more young lady friends too," she resumed in a moment. She paused again for an instant; she was looking at Winterbourne with all her prettiness in her frank gay eyes and in her clear rather uniform smile. "I've always had," she said, "a great deal of gentlemen's society."

Poor Winterbourne was amused and perplexed—above all he was charmed. He had never yet heard a young girl express herself in just this fashion; never at least save in cases where to say such things was to have at the same time some rather complicated consciousness about them. And yet was he to accuse Miss Daisy Miller of an actual or a potential *arriere-pensee*,[12] as they said at Geneva? He felt he had lived at Geneva so long as to have got morally muddled; he had lost the right sense for the young American tone. Never indeed since he had grown old enough to appreciate things had he encountered a young compatriot of so "strong" a type as this. Certainly she was very charming, but how extraordinarily communicative and how tremendously easy! Was she simply a pretty girl from New York State—were they all like that, the pretty girls who had a good deal of gentlemen's society? Or was she also a designing, an audacious, in short an expert young person? Yes, his instinct for such a question had ceased to serve him, and his reason could but mislead. Miss Daisy Miller looked extremely innocent. Some people had told him that after all American girls *were* exceedingly innocent, and others had told him that after all they weren't. He must on the whole take Miss Daisy Miller for a flirt—a pretty American flirt. He had never as yet had relations with representatives of that class. He had known here in Europe two or three women—persons older than Miss Daisy Miller and provided, for respectability's sake, with husbands—who were great coquettes; dangerous terrible women with whom one's light commerce might indeed take a serious turn. But this charming apparition wasn't a coquette in that sense; she was very unsophisticated; she was only a pretty American flirt. Winterbourne was almost graterul for having found the formula that applied to Miss Daisy Miller. He leaned back in his seat; he remarked to himself that she had the finest little nose he had ever seen; he wondered what were the regular conditions and limitations of one's intercourse with a pretty American flirt. It presently became apparent that he was on the way to learn.

"Have you been to that old castle?" the girl soon asked, pointing with her parasol to the far-shining walls of the Chateau de Chillon.

"Yes, formerly, more than once," said Winterbourne. "You too, I suppose, have seen it?"

"No, we haven't been there. I want to go there dreadfully. Of course I mean to go there. I wouldn't go away from here without having seen that old castle."

"It's a very pretty excursion," the young man returned, "and very easy to make. You can drive, you know, or you can go by the little steamer."

"You can go in the cars," said Miss Miller.

"Yes, you can go in the cars," Winterbourne assented.

"Our courier says they take you right up to the castle," she continued. "We were going last week, but mother gave out. She suffers dreadfully from dyspepsia. She said she couldn't any more go—!" But this sketch of Mrs. Miller's plea remained unfinished. "Randolph wouldn't go either; he says he don't think much of old castles. But I guess we'll go this week if we can get Randolph."

"Your brother isn't interested in ancient monuments?" Winterbourne indulgently asked.

He now drew her, as he guessed she would herself have said, every time. "Why no, he says he don't care much about old castles. He's only nine. He wants to stay at the hotel. Mother's afraid to leave him alone, and the courier won't stay with him; so we haven't been to many places. But it will be too bad if we don't go up there." And Miss Miller pointed again at the Chateau de Chillon.

"I should think it might be arranged," Winterbourne was thus emboldened to reply. "Couldn't you get some one to stay—for the afternoon—with Randolph?"

Miss Miller looked at him a moment, and then with all serenity, "I wish you'd stay with him!" she said.

He pretended to consider it. "I'd much rather go to the Chillon with you."

"With me?" she asked without a shadow of emotion.

She didn't rise blushing, as a young person at Geneva would have done; and yet, conscious that he had gone very far, he thought it possible she had drawn back. "And with your mother," he answered very respectfully.

But it seemed that both his audacity and his respect were lost on Miss Daisy Miller. "I guess mother wouldn't go—for you," she smiled. "And she ain't much bent on going, anyway. She don't liked to ride round in the afternoon." After which she familiarly proceeded: "But did you really mean what you said just now—that you'd like to go up there?"

"Most earnestly I meant it," Winterbourne declared.

"Then we may arrange it. If mother will stay with Randolph I guess Eugenio will."

"Eugenio?" the young man echoed.

"Eugenio's our courier.[13] He doesn't like to stay with Randolph—he's the most fastidious man I ever saw. But he's a splendid courier. I guess he'll stay at home with Randolph if mother does, and then we can go to the castle."

Winterbourne reflected for an instant as lucidly as possible: "we" could only mean Miss Miller and himself. This prospect seemed almost too good to believe; he felt as if he ought to kiss the young lady's hand. Possibly he would have done so, —and quite spoiled his chance; but at this moment another person—presumably Eugenio—appeared. A tall handsome man, with superb whiskers and wearing a velvet morning-coat and a voluminous watch-guard, approached the young lady, looking sharply at her companion. "Oh Eugenio!" she said with the friendliest accent.

Eugenio had eyed Winterbourne from head to foot; he now bowed gravely to Miss Miller. "I have the honour to inform Mademoiselle that luncheon's on table."

Mademoiselle slowly rose. "See here, Eugenio, I'm going to that old castle anyway."

"To the Chateau de Chillon, Mademoiselle?" the courier enquired. "Mademoiselle has made arrangements?" he added in a tone that struck Winterbourne as impertinent.

Eugenio's tone apparently threw, even to Miss Miller's own apprehension, a slightly ironical light on her position. She turned to Winterbourne with the slightest blush. "You won't back out?" "I shall not be happy till we go!" he protested.

"And you're staying in this hotel?" she went on. "And you're really American?"

The courier still stood there with an effect of offence for the young man so far as the latter saw in it a tacit reflexion on Miss Miller's behaviour and an insinuation that she "picked up" acquaintances. "I shall have the honour of presenting to you a person who'll tell you all about me," he said, smiling, and referring to his aunt.

"Oh well, we'll go some day," she beautifully answered; with which she gave him a smile and turned away. She put up her parasol and walked back to the inn beside Eugenio. Winterbourne stood watching her, and as he moved away, drawing her muslin furbelows over the walk, he spoke to himself of her natural elegance.

Notes:

1. *Daisy Miller* first appeared in *Cornhill Magazine* in July, 1978, was reprinted (and pirated) many times in James' lifetime, and was carefully revised for inclusion in the New York edition, Vol. XVIII(1909), the source of the present text.
2. Lac Leman, or Lake of Geneva.
3. Newport, Rhode Island, and Saratoga, New York, resort areas for the rich, where the Ocean House and Congress Hall are located.
4. "Three Crowns."
5. A peak of Mont Blanc; "Castle of Chillon": the setting for Byron's The Prisoner of Chillon.
6. Geneva, where John Calvin (1509—1564) centered his Protestant regime.
7. I.e., University of Geneva.
8. I.e., like members of the diplomatic corps.
9. A pass in the Alps between Switzerland and Italy.
10. Intergrated whole.
11. Railway cars.
12. Mental reservation.
13. Social guide.

Question for Consideration:

In this novelette, James showed how the frank and self-confident behavior of a young American girl offends the delicate social sense of various Europeans and Europeanized Americans. What is your opinion of the girl's behaviour?

Chapter Ⅲ Four Novelists of Naturalism

——Stephen Crane, Frank Norris, Jack London, and Theodore Dreiser

Stephen Crane (1871—1900)

① ***Biographical Introduction***

Stephen Crane, the fourteenth child of a Methodist minister in Newark, New Jersey, spent most of his boyhood and youth in upstate New York, where he was a student at a military academy at Claverock and at Lafayette College and Syracuse University. Tired of college life, he left it and set out as a roving reporter and free-lance writer. His first book. *Maggie*: *A Girl of the Streets* (1992), was not widely noticed. His second novel, *The Red Badge of Courage* (1895) was a critical and popular success. Then Crane tried his hand at short stories and poetry. His main collections of short stories include: *The Little Regiment* (1986) focusing on the Civil War, and *Whilomville Stories* (1900) about childhood in a small town in New York. His poems were collected under the title *The Black Rider* (1895) and *War Is Kind* (1900), which were stylistically influenced by the poetry of Emily Dickinson. Crane died of tuberculosis at the age of twenty-nine, largely because of his roving irregular life pattern.

② *Crane's View and Theme*

As a naturalist, Crane shares the naturalistic belief that the destiny of human beings, like the biological fate of other creatures, is so much determined by factors beyond the control of individual will or choice that ethical judgement or moral comment by the author is irrelevant or impertinent. In correspondence with this belief, Crane's works are mostly concerned with the brutality and degradation of slum life, the actualities of war, vain illusion in context of a sombre nature, and the indifference and hostility of the universe. With these themes, Crane developed a character type: the poignantly muddled, morally powerless egotist victimized by both the environment and heredity and his sentimental heroic fantasies and delusions.

③ *Crane's Form and Style*

Crane is noted for his brilliant and innovative form and style. He avoided the conventional plot, shifting the focus from the drama of external event or situation to the drama of thought and feeling in the mental life of his subjects. He substituted for the conventional expository, descriptive style a highly metaphorical, imagistic representation of psychological effects. And he denied assumptions about norms of reality, often depicting unfolding experience as gradual revelation of its ultimate mystery. An ironist and impressionist with a mind swift to seize even fleeting impressions he anticipated the modernsim of Ernest Hemingway, F. Scott Fitzgerald, Anderson, and William Faulkner by thirty years. Like Hemingway, he was preoccupied with violence, finding in the reaction of his hero under the stress of ultimate crisis the mystery and poignancy of the hero's character and fate. Like Anderson, Fitzgerald, and Faulkner, he dramatized the powers of illusion to shape events and destinies.

④ *Crane's Major Works*

Maggie is claimed by some critics as the first American naturalistic novel. It does very vividly describe slum life as Zola's naturalism urged the writer to do. It makes us feel we are observing wild animals in a zoo or in a jungle. The story is a very simple one. Maggie, a factory girl, is seduced by a swaggering bartender, a friend of her truck-driver brother. When she becomes pregnant, she is thrown out of her home by her brutal, alcoholic mother, rejected by her lover and forced into prostitution. Finally, in a fit of despair, she drowns herself. It is not the plot but the physical description of the sordid life of the slums that has made the book so widely noted today. In the novel, Crane is very much on the side of Maggie and very contemptuous of those around her, who have, apparently, been brutalized by the environment. Maggie has been a rose in the mud-puddle of the slum. All her short life she has been struggling to escape her mud-puddle prison but all in vain. As Crane states, environment is a tremendous thing for an insignificant human being to battle against.

The Red Badge of Courage, the novel of the Civil War, is Crane's most famous work and has long been regarded as one of the classics of American literature. It is a story about a raw recruit at an unnamed battle, who moves from one mental state to another, bewildered, driven by forces outside and within himself. From anxiety to be in a battle to prove himself heroic he passes into doubt about his personal courage and then the dissipation of his heroic illusions. In face of danger, he is seized with panic which causes him to run. Caught in the lines of the wounded and then in a renewed attack he passes through shame to renewed courage which takes him into and through battle. Henry Fleming, the hero. like Maggie, stands for man opposing his environment, worked upon by pressures and tensions both within and beyond himself. Against the romantic view of war as a symbol of courage and heroism, Crane debunks war as a slaughter house, where there is nothing like valor or heroism but fear and cowardice. Crane's deglorification of war initiated the modern tradition of telling the truth at all costs about the elemental human experience , and produced a far-reaching influence on later writers like Hemingway, Do Passos, and Kurt Vonnegut.

The Open Boat and Other Tales of Adventure(1898) contains the best Crane short stories. The dominating naturalistic theme is the indifference of the universe to man.

"The Open Boat," his most naturalistic work, was based on his lifeboat experiences after a shipwreck. The four castaways in the boat win to sight of shore and human beings only to be frustrated by the violent surf in their attempt to land. After a night at sea, having exhausted past desperation, they make a second try, in which three are successful. Billy, the oiler in the struggling group, is lost to the sea. The musing "correspondent" concludes about the Nature they have been battling: "she did not seem cruel to him then, nor beneficent, nor treacherous, nor wise. But she was indifferent, flatly indifferent."

THE RED BADGE OF COURAGE
An Episode of The American Civil War[1]

Chapter 1

The cold passed reluctantly from the earth, and the retiring fogs revealed an army stretched out on the hills, resting. As the landscape changed from brown to green, the army awakened, and began to tremble with eagerness at the noise of rumors. It cast its eyes upon the roads, which were growing from long troughs of liquid mud to proper thoroughfares. A river, amber-tinted in the shadow of its banks, purled at the army's feet; and at night, when the stream had become of a sorrowful blackness, one could see across it the red, eyelike gleam of hostile campfires set in the low brows of distant hills.

Once a certain tall soldier developed virtues and went resolutely to wash a shirt. He came flying back from a brook waving his garment bannerlike. He was swelled with a tale he had heard from a reliable friend, who had heard it from a truthful cavalryman, who had heard it from his trustworthy brother, one of the orderlies at division headquarters. He adopted the important air of a herald in red and gold.

"We're goin't' move t' morrah-sure," he said pompously to a group in the company street. "We're goin't way up the river, cut across, an' come around in behint' em."

To his attentive audience he drew a loud and elaborate plan of a very brilliant campaign. When he had finished, the blue-clothed men scattered into small arguing groups between the rows of squat brown huts. A negro teamster who had been dancing upon a cracker box with the hilarious encouragement of twoscore soldiers was deserted. He sat mournfully down. Smoke drifted lazily from a multitude of quaint chimneys.

"It's a lie! that's all it is—a thunderin'lie!" said another private loudly. His smooth face was flushed, and his hands were thrust sulkily into his trousers' pockets. He took the matter as an affront to him. "I don't believe the damned old army's ever going to move. We're set. I've got ready to move eight times in the last two weeks, and we ain't moved yet."

The tall soldier felt called upon to defend the truth of a rumor he himself had introduced. He and the loud one came near to fighting over it.

A corporal began to swear before the assemblage. He had just put a costly board floor in his house, he said. During the early spring he had refrained from adding extensively to the comfort of his environment because he had felt that the army might start on the march at any moment. Of late, however, he had been impressed that they were in a sort of eternal camp.

Many of the men engaged in a spirited debate. One outlined in a peculiarly lucid manner all the plans of the commanding general. He was opposed by men who advocated that there were other plans of campaign. They clamored at each other, numbers making futile bids for the popular attention. Meanwhile, the soldier who had fetched the rumor bustled about with muhk importance. He was continually assailed by questions.

"What's up, Jim?"

"Th' army's goin't move."

"Ah, what yeh talkin' about? How yeh know it is?"

"Well, yeh kin b'lieve me er not, just as yeh likd. I don't care a hang."

There was much food for thought in the manner in which he replied. He came near to convincing them by disdaining to produce proofs. They grew much excited over it.

There was a youthful private who listened with eager ears to the words of the tall soldier and to the varied comments of his comrades. After receiving a fill of discussions concerning marches and attacks, he went to his hut and crawled through an intricate hole that served it as a door. He wished to be alone with some new thoughts that had lately come to him.

He lay down on a wide bunk that stretched across the end of the room. In the other end, cracker boxes were made to serve as furniture. They were grouped about the fireplace. A picture from an illustrated weekly was upon the log walls, and three rifles were paralleled on pegs. Equipments hung on handy projections, and some tin dishes lay upon a small pile of firewood. A folded tent was serving as a roof. The sunlight, without, beating upon it, made it glow a light yellow shade. A small window shot an oblique square of whiter light upon the cluttered floor. The smoke from the fire at times neglected the clay chimney and wreathed into the room, and this flimsy chimney of clay and sticks made endless threats to set ablaze the whole establishment.

The youth was in a little trance of astonishment. So they were at last going to fight. On the morrow, perhaps, there would be a battle, and he would be in it. For a time he was obliged to labor to make himself believe. He could not accept with assurance an omen that he was about to mingle in one of those great affairs of the earth.

He had, of course, dreamed of battles all his life—of vague and bloody conflicts that had thrilled him with their sweep and fire. In visions he had seen himself in many struggles. He had imagined peoples secure in the shadow of his eagle-eyed prowess. But awake he had regarded battles as crimson blotches on the pages of the past. He had put them as things of the bygone with his thought-images of heavy crowns and high castles . There was a portion of the world's history which he had regarded as the time of wars, but it, he thought, had been long gone over the horizon and had disappeared forever.

From his home his youthful eyes had looked upon the war in his own country with distrust. It must be some sort of a play affair. He had long despaired of witnessing a Greeklike struggle. Such would be no more, he had said. Men were better, or more timid. Secular and religious education had effaced the throatgrappling instinct, or else firm finance held in check the passions.

He had burned several times to enlist. Tales of great movements shook the land. They might not be distinctly Homeric, but there seemed to be much glory in them. He had read of marches, sieges, conflicts, and he had longed to see it all. His busy mind had drawn for him large pictures extravagant in color, lurid with breathless deeds.

But his mother had discouraged him. She had affected to look with some contempt upon the quality of his war ardor and patriotism. She could calmly seat herself and with no apparent difficulty give him many hundreds of reasons why he was of vastly more importance on the farm than on the field of battle. she had certain ways of expression that told him that her statements on the subject came from a deep conviction. Moreover, on her side, was his belief that her ethical motive in the argument was impregnable.

At last, however, he hand made firm rebellion against this yellow light thrown upon the color of his ambitions. The newspapers, the gossip of the village, his own picturings, had aroused him to an uncheckable degree. They were in truth fighting finely down there. Almost every day the newspapers printed accounts of a decisive victory.

One night, as he lay in bed, the winds had carried to him the clangoring of the church bell as some enthusiast jerked the rope frantically to tell the twisted news of a great battle. This voice of the people rejoicing in the night had made him shiver in a prolonged ecstasy of excitement. Later, he had gone down to his mother's room and had spoken thus: "Ma, I'm going to enlist."

"Henry, don't you be a fool," his mother had replied. She had then covered her face with the quilt. There was an end to the matter for that night.

Nevertheless, the next morning he had gone to a town that was near his mother's farm and had enlisted in a company that was forming[2] there. When he had returned home his mother was milking the brindle[3] cow. Four others stood waiting. "Ma, I've enlisted," he had said to her diffidently. There was a short silence. "The Lord's will be done, Henry," she had finally replied, and had then continued to milk the brindle cow.

When he had stood in the doorway with his soldier's clothes on his back, and with the light of excitement and expectancy in his eyes almost defeating the glow of regret for the home bonds, he had seen two tears leaving their trails on his mother's scarred cheeks.

Still, she had disappointed him by saying nothing whatever about returning with his shield or on it.[4] He had privately primed himself for a beautiful scene. He had prepared certain sentences which he thought could be used with touching effect. But her words destroyed his plans. She had doggedly peeled potatoes and addressed him as follows: "You watch out, Henry, an' take good care of yerself in this here fighting business—you watch out, an' take good care of yerself. Don't go a-thinkin' you can lick the hull rebel army at the start, because yeh can't. Yer jest one little feller amongst a hull lot of others, and yeh've got to keep quiet an' do what they tell yeh. I know how you are, Henry.

"I've knet yeh eight pair of socks, Henry, and I've put in all yer best shirts, because I want my boy to be jest as warm and comf'able as anybody in the army. Whenever they get holes in' em, I want yeh to send'em right-away back to me, so' I kin dern' em.

"An' allus be careful an' choose yer comp'ny. There's lost of bad men in the army, Henry. The army makes'em wild, and they liked nothing better than the job of leading off a young feller like you, as ain't never been away from home much and nas allus had a mother, an' a-learning'em to drink and swear. Keep clear of them folks, Henry. I don't wnat yeh to ever do anything, Henry, that yeh would be' shamed to let me know about. Jest think as if I was a-watchin'yeh. If yeh keep that in yer mind allus, I guess yeh'll come out about right.

"Yeh much allus rember yer father, too, child, an' remember he never drunk a drop of licker in his life, and seldom swore a cross oath.

"I don't know what else to tell yeh, Henry, excepting that yeh must never do no shirking, child, on my account. If so be a time comes when yeh have to be kilt or do a mean thing, why, Henry, don't think of anything 'cept what's right, because there's many a woman has to bear up' ginst sech things these times, and the Lord'll take keer of us all.

"Don't forget about the socks and the shirts, child; and I've put a cup of blackberry jam with yer bundle, because I know yeh like it above all things. Good-by, Henry. Watch out, and be a good boy."

He had, of course, been impatient under the ordeal of this speech. It had not been quite what he expected, and he had borne it with an air of irritation. He departed feeling vague relief.

Still, when he had looked back from the gate, he had seen his mother kneeling among the potato parings. Her brown face, upraised, was stained with tears, and her spare form was quivering. He bowed his head and went on, feeling suddenly ashamed of his purposes.

From his home he had gone to the seminary[5] to bid adieu to many schoolmates. They had thronged about him with wonder and admiration. He had felt the gulf now between them and had swelled with calm pride. He and some of his fellows who had donned blue were quite overwhelmed with privileges for all of one afternoon, and it had been a very delicious thing. They had strutted.

A certain light-haired girl had made vivacious fun at his martial spirit, but there was another and darker girl whom he had gazed at steadfastly, and he thought she grew demure and sad at sight of his blue and brass. As he had walked down the path between the rows of oaks, he had turned his head and detected her at a window watching his departure. As he perceived her, she had immediately begun to stare up through the high tree branches at the sky. He had seen a good deal of flurry and haste in her movement as she changed her attitude. He often thought of it.

On the way to Washington[6] his spirit had soared. The regiment was fed and caressed at station after station until the youth had believed that he must be a hero. There was a lavish expenditure of bread and cold meats, coffee, and pickles and cheese. As he basked in the smiles of the girls and was patted and complimented by the old men, he had felt growing within him the strength to do mighty deeds of arms.

After complicated journeyings with many pauses, there had come months of monotonous life in a camp. He had the belief that real war was a series of death struggles with small time in between for sleep and meals; but since his regiment had come to the field the army had done little but sit still and try to keep warm.

He was brought then gradually back to his old ideas. Greek-like struggles would be no more. Men were better, or more timid. Secular and religious education had effaced the throat-grappling instinct, or else firm finance held in check the passions.

He had grown to regard himself merely as a part of a vast blue demonstration. His province was to look out, as far as he could, for his personal comfort. For recreation he could twiddle his thumbs and speculate on the thoughts which must agitate the minds of the generals. Also, he was drilled and drilled and reviewed, and drilled and drilled and reviewed.

The only foes he had seen were some pickets[7] along the river bank. They were a sun-tanned, philosophical lot, who sometimes shot reflectively at the blue[8] pickets. When reproached for this afterward, they usually expressed sorrow, and swore by their gods that the guns had exploded without their permission. The youth, on guard duty one night, conversed across the stream with one of them. He was a slightly ragged man, who spat skillfully between his shoes and possessed a great fund of bland and infantile assurance. The youth liked him personally.

"Yank," the other had informed him, "yer a right dum good feller." This sentiment, floating to him upon the still air, had made him temporarily regret war.

Various veterans had told him tales. Some talked of gray, bewhiskered hordes who were advancing with relentless curses and chewing tobacco with unspeakable valor; tremendous bodies of fierce soldiery who were sweeping along like the Huns.[9] Others spoke of tattered and eternally hungry men who fired despondent powders. "They'll charge through hell's fire an' brimstone t' git a holt on a haversack, an sech stomachs ain's a-lastin' long," he was told. From the stories, the youth imagined the red, live bones sticking out through slits in the faded uniforms.

Still, he could not put a whole faith in veterans' tales, for recruits were their prey. They talked much of smoke, fire, and blood, but he could not tell how much might be lies. They persistently yelled "Fresh fish!"[10] at him, and were in no wise to be trusted.

However, he perceived now that it did not greatly matter what kind of soldiers he was going to fight, so long as they fought, which fact no one disputed. There was a more serious problem. He lay in his bunk pondering upon it. He tried to mathematically prove to himself that he would not run from a battle.

Previously he had never felt obligated to wrestle too seriously with this question. In his life he had taken certain things for granted, never challenging his belief in ultimate success, and bothering little about means and roads. But here he was confronted with a thing of moment. It had suddenly appeared to him that perhaps in a battle he might run. He was forced to admit that as far as war was concerned he knew nothing of himself.

A sufficient time before he would have allowed the problem to kick its heels at the outer portals of his mind, but now he felt compelled to hive serious attention to it.

A little panic-fear grew in his mind. As his imagination went forward to a fight, he saw hideous possibilities. He contemplated the lurking menaces of the future, and failed in an effort to see himself standing stoutly in the midst of them. He recalled his visions of broken-bladed glory, but in the shadow of the impending tumult he suspected them to be impossible pictures.

He sprang from the bunk and began to pace nervously to and fro. "Good Lord, what's th' matter with me?" he said aloud.

He felt that in this crisis his laws of life were useless. Whatever he had learned of himself was here to no avail. He was an unknown quantity. He saw that he would again be obliged to experiment as he had in early youth. He must accumulate information of himself, and meanwhile he resolved to remain close upon his guard lest those qualities of which he knew nothing should everlastingly disgrace him. "Good Lord!" he repeated in dismay.

After a time the tall soldier as he entered. He waved his hand expressively. "You can believe me or not, jest as you like. All you got to do is to sit down and wait as quiet as you can. Then pretty soon you'll find out I was right."

His comrade grunted stubbornly. For a moment he seemed to be searching for a formidable reply. Finally he said: "Well, you don't know everything in the world, do you?"

"Didn't say I knew everything in the world," retorted the other sharply. He began to stow various articles snugly into his knapsack.

The youth, pausing in his nervous walk, looked down at the busy figure. "Going to be a battle, sure, is there, Jim?" he asked.

"Of course there is," replied the tall soldier. "Of course there is. You jest wait'til to-morrow, and you'll see one of the biggest battles ever was. You jest wait."

"Thunder!" said the youth.

"Oh, you'll see fighting this time, my boy, what'll be regular out-and-out fighting," added the tall soldier, with the air of a man who is about to exhibit a battle for the benefit of his friends.

"Huh!" said the loud one from a corner.

"Well," remarked the youth, "like as not this story'll turn out jest like them others did."

"Not much it won't," replied the tall soldier, exasperated.

"Not much it won't. Didn't the cavalry all start this morning?" He glared about him. No one denied his statement. "The cavalry started this morning," he continued. "They say there ain't hardly any cavalry left in camp. They're going to Richmond, or some place, while we fight all the Johnnies.[11] It's some dodge like that. The regiment's got orders, too. A feller what seen'em go to headquarters told me a little while ago. And they're raising blazes all over camp—anybody can see that."

"Shucks!" said the loud one.

The youth remained silent for a time. At last he spoke to the tall soldier. "Jim!"

"What?"

"How do you think the reg'ment 'll do?"

"Oh, they'll fight all right, I guess, after they once get into it," said the other with cold judgment. He made a fine use of the third person. "There's been heaps of fun poked at 'em because they're new, of course, and all that; but they'll fight all right, I guess."

"Think any of the boys 'll run?" persisted the youth.

"Oh, there may be a few of 'em run, but there's them kind in every regiment, 'specially when they first goes under fire," said the other in a tolerant way. "Of course it might happen that the hull kit-and-boodle might start and run, if some big fighting came first-off, and then again they might stay and fight like fun. But you can't bet on nothing. Of course they ain't never been under fire yet, and it ain't likely they'll lick the hull rebel army all-to-oncet the first time; but I think they'll fight better than some, if worse than others. That's the way I figger. They call the reg'ment 'Fresh fish' and everything; but the boys come of good stock, and most of 'em 'll fight like sin after they oncet git shootin'," he added, with a mighty emphasis on the last four words.

"Oh, you think you know—" began the loud soldier with scorn.

The other turned savagely upon him. They had a rapid altercation, in which they fastened upon each other various strange epithets.

The youth at last interrupted them. "Did you ever think you might run yourself, Jim?" he asked. On concluding the sentence he laughed as if he had meant to aim a joke. The loud soldier also giggles.

The tall private waved his hand. "Well," said he profoundly, "I've thought it might get too hot for Jim Conklin in some of them scrimmages, and if a whole lot of boys started and run, why, I s'pose I'd start and run. And if I once started to run, I'd run like the devil, and no mistake. But if everybody was a-standing and a-fighting, why, I'd stand and fight. Be jiminey, I would. I'll bet on it.

"Huh!" said the loud one.

The youth of this tale felt gratitude for these words of his comrade. He had feared that all of the untried men possessed a great and correct confidence. He now was in a measure reassured.

Notes:

1. Although the battle described in the novel is unidentified, the details of the action most nearly resemble those of the Battle of Chancellorsville, fought in Virginia in May 1863.
2. In spite of a conscription law, passed in 1863, the North relied primarily on volunteers who enlisted for a period of three years. Most companies in the Union Army were raised by local citizens and then were joined to state militia regiments and sent into battle.
3. Gray or brown with dark streaks.

4. According to Plutarch, Spartan warriors went off to war bidden by their mothers to return "with your shield or upon it," i. e., either undefeated or dead.
5. A high school.
6. Northern troops to be used in the Virginia campaigns were first sent to Washington, D.C., before proceeding south into Virginia.
7. Sentries.
8. Union troops were dressed in blue.
9. Nomadic tribesment from the East who had invaded and pillaged Europe around A.D. 450.
10. I.e., "Rooky!"
11. The Confederate soldier was nicknamed Johnny Reb; the Union soldier, Billy Yank.

Questions for Consideration:

1. What kind of atmosphere does the author introduce here?
2. The chapter reveals that the book has two settings, one physical and one emotional. Can you explain what they are?
3. What illusion does the main character have about himself and the nature of war?

Frank Norris (1870—1902)

① *Biographical Introduction*

Frank Norris was born of wealthy Chicago parents. When he was twelve, they moved to San Francisco. Frank was sent to a private school and then to study painting in Paris. After a year, he returned to attend the Nniversity of California. He left the university to study writing at Harvard but soon he went to work as a war correspondent and a magazine writer. At Harvard, he began to write novels, one of which is the famous *McTeague*. Then he attempted to write a trilogy on wheat, of which he finished the first two. The third never came into being because of his sudden death of a mis-diagnosed appendicitis at the age of thirty-two.

② *Norris's View and Theme*

Norris leaned toward naturalism. The French naturalist Zola made an early and lasting impression on him so much, so that he absorbed some of Zola's romantic overtones as well. In addition to accepting Zola's idea that naturalism was a further extention of realism privileged to explore every aspect of life, particularly those earlier considered unmentionable, Norris felt that naturalism should deal with the exceptional, the grotesque, the violent, and that naturalism was in fact romanticism set in the milieu of actual social conditions. He said that true romance, unlike realism which notes only the surface of things, penetrates to "the real, living heart of things... the unplumed depths of the human heart, and the mystery of sex, and the problems of life, and the black, unsearched penetralia of the soul of man."

Norris observed his naturalism or romantic realism in all his major works, the main theme of which is the inevitable effect of environment and heredity on human lives. Norris created a harsh world of the late-nineteenth century America, in which people, driven by social, cultural, moral, commercial, and temperamental forces, are like wild unhappy animals destroying each other in their struggles for satisfaction and survival.

③ *Norris's Style*

Norris is not much read now. This is perhaps because of his unbridled melodrama, bombastic language, irritating anticlimaxes, and overwrought allegorical characterizations. But the richness and exuberance of his materials, his vibrant and fresh imagery, his poetic mode of fiction, as in the choice of words for their precise and exact effect, were all part of the literary legacy of the period under discussion.

④ *Norris's Major Works*

McTeague (1899) has been called "the first full-bodied naturalistic American novel and a consciously naturalistic manifesto" of naturalism. It is a story of a violent, murderous human brute whose tragedy lies in the fact that he could not shake himself free of the brutalizing forces of his wild birthplace and his alcoholic father, which are destined to destroy him as a man. Having learned the rudiments of dentistry from a journey man McTeague sets up an unlicensed practice in San Francisco. He marries Trina Sieppe, a girl met through his best friend, Marcus Schoulder, to whom the girl is half engaged. After Trina wins $ 5000 in a lottery, she becomes increasingly grasping and tight-fisted. Meanwhile, Marcus has become bitter over losing Trina. He falls out with McTeague, then reports him for practicing illegally. Unable to settle in other employment, McTeague dissipates his remaining funds and deserts his wife, later to return and murder her for the $ 5000. His flight from the police brings him ultimately to Death Valley, where he perishes with Marcus, who has pursued him there.

The Octopus (1901) is the first of Norris's projected trilogy on wheat. In it Norris illustrates how social and economic conditions ruined the lives of innocent, powerless people. The Pacific and Southwestern Railraid (the octopus) has encouraged wheat farmers to settle on its land by offering certain price concessions. Once the land is under cultivation, however, the railroad raises the price of the land which it has rented to the people and its policy becomes one of manifold exploitation. The rankers unite to resist, but in vain. Finally the wheat growers capitulate to the railroad monopoly, and the high freight rates charged by the railroad force all the farmers and the poor in general to end up in bankruptcy and ruin.

The Pit (1903) is the second of the trilogy, concerning the manipulation of the wheat market in Chicago. In it Norris shows that the laws of nature like supply and demand can ruin a financial superman if he challenges them. Curtis Jadwin, a millionaire, is trying to corner the wheat market and has little time for his wife Laura. When Jadwin overextends himself and is ruined, Laura is about to elope with her lover, but responding to her husband's need he chooses to accompany him westward to a new life. One of the novel's highlights is Grain Pit, where Jadwin is battling for monopoly.

Jack London (1871—1916)

① *Biographical Introduction*

John Ariffith London, born in San Francisco, was probably the illegitimate child of Wellman H. Chaney, a professional astrologer. His mother married a John London, who gave his surname to the infant. As a boy Jack lived on the Oakland waterfront, reading avidly between various menial but adventurous jobs. He was once an oyster pirate, and he also spent a month in prison for vagrancy. His contact with the under-privileged taught him the struggle for survival, developed his social consciousness, and early convinced him that he must get the things he coveted by intellectual rather than manual labor. By prodigious effort he prepared himself for college in less than two years; but after a few months at the University of California he withdrew and shortly after, in 1897, joined the rush to the Klondike, whence he returned without gold but with literary ore of great potential value. By sheer determination he taught himself enough of the writer's craft to sell stories and articles to magazines. The wealth that came from his writing he lavished on his enthusiasms, including travel and politics. Exhausted physically, mentally, and emotionally, he was said to commit suicide at the age of forty.

② *London's View and Theme*

London was logically inconsistent in his viewpoint. On the one hand, he took faith in Herbert Spencer's evolutionary concept of progress, Darwin's survival of the fittest, and the Neitzchean concept of the superman, and on the other hand, he embraced the socialist doctrines of Marx. His belief in evolution was compatible with socialism, but his glorification of Anglo-Saxon supremacy, Darwinism and the Neitzchean superman notion were antithetical to social and economic equalitarianism. These conflicting ideas colored his writing, alternately or simultaneously. His sincere intellectual and personal involvement in the socialist movement is recorded in such novels and polemical works as *The People of the Abyss* (1903), *The Iron Heel* (1908), *The War of the Classes*, and *Revolution* (1910); his commitment to the fundamental reality of the law of survival and the will to power is dramatised in his most popular novels, *The Call of the Wild* (1903) and *The Sea Wolf* (1904); and the contradiction between these competing beliefs is most vividly projected in his autobiographical novel *Martin Eden* (1909).

London wrote on many subjects and themes which centred around primitive violence, Anglo-Saxon supremacy, atavism, biological evolution, class warfare, and mechanistic determinism. His heroes are physically robust and rugged but often psychologically harried. His heroines are athletic, daring, yet intensely feminine. They are man's intellectual equal and his emotional superior.

③ *London's Form and Style*

London's work mingles naturalism with sheer romance, and his bald realism pushes against conventionality. No writer of his generation was more uneven, not only because he wrote too much but because his technique, with rare exceptions, was inadequate. He had little sense of form, depending too much upon explanation rather than dramatic portrayal. His characterization was stiff with stereotyped dialogue, and his ideas and emotions were discordant and conflicting. Yet his style is singularly forcible and free from all affectation. His crude vigor, his imaginative fertility, his vividness and animation hold him a position in American literature.

④ *London's Major Works*

The Call of the Wild is the story of Buck, a giant California dog stolen and shipped to the Klondike as a sled dog. He passes through the hands of several harsh owners while learning to master the environment and the rivalry of his peers. Buck is delivered at last by the sympathetic John Thornton. Dog and man develop strong bonds of love and devotion, but an awaking instinct in Buck begins to draw him to the wildness. When Thornton is killed in an Indian attack, Buck reverts to the wild to lead a wolf pack. London's primitive satisfaction in physical struggle finds its best expression in the dog hero, who is uncomplicated by human repressions and ambitions.

The Sea Wolf is the study of Wolf Larsen, a ruthless and brutal sea captain, who lives by the code of survival of the fittest. Humphrey Van Wegden and Maude Brewster, two ship-wrecked refugees from a more civilized world, are pressed into Larson's crew. They are drawn together by their common plight, and when Humphrey manages to foil an assault on Maude by the Wolf, the two seize the opportunity to escape. The small Arctic, the land they attain, is visited weeks later by the wreck of Larson's schooner. Larsen alone is aboard, dying of a cerebral tumor. Maude and Humphrey are rescued soon after.

Martin Eden is essentially autobiographical. London sees in Eden his own early aspirations to achieve status with fame and fortune. It is thus that Eden becomes infatuated with the wealthy, charming, and cultivated Ruth Morse. In time Eden becomes convinced that status and fortune carry with them greed, materialism, and meaningless conformity. Rejecting these, he commits suicide.

Theodore Dreiser (1871—1945)

① *Biographical Introduction*

Dreiser was born in Terre Haute, Indiana, the ninth child of German immigrant parents. His early years were a series of exposures to poverty, emotional instability, and religious bigotry in the home, and of frequent moves dictated by financial necessity. At fifteen, he went to Chicago, where he had a succession of minor jobs.

After a year at Indiana University, he returned to Chicago, where he became a reporter on the Chicago Globe. He also worked for newspapers in St. Louis and Pittsburg before he arrived in New York in 1894.

Dreiser's first two novels, *Sister Carrie* (1900) and *Jennie Gerhardt*, were attacked by the American reading public for their candid depiction of Amerian life and for their unconventional subject matters. In 1912 Dreiser published *The Financeer*, the first of his "Cowperwood" trilogy, the other two of which are *The Titan* (1914) and *The Stoic*, published posthumously in 1947. In 1915 he published *The Genius*, which was censured for his stark use of sex. Dreiser's popular claim came only with the publication of *An American Tragedy* (1925). His last book is *The Bulwark*, which reflects Dreiser's concern with religious mysticism.

Dreiser was a prolific writer. In the process of his creation he tried his hand at various mediums, publishing collections of short stories, poems, plays, travel books, and essays, often of a political nature. He also wrote a number of autobiographical books.

② *Dreiser's View and Theme*

Dreiser is one of the most significant of American naturalists. Profoundly influenced by Herbert Spenser, Dreiser embraced the idea of social Darwinism. He learned to regard man as merely an animal driven by greed and lust in a struggle for existence in which only the "fittest", the most ruthless, survive. To him, the world is a machine and man is only its mechanism, who has no control over his destiny; and human tragedy results from the collision between man's biological needs and society's ruthless manipulatoin.

Yet in the late 1920s, Dreiser took increasing interest in communism, in American social problems, and in the efforts of the poor and oppressed to gain a better life. This development of belief in man's ability to improve his condition through conscious effort appears to be in contradiction with his determinism. To Dreiser, however, these positions were not irreconcilable. He had come to view the mechanistic foundations of life not so much as imprisoning but a vast and intricate complex of beauty and wonder in which the destructive forces could be lessened through social change. Dreiser achieved the reconciliation of these positions in his final book *The Bulwark*.

Dreiser's works are mainly concerned with the tragic nature of the human condition by depicting the coarse, vulgar, cruel, and terrible aspects of life like sex and crime.

③ *Dreiser's Style*

In terms of style, Dreiser has sometimes been censured for his clumsy syntax, deficient characterization, and inept and dull prose. Yet his accumulated detail, carefully selected and faithfully recorded, is a technique of power. Like the other naturalists, he refused to judge—to consider people as good or evil. He clothed his concepts symbolically in the details of reality. It is his journalistic method that has made him one of America's foremost novelists.

④ *Dreiser's Major Works*

Sister Carrie, Dreiser's first novel, is the story of the rise of Carrie Meeber and the fall of George Hurstwood, who are the victims of forces beyond their control.

Carrie, a pretty, poor country girl, comes to Chicago for a better life. She first stays with her sister, whose working-class home is too poor to keep her, and she has to roam about looking for a job. Then winter is coming and she is seriously ill. A traveling man, Drouet by name, comes to her rescue and takes her home as his mistress. Through Drouet, she meets Hurstwood, manager of a well known bar, who deserts his comfortable home and tricks her to elope with him first to Canada and then to New York after he has robbed his employer's safe. Tracked down and forced to surrender the money, Hurstwood begins to disintegrate. Carrie goes out to find work on the stage and steadily rises to fame. She leaves Hurstwood, who sinks lower and lower until he commits suicide. Carrie succeeds, yet she is not happy. She is a wisp in the wind of her environmental forces, moving along and catching blindly at any opportunities for a better existence without any respect to morality. Dreiser does not blame her as he feels she simply does what she has to do for a survival. Hursthood is one of the impotent modern man unfit to survive.

The Cowperwood Trilogy—*The Financier*, *The Titan*, and *The Stoic*—form a thorough study of the big business man whose ruthlessness and drive for power are, in Dreiser's mind, related to the natural laws of the universe as conceived by Darwin and Spencer. Cowperwood, driven by the desire for wealth, social position, beauty, and sexual satisfaction, overrides every obstacle and secures what he wishes until he is caught in the misuse of city funds and imprisoned. After his release, he divorces his wife, marries his mistress, Aileen, the daughter of one of the late city bosses, and amasses an even greater fortune. Powerful, he becomes tired of Aileen, forms a number of temporary attachments, and forces her to seek a succession of lovers. Finally he establishes himself in New

York, meets the lovely, young Bernice Fleming, and goes with her to Europe, where there are new worlds to conquer. In the first two books Cowperwood's actions are explained by biological and social determinism. With *The Stoic* there is a turning toward religion, especially the mystical element.

An American Tragedy, Dreiser's best known novel, is the story of a poor boy, who is propelled to destruction by the desire for wealth and the drive of sex. He is the victim of social and biological forces, felt but not understood.

Clyde Griffiths, the son of Kansas city street evangelist, wants to get away from his environment. He starts out as a bellboy in a hotel. Forced to leave town because of an automobile accident, he gets a job in a collar factory in New York, where he falls in love with Roberta Alden, a girl of his own class whom he makes pregnant. Then he has met the wealthy Sondra Finchley, through marriage with whom he can rise. Thinking about murder but unable to act, he takes Roberta out on a deserted lake. There when she sees his grim face, she is frightened and moves. The boat overturns, and Clyde leaves Roberta to drown. The long trial scene follows, ending with the death sentence.

THE TITAN

Chapter 11 The Fruits of Daring

Next morning, over the breakfast cups at the Norrie Simmses'[1] and elsewhere, the import of the Cowperwoods' social efforts was discussed and the problem of their eventual acceptance or non-acceptance[2] carefully weighted.

"The trouble with Mrs. Cowperwood," observed Mrs. Simms, "is that she is too *gauche*. The whole thing was much too showy. The idea of her portrait at one end of the gallery and that Gerôme at the other[3]! And then this item in the *Press*[4] this morning! Why, you'd really think they were in society[5]." Mrs. Simms was already a little angry at having let herself be used, as she now fancied she had been, by Taylor Lord and Kent McKibben[6], both friends of hers.

"What did you think of the crowd?" asked Norrie, buttering a roll.

"Why, it wasn't representative at all, of course. We were the most important people they had there, and I'm sorry now that we went. Who are the Israelses and the Hoecksemas[7], anyhow? That dreadful woman!" (She was referring to Mrs. Hoecksema.) "I never listened to duller remarks in my life."

"I was talking to Haguenin of the *Press* in the afternoon," observed Norrie. "He says that Cowperwood failed in Philadelphia before he came here, and that there were a lot of lawsuits. Did you ever hear that?"

"No. But she says she knows the Drakes and the Walkers[8] there. I've been intending to ask Nellie[9] about that. I have often wondered why he should leave Philadelphia if he was getting along so well. People don't usually do that."

Simms was envious already of the financial showing Cowperwood was making in Chicago. Besides, Cowperwood's manner bespoke supreme intelligence and courage, and that is always resented by all save the suppliants[10] or the triumphant masters of other walks in life. Simms was really interested at last to know something more about Cowperwood, something definite.

Before this social situation had time to adjust itself one way or the other, however, a matter arose which in its way was far more vital, though Alieen[11] might not have thought so. The feeling between the new and old gas companies was becoming strained; the stockholders of the older organization were getting uneasy. They were eager to find out who was back of these new gas companies which were threatening to poach on their exclusive preserves. Finally one of the lawyers who had been employed by the North Chicago Gas Illuminating Company to fight the machinations of De Soto Sippens and old General Van Sickle[12], finding that the Lake View Council had finally granted the franchise to the new company and that the Appellate Court was about to sustain it, hit upon the idea of charging conspiracy and wholesale bribery of councilmen. Considerable evidence had accumulated the Duniway, Jacob Gerecht, and others on the North Side had been influenced by each, and to bring legal action would delay final approval of the franchises and give the old company time to think what else to do. This North Side company lawyer, a man by the name of Parsons, had been following up the movements of Sippens and old General Van Sickle, and had finally concluded that they were mere dummies and pawns, and that the real instigator in all this excitement was Cowperwood, of, if not be, then men whom he represented. Parsons visited Cowperwood's office one day in order to see him;

getting no satisfaction, he proceeded to look up his record and connections. These various investigations and counter-schemings[13] came to a head in a court proceeding filed in the United States Circuit Court late in November, charging Frank Algernon Cowperwood, Henry De Soto Sippens, Judson P. Van Sickle, and others with conspiracy; this again was followed almost immediately by suits begun by the West and South Side companies charging the same thing. In each case Gowperwood's name was mentioned as the secret power behind the new companies, conspiring to force the old companies to but him out. His Philadelphia history was published, but only in part—a highly modified account he had furnished the newspapers some time before. Though conspiracy and bribery are ugly words, still lawyers' charges prove nothing. But a penitentiary record[14], for whatever reason served, coupled with previous failure, divorce, and scandal (though the newspapers made only the most guarded reference to all this), served to whet public interest and to fix Cowperwood and his wife in the public eye.

Cowperwood himself was solicited for an interview, but his answer was that he was merely a financial agent for the three new companies, not an investor; and that the charges, in so far as he was concerned, were untrue, mere legal fol-de-rol[15] trumped up to make the situation as annoying as possible. He threatened to sue for libel. Nevertheless, although these suits eventually did come to nothing (for he had fixed it so that he could not be traced save as a financial agent in each case), yet the charges had been made, and he was now revealed as a shrewd, manipulative factor, with a record that was certainly spectacular.

"I see," said Anson Merrill to his wife, one morning at breakfast, "that this man Cowperwood is beginning to get his name in the papers." He had the *Times* on the table before him, and was looking at a headline which, after the old-fashioned pyramids[16] then in vogue, read: "Conspiracy charged against various Chicago citizens. Frank Algernon Cowperwood, Judson P. Van Sickle, Henry De Soto Sippens, and others named in Circuit Court complaint." It went on to specify other facts. "I supposed he was just a broker."

"I don't know much about them," replied his wife, "except what Bella Simms tells me. What does it say?"

He handed her the paper.

"I have always thought they were merely climbers," continued Nrs. Merrill. "From what I hear she is impossible. I never saw her."

"He begins well for a Philadelphian" smiled Merrill. "I've seen him at the Calumet[17]. He looks like a very shrewd man to me. He's going about his work in a brisk spirit, anyhow."

Similarly Mr Norman Schryhart, a man who up to this time had taken no thought of Cowperwood[18], although he had noted his appearance about the halls of the Calumet and Union League Clubs, began to ask seriously who he was. Schryhart, a man of great physical and mental vigor, six feet tall, hale and stolid as an ox, a very different type of man from Anson Merrill, met Addison[19] one day at the Calumet Club shortly after the newspaper talk began. Sinking into a great leather divan beside him, he observed:

"Who is this man Cowperwood whose name is in the papers these days, Addison? You know all these people. Didn't you introduce him to me once?"

"I surely did," replied Addison, cheerfully, who, in spite of the attacks on Cowperwood, was rather pleased than otherwise. It was quite plain from the concurrent excitement that attended all this struggle, that Cowperwood must be managing things rather adroitly, and, best of all, he was keeping his backers' names from view. "He's a Philadelphian by birth. He came out here several years ago, and went into the grain and commission business. He's a banker now. A rather shrewd man, I should say. He has a lot of money."

"Is it true, as the papers say, that he failed for a million in Philadelphia in 1871[20]?"

"In so far as I know, it is."

"Well, was he in the penitentiary down there?"

"I think so—yes. I believe it was for nothing really criminal, though. There appears to have been some political financial mix-up, from all I can learn."

"And is he only forty, as the papers say?"

"About that, I should judge. Why?"

"Oh, this scheme of his looks rather pretentious to me holding up the old gas companies here. Do you suppose he'll manage to do it?"

"I dont's know that. All I know is what I have read in the papers," replied Addison, cautiously. As a matter of fact, he did not care to talk about this business at all. Cowperwood was busy at this very time, through an agent, attempting to effect a compromise and union of all interests[21] concerned. It was not going very well.

"Humph!" commented Schryhart. He was wondering why men like himself, Merrill, Arneel, and others had not worked into this field long ago or bought out the old companies. He went away interested, and a day or two later—even the next morning—had formulated a scheme. Not unlike Cowperwood, he was a shrewd, hard, cold man. He believed in Chicago implicitly and in all that related to its future. This gas situation, now that Cowperwood had seen the point, was very clear to him. Even yet it might not be impossible for a third party to step in and by intricate manipulation secure the much coveted rewards. Perhaps Cowperwood himself could be taken over—who could tell?

Mr. Schryhart, being a very dominating type of person, did not believe in minor partnerships or investments. If he went into a thing of this kind it was his preference to rule. He decided to invite Cowperwood to visit the Schryhart office and talk matters over. Accordingly, he had his secretary pen a note, which in rather lofty phrases invited Cowperwood to call "on a matter of importance."

Now just at this time, it so chanced, Cowperwood was feeling rather secure as to his place in the Chicago financial world, although he was still smarting from the bitterness of the aspersions recently cast upon him from various quarters. Under such circumstances it was his temperament to evince a rugged contempt for humanity, rich and poor alike. He was well aware that Schryhart, although introduced, had never previously troubled to notice him.

"Mr. Cowperwood begs me to say," wrote Miss Antoinette Nowak[22], at his dictation, "that he finds himself very much pressed for time at present, but he would be glad to see Mr. Schryhart at his office at any time."

This irritated the dominating, self-sufficient Schryhart a little, but nevertheless he was satisfied that a conference could do no harm in this instance—was advisable, in fact. So one Wednesday afternoon be journeyed to the office of Cowperwood, and was most hospitably received.

"How do you do, Mr. Schryhart," observed Cowperwood, cordially, extending his hand. "I'm glad to see you again. I believe we met once before several years ago."

"I think so myself," replied Mr. Schryhart, who was broad-shouldered, square-headed, black-eyed, and with a short black mustache gracing a firm upper lip. He had hard, dark, piercing eyes. "I see by the paper, if they can be trusted," he said, coming direct to the point, "that you are interesting yourself in localges. Is that true?"

"I'm afraid the papers cannot be generally relied on," replied Cowperwood, quite blandly. "Would you mind telling me what makes you interested to know whether I am or not?"

"Well, to tell the truth," replied Schryhart, staring at the financier, "I am interested in this local gas situation myself. It offers a rather profitable field for investment, and several members of the old companies have come to me recently to ask me to help them combine." (This was not true at all.) "I have been wondering what chance you thought you had of winning along the lines you are now taking."

Cowperwood smiled. "I hardly care to discuss that," he said, "unless I know much more of your motives and connections than I do at present. Do I understand that you have really been appealed to by stockholders of the old companies to come in and help adjust this matter?"

"Exactly," said Schryhart.

"And you think you can get them to combine? On what basis?"

"Oh, I should say it would be a simple matter to give each of them two or three shares of a new company for one in each of the old. We could then elect on set of officers, have one set of offices, stop all these suits, and leave everybody happy."

He said this in an easy, patronizing way, as though Cowperwood had not really thought it all out years before. It amazed the latter no little to see his own scheme patronizingly brought back to him, and that, too, by a very powerful man locally—one who thus far had chosen to overlook him utterly.

"On what basis," asked Cowperwood, cautiously, "would you expect these new cempanies to come in?"

"On the same basis as the others, if they are not too heavily capitalized. I haven't thought out all the details. Two or three for one, according to investment. Of course, the prejudices of these old companies have to be considered."

Cowperwood meditated. Should or should he not entertain this offer? Here was a chance to realize quickly by selling out to the old companies. Only Schryhart, not himself, would be taking the big end in this manipulative deal. Whereas if he waited—even if Schryhart managed to combine the three old companies into one—he might be able to force better terms[24]. He was not sure. Finally he asked, "How much stock of the new company would be left in your hands—or in the hands of the organizing group—after each of the old and new companies had been provided for on this basis?"

"Oh, possibly thirty-five or forty per cent of the whole," replied Schryhart, ingratiatingly. "The laborer is worthy of his hire."

"Quite so," replied Cowperwood, smiling, "but, seeing that I am the man who has been cutting the pole to knock this persimmon it seems to me that a pretty good share of that should come to me; don't you think so?"

"Just what do you mean?"

"Just what I have said. I personally have organized the new companies which have made this proposed combination possible. The plan you propose is nothing more than that I have been proposing for some time. The officers and directors of the old companies are angry at me merely because I am supposed to have invaded the fields that belong to them. Now, if on account of that they are willing to operate through you rather than through me, it seems to me that I should have a much larger share in the surplus. My personal interest in these new companies is not very large. I am really more of a fiscal agent than anything else." (This was not true, but Cowperwood preferred to have his guest think so.)

Schryhart smiled. "But, my dear sir," he explained, "you forget that I will be supplying nearly all the capital to do this."

"You forget," retorted Cowperwood, "that I am not a novice. I will guarantee to supply all the capital myself, and give you a good homour for your services, if you want that. The plans and franchises of the old and new companies are worth something. You must remember that Chicago is growing."

"I know that," replied Schryhart, evasively, "but I also know that you have a long, expensive fight ahead of you. As things are now you cannot, of yourself, expect to bring these old companies to terms. They won't work with you, as I understand it. It will require an outsider like myself—some one of influence, or perhaps, I had better say, of old standing in Chicago, some one who knows these people—to bring about this combination. Have you any one, do you think, who can do it better than I?"

"It is not at all impossible that I will find some one," replied Cowperwood, quite easily.

"I hardly think so; certainly not as things are now. The old companies are not disposed to work through you, and they are through me. Don't you think you had better accept my terms and allow me to go ahead and close this matter up?"

"Not at all on that basis," replied Cowperwood, quite simply. "We have invaded the enemies' country too far and done too much. Three for one or four for one—whatever terms are given the stockholders of the old companies—is the best I will do about the new shares, and I must have one-half of whatever is left for myself. At that I will have to divide with others." (This was not true either.)

"No," replied Schryhart, evasively and opposingly, shaking his square head. "It can't be done. The risks are too great. I might allow you one-fourth, possibly I can't tell yet."

"One-half or nothing," said Cowperwood, definitely.

Schryhart got up. "That's the best you will do, is it?" he inquired.

"The very best."

"I'm afraid then," he said, "we can't come to terms. I'm sorry. You may find this a rather long and expensive fight."

"I have fully anticipated that," replied the financier.

Chapter Ⅳ Other Writers of Social Criticism

Bret Harte (1836—1902)

Bret Harte was the first writer of American local colorism. He was born in Albany, New York, and went to California with his remarried mother in 1853. In the west he taught school, mined for gold, worked as a drug clerk, and in 1858 became printer and assistant editor. Beginning with humorous sketches, he proceeded to humorous verse, and eventually won fame through his short stories.

Harte's *West* is one of picturesque melodrama, a rough violent society set against spectacular scenery. His pre-eminent appeal was the romantic California of the 1850s, where civilized man lived in elemental, free-wheeling fashion. Dangers of a raw land and lawless men produced almost a medieval indifference to death and fortune. Harte's favorite subjects are miners, gamblers, prostitutes, and adventures, who have the heart of gold beneath the rough exterior. Harte's style is sharp, clear, direct, reportorial, and rapid. Harte's best collection is the *Luck of Roaring Camp and Other Sketches* (1870), the fount of all Western local color stories, among which are the best known "The luck", "The Outcasts of Poker Flat", "Tennessee's Partner," and "Miggles".

Harriet Beecher Stowe (1811—1896)

Stowe, born in Connecticut, was the seventh child of a respectable family. Influenced by the Calvinist rigor in her family, Stowe remained essentially a religious writer. She held that politics and art were always framed by standards of moral purity and questions of salvation. In 1836, she married the widower Calvin E. Stowe, with whom she went to Maine in 1850, where, amid house hold cares, Harriet wrote her first novel *Uncle Tom's Cabin*. Like most of her subsequent novels, it was written as a serial, and began appearing in the National Era magazine in 1851. It was an immediate success both in the U. S. and abroad, not only because of its truthful presentation of the evils of slavery, which made a great influence on American attitudes toward slavery, but because its realism was added to by moral fervor and the author's artistic skill. In 1856, Stowe published her second anti-slavery novel, *Dred: A Tale of Great Dismal Swamp*, which told the story of a dramatic attempt at a slave rebellion, while attacking ministers who failed to bake a strong anti-slavery stand and demonstrating the redemptive powers of Christian womanhood. Stowe also wrote children's books, travelogues, and purely theological works, which are in no way comparable with her first anti-slavery novel, on which her reputation rests.

Edith Wharton (1862—1937)

Edith Wharton was best known for her stories and ironic novels about upper class people. Wharton's central subjects were the conflict between social and individual fulfillment, repressed sexuality, and the manners of old families and the new rich.

Edith Wharton was born on January 24, 1862 in New York, into a wealthy and socially prominent family. She was educated privately by European governesses. In 1885 she married Edward Wharton, a Boston banker, who was twelve years her senior. Wharton's role as a wife with social responsibilities and her writing ambitions resulted in nervous collapse. She had started to compose poems in her teens and she was advised that writing might help her recover. Her first book, *The Decoration of Houses*, appeared in 1897. Her husband started to show increasing signs of mental instability. In 1906—1909 Wharton had an affair with the American journalist Morton Fullerton, the great love of her life. The Whartons were divorced in 1913 and Edith spent the rest of her life in France.

Wharton gained her first literary success with her book *The House of Mirth* (1905), a story of a beautiful but poor woman, Lily Bart, trying to survive in the pitiless New York City. *The Custom of the Country* (1913) was a story of a young ambitious woman. Among Wharton's most famous novels is *The Age of Innocence* (1920), which was awarded the Pulitzer Prize. Wharton's other major works include the long tale *Ethan Frome* (1911), which was set in impoverished rural New England and

The Reef (1912). The novel *Hudson River Bracketed* (1929) and its sequel *The Gods Arrive* (1932) compared the cultures of Europe and the sections of the U. S. she knew. Wharton also wrote poems, essays, travel books and her autobiography, *A Backward Glance* (1934).

The House of Mirth is a novel of manners, one of the first to emerge in American literature. Lily Bart is an attractive woman with some important social and family ties, but at the age of 29, she is still not married. Since the death of her mother, who had an intense hatred for "dinginess", Lily began to live with her aunt, Mrs. Peniston. However, Lily spends much of her time staying at the Bellomont, the out-of-town estate of the wealthy and well-established Gus and Judy Trenor. At the Bellomont, Judy regularly throws extravagant parties that are attended by most of the New York upper-crust. They play bridge for money, which is problematic for Lily because she has a gambling addiction and cannot stop gambling, even though it ruins her financially. Lily's slide down the social ladder, in which each rung is a mere imitation of the one above it, has been compared to the determinist fiction of Flaubert and Zola. The real reason for her destruction is a simple lack of money.

Kate Chopin (1851—1904)

Kate Chopin was born in St. Louis. Her father died when she was four, and she was raised by her Creole mother's family. In 1870 she married Oscar Chopin, a cotton broker. They lived in Louisiana, first in New Orleans and then on a large plantation among the French speaking Acadians. Upon her husband's death, Chopin tried to run his business herself but in 1884 decided to return to her mother's home in St. Louis.

Friends encouraged her to write, and when she was nearly forty years old she published her first novel, *At Fault* (1890). Her stories began to appear in *Century and Harper's Magazine*, and two collections followed: *Bayou Folk* (1894) and *A Night in Arcadie* (1897). Her last major work, the novel *The Awakening* (1899), is her masterpiece, but its sympathetic treatment of adultery shocked reviewers and readers throughout America. In St. Louis the novel was taken out of the libraries, and Chopin was denied membership in the St. Louis Fine Arts Club. When her third collection of stories was rejected by her publishers at the end of 1899, Chopin felt herself a literary outcast; she wrote very little in the last years of her life.

What affronted the genteel readers of the 1890s was Chopin's attempt to write frankly about women's emotions in their relations with men, children, and their own sexuality. After her mother's death in 1885, she stopped being a practicing Catholic and accepted the Darwinian view of human evolution. Seeking God in nature rather than through the Church, Chopin wrote freely on the subjects of sex and love, but she said she sadly learned that for American authors, "the limitations imposed upon their art by their environment hamper a full and spontaneous expression." Chopin's work was rediscovered in the 1960s, and a third collection of stories *A Vocation and a Voice* was published posthumously in 1991.

The Awakening tells the story of Edna Pontellier and the

changes that occur in her thinking and lifestyle as the result of a summer romance. At the start of the story, Edna is a young mother of two and the life of a successful New Orleans businessman. While the family is vacationing at a seaside resort, Edna becomes acquainted with Robert Lebrun, a younger man who pays special attention to her. Moonlit walks and intimate conversations with Robert spark feelings that Edna has forgotten. When she returns to the city, Edna throws off the trappings of her old life—devotion to family, attention to societal expectations, and adherence to tradition—to explore independence in love, life, and sexual fulfillment. As evidenced by the many reprints of the book, modern critics appreciate Chopin's skill and artistry-particularly her use of psychological realism, symbolic imagery, and sensual themes. The feminist movement lauds Chopin's portrayal of Edna and the restraints tradition places on women.

William Sidney Porter (1862—1910)
(O. Henry)

Born in North Carolina, Porter lived in poverty as a young man, trying his hand at a number of pedestrian jobs: clerk, bookkeeper, draftsman, and bank teller. In 1894, he founded *The Rolling Stone*, a comic weekly magazine. Five years later, while serving a three-year prison sentence for alleged embezzlement in Columbus, Ohio, he began to write short stories published under the pseudonym of O. Henry.

After his release from prison in 1902 he went to New York

City, where he became a popular and prolific writer of short stories for magazines. His stories are characteristically marked by a twist of plot which turns on an ironic or coincidental circumstance. He is a master of the surprise ending. The basic themes of his stories are concerned with pretense (the desire to pose as what one is not) and reversal of fortune, discovery and initiation through adventure, the city as playground for the imagination, and the basic yearning of all humanity.

The Four Million (1906) is generally considered as O. Henry's best single collection of short stories. It is intended to explore the lives of the multitude of New Yorkers, who jostle each other with their comedies and tragedies mingling against the glittering, beautiful ignoble, crowded, lonely city. Some stories in this collection, such as "The Gift of the Magi," "The Skylight Room," "The Cop and the Anthem," and "The Furnished Room" are well-known.

"The Gift of the Magi" has become almost as much a Christmas classic as Dickens' "Christmas Carol." It is a story about the true love of a poor married couple, each of whom sacrifices their most cherished possession to buy the other a gift. Della sells her long hair to buy Jim a watch fob, and Jim sells his grandfather's watch to buy her fancy hair combs. The gift is now useless, but love, not gain, is the meaning of Christmas.

"The Cop and the Anthem" is about a tramp named Soapy, who tries to get arrested and thus comfortably lodged in jail as winter approaches. But the police prod him onward, refusing to arrest him. Lingering near a church, Soapy is moved by the church anthem and decides to reform and live a productive life.

Then a policeman nabs him for loitering.

"An Unfinished Story" condemns employers for the meager pay given to women workers, who are thereby forced into immorality to live.

"The Furnished Room" brings a disconsolate young man to the boarding-house where his sweetheart committed suicide. The landlady conceals the tragedy in order to have the room rented. He, too, kills himself in the room.

Other volumes of O. Henry's short stories are *Cabbages and Kings* (1904), *Roads of Destiny* (1909), and *The Trimmed Lamp* (1907), the last of which included "The Last Leaf". Henry's best-known work is perhaps the much anthologized "The Ransom of Red Chief", included in the collection *Whirligigs* (1910). *The Heart of the West* (1907) presented tales of the Texas range. O. Henry published 10 collections and over 600 short stories during his lifetime. O. Henry's last years were shadowed by alcoholism, ill health, and financial problems. He married Sara Lindsay Coleman in 1907, but the marriage was not happy, and they separated a year later. O. Henry died of cirrhosis of the liver on June 5, 1910, in New York. Three more collections, *Sixes and Sevens* (1911), *Rolling Stones* (1912) and *Waifs and Strays* (1917), appeared posthumously.

AN UNFINISHED STORY

O. Henry

We no longer groan and heap ashes upon our heads when the flames of Tophet are mentioned. For, even the preachers have begun to tell us that God is radium, or ether or some scientific compound, and that the worst we wicked ones may expect is a chemical reaction. This is a pleasing hypothesis; but there lingers yet some of the old, goodly terror of orthodoxy.

There are but two subjects upon which one may discourse with a free imagination, and without the possibility of being controverted. You may talk of your dreams; and you may tell that you heard a parrot say. Both Morpheus and the bird are incompetent witnesses; and your listener dare not attack your recital. The baseless fabric of a vision, then, shall furnish my theme—chosen with apologies and regrets instead of the more limited field of pretty Pelly's small talk.

I had a dream that was so far removed from the higher criticism that it had to do with the ancient, respectable, and lamented bar-of-judgment theory.

Gabriel had played his trump; and those of us who could not follow suit were arraigned for examination. I noticed at one side a gathering of professional bondsmen in solemn black and collars that buttoned behind; but it seemed there was some trouble about their real estate titles; and they did not appear to be getting any of us out.

A fly cop—an angel policeman—flew over to me and took me by the left wing. Near at hand was a group of very prosperous-looking spirits arraigned for judgment.

"Do you belong with that bunch?" the policeman asked.

"Who are they?" was my answer.

"Why," said he, "they are"

But this irrelevant stuff is taking up space that the story should occupy.

Dulcie worked in a department store. She sold Hamburg edging, or stuffed peppers, or automobiles, or other little trinkets such as they keep in department stores. Of what she earned, Duicie received six dollars per week. The remainder was credited to her and debited to somebody else's account in the ledger kept by G—Oh, primal energy, you say, Reverend Doctor—Well then, in the Ledger of Primal Energy.

During her first year in the store, Dulcie was paid five dollars per week. It would be instructive to know how she lived on that amount. Don't care? Very well; probably you are interested in larger amounts. Six dollars is a larger amount. I will tell you how she lived on six dollars per week.

One afternoon at six, when Dulcie was sticking her hat-pin within an eighth of an inch of her *medulla oblongata*, she said to her chum, Sadie—the girl that waits on you with her left side:

"Say, Sadie, I made a date for dinner this evening with Piggy."

"You never did!" exclaimed Sadie admiringly. "Well, ain't you the lucky one? Piggy's an awful swell; and he always takes a girl to swell places. He took Blanche up to the Hoffman House one evening, where they have swell music, and you see a lot of swells. You'll have a swell time, Dulcie."

Dulcie hurried homeward. Her eyes were shining, and her cheeks showed the delicate pink of life's—real life's—approaching dawn. It was Friday; and she had fifty cents left of her last week's wages.

The streets were filled with the rush-hour floods of people. The electric lights of Broadway were glowing—calling moths from miles, from leagues, from hundreds of leagues out of darkness around to come in and attend the singeing school. Men in accurate clothes, with faces like those carved on cherry-stones by the old salts in sailors' homes, turned and stared at Dulcie as she sped, unheeding, past them. Manhattan, the night-blooming cereus, was beginning to unfold its dead-white, heavy-adored petals.

Dulcie stopped in a store where goods were cheap and bought

an imitation lace collar with her fifty cents. That money was to have been spent otherwise—fifteen cents for supper, ten cents for breakfast, ten cents for lunch. Another dime was to be added to her small store of savings; and five cents was to be squandered for liquorice drops—the kind that made your check look like the toothache, and last as long. The liquorice was an extravagance—almost a carouse—but what is life without pleasures?

Dulcie lived in a furnished room. There is this difference between a furnished room and a boarding house. In a furnished room, other people do not know it when you go hungry.

Dulcie went up to her room—the third floor back in a West Side brownstone-front. She lit the gas. Scientists tell us that the diamond is the hardest substance linown. Their mistake. Landladies know of a compound beside which the diamond is as putty. They pack it in the tips of gas-burners; and one may stand on a chair and dig at it in vain until one's fingers are pink and bruised. A hairpin will not remove it; therefore let us call it immovable.

So Dulcie lit the gas. In its one-fourth-candle-power glow we will observe the room.

Couch-bed, dresser, table, washstand, chair—of this much the landlady was guilty. The rest was Dulcie's. On the dresser were her treasures—a gilt china vase presented to her by Sadie, a calendar issued by a pickle works, a book on the divination of dreams, some rice powder in a glass dish, and a cluster of artificial cherries tied with a pink ribbon.

Against the wrinkly mirror stood pictures of General Kitchener, William Muldoon, the Duchess of Marlborough, and Benvenato Cellini. Against one wall was a plaster of Paris plaque of an O'Callahan in a Roman helmet. Near it was a violent oleograph of a lemon-coloured child assaulting an inflammatory butterfly. This was Dulcie's final judgment in art; but it had never been upset. Her rest had never been disturbed by whispers of stolen copes; no critic had never been disturbed by whispers of stolen copes; no critic had elevated his eyebrows at her infantile entomologist.

Piggy was to call for her at seven. While she swiftly makes ready, let us discreetly face the other way and gossip.

For the room, Dulcie paid two dollars per week. On week-days her breakfast cost ten cents; she made coffee and cooked an egg over the gaslight while she was dressing. On Sunday mornings she feasted royally on veal chops and pineapple fritters at "Billy's" restaurant, at a cost of twenty-five cents—and tipped the waitress ten cents. New York presents so many temptations for one to run into extravagance. She had her lunches in the department-store restaurant at a cost of sixty cents for the week; dinners were $ 1.05. The evening papers—show me a New Yorker going without his daily paper—came to six cents; and two Sunday papers—one for the personal column and the other to read—were ten cents. The total amounts to $ 476. Now, one has to buy clothes, and—I give it up. I hear of wonderful bargain in fabrics, and of miracles performed with needle and thread; but I am in doubt. I hold my pen poised in vain when I would add to Dulcie's life some of those joys that belong to woman by virtue of all the unwritten, sacred, natural, inactive ordinances of the equity of heaven. Twice she had been to Coney Island and had ridden the hobby-horses. 'Tis a weary thing to count your pleasure by summers instead of by hours.

Piggy needs but a word. When the girls named him, an undeserving stigma was cast upon the noble family of swine. The words-of-three-letters lesson in the old blue spelling book begins with Piggy's biography. He was fat; he had the soul of a rat, the habits of a bat, and the magnanimity of a cat... He wore expensive clothes; and was a connoisseur in starvation. He could look at a shop-girl and tell you to an hour how long it had been since she had eaten anything more nourishing than marshmallows and tea. He hung about the shopping districts, and prowled around in department stores with his invitations to dinner. Men who escort dogs upon the streets at the end of a string look down upon him. He is a type; I can dwell upon him no longer; my pen is not the kind intended for him; I am no carpenter.

At ten minutes to seven Dulcie was ready. She looked at herself in the wrinkly mirror. The reflection was satisfactory. The dark blue dress, fitting without a wrinkle, the hat with its jaunty black feather, the but-slightly-soiled gloves—all representing selfdenial, even of food itself—were vastly becoming.

Dulcie forgot everything else for a moment except that she was beautiful, and that life was about to lift a corner of its mysterious veil for her to observe its wonders. No gentleman had ever asked her out before. Now she was going for a brief moment into the glitter and exalted snow.

The girls said that Piggy was a "spender". There would be a grand dinner, and music, and splendidly dressed ladies to look at, and things to eat that strangely twisted the girl's jaws when they tried to tell about them. No doubt she would be asked out again.

There was a blue pongee suit in a window that she knew—by saving twenty cents a week instead of ten, in—let's see—Oh, it would run into years. But there was a second-hand store in Seventh Avenue where—

Somebody knocked at the door. Dulcie opened it. The landlady stood there with a spurious smile, sniffing for cooking by stolen gas.

"A gentleman's downstairs to see you," she said. "Name is Mr. Wiggins."

By such epithet was Piggy known to unfortunate ones who had to take him seriously.

Dulcie turned to the dresser to get her handkerchief; then she stopped still, and bit her underlip hard. While looking in her mirror she had seen fairyland and herself, a princess, just awakening from a long slumber. She had forgotten one that was watching her with sad, beautiful, stern eyes—the only one there was to approve or condemn what she did. Straight and slender and tall, with a look of sorrowful reproach on his handsome, melancholy face, General Kitchener fixed his wonderful eyes on her out of his gilt photograph frame on the dresser.

Dulcie turned like an automatic doll to the landlady.

"Tell him I can't go," she said dully. "Tell him I'm sick, or something. Tell him I'm not going out."

After the door was closed and locked, Dulcie fell upon her bed, crushing her black tip, and cried for ten minutes. General Kitchener was her only friend. He was Dulcie's ideal of a gallant knight. He looked as if he might have a secret sorrow, and his wonderful moustache was a dream, and she was a little afraid of that stern yet tender look in his eyes. She used to have little fancies that he would call at the house sometimes, and ask for her, with his sword clanking against his high boots. Once, when a boy was rattling a piece of chain against a lamp-post, she had opened the window and looked out. But there was no use. She knew that General Kitchener was away over in Japan, leading his army against the savage Turks; and he would never step out of his gilt frame for her. Yet one look from him had vanquished Piggy that night. Yes, for that night.

When her cry was over Dulcie got up and took off her best dress, and put on her old blue kimono. She wanted no dinner. She sang two verses of "Sammy". Then she became intensely interested in a little red speck on the side of her nose. And after that was attended to, she drew up a chair to the rickety table, and told her fortune with an old deck of cards.

"The horrid, impudent thing!" she said aloud. "And I never gave him a word or a look to make him think it!"

At nine o'clock Ducie took a tin box of crackers and a little pot of raspberry jam out of her trunk, and had a feast. She offered General Kitchener some jam on a cracker; but he only looked at her as the sphinx would have looked at a butterfly—if there are butterflies in the desert.

"Don't eat it if you don't want to," said Dulcie. "And don't put on so many airs and scold so with your eyes. I wonder if you'd be so superior and snippy if you had to live on six dollars a week."

It was not a good sign for Dulcie to be rude to General Kitchener. And then she turned Benvenuto Cellini face downward with a severe gesture. But that was not inexcusable; for she had always thought he was Henry Ⅷ, and she did not approve of him.

At half past nine Dulcie took a last look at the pictures on the dresser, turned out the light, and skipped into bed. It's an awful thing to go to bed with a good night look at General Kitchener, William Muldoon, the Duchess of Marlborough, and Benvenuto Cellini.

This story really doesn't get anywhere at all. The rest of it comes later—sometime when Piggy asks Dulcie again to dine with him, and she is feeling lonelier than usual, and General Kitchener happens to be looking the other way, and then—

As I said before, I dreamed that I was standing near a crowd of prosperous-looking angels, and a policeman took me by the wing and asked if I belonged with them.

"Who are they?" I asked.

"Why," said he, "they are the men who hired working-girls, and paid them five or six dollars a week to live on. Are you one of the bunch?"

"Not on your immortality," said I. "I'm only the fellow that set fire to an orphan asylum, and murdered a blind man for his pennies".

Part Five The Age of Modernism

Chapter Ⅰ The Rise of Modernism

1. Modernism

Modernism was a complex and diverse international literary movement, originating at about the end of the 19th century and reaching its maturity in the mid 20th. It was rooted in the social upheavals, and promoted by the new ideas and thoughts such as Nietzsche's philosophy of subconsciousness, Sigmund Freud's psychoanalysis, Bergson's intuitionism, and Darwinism.

It is usually regarded that the time between the publication of Baudelaire's *The Flower of Evils* (1857) and World War Ⅰ was the originating period of modernism. During this period of time, free capitalism was on its way to monopolistic capitalism. The innate social contradictions in capitalist countries were becoming increasingly acute and complex. In accordance to the unreasonable development of social economy was the cultural life, which also tended to be more and more irrational. It was from the social and cultural irrationality that arose the modernist literature, which fully developed between the two world wars.

The great tragedy of the wars, together with the Great Depression of the 1930s, shaked people's trust and belief in the values of capitalism. A large group of writers took up pens to express people's frustration and perplexity, especially to present how people were distorted and dislocated under the irrational forces of the modern world. These writers, profoundly influenced by new philosophical ideas like Freud's psychoanalysis, later strove to explore the inner reality of the modern man in many of their works.

After the 1950s, Modernism began to lose its wail, but its artistic technique has been still exerting influence on contemporary writers. Thus, the time between the 1950s and the present day is generally regarded by some Western critics as the period of postmodernism, which is related to modernism in that it intensifies the modernist feeling of the world as a random, contingent, and chaotic place, and different from Modernism in that it rejects modernist attempt to control the meaningless and disorder through the agency of art and instead tends to accept the world as it is by trying to generate meaning in the face of chaos and absurdity.

2. Features of Modernism

Based on different social realities and influenced by different ideas and thoughts, Modernism has been made up of many facets—symbolism, surrealism, expressionism, existentialism, stream of consciousness, Black Humor, The Theatre of the Absurd, and other minor trends. These sub-schools differ from each other, but only in subtle ways. They have some features in common.

In a broad sense Modernism is applied to writing marked by a strong and conscious break with traditional forms and techniques of expression. It employs a distinctive kind of imagination, one that insists on having its general frame of reference within itself. Modernism implies a historical discontinuity, a sense of alienation, loss, and despair. It not only rejects history but also rejects the society of whose fabrication history is a record. It rejects traditional values and assumptions, and rejects equally the rhetoric by which they were communicated. It elevates the individual and the inner being over the social human being and prefers the unconscious to the self-conscious. Modernism revels in a dense and often morbid actuality, as opposed to the practical and systematic, and in exploring that actuality as it exists in the mind of the writer it has been richly experimental with language, form, symbol, and myth.

3. Historical Introduction of American Modernism

The beginning of the 20th century brought vast changes to the character of American society. Scientific advances were causing an increase in industry; people were moving by the thousands from the farms to the cities; and millions of Americans were changing their manners, morals, and ideas. Writers were no longer content to follow familiar patterns of the past. They introduced new and sometimes radical methods and styles that gradually came to be accepted.

By the end of World War Ⅰ, many American authors had already created a new literature of enduring merits, characterized by aesthetic originality and rebellion, by the determination to shatter conventional taboos in their expression of physical and psychological actuality, by a mystical hunger for spiritual enlightenment which attracted them toward symbolic or primitivistic expression, and by a growing sense of responsibility for their fellow human beings, expressed in the directness of their attack upon the falseness of the contemporary social order. Through their writing they intended to confirm the dignity and value of man who was facing complex new forces and ideas that threatened his humanity and individuality.

American Modernism divides into three periods, with the two world wars marking the transitions. Between 1910 and 1917, modern American drama and poetry came of age. The second decade of the century was a time of rebellion and experiment which produced writers with extraordinary literary talent, such as Pound, Robinson, Frost, T. S. Eliot, Sandburg, Anderson, and Sinclair, who have left marks upon subsequent literature in the United States. World War Ⅰ marked a hiatus, but it was followed by a similar awakening in fiction, which, particularly after the stock market crash of 1929, became strongly social in flavor. With the appearance of Fitzgerald, Hemingway, and Faulkner, the American novel commanded a new respect around the world. Drama and poetry developed steadily between the wars, and there arose what amounted to a revolution in criticism, which substituted the conventional historical approach for the close analysis of a literary work itself. Since 1945, finally, while there has been no sharp break with the earlier periods, American writers have in a sense turned inward, toward an appraisal of what an honest man can do in a world fractured by the overwhelming complexities of contemporary life.

4. Modern American Poetry

Although various dates have been mentioned as marking the beginning of the American modern poetry, the date most widely accepted is 1912, the year of the founding of *Poetry, A Magazine of Verse* by Harriet Monroe (1860—1936). This monthly magazine introduced to the public many new poets including Ezra Pound, T. S. Eliot, Edwin Arlington Robinson, Carl Sandburg, Robert Frost, Wallace Stevens, Robinson Jeffers, and Hart Crane. These poets took interest in experimenting with new poetry and shared a common attitude—the rebellion against Victorian poetry. They rebelled not only against conventional beliefs but also against conventional poetic techniques.

First, modern American poets discard the conventional ideas about the "seriousness" proper to poetry. According to conventional critics, the best poetry was concerned with "high seriousness"—serious subjects like love, hate or sorrow, dealt with in a serious way. Poets had values about which they cherished no doubts, and though their poems sometimes showed vacillations, they moved forward steadily to firm conclusions. Modern poets, feeling that life is complicated, reveal its conflicting aspects, its colliding values. Therefore, their poems deal with incongruities; and humor, wit, or irony of varied shade become important even in very serious poems. Sandburg, Robinson, and Frost recreate in serious poetry the extravagant humor of the old West or the dry humor of Down East. T. S. Eliot, Wallace Stevens, and many others embody more subtle and ironic incongruities.

Secondly, modern American poets are against conventional versification. Contrary to the strict iambic meter of the past are the modern flexible rhythms in free verse. During the early years of the 20th century, one great battle was for the recognition of free verse. Among the writers of such verse, obviously in the tradition of Walt Whitman, are Carl Sandburg and Wallace Stevens. Free Verse won its spurs, but after a period it lost its wail. Nevertheless, it had important effects, for it offered clues about possible variations in verse forms. Robinson, for instance, in some ways highly conventional in his prosody, diverged from regularity sometimes. Even so "classical" a poet as Robert Frost deviated from the regular iambic pattern in some places. The wide range of modern rhythmic patterns became highly appropriate to the expression of the contrasts and the incongruities so important in many modern poems.

Thirdly, modern American poets are opposed to conventional "poetic" diction. After 1914 there was about as much variety in the kinds of language used as there was in the kinds of rhythms. Some poets like Robinson, in general, used the same diction as had been used in the Victorian period, though short of many of its ornaments. Other poets consciously rebelled against what they believed to be unnatural ways of saying things, characteristic of older poetry. They advocated the use of the common speech. However, some modem poets, for all their approval of the use of conversational language, often depart from the simplicities of social talk and get into being obscure. Such obscurity is said to express the complex meanings about the modern world which are hard to decipher.

After the Second World War a new generation of American poets emerged, along with some of the older modern poets who still kept their significance. The outstanding post-war poets are Theodore Roethke, Randall Jarrel, Robert Lowell, and some others, many of whom are college teachers. Their works are basically founded on the achievements of modem poets in the first half of the century. What is new in their works is the sense of living on the brink of disaster. Their visions are for the most part bleak, and their awareness of the forces arrayed against common humanity is keen. Besides these academic poets, there are the beat poets—Allen Ginsberg and Lawrence Ferlinghetti, who wrote candidly about their own life and bouts of insanity.

5. Modern American Drama

Although the theatre was popular in America from colonial times, and although many Americans wrote plays which were produced, American drama of a quality to command respect abroad is the product of the 20th century. It began in rebellion.

Stimulated by the naturalistic, symbolic, and critical drama of Europe, experimental theatres sprang up in America in the 1910s. In the meantime, modern American dramatists began to attract attention. Among them, Paul Green, Eugene O'Neill, Cliffod Odets, and Maxwell Anderson were standing out. These authors wrote for the new theatre. They not only tried to avoid the cliches of plot, characterization, dialog, acting, and staging which had stultified the older drama, but they experimented imaginatively in numerous ways. One development of their experimentation peculiar to the period was expressionism—the mingling of the realistic and the fantastic or symbolic. Experiments of this kind abound in the work of Eugene O'Neill, the greatest American dramatist of the inter-war period. In his *The Hairy Ape* some of the scenery and much of the dialogue and action are realistic. In some scenes, however, masked characters, marionette-like processions and monologs lift the action into the realm of fantasy. Another great play of expressionist experiments was Elmer Rice's *The Adding Machine*, a clear indictment of the systematic application of commercial values to crush the soul of the individual.

The modern drama was marked not only by its experimentation but also by its greater concern with social problems. Anderson's *What Price Glory*? (1924) was only one of many plays showing the American disillusionment with a war which was supposed to make the world safe for democracy. The heyday of the so-cial drama, however, was the thirties. Odets' *Waiting for Left* (1935), a depiction of a strike of taxicab drivers, remains the best known of the so-called proletarian plays.

All through the forties and in the post-war period, new plays kept appearing and with them new emerged playwrights, among whom Tennessee Williams, Arthur Miller, and Edward Albee are dominant figures. The central theme of the new dramatists is mans' search for identity and integrity in a complex and confusing world.

6. Modern American Fiction

Modern American Fiction won its recognition in the 1920s, when a number of novelists came into the scene with a list of bestsellers. The new novelists, with Hemingway and Faulkner taking the lead, departed from the traditions and values of the past and searched for new techniques to tell the real truth about life as it was. To achieve their purpose to make the novel true, they handled detail, plot, and characterization in completely new ways.

The outstanding way of handling detail in modern fiction is the documentary method, discoverable in the writings of Fitzgerald, Lewis, Passos, and many other modern novelists. This method is notable for its mass of detail and its ideal is something like scientific accuracy and completeness. A typical example of this method is Lewis' *Main Street* in which the author tells about the street and its buildings in very fine details. The intention behind it is to give such overwhelming documentation that the reader feels that the picture must be accurate.

In terms of plot, modern novelists, like modern dramatists, refuse to arrange happenings in neat and complete patterns comparable to those in older fiction, as they see life as not to be neatly arranged in the study of a scholar but as a terrifying thing like the tornado, the earthquake, and the devastating fire. To correspond to such a life, they are satisfied to write simply the biographies of characters—sometimes from birth to death, sometimes from day to day over a shorter but not particularly exciting period. Such biographies often tell of characters who do not change: like picaresque figures they merely do various things and meets a series of people. Dos Passos' *U. S. A.* is a picture of chaos in which each chapter is a loose bundle of incidents from the lives of twelve people who encounter many characters that move in and out of their lives. There are many modern narratives, nevertheless, which do show developments, developments which occur when the characters discover something. Faulkner's narratives often show a discovery of the terrible in human existence.

In characterization, modern novelists avoid showing the characteristics of the people by commenting upon them. They tend to drop out of their stories and to become relatively objective in their characterization. Although some authors still use detailed description of background and physical appearance as a characterizing device, modern fiction writers, for the most part, rely for characterization upon the presentation of the words, deeds and thoughts of their characters. This way of characterization was largely shaped by the science of psychology. By exploiting their concepts of psychology, modern fictionists attempt to penetrate into the minds of their characters. Sherwood Anderson, for instance, was strongly influenced by the Freudian concept of human behavior, and his stories in *Winesbury*, *Ohio* almost all deal with complexes or phobias.

Since World War Ⅱ, many literary trends in fiction have come into being. The various experimental fiction of the postwar years has been variously described as "metafiction," "transfiction," "surfiction," or, more commonly, "postmodernism." If the writers included in these categories differ widely in their technical innovations, they do share a common refusal of conventional forms of fiction and a search for drastically new narrative modes able to accommodate their post-apocalyptic era. Thus, what is at stake in postmodernism is a deep cultural crisis, not only a distrust of the assumptions and values that had sustained the modernist writers—in particular that of the salvaging power of art in a disordered world—, but also a radical questioning of the forms and strategies of literary discourse perfected by the great modernists in their effort to give a shape and significance to the chaotic wasteland. In the face of a meaningless, stupefying world, in which history itself becomes the plot of an absurd fiction, the new fictionalists confront the task of perfecting tools adequate to portray the grotesque and fantastic factuality surrounding them: turning away from realism, they elaborate a kind of "fabulation" akin to surrealism and fantasy, privileging parody, ironic inversion, burlesque or absurdist techniques, and stressing the metafictional character of their writing—fiction in the making, fiction as game and fiction as self-reflexive literary criticism. The modes chosen by the different postmodern writers obviously vary greatly, ranging from minimalism or distinctive processes, opening onto a literature of silence, to exuberant, encyclopedic proliferations, loaded with hidden systems and ultimately untractable. One of the most important has been the emergence of the so-called "ethnic novel". This was first apparent with the growth of a substantial group of American Jewish novelists: Saul Bellow, Isaac Bashevis Singer, J. D. Salinger, Bernard Malamud, Herbert Gold, and Philip Roth. These writers write about the anxieties of urban man, alternating between exuberant picaresque comedy and wry sadness. A parallel school of Negro fiction has developed. Its representatives are Richard Wright, Ralph Ellison, and James Baldwin, who, like the Jewish novelists, concentrate on urban man. But for obvious sociological reasons they sound a deeper and more urgent note of discontent. Besides the ethnic novel, there are the south novel represented by Faulkner, Katherin Anne Porter, Eudora Welty, Carson McCullers, and Flannery O'Connor; the war novel led by Norman Mailer, Joseph Heller, and Kurt Vonnegut; and other post modern novels like Jack Kerouac's beat novel and John Updike's middle class novel. All the post-war novelists, as a whole, are preoccupied with modern man's isolation, identity, and dislocation in the fragmented and fractured society.

Chapter Ⅱ Modern Poets

1. Poets of Native Traditions

In speaking of poets of native traditions, we refer to those who kept pretty much to American settings and experiences, and who drew upon techniques developed by their American predecessors. These poets include Edwin Arlington Robinson, Edgar Lee Masters, Carl Sandburg, Vachel Lindsay, and Robert Frost. Each of them, unlike their contemporaries such as Lowell, Pound, and Eliot who tended to engage European subjects and poetic methods, attached himself imaginatively to one or another distinctive feature of the American scene: a mild town in Maine; rural life in the Midwest; the city of Chicago; Springfield, Illinois; New England farming country. Besides, we find in their works an attachment to certain traditional themes and attitudes that themselves represent a gathering response to experience in

America. And if they are remarkably different one from another in poetic technique, the differences depend largely upon which segment of the American literary tradition each has chosen to ally himself with: whether it be, for example, the free verse of Whitman adopted by Masters and Sandburg; the rousing evangelical hymn-singing echoed in Vachel Lindsay; or as with Robinson, the storytelling methods of realistic fiction.

Edwin Arlington Robinson (1869—1935)

① *Biographical Introduction*

E. A. Robinson, the first major poet of the 20th century was born in Head Tide, Maine. His childhood in Gardiner, Maine, provided the background for "Tilbury Town", the fictional location of many of his poems. He studied at Harvard for a time, but the death of his father and other family difficulties forced him to leave in 1893. He published his first collection of poems, *The Torrent and Night Before* (1896), at his own expense. In 1897 this volume was revised, expanded, and reissued as *The Children of the Night*. Following the publication of his third book, *Captain Craig* in 1902, he received, with the help of President Theodore Roosevelt, a job at the New York Customs House, and in 1910 he published his fourth book of poems, *The Town Down the River*. *The Man Against the Sky* appeared in 1916, and was followed in 1917 by the first part of his Arthurian trilogy, *Merlin*. The volumes *Lancelot* (1920) and *Tristram* (1927) completed his reworking of the medieval legend. The 1920s and 1930s were the poet's most productive years. He published *The Three*

Taverns in 1920 and *Avon's Harvest* in 1921. His *Collected Poems* (1921) brought him the first of three Pulitzer Prizes, and his other publications include *The Man Who Died Twice* (1924), *Roman Bartholow* (1923), *Dionysus in Doubt* (1925), *Cavender's House* (1929), *The Glory of the Nightingales* (1930), and *King Gasper* (1935).

② Robinson's View and Theme

Through much of his life Robinson experienced personal tragedy, poverty, and public disregard, all of which made his world naturalistic in nature. Here God is no longer caring, men suffer from frustrations and want of mutual understanding, and life is in general futile and meaningless. Such a tragic vision in step with the modern spirit resulted in his fascination with the interior drama of human defeat which earned him a reputation for pessimism. But it was a pessimism qualified by the positive values of a New England conscience—endurance, moral courage, and the conviction that, as he once put it, "There's a good deal to live for, but a man has to go through hell really to find it out", so the pain of life balanced only by those gleams of meaning which come to those who suffer and endure became Robinson's major repeated theme.

③ Robinson's Style

Robinson was a transitional figure between the 19th and 20th centuries. His life spanned the waning years of the genteel era and the rebellions period of disillusionment that followed World War Ⅰ. Robinson's poetry was transitional, evaluating the present by using traditional forms and by including elements of transcendentalism and Puritanism. An older generation found his poetry dangerously radical, marred by formlessness, and the modernists found it tamely conservative. In spite of the contradictory view, Robinson's poetry is noted for the uniform mastery of varieties of meters, the dry New England humor, the telling economy of language, the obscure and beautiful symbolism, and the charm and elegance of the phrase.

④ Robinson's Major Poems

"Captain Craig" is Robinson's first major poem, published in *Captain Craig*. In this poem, Robinson, with power and humor, drew the portrait of Capt. Craig, the wise and witty observer of New England life, of its social and literary phenomena, the failure of Tillbury Town who had saved his soul alive in defiance of conventionality and had glimpsed the underlying meaning of life.

"The Man Against the Sky" is the title piece in *The Man Against the Sky*. Here the man against the sky is Everyman, is the man kind examined for a brief moment before beggar and king alike approach the grave. In the short time of life, man moves through sorrow, bitterness, defeat, despair, frustration, moves blindly through a dark world lit only by the fitful, "incommunicable gleam" of meaning, "Man's immortal vision", that is, man's capacity to perceive his relationship with reality.

Merlin and *Lancelot* are his first book-length, narrative poems, written under the pressure of World War Ⅰ to convey through a familiar subject Robinson's growing concern with the possible collapse of Western civilization. Merlin is one of his wise men, who moves alone through darkness guided by insights springing from wisdom, suffering, and self-knowledge.

Tristram is the last of the Arthurian poems. In it a flood tide of pent-up emotion seeks release through romance. With a blend of idealism and naturalism Robinson tells the familiar story of love, jealousy, and thwarted desire, the familiar story of storm-tossed lovers whose passion is identified with the restless sea and death.

Roman Bartholow and *Cavender's House*, together with some shorter poems like "Riclard Cory", deal with the spiritual failure of the American businessmen. *Roman Bartholow* is a difficult narrative of the soul sickness of a man of inherited wealth who destroys his wife through jealousy and by his failure to understand her character and her needs. In *Cavender's House*, Robinson introduces Cavender, captain of industry, alone in an empty house at night, debating with the image of his murdered wife, the projection of his own imagination, his self-accuser and his judge. Slowly, as the poet follows the struggle within Cavender's mind, the reader becomes aware of the situation, of Cavender's marriage, domination, jealousy, guilt, of his gradual release from self-torture as he comes to admit he had failed to respect his wife's personality.

"The Man Who Died Twice" deals with the problem of the artist, willing to compromise with the world. Fernando Nash, a musician, buries his talent and dissipates his strength in sensual pleasures until, when inspiration comes, he is too weak to translate or convey the experience. Spiritually dead, he awaits in remorse his body's death.

RICHARD CORY

Whenever Richard Cory went down town,
We people on the pavement looked at him:
He was a gentleman from sole to crown,
Clean favored, and imperially slim.

And he was always quietly arrayed,
And he was always human when he talked;
But still he fluttered pulses when he said
"Good-morning," and he glittered when he walked.

And he was rich—yes, richer than a king—
And admirably schooled in every grace:
In fine, we thought that he was everything
To make us wish that we were in his place.

So on we worked, and waited for the light,
And went without the meat, and cursed the bread;
And Richard Cory, one calm summer night,
Went home and put a bullet through his head

CLIFF KLINGENHAGEN

Cliff Klingenhagen had me in to dine
With him one day; and after soup and meat,
And all the other things there were to eat,
Cliff took two glasses and filled one with wine
And one with wormwood. Then without a sign
For me to choose at all, he took the draught
Of bitterness himself, and lightly quaffed
It off, and said the other one was mine.

And when I asked him what the deuce he meant

By doing that, he only looked at me
And smiled, and said it was a way of his.
And though I know the fellow, I have spent
Long time a-wondering when I shall be
As happy as Cliff Klingenhagen is.

MINIVER CHEEVY

Miniver Cheevy, child of scorn,
  Grew lean while he assailed the seasons;
He wept that he was ever born,
  And he had reasons.

Miniver loved the days of old
  When swords were bright and steeds were prancing;
The vision of a warrior bold
  Would set him dancing.

Miniver sighed for what was not,
  And dreamed, and rested from his labors;
He dreamed of Thebes and Camelot[1],
  And Pram's[2] neighbors.

Miniver mourned the ripe renown
  That made so many a name so fragrant;
He mourned Romance, now on the town,
  And Art, a vagrant.

Miniver loved the Medici,[3]
  Albeit he had never seen one;
He would have sinned incessantly
  Could he have been one.

Miniver cursed the commonplace
  And eyed a khaki suit with loathing;
He missed the medieval grace

Of iron clothing.

Miniver scorned the gold he sought,
But sore annoyed was he without it;
Miniver thought, and thought, and thought,
And thought about it.

Miniver Cheery, born too late,
Scratched his head and kept on thinking;
Miniver coughed, and called it fate,
And kept on drinking.

Notes:

1. Thebes: name of cities in ancient Egypt and Greece; Camelot: legendary site of King Arthur's palace.
2. Pram: Mythological king of Troy during the Trojan War.
3. the Medici: Powerful family of Renaissance Florence, Italy, with a reputation for predatory ruthlessness and sinfulness.

Carl Sandburg (1878—1967)

① *Biographical Introduction*

Carl Sandburg was born in Galsburg, Illinois, of Swedish emigrant parents. He grew up poor and ill educated, spent a little time in the army, then worked as an organizer for Wisconsin's Social Democratic Party, as secretary to the socialist mayor of Milwaukee, and a writer for the radical *Milwaukee Leader*. In 1916 the publication of his *Chicago Poems* established his reputation as a major poet of the Midwest. Then other collections of poetry followed: *Cornhuskers* (1918), *Smoke and Steel* (1920),

Slabs of the Sunburnt West (1922), *Good Morning, America* (1928), and *The People, Yes* (1936). His *Complete Poems* (1950) was awarded the Pulitzer Prize. In addition to his poetry, Sandburg is known for his two-part biography of Abraham Lincoln: *The Prairie Years* (1926) and *The War Years* (1934). For this biography, he was awarded the Pulitzer Prize again.

② Sandburg's View and Theme

As a poet of Chicago, Sandburg knew the countryside, towns, and cities of the Middle West at first hand and looked upon them with affection and understanding, loving their vital force. His most cherished ideal in life was to be "the word of the people," and his poetry articulated in song the thoughts, feelings, and aspirations of the common man confronted with the complexities of the new industrial civilization. Sandburg's celebrations of city low lives and prairie immigrants proved irresistible to an audience that mistrusted refinement and craved an opportunity to admire its own crudity. Sandburg's most serious creative thought centered on history, on the American Civil War in general, and on the figure of Lincoln in particular. A handful of poems celebrated Lincoln and the war: "The Cool Tombs," "Grass," and "Old Timers." Sandburg was the great poet who wrote in the tradition of Whitman. His writing is an expression of Whitmanian optimism and democratic sentiment. Like Whitman, Sandburg draws upon ordinary folk. In the service of those people, he devised a sort of roughneck aesthetic: prosy rhythms, street-smart, slangy diction, and direct, emphatic, and declamatory statement. His poetry ranges from the abbreviated imagism of "Fog" to such free-verse effusions as "Chicago". Sandburg's lively, colloquial, and bragging style made an undeniable contribution to the reclamation of American poetry.

③ *Sandburg's Major Works*

Chicago Poems is a volume of free-verse poems of 20-century urban theme. Here Sandburg caught the strident, arrogant, husky notes of a harsh, brawling, vital city, caught the tempo, movement, color, life of America, caught those things in easy flowing speech, clear, simple, and direct that even school children could understand. In the poem "Chicago", the city of Chicago is singing, building, breaking, rebuilding and laughing in spite of its wickedness, brutalities, hunger and suffering.

The People, Yes is a book of many forms with its organic unity maintained by its single theme, the virtues of the ordinary people. For Sandburg, it is the people who have done the great work of the world, who have invented and produced food and clothes, witnessed history and sent forth great men like Napoleon and Lincoln, and the people will one day rise and come into their own. In "I am the People, the Mob", the poet identifies himself with the people he speaks for and reveals himself as one with the masses.

Abraham Lincoln is a monumental and excellent six-volume biography of Lincoln, written over a period of fifteen years. It appeared sectionally at in *The Prairie Years* and *The War Years*. Sandburg revered Lincoln as the pre-eminent American hero. His humor, wit, and warmth, his use of the homely image, the racy figure of speech is in the tradition of Lincoln.

CHICAGO

Hog butcher for the World,
Tool Maker, Stacker of Wheat,
Player with Railroads and the Nation's Freight Handler;
Stormy, husky, brawling, City of the Big Shoulders:
They tell me you are wicked and I believe them, for I have seen your painted women under the gas lamps luring the farm boys.
And they tell me you are crooked and I answer: Yes, it is true I have seen the gunman kill and go free to kill again.
And they tell me you are brutal and my reply is: On the faces of
women and children I have seen the marks of wanton hunger.
And having answered so I turn once more to those who sneer at this my city, and I give them back the sneer and say to them:
Come and show me another city with lifted head singing so proud to be alive and coarse and strong and cunning.
Flinging magnetic curses amid the toil of piling job on job, here is a tall bold slugger set vivid against the little soft cities;
Fierce as a dog with tongue lapping for action, cunning as a savage pitted against the wilderness,
Bareheaded,
Shoveling,
Wrecking,
Planning,
Building, breaking, rebuilding,
Under the smoke, dust all over his mouth, laughing with white teeth,

Under the terrible burden of destiny laughing as a young man laughs,

Laughing even as an ignorant fighter laughs who has never lost a battle,

Bragging and laughing that under his wrist is the pulse, and under his ribs the heart of the people,

Laughing!

Laughing the stormy, husky, brawling laughter of Youth, halfnaked, sweating, proud to be Hog Butcher, Tool Maker, Stacker of Wheat, Player with Railroads and Freight Handler to the Nation.

THE HARBOR

Passing through huddled and ugly walls
By doorways where women
Looked from their hunger-deep eyes,
Haunted with shadows of hunger-hands,
Out from the huddled and ugly walls,
I came sudden, at the city's edge,
On a blue burst of lake,
Long lake waves breaking under the sun
On a spray-flung curve of shore;
And a fluttering storm of gulls,
Masses of great gray wings And flying white bellies
Veering and wheeling free in the open.

HAPPINESS

I asked professors who teach the meaning of life to tell me what is happiness.

And I went to famous executives who boss the work of thousands of men.

They all shook their heads and gave me a smile as though I was trying to fool with them.
And then one Sunday afternoon I wandered out along the Desplaines river.
And I saw a crowd of Hungarians under the trees with their women and children and a keg of beer and an accordion.

GRACELAND

Tomb of a millionaire,
A multi-millionaire, ladies and gentlemen,
Place of the dead where they spend every year
The usury of twenty-five thousand dollars
For upkeep and flowers
To keep fresh the memory of the dead.
The merchant prince gone to dust
Commanded in his written will
Over the signed name of his last testament
Twenty-five thousand dollars be set aside
For roses, lilacs, hydrangeas, tulips,
For perfume and color, sweetness of remembrance
Around his last long home.

(Ahundred cash girls want nickels to go. to the movies tonight
In the back stalls of a hundred saloons, women are at tables
Drinking with men or waiting for men jingling loose silver dollars in their pockets.
In a hundred furnished rooms is a girl who sells silk or dress goods or leather stuff for six dollars a week wages
And when she pulls on her stockings in the morning she is reckless about God and the newspapers and the police, the talk of her home town or the name people call her.)

FOG

The fog comes
on little cat feet.
It sits looking over harbor and city
on silent haunches
and then moves on.

COOL TOMBS

When Abraham Lincoln was shoveled into the tombs, he forgot the copperheads[1] and the assassin[2]... in the dust, in the cool tombs.
And Ulysses Grant lost all thought of con men and Wall Street. cash and collateral turned ashes... in the dust, in the cool tombs.
Pocahontas' body, lovely as a poplar, sweet as a red haw[3] in November or a pawpaw[4] in May, did she wonder? Does she remember? ... in the dust, in the cool tombs?
Take any streetful of people buying clothes and groceries, cheering a hero or throwing confetti and blowing tinhorns... tell me
if the lovers are losers.., tell me if any get more than the
lovers... in the dust... in the cool tombs.

Notes:

1. the copperheads: Northerners who supported the Confederacy during the Civil War.
2. the assassin: John Wilkes Booth (1838—1865).
3. red haw: Hawthorn berry.
4. pawpaw: The fruit of the papaw tree.

Questions for Consideration:

1. What does the image "fog" stand for?
2. What images are associated with each of the persons mentioned in the poem "Cool Tombs"?

Robert Frost (1874—1963)

① *Biographical Introduction*

Robert Frost was born in San Francisco. When he was eleven, at the death of his father, his mother brought him to New England, his family's native region, with which his poetry has always been associated. After graduating from high school as class poet in 1892, Frost entered Dartmouth College but soon left to work at old jobs and to write poetry. In 1897, he was accepted as a special student by Harvard but withdrew after two years because of his increasing dislike for academic convention. For the next twelve years, Frost made a minimal living by teaching and farming while continuing to write his poems. In 1912, he and his family moved to England, where he found a publisher for his first book of verse, *A Boy's Will* (1913). This collection was well received and was soon followed by a second, *North of Boston* (1914). Determined to win recognition in his native land, Frost returned to the U. S. and settled on a farm in New Hampshire. His fame grew with the appearance of a succession of books: *Mountain Interval* (1916), *New Hampshire* (1923), *West-Running Brook* (1928), *A Further Range* (1936), *A Witness Tree*

(1942), *Steeple Bush* (1947), *In the Clearing* (1962). By the end of his life he had become a national poet; he received honorary degrees from forty-four colleges and universities and won four Pulitzer Prizes; the United States senate passed resolutions honoring his birthdays, and when he was eighty-seven he read his poetry at the inauguration of President John F. Kennedy.

② Frost's View and Theme

Frost, being determined to ground himself in the living traditions in his own country, wrote about the landscapes and people of America's far North-east in many moods. As a poet of nature he had obvious affinities with romantic writers, notably Wordsworth and Emerson. He saw nature as a storehouse of analogy and symbol, announcing, "I'm always saying something that's just the edge of something more," but he had little faith in religious dogma or speculative thought. His concern with nature reflected deep moral uncertainties. He understood the terror and tragedy, and at the same time, its beauty. His poetry often probes mysteries of darkness and irrationality in the bleak and chaotic landscapes of an indifferent universe where men and women stand alone, bereft, un-aid, perplexed, and seeking to make sense of it. The quest of the solitary person to make sense of the world has become the central theme of all Frost's collections and made his poetry among the most accessible of modern writers.

③ Frost's Style

Frost took no part in the literary movements of the 20th century. He did not experiment with form, as many poets did in the

1920s, but used traditional forms such as the blank verse, plain language, and a graceful style. In his poetry, there is a steady tone of wry Yankee humor, and a virtually inexhaustible verbal grace. Many of his poems take the form of dramatic monologues or dialogues, using and transforming the New Englander's patterns of speech which he heard each day on his farm. He used symbols from everyday country life to express his deep ideas. As a whole, Frost's art is an act of clarification, which, without simplifying the truth, renders it in some degree accessible to everyone.

④ *Frost Major Works*

A Boy's Will is one of Frost's most important books. In it there are echoes of earlier poets, and many of the poems are in the tradition of Wordsworth. Yet, the book is distinctively Frost's own, and it is New England in tone and language. Most of the poems deal with the joys and griefs of country lives. One example is the pastoral poem, "Mowing", in which the poet points out the truth that working is a pleasure, a reward in itself, and so it is significant, by presenting an ordinary farmer's meditation on the noise of his mower.

North of Boston is filled with poems that turned the terse speech of New England into poetry. Here Frost used with considerable craftsmanship the narratives, dialogues, and dramatic monologues in such poems as "The Death of the Hired Man", "Home Burial", and "A Servant to Servants". Perhaps the best known and most frequently cited is "Mending Wall", a delightful picture of two farmers repairing the damages of frost and ice to the stone walls that mark their boundaries.

Mountain Interval continued the use of the dramatic dialogue. But in it Frost began to move out from some single object, event, or person to the wider realm of meditation so that the apparently simple thing gathered complexity of meaning. The best known poem is "Birches", the simple account of a boy swinger of birches which slowly builds up into a meditation on the infinitely larger and dual movement from earth to heaven and from heaven to earth. Here the poet craves for a momentary relief from the disorder of earthly life in the way the boy, swinging, leaves the ground but returns when "the tree could bear no more."

New Hampshire contains a number of long narrative poems such as "Maple", the title poem, which expresses Frost's preference for New Hampshire, glitters with satirical comments on places and people. Sprinkled among the longer poems are some of his clear and beautifully simple lyrics, such as the "Stopping by Woods on a Snowy Evening", which represents a moment of relaxation from the hard journey of life in the natural beauty.

West-Running Brook has the tone and thought of the title poem, in which the brook, running west rather than east, as though it were attempting to move backward to the source, is symbolical of the nature of man. The poet's thought is concerned with the relation of man and nature, though he now sees a tension between them as man has a sense of loneliness and futility in the hostile universe. Here Frost is groping for the meaning of a man's life in a universe that overwhelms him and beats him down.

STOPPING BY WOODS ON A SNOWY EVENING

Whose woods these are I think I know.
His house is in the village though;
He will not see me stopping here
To watch his woods fill up with snow.

My little horse must think it queer
To stop without a farmhouse near
Between the woods and frozen lake
The darkest evening of the year.

He gives his harness bells a shake
To ask if there is some mistake.
The only other sound's the sweep
Of easy wind and downy flake.

The woods are lovely, dark and deep.
But I have promises to keep,
And miles to go before I sleep,
And miles to go before I sleep.

THE ROAD NOT TAKEN

Two roads diverged in a yellow wood,
And sorry I could not travel both
And be one traveler, long I stood
And looked down one as far as I could
To where it bent in the undergrowth;

Then took the other, as just as fair,
And having perhaps the better claim,
Because it was grassy and wanted wear;
Though as for that, the passing there

Had worn them really about the same,
And both that morning equally lay
In leaves no step had trodden black.
Oh, I kept the first for another day!
Yet knowing how way leads on to way,
I doubted if I should ever come back.

I shall be telling this with a sigh
Somewhere ages and ages hence:
Two roads diverged in a wood, and I—
I took the one less traveled by,
And that has made all the difference.

BIRCHES

When I see birches bend to left and right
Across the lines of straighter darker trees,
I like to think some boy's been swinging them.
But swinging doesn't bend them down to stay
As ice storms do. Often you must have seen them
Loaded with ice a sunny winter morning
After a rain. They click upon themselves
As the breeze rises, and turn many-colored
As the stir cracks and crazes their enamel.
Soon the suns' warmth makes them shed crystal shells
Shattering and avalanching on the snow-rust—
Such heaps of broken glass to sweep away
You'd think the inner dome of heaven had fallen.
They are dragged to the withered bracken by the load,
And they seem not to break; though once they are bowed
So low for long, they never right themselves:
You may see their trunks arching in the woods
Years afterwards, trailing their leaves on the ground.

Like girls on hands and knees that throw their hair
Before them over their heads to dry in the sun.
But I was going to say when Truth broke in
With all her matter of fact about the ice storm
I should prefer to have some boy bend them
As he went out and in to fetch the cows—
Some boy too far from town to learn baseball,
Whose only play was what he found himself,
Summer or winter, and could play alone.
One by one he subdues his father's trees
By riding them down over and over again
Until he took the stiffness out of them,
And not one but hung limp, not one was left
For him to conquer. He learned all there was
To learn about not launching out too soon
And so not carrying the tree away
Clear to the ground. He always kept his poise
To the top branches, climbing carefully
With the same pains you use to fill a cup
Up to the brim, and even above the brim.
Then he flung outward, feet first, with a swish,
Kicking his way down through the air to the ground.
So was I once myself a swinger of birches.
And so I dream of going back to be.
It's when I'm weary of considerations,
And life is too much like a pathless wood
Where your face burns and tickles with the cobwebs
Broken across it, and one eye is weeping
From a twig's having lashed across it open.
I'd like to get away from earth awhile
And then come back to it and begin over.
May no fate willfully misunderstand me

And half grant what I wish and snatch me away
Not to return. Earth's the right place for love:
don't know where it's likely to go better,
I'd like to go by climbing a birch tree,
And climb back branches up a snow-white trunk
Toward heaven, till the tree could bear no more,
But dipped its top and set me down again,
That would be good both going and coming back,
One could do worse than be a swinger of birches.

FIRE AND ICE

Some say the world will end in fire,
Some say in ice.
From what I've tasted of desire
I hold with those who favor fire.
But if it had to perish twice,
I think I know enough of hate
To say that for destruction ice
Is also great
And would suffice.

Questions for Consideration:

1. Who says "the world will end in fire" and who says "it will end in ice"?
2. In "Birches", is Frost celebrating the events of his boyhood, or is he using the images of bent-over birches and youthful game to say something about the fatigue one feels as the result of life's struggle?

2. *Imagist and Symbolist Poets*

Imagism was a poetic movement in England and the U. S. from 1909 to 1917. It rose as a protest against the conventional Victorian poetry that was loaded with abstraction, windy rhetoric, and moralization. The movement, with Ezra Pound and Amy Lowell as its leading spokesmen, strove for a freedom in the selection of subject matter, clarity of images, exact unfrilled language, and musical rhythm. Imagism as a movement flourished only briefly, but it had considerable influence on the development of form and subject matter in modern poetry. Poets like T. S. Eliot, William Carlos Williams, Wallace Stevens, and E. E. Cummings, recognizing strengths in imagist philosophies, made poems of the Imagist type.

Ezra Pound (1885—1975)

① *Biographical Introduction*

Pound was born in Hailey, Idaho, and raised in Pennsylvania. He studied Romance languages at Hamilton College and the university of Pennsylvania. In 1908 he left the U. S. for Europe. In London he came into contact with F. E. Hulme, with whom he founded the "imagist" movement. He helped to start the literary career of some struggling talents like Robert Frost and T. S. Eliot, and at the same time he began writing the *Cantos* which he continued for the next thirty years. In 1920, he moved to Paris, where, as part of Gertrude Stein's circle, he helped Eliot and Hemingway by editing their early writings. In 1924, He went to

Italy and made his home there. He continued to write the *Cantos* and produced many books of translation and literary criticism. With the outbreak of World War Ⅱ, he began broadcasting pro-fascist propaganda to the U. S., for which he was charged with treason and was arrested by the U. S. military authorities at Pisa. There he wrote the first draft of his Pisan Cantos in prison. He was brought back to the States to stand trial, but was sent, instead, to a hospital for the criminally insane in Washington. He spent his time translating works of ancient Greek and ancient Chinese literature. While in prison, he was awarded a prestigious poetry prize for his last *Cantos*. In 1958, Pound was released at the age of 73. He returned to Italy where he continued to write and make translations until he died at the age of 87.

② *Pound's View and Theme*

When Ezra Pound appeared on the scene in the first years of the present century, the West presented a panorama of a waste-land. It was a world in which Pound saw pervasive and impenetrable gloom, and chaos and disorder and barbarism everywhere. To him life was sordid personal crushing oppression, and culture produced nothing but "intangible bondage". He considered it his mission to save a tottering civilization. To derive standards from the cultures of the past and resurrect lost principles of order, he surveyed earlier literatures and cultures, made a synthesis out of bits of history, and adapted their conventions to his own purposes. His mature poetry became a diagnosis of cultural worth. He celebrates the glory of those periods in the past which he found admirable, or he angrily denounces those in which civilization had become coarse, weak, or corrupt.

③ *Pound's Style*

Pound's poetry represent a wide diversity of forms. Believing that all ages were contemporaneous, Pound drew from past and present, drawing upon the Latin lyric, Provencal ballad, Italian and Elizabethan song, French symbolist technique, Chinese and Japanese poetry, and modern imagism. In his early work, Pound battled gentility, didacticism, and academicism. His verse, however experimental, was fresh, invigorating, and direct. In his later work, his innovative techniques often failed him, yet some individual passages in his Cantos contain his great work.

④ *Pound's Major Works*

The *Cantos* is a long poem written in sections over a period of over thirty years. It was meant to be considered as a whole, as forming a pattern in the contrast of past and present. In fact, the *Cantos* are unconnected poems, disjointed and fragmentary. They are conversations on a wide variety of unrelated subjects. In them, the poet talked about the rise and fall of eastern and western empires, the destruction of civilization caused by greed and materialism, the corruption of American after the heroic time of Jefferson, and even his own suffering. On the whole, the *Cantos* present a world of cheerlessness and somberness. They are difficult to read.

Hugh Selwyn Mauberley (1920) is one of Pound's best poems. It summarized Pound's literary career in London from 1908 to 1920, and expressed Pound's disillusionment with the war and England, through the life of Mauberley. Mauherley is Pound, who sees himself born too late and in a "half-savage country". London, the symbol of Modern civilization, has no place for him as an artist, for he cannot recognize what he is trying to do or by what principles he lives. In the speaker's embittered gaze, much more is involved than an indifference to the arts bred by the desire to make money or to live by commercial values. Those values themselves destroy not only art but with it human integrity. The poem is considered as a satire of the materialistic forces involved in World War Ⅰ.

⑤ *Pound's Contribution to American Poetry*

Pound was a great poet, critic, and translator, who contributed a lot to open the way to modern poetry. As a critic he was important to his own time, the first half of twentieth century, and, in some respects, to future time. Born in an age of poetic doldrums, he introduced new ideas and new poets and reintroduced old poets and their thoughts. As a translator, Pound produced some of his most creative work. His translations, though inexact, remain true to the spirit, form, feeling, and essential meaning of the original. His translations from the Chinese and Japanese not only stimulated interest in Oriental culture and art, but introduced new techniques in poetry and strengthened his Imagist concepts of compression, word-painting, image and symbol. As an original poet, Pound's fame lies not so much in his poetry as in his ability to stimulate others. His early lyrics and his cantos with their fresh images, starling phrases, fluid form, and brilliant hotchpotch of association are less beautiful and original poetry than they are rich-veined mines for other poets to excavate. This ability to excite, to startle, and to open up broad vistas and new areas made him one of the great creators of the modern movement in poetry.

A PACT

I make a pact with you, Walt Whitman—
I have detested you long enough.
I come to you as a grown child
Who has had a pig-headed father;
I am old enough now to make friends
It was you that broke the new wood,
Now is a time for carving.
We have one sap and one root—
Let there be commerce between us.

IN A STATION OF THE METRO

The apparition of these faces in the crowd;
Petals on a wet, black bough.

THE RIVER-MERCHANT'S WIFE: A LETTER

While my hair was still cut straight across my forehead
I played about the front gate, pulling flowers.
You came by on bamboo stilts, playing horse,
You walked about my seat, playing with blue plums.
And we went on living in the village of Chokan:
Two small people, without dislike or suspicion.
At fourteen I married My Lord you.
I never laughed, being bashful.
Lowering my head, I looked at the wall.
Called to, a thousand times, I never looked back.

At fifteen I stopped scowling,

I desired my dust to be mingled with yours
Forever and forever and forever.
Why should I climb the look out?

At sixteen you departed,
You went into far Ku-to-yen, by the river of swirling eddies,
And you have been gone five months.
The monkeys make sorrowful noise overhead.

You dragged your feet when you went out.
By the gate now, the moss is grown, the different mosses,
Too deep to clear them away!
The leaves fall early this autumn, in wind.
The paired butterflies are already yellow with August
Over the grass in the West garden;
They hurt me. I grow older.
If you are coming down through the narrows of the river Kiang,
Please let me know beforehand,
And I will come out to meet you As far as Cho-fu-Sa.

By Rihcaku[1]

Notes:

1. Rihcaku: Japanese name for the Chinese poet Li Po(701—762) whose poem Pound translates and adapts.

Question for Consideration:

What do the first two poems do with imagist techniques?

T. S. Eliot (1888—1965)

① *Biographical Introduction*

T. S. Eliot was the single dominant figure in poetry and criticism in the period between the two world wars. With the encouragement and help of his teacher, Ezra Pound, he made a new poetry for America in the twenties, and shaped the tastes and the critical vocabulary of a new generation.

Eliot was born in Saint Louis, Missouri. His family encouraged his interest in poetry and gave him a thorough training in the classics before sending him to Harvard to study literature and philosophy. At Harvard, he began to write poetry and finished his first major poem "The Love Song of J. Alfred Prufrock", which was collected in his first volume, *Prufrock and Other Observations* (1917). In 1914, Eliot went to Europe, and after studying in Germany, Paris, and at Merton College, Oxford, settled in London, where he worked successively as a school teacher, a bank clerk, and an editor. In 1922, he published his best-known poem *The Waste Land*, which was followed by many others including "The Hollow Men", "Ash Wednesday", "The Journey of the May," and *Four Quartets*. In his later years, Eliot devoted himself mainly to verse drama. His first play, based upon the martyrdom of Saint Thomas Becket, *Murder in the Cathedral* (1935), met with some success. The later plays, in contemporary settings, include *The Family Reunion* (1939), *The Cocktail Party* (1950) and *The Confidential Clerk* (1954). Eliot's collections of critical essays include *The Sacred Wood*

(1920), *Homage to John Dryden* (1924), *Selected Essays* (1932) and some others. In 1948, Eliot was awarded the Nobel Prize for literature.

② *E1iot's View and Theme*

Eliot shared the modern view that the world is chaotic and its life is futile and fragmentary. Most of his poetry concern various aspects of the frustration and enfeeblement of individual characters caught in a world of monotonous repetition, a world of aimless circling about, without end or purpose, and the quest for order and discipline became Eliot's major theme, which led him toward conservatism and to religion for salvation. In 1927, Eliot conversed to the Church of England and announced that he was a royalist in politics, a classicist in literature, and an Anglo-catholic in religion. His poetry moved from the secular to the ascetic, from pessimism to religious faith. Most of his verse dramas and late poetry deal with religious themes.

③ *Eliot's Literary Criticism*

Eliot was a distinguished literary critic whose criticism sheds light on poetry in general and on his poetry in particular. The basic themes of his criticism are concerned with the relationship between tradition and individual talent, and between the past, the present, and the future. In his first critical work, *The Sacred Wood*, Eliot focused his attention on the English writers of the sixteenth and seventeenth centuries. It started the revaluation of poets like Milton and the Romantics, popularized the "metaphysical poets" such as John Donne, and emphasized the need to see the vitality of the literature of the past. It is also in this work, especially in the essay "Tradition and the Individual Talent", that Eliot made the earliest statement of his aesthetic principle that the poem is an organic thing in itself, whose concrete elements are true correlatives of the artist's imagination and experience with respect to that poem. The degree to which fusion and concentration of intellect, feeling, and experience were achieved was Eliot's criterion for judging the poem. Such ideas he developed in his other critical works.

④ *Eliot's Style*

First of all, Eliot's poetry is noted for its images. Eliot's images were not romantic, feminine, delicate, and charming. They were vigorous, masculine, ugly, and sordid. Nor did he allow the single image, beautiful and bare, to carry the weight of meaning and emotion. Rather he piled image upon image, each precise and sharp, using a series of pictures to build up by association intense feeling, and allowing the images to develop into a symbol, to become something greater, than the sum of the images. For example, the succession of unrelated images in *The Wasteland* combine to form an impression of modern man's despair.

Secondly, like Ezra Pound, Eliot used abundantly literary reference in his works; he fused the present with an unfaltering sense of the past, mingling the big city life with the primitive society, and he pressed for a greater attention to myth and legend as clues to understanding contemporary dilemmas. Eliot's abrupt movement of disassociated images, together with his learned quotations and allusions, has made his poetry too demanding for the reader.

⑤ *Eliot's Major Works*

"The Love Song of J. Alfred Prufrock" is Eliot's first major poem. It has been called the first masterpiece of modernism in English. It depicts a repressed, weak, balding middle-aged man who is thinking of going to propose marriage to a lady but hesitating all the way there. The poem takes the form of an interior monologue and expresses the disillusionment and despair of the twentieth-century Western man, who is caught in the dilemma of desire and impotence.

The Waste Land is Eliot's most memorable poem and one that set the tone of the postwar era. It contrasts the spiritual weakness and vulgarity of Europe and America with the beauty, the values and the unity of the past. To emphasis the inhumanity, decadence, and fragmentation of Western life, Eliot developed the fragmentary style. The poem was divided into five sections: "The Burial of the Dead," "A Game of Chess," "The Fire Sermon," "Death by Water," and "What the Thunder Said". Between these parts there is no logical transitions either in themselves or in relation to each other. The whole poem is just an accumulation of disconnected images that are subsumed into the central theme, desperation.

Four Quartets, Eliot's culmination in religious themes, comprises four poems: "Burnt Norton", "East Coker," "The Dry Salvages," and "Little Gidding," These poems provide a reasoned philosophical discussion of the foundations of Christian faith, involving the nature of time, the significance of history, the religious psychology of man, and the nature of his experience. Most importantly, they attempt, by means of lofty poetic feeling and metaphysical insight, to suggest the actuality and meaning of such Christian mysteries as incarnation and Pentecost.

THE LOVE SONG OF J. ALFRED PRUFROCK[1]

S'io credesse che mia risposta fosse
A persona che mai tornasse al mondo,
Questa fiamma staria senza piu scosse.
Ma perciocche giammai di questo fondo
Non torno vivo alcun, s'i'odo il vero,
Senza tema d'infamia ti rispondo.[2]

Let us go then, you[3] and I,
When the evening is spread out against the sky
Like a patient etherized upon a table;[4]
Let us go, through certain half-deserted streets
The muttering retreats
Of restless nights in one-night cheap hotels
And sawdust restaurants with oyster-shells:
Streets that follow like a tedious argument
Of insidious intent
To lead you to an overwhelming question...
Oh, do not ask, 'What is it?'
Let us go and make our visit.

In the room the women come and go
Talking of Michelangelo.

The yellow fog that rubs its back upon the window-panes,
The yellow smoke that rubs its muzzle on the window-panes
Licked its tongue into the corners of the evening,
Lingered upon the pools that stand in drains,
Let fall upon its back the soot that falls from chimneys,

Slipped by the terrace, made a sudden leap,
And seeing that it was a soft October night,
Curled once about the house, and fell asleep.

And indeed there will be time[5]
For the yellow smoke that slides along the street,
Rubbing its back upon the window-panes;
There will be time, there will be time
To prepare a face to meet the faces that you meet;
There will be time to murder and create,
And time for all the works and days of hands
That lift and drop a question on your plate;
Time for you and time for me,
And time yet for a hundred indecisions,
And for a hundred visions and revisions,
Before the taking of a toast and tea.

In the room the women come and go
Talking of Michelangelo.

And indeed there will be time T
To wonder, 'Do I dare?' and, 'Do I dare?'
Time to turn back and descend the stair,
With a bald spot in the middle of my hair—
(They will say: 'How his hair is growing thin!')
My morning coat, my collar mounting firmly to the chin,
My necktie rich and modest, but asserted by a simple pin—
(They will say: 'But how his arms and legs are thin!')
Do I dare
Disturb the universe?
In a minute there is time.
For decisions and revisions which a minute will reverse.

For I have known them all already, known them all;
Have known the evenings, mornings, afternoons,

I have measured out my life with coffee spoons;
I know the voices dying with a dying fall
Beneath the music from a farther room.
So how should I presume?

And I have known the eyes already, known them all—
The eyes that fix you in a formulated phrase,
And when I am formulated, sprawling on a pin,
When I am pinned and wriggling on the wall,
Then how should I begin
To spit out all the butt-ends of my days and ways?
And how should I presume?
And I have known the arms already, known them all—
Arms that are braceleted and white and bare
(But in the lamplight, downed with light brown hair!)
Is it perfume from a dress
That makes me so digress?
Arms that lie along a table, or wrap about a shawl.
And should I then presume?
And how should I begin?

Shall I say, I have gone at dust through narrow streets
And watched the smoke that rises from the pipes
Of lonely men in shirt-sleeves, leaning out of windows?...

I should have been a pair of ragged claws
Scuttling across the floors of silent seas.

And the afternoon, the evening, sleeps so peacefully!
Smoothed by long fingers, Asleep... tired... or it malingers,
Stretched on the floor, here beside you and me.
Should I, after tea and cakes and ices,
Have the strength to force the moment to its crisis?
But though I have wept and fasted, wept and prayed,
Though I have seen my head (grown slightly bald) brought in

upon a platter,[6]
I am no prophet—and here's no great matter;
I have seen the moment of my greatness flicker,
And I have seen the eternal Footman hold my coat and snicker,
And in short, I was afraid

And would it have been worth it, after all,
After the cups, the marmalade, the tea,
Among the porcelain, among some talk of you and me
Would it have been worth while,
To have bitten off the matter with a smile,
To have squeezed the universe into a ball
To roll it toward some overwhelming question
To say: 'I am Lazarus, come from the dead,[7]
Come back to tell you all, I shall tell you all'—
If one, settling a pillow by her head,
Should say: 'That is not what I meant at all.
That is not it, at all.'

And would it have been worth it, after all,
Would it have been worth while
After the sunsets and the dooryards and the sprinkled streets,
After the novels, after the teacups, after the skirts that trail along the floor
And this, and so much more? —
It is impossible to say just what I mean!
But as if a magic lantern threw the nerves in patterns on a screen:
Would it have been worth while
If one, settling a pillow or throwing off a shawl,
And turning toward the window, should say:
'That is not it at all,
That is not what I mean, at all.'

No! I am not Prince Hamlet, nor was meant to be;
Am an attendant lord, one that will do,
To swell a progress,[8] start a scene or two,
Advise the prince; no doubt, an easy tool,
Deferential, glad to be of use,
Politic, cautious, and meticulous;
Full of high sentence,[9] but a bit obtuse;
At times, indeed, almost, ridiculous—
Almost, at times, the Fool.

I grow old... I grow old...
I shall wear the bottoms of my trousers rolled.

Shall I part my hair behind? do I dare to eat a peach?
I shall wear white flannel trousers, and walk upon the beach.
I have heard the mermaids[10] singing, each to each.

I do not think that they will sing to me.

I have seen them riding seaward on the waves
Combing the white hair of the waves blown back
When the wind blows the water white and black.

We have lingered in the chambers of the sea
By sea-girls wreathed with seaweed red and brown
Till human voices wake us, and we drown.

Notes:

1. The poem presents with irony and pathos the musings of an aging young man, uncertain, unable to commit himself to the love he desires or to life at all, a figure representative of the frustrations in modern life and of the aridity of a sterile supper-class culture.
2. This stanza is taken from Dante's Inferno, meaning "if I thought that my reply would be given to one who would ever return to the world, this flame world stay without further movement; but since none has ever returned a-

live from this depth, if what I hear is true, I answer you without fear of infamy."

3. "you" probably refers to his soul.
4. The evening is compared to a patient lying numb on a table of operation.
5. A reference to "Works and Days", a poem by the Greek Hesiod, on the rural life and labors of a peasant.
6. The prophet John the Baptist was beheaded and his head brought a platter to Salome, the daughter of Heodias Mather.
7. Jesus raised Iazarus from the dead, John Ⅱ.
8. To be part of a royal procession.
9. Judgment, pronouncement.
10. Mythical alluring creatures, half woman and half fish.

Questions for Consideration:

1. What are some of the factors weighing for and against Prufrock's declaration of his love?
2. Is the poet making a comment about contemporary society?
3. How do you explain the irony of the title?

Wallace Stevens(1879—1955)

①*Biographical Introduction*

Wallace Stevens was an unusual poet in modern American literary history, who combined a business career with a genuine vocation for poetry. A native of Reading, Pennsylvania, he showed at an early age both the artistic tendency and the clear mind that was to develop in divergent directions. After three years at Harvard, where he published poems in the *Harvard Advocate*, he attended New York Law School. Admitted to the bar in 1904, he worked for several law firms before marrying and moving to Connecticut, where he eventually rose to the position of vice-president of the Hartford Accident and Indemnity Company. During his years in New York, with the modernist movement gaining momentum, Stevens became acquainted with a number of young writers such as William Carlos Williams, and began submitting his poems to little magazines, especially *Poetry: A Magazine of Verse*, the most popular magazine for the new revolutionary poets. It was not until 1923, however, that Stevens, at the age of 44, was finally persuaded to publish a book of poems, *Harmonium*. His later volumes, which followed slowly for he was in no hurry to publish, include: *Ideas of Order* (1935), *The Man with the Blue Guitar* (1937), Parts *of a World* (1942), *Transport to Summer* (1947), and *The Auroras of Autumn* (1950). His collected poems, published in 1954, won him the Pulitzer Prize.

② *Stevens' View and Theme*

Stevens was absolutely committed to the notion that a poet lives in two worlds: the world of reality and the world of imagination. The problem of the relation between the real and the ideal become a constant theme in his poetry, and he elaborated a series of oppositions between inner and outer worlds—between subject and object, the self and the world, fiction and fact. To Stevens, it is the poet's primary concern to overcome these contraries. The means is the imagination, the "acute intelligence," whose power lies in its ability to bring order and meaning to the chaos and nothingness of modern existence. Stevens deals repeatedly in his poetry with the role of imagination, and his exaltation of its power reaches the highest point in modern American literary history. With all of his praise of imagination and the way it shapes our notions of the world, Stevens is tremendously interested in the brute fact of reality. The world of reality exists to determine the limits of art, and imagination can construct only on the basis of the world of nature. At the bottom of Stevens' poetry there is man's joy in his own existence, and thankfulness of it.

③ *Stevens' Style*

In form Stevens is a modern. He rebelled against the "stale intelligence" of the past. Setting out "to make a new intelligence prevail", he invoked the comic, the strange, the bizarre. He adopted a variety of experimental styles, created poetic surfaces of elegant language, exotic imaging, odd sounds, curious analogies, and inscrutable titles. Stevens reveled in outer expressions and foreign phrases and his poetry is highly suggestive and capable of more than one interpretation. But whatever the highly polished and grandest surfaces of his verse might suggest, the body of his poetry is in no way frivolous. He used his prodigious technique to probe serious issues such as those of life and death, and belief and value.

④ *Stevens' Major Poems*

"Anecdote of the Jar" is a highly symbolic poem. Here lies the wild rural Tennessee, which can be assumed as a symbol of the world of nature. Then the "I" of the poem places in it a tall, round jar, a man-made object, which is suggestive of the world of art, and by extension, the world of imagination. What happens when the jar is standing there is almost a miracle: it controls the whole disorderly landscape, so that "the wildness up to it, And sprawled around, no longer wild." The poem seems to be talking about the relationship between art and nature. The world of nature, shapeless and chaotic, takes shape and order from the presence of the jar, the world of art and imagination.

"The Idea of Order at Key West" is one of the most eloquent poems of the modern period, and it is one of Stevens finest tributes to the power of the imagination. Here a girl is singing by the sea and her song causes the poet to mediate on the whole problem of the relation of poetry to reality and the power of imagination. The girl, whose sing gives ordered significance to the scene, stands for the poet. The sea, in its ever-changing panorama, its ever-shifting moods and sights and sounds, constitutes a perfect example of the chaotic and disordered world of our experience which the poet needs to arrange, enchant, and put into order.

"Sunday Morning" is one example of Stevens' view of an age of disbelief, a world emptied of the gods. Here a woman sits over a late breakfast on a sunny porch. She is evidently not going to church this morning. Through the woman's reverie, Stevens urges human self-sufficiency against dependence on the pallid ghost of dead gods. The poem asks what divinity is, "if it can come only in silent shadows and in dreams." Upending the claims of religion to rule the realm of permanence, the poem argues that life in its transience is more durable than any supernatural abstraction, and that man can discover in his own human resources, in his powers of imagination, all that he needs in order to cope with the crisis in culture.

ANECDOTE OF THE JAR

I placed a jar in Tennessee,
And round it was, upon a hill.
It made the slovenly wilderness
Surround that hill.

The wilderness rose up to it,
And sprawled around, on longer wild.
The jar was round upon the ground
And tall and of a port in air.

It took dominion everywhere.
The jar was gray and bare.
It did not give of bird or bush,
Like nothing else in Tennessee.

THE SNOW MAN

One must have a mind of winter
To regard the frost and the boughs
Of the pine-trees crusted with snow;

And have been cold a long time
To behold the junipers shagged with ice,
The spruces rough in the distant glitter

Of the January sun; and not to think
Of any misery in the sound of the wind
In the sound of a few leaves,

Which is the sound of the land
Full of the same wind
That is blowing in the same bare place

For the listener, who listens in the snow,

And, nothing himself, beholds
Nothing that is not there and the nothing that

THE EMPEROR OF ICE-CREAM

Call the roller of big cigars,
The muscular one, and bid him whip
In kitchen cups concupiscent curds.
Let the wenches dawdle in such dress
As they are used to wear, and let the boys
Bring flowers in last month's newspapers.
Let be finale of seem.
The only emperor is the emperor of ice-cream

Take from the dresser of deal[1]
Lacking the three glass knobs, that sheet
On which she embroidered fantails[2] once
And spread it so as to cover her face.
If her horny feet protrude, they come
To show how cold she is, and dumb.
Let the lamp affix its beam.[3]
The only emperor is the emperor of ice-cream.

Notes:

1. Made of cheap pine or fir planks.
2. Fan-shaped designs, like the tails of birds.
3. Let the truth assert itself.

Questions for Consideration:

1. What is "Jar" associated with? In what way does it function?
2. What does the snow man, himself a kind of nothing, with "a mind of winter", see and hear in the bleak scene?

3. What experience is being communicated in "The Emperor of Ice-Cream"?

William Carlos Williams (1883—1963)

① *Biographical Introduction*

Williams was a hard-working physician all his life just as Wallace Stevens was a successful businessman. For them, poetry was only an avocation. Williams was born in Rutherford, New Jersey. He attended Swiss and French schools before studying medicine at the University of Pennsylvania, where he made friends with Ezra Pound. After further medical study in New York where he met Wallace Stevens and a postgraduate year in Germany studying pediatrics, Williams returned to his birthplace, Rutherford, and there he practiced medicine for forty years, until his retirement in 1951. Williams' interest in poetry was aroused early. In 1909, the year before he began his medical practice, he published his first volume, *Poems*, which was followed by a succession of other volumes of poetry, including *The Tempers* (1913), *Kora in Hell* (1920), *Sour Grapes* (1921), *Spring and All* (1923), *Paterson* (1946), and *The Desert Music* (1954). Besides poetry, Williams also experimented with prose, writing essays, short stories, plays and novels. But today, Williams is best known as a poet, especially as the creator of that imagistic red wheelbarrow, glistening in the rain.

② *Williams' View, Theme, and Style*

Williams wrote several times "Say it, no ideas but in

things", summarizing his poetic credo. Repudiating what he considered to be the learned rhetoric of such literary patricians as T. S. Eliot and Wallace Stevens, Williams placed himself in the line of Whitman and argued for the integrity of the commonplace and the primacy of the object. He repeatedly insisted that the job of the poet was to illuminate the here and now, to lift up to the imagination "those things which lie under the direct scrutiny of the senses, close to the nose." Like Whitman he used commonplace American scenes and speech to portray contemporary urban America. And like Whitman he was a significant force in the freeing of poetry from the restraints and predictive regularity of traditional rhythms and meters. His poetry is simple, direct, and apparently formless. His earlier poems, present homely images and show the influence of imagism in its objective, precise manner of description. His later poems, however, went beyond the interest of that movement, and shows a greater control of form, a deeper sympathy for humanity, and a more sensitivity to the sumptuous squalor of modern America.

③ *Williams' Major Poems*

"The Red Wheelbarrow" is Williams' best imagistic poem, in which the poet tried to convey a simple experience through sheer simplicity of statement. The poem only contains sixteen simple words separated in eight lines. Yet it appeals to the imagination and forces the reader to visualize and derive an aesthetic pleasure from reading it. With the animate "chickens" juxtaposed with the inanimate "barrow" and the white color in contrast with the red, we have in our mind's eye meaningful textures and clear, delightful colors. We become aware that it is important to perceive them to make fuller, and that so much depends on how we perceive them both in our life and in our writing of poetry.

Paterson, Williams' most ambitious work, is a long, epic poem of six books. Set in Paterson, New Jersey, the poem deals with the history and people of the town from its origins to modern times. The poem is a bodying forth of Williams' aesthetics. In it, Williams, keeping his eyes and ears on the vivid concrete particulars of his homeland, tried to pull together his isolated observations and experiences to achieve the profound universal meaning through the representation of the local. Paterson is innovative in technique. It faith fully reproduces the quiet, serene rhythm of life itself in its natural flow, now in prose, now in verse, with interpolations of monologues, conversations, and letters in between the unhurried narrative. The form of the poem is highly flexible to accommodate the variety of themes which keep coming into it.

PORTRAIT OF A LADY

Your thighs are apple trees
whose blossoms touch the sky.
Which sky? The sky
where Watteau[1] hung a lady's
slipper. Your knees
are a southern breeze— or
a gust of snow. Agh! what
sort of man was Fragonard?[2]
—as if that answered
anything. Ah, yer—below
the knees, since the tune

drops that way, it is
one of those white summer days,
the tall grass of your ankles
flickers upon the shore—
Which shore? —
the sand clings to my lips—
Which shore?
Agh, petals maybe. How
should I know?
Which shore? Which shore?
I said petals from an appletree.

TRACT

I will teach you my townspeople
how to perform a funeral—
for you have it over a troop
of artists—
unless one should scour the world—
you have the ground sense necessary.

See! the hearse leads.
I begin with a design for a hearse.
For Christ's sake not black[3]
nor white either—and not polished!
Let it be weathered—like a farm wagon—
with gilt wheels (this could be
applied fresh at small expense)
or no wheels at all.
a rough dray to drag over the ground.

Knock the glass out!
My God—glass, my townspeople!
For what purpose? Is it for the dead

to look out or for us to see
how well he is housed or to see
the flowers or the lack of them—
or what?
To keep the rain and snow from him?
He will have a heavier rain soon.
pebbles and dirt and what not.
Let there be no glass—
and no upholstery! phew!
and no little brass rollers
and small easy wheels on the bottom—
my townspeople what are you thinking of!

A rough plain hearse then
with gilt wheels and no top at al
On this the coffin lies
by its own weight.

NO WREATHS PLEASE—

especially no hot-house flowers.
Some common memento is better,
something he prized and is known by:
his old clothes—a few books perhaps—
God knows what! You realize
how we are about these things,
my townspeople—
something will be found—anything—
even flowers if he had come to that.
So much for the hearse.

For heaven's sake though see to the driver!
Take off the silk hat! In fact
that's no place at all for him up there unceremoniously

dragging our friend out of his own dignity!
Bring him down—bring him down!
Low and inconspicuous! I'd not have him ride
on the wagon at all—damn him—
the undertaker's understrapper!
Let him hold the reins and walk at the side
and inconspicuously too!

Then briefly as to yourselves:
Walk behind—as they do in France,
seventh class, or if you ride
Hell take curtains! Go with some show
of inconvenience; sit openly—
to the weather as to grief.
Or do you think you can shut grief in?
What—from us? We who have perhaps
nothing to lose? Share with us
share with us—it will be money
in your pockets.
Go now
think you are ready.

THE YOUNG HOUSEWIFE

At ten A.M. the young housewife
moves about in negligee behind
the wooden walls of her husband's house.
I pass solitary in my car.

Then again she comes to the curb
to call the ice-man, fish-man, and stands
shy, un-corseted, tucking in
stray ends of hair, and I compare her
to a fallen leaf. The noiseless wheels of my car

rush with a crackling sound over
dried leaves as I bow and pass smiling.

QUEEN ANNE'S LACE

Her body is not so white as
anemone petals nor so smooth—nor
so remote a thing. It is a field
of the wild carrot taking
the field by force; the grass
does not raise above it.
Here is on question of whiteness,
white as can be, with a purple mole[4]
at the center of each flower.
Each flower is a hand's span
of her whiteness. Wherever
his hand has lain there is
a tiny purple blemish.
Each part is a blossom under his touch
to which the fibers of her being
stem one by one, each to its end,
until the whole field is a
white desire, empty, a single stem,
a cluster, flower by flower,
a pious wish to whiteness gone over—
or nothing.

THE RED WHEELBARROW

So much depends
upon

a red wheel

barrow
glazed with rain
water

beside the white
chickens.

THIS IS JUST TO SAY

I have eaten
the plums
that were in
the icebox

and which
you were probably
saving
for breakfast

Forgive me
they were delicious
so sweet
and so cold

Notes:

1. Jena Antoine Watteau (1684—1721), French Painter celebrated for romantic, idealized outdoor scenes. See Fragonard, below.
2. Jean Honore Fragonard (1732—1806), French court painter of scenes of love and gallantry. His familiar painting, "The Swing," with a girl who has just kicked her shoe in air, is suggestive. Ascribing this gay jest to Watteau may have been intentional, since Fragonard did paint scenes regarded as salacious.
3. Cf. the persistent biblical concept of God as immortal Light, and the identification of Christ with the Light in the Gospels, especially John Ⅰ: 1-9

and iii:19.

4. A single purple blossom in the center of the flower queen Anne's lace, or wild carrot. Actually, the "flower" is an umbel composed of a multitude of tiny blossoms, all white except this one, and all joined downward to the top of the main stalk by an intricate system of tiny stems.

Questions for Discussion:

1. The short poem "The Red Wheelbarrow" describes a simple scene. What images does the poet use?
2. Note the structure of the poem. What effect do you think the use of rhyme would have had?

E. E. Cummings (1894—1962)

Cummings was born in Cambridge, Massachusetts, to liberal, indulgent parents who from early on encouraged him to develop his creative gifts. While at Harvard, where his father had taught before becoming a Unitarian minister, he delivered a daring commencement address on modernist artistic innovations, thus announcing the direction his own work would take. In 1917, after working briefly for a mail-order publishing company, the only regular employment in his career, Cummings volunteered to serve in the Norton-Harjes Ambulance group in France. Here he and a friend were imprisoned (on false grounds) for three months in a French detention camp. *The Enormous Room* (1922), his witty and absorbing account of the experience, was also the first of his literary attacks on authoritarianism. *Eimi* (1933), a later travel journal, focused with much less successful results on the collectivized Soviet Union.

At the end of the First World War Cummings went to Paris to study art. On his return to New York in 1924 he found himself a celebrity, both for *The Enormous Room* and for *Tulips and Chimneys* (1923), his first collection of poetry (for which his old classmate John Dos Passos had finally found a publisher). Clearly influenced by Gertrude Stein's syntactical and Amy Lowell's imagistic experiments, Cummings's early poems had nevertheless discovered an original way of describing the chaotic immediacy of sensuous experience. The games they play with language (adverbs functioning as nouns, for instance) and lyric form combine with their deliberately simplistic view of the world (the individual and spontaneity versus collectivism and rational thought) to give them the gleeful and precocious tone, which became, a hallmark of his work. Love poems, satirical squibs, and descriptive nature poems would always be his favored forms.

In later life Cummings divided his time between their apartment in New York and his family's farm in New Hampshire. His many later books of poetry, from *VV* (1931) and *No Thanks* (1935) to *Xaipe* (1950) and *95 Poems* (1958), took his formal experiments and his war on the scientific attitude to new extremes, but showed little substantial development.

3. *Confessional Poets*

Confessional poetry is a term used in 1967 by M. L. Rosenthal to describe an influential tread apparent since the 1950s. In confessional writing the poet's personal experience is accorded particular prominence and the conventional gap between poet and poetic persona seems to have been extinguished. The poetry of Robert Lowell, John Berryman, Anne Sexton, Sylvia Plath, and to a lesser degree, of Theodore Roethke, Randall Jarrell, and Allen Ginsberg, has been called confessional, and the books *Heart's Needle* (1959) by W. D. Snodgrass and Lowell's *Life Studies* (1959) are often taken as initiating the style.

Although confessional poetry varies considerably, there are shared aspects. The poets termed confessional were among the first to undergo psychoanalysis and to incorporate it into poetry; for instance, by exploring childhood experience as the source of adult difficulties. Accordingly, "confessional" is sometimes used to describe the representation of extreme, personal, possibly painful, experience, for therapeutic or cathartic effect. However, confessional poetry is not merely private. Much confessional poetry actually demonstrates an engagement with public, social and political concerns, and explores how these impinge on the individual.

Robert Lowell (1917—1977)

Among the most acclaimed and influential 20th century poets, Robert Lowell was born into one of Boston's oldest and most prominent families. He attended Harvard College for two years before transferring to Kenyon College, where he studied poetry under John Crowe Ransom and received an undergraduate degree in 1940. He took graduate courses at Louisiana State University where he studied with Robert Penn Warren and Cleanth Brooks. His first and second books, *Land of Unlikeness* (1944) and *Lord Weary's Castle* (for which he received a Pulitzer Prize in 1946, at the age of thirty), were influenced by his conversion from Episcopalianism to Catholicism and explored the dark side of America's Puritan legacy. Under the influence of Allen Tate and the New Critics, he wrote rigorously formal poetry that drew praise for its exceptionally powerful handling of meter and rhyme. Lowell was politically involved—he became a conscientious objector during the Second World War and was imprisoned as a result, and actively protested against the war in Vietnam—and his personal life was full of marital and psychological turmoil. He suffered from severe episodes of manic depression, for which he was repeatedly hospitalized.

Partly in response to his frequent breakdowns, and partly due to the influence of such younger poets as W. D. Snodgrass and Allen Ginsberg, Lowell in the mid-fifties began to write more directly from personal experience, and loosened his adherence to traditional meter and form. The result was a watershed collection, *Life Studies* (1959), which forever changed the landscape of modern poetry, much as Eliot's *The Waste Land* had three decades before. Considered by many to be the most important poet in English of the second half of the twentieth century, Lowell continued to develop his work with sometimes uneven results, all along defining the restless center of American poetry, until his sudden death from a heart attack at the age of sixty. Robert Lowell served as a Chancellor of The Academy of American Poets from 1962 until his death in 1977.

Life Studies comprises four interrelated parts. The first is mainly devoted to historical figures; the second "91 Revere Street", is a prose memoir of Lowell's childhood; the third section comprises four poems on writers, and the final part, "Life Studies", contains a sequence of poems on Lowell's own life. The book is broadly sequential, with recurring images, and there is a notable shift from dramatic monologue by assumed personae towards the poet speaking in his own voice and exploring personal, familial and public crisis. It was this aspect of *Life Studies* that accounted for its impact and led to its being considered a key work of Confessional Poetry. Lowell explores various aspects of loss and breakdown in cultural, historical and individual terms, and examines how far these may result in the generation of significant energies. The book is also elegiac to a large extent, and includes powerful poems on the deaths of Lowell's parents. Stylistically, Lowell moved away from the allusive, dense texture of his earlier poetry to a more informal, apparently freer style.

Sylvia Plath (1932—1963)

Sylvia Plath was born in Boston in 1932. She grew up in a comfortably middle-class style and attended Smith College. She suffered a breakdown at the end of her junior year of college, but recovered well enough to return and excel during her senior year, receiving various prizes and graduating *summa cum laude*. In 1955, having been awarded a Fulbright scholarship, she began two years at Cambridge University. There she met and married the British poet Ted Hughes and settled in England, bearing two children. Her first book of poems, *The Colossus* (1960), demonstrated her precocious talent, but was far more conventional than the work that followed. Having studied with Robert Lowell in

1959 and been influenced by the "confessional" style of his collection Life Studies, she embarked on the new work that made her posthumous reputation as a major poet. A terrifying record of her encroaching mental illness, the poems that were collected after her suicide (at age 30) in 1963 in the volumes *Ariel*, *Crossing the Water*, and *Winter Trees* are graphically macabre, hallucinatory in their imagery, but full of ironic wit, technical brilliance, and tremendous emotional power. Her *Selected Poems* were published by Ted Hughes in 1985. Plath's best-known poems are noted for their personal imagery and intense focus. Her posthumous *Ariel* (1965) astonished the literary world with its power, and has become one of the best-selling volumes of poetry published in England and America in the 20th century.

Ariel includes forty poems. It explores a nightmarish world of menace, horror and repression in which an individual self, closely aligned with Plath herself, struggles to maintain integrity and resist the temptation to surrender to the forces that threaten to shape or destroy it. The book's tone varies between angry resentment, resignation, grim comedy, affection and hope for the future. The poems are highly sophisticated in formal terms and imaginatively connected through recurrent imagery and through references to Shakespeare's Ariel from *The Tempest*. Although deeply personal at times, the collection has a significant public dimension, reflecting Plath's concern with public matters such as the aftermath of World War Ⅱ and the proliferation of nuclear weapons.

4. *Beat Poets*

Beat movement was a literary group, also known as the Beats or the Beat generation, that flourished from the mid-1950s until the early 1960s. Its most prominent members were the novelists John Clellon Holmes (1926—1988) and Jack Kerouac (1922—1969), and the poets Allen Ginsberg, Lawrence Ferlinghetti (b. 1919), Philip Whalen (b. 1923), Gary Snyder (B. 1930) and Gregory Corso (1930—2001). The group was mainly located in San Francisco and in Green Village, New York City. Much Beat poetry was published by Ferlinghetti's "City Lights" imprint, and his "City Lights" bookstore in San Francisco was an important meeting-place for the group. Gregory Stephenson has suggested that the beat movement had two distinct phases: the underground, from 1944 to 1956, and the public, 1956 to 1962.

Holmes introduced the term "Beat generation" in a 1952 essay on his novel *Go* (1952), and later Kerouac suggested that "Beat" meant being socially marginalized and exhausted and blessed. There are also musical connotations to the name as many members were jazz enthusiasts. Socially the Beats, many of whom were homosexual or bisexual, extolled individual freedom and attacked what they saw as the materialism, militarism, consumerism and conformity of the 1950s. America was a place "where everyone is always doing what they ought," as Kerouac put it in one of Beat's defining works, the novel *On the Road* (1957). To this end they affected non-conformist styles of dress and speech and, avowedly anti-materialist, they cultivated mystical experiences by the use of drugs or by meditation—many members developed an interest in forms of mysticism and Zen Buddhism. The Beats were politically radical, and to some degree their anti-authoritarian attitudes were taken up by activists in the 1960s. In their writing they encouraged direct and frank communication and, rejecting the formalist, impersonal writing encouraged by the New Criticism, they cultivated styles that gave the impression of spontaneity and improvisation. Much of Beat poetry was performance orientated (often read in public with jazz accompaniment). The Beats brought fresh energies to American writing and their influence has been significant.

Allen Ginsberg (1926—1997)

Ginsberg was born into a Jewish family in Newark, New Jersey. He attended the University of Columbia, where he met William Burroughs and Jack Kerouac. After his graduation, he worked at a variety of jobs before moving to San Francisco, where he became a leading member of the Beats. In 1956 he published his first book, *Howl and Other Poems*. Although its critical reception was mixed, the book, and especially the title poem "Howl", proved influential in the development of American poetry. No subsequent book by Ginsberg had the same impact. The title poem of *Kaddish and Other Poems* (1961) is a moving elegy for his mother, who had experienced periods of madness. From the 1960s onwards Ginsberg became a celebrity who traveled widely and spoke eloquently for many social causes.

Ginsberg absorbed a wide range of influences, notably William Blake, What Whitman and William Carlos Williams, and his poetry reflects his often troubled engagement with the contemporary political and social situation. Using often-robust vocabulary, his poems can shift impressively between outrage, comic self-regard, apocalyptic prophecy, satire and tenderness. Ginsberg tended to use speech-based free verse in long lines, but as he became increasingly interested in creative fusions of poetry and music, he considered the poem as a public utterance requiring performance. His writing is highly innovative and yet also self-consciously traditional, resorting a bardic, prophetic voice to poetry. Overall, his work is driven by his personal and social concerns, such as his intense sympathy for the marginalized, his disgust with materialism and with the spiritual vacancy that he considered characteristic of post-war consumerist America, his homoeroticism and his varied interests, such as Buddhism. Consistent with the bardic tradition, his ambition was for poetry that would raise political consciousness and effect social change.

"Howl", the key work of the beat Movement, was first published by the City Lights Press of San Francisco in 1956. Its frank language caused its publisher, the poet Lawrence Ferlinghetti to be tried for obscenity. "Howl", in its final text (1986) comprises three sections and an epigraphic "Footnote." Dedicated to a mentally troubled friend, Carl Solomon, the poem asserts that his condition is a result of the intolerant repressive age. The poem ranges widely in tone and subject, angrily condemning the materialism and aggression of Cold War American, expressing an apocalyptic view of the future, both lamenting and affirming homosexual alienation, and declaring profound affection for Solomon and others. Much of the poem's success derives from

Ginsberg's choice of an incantatory form that flexibly accommodates shifting moods and subjects.

Chapter Ⅲ Modern Novelists

1. Midwest Novelists

As urbanization and industrialization invaded the American scene at the turn of the 20th century, some writers discarded the big cities and turned to the slumbering Midwestern small towns. One famous example of this Midwest revisited was *Spoon River Anthology* (1951). Edgar Lee Masters' work was a collection of over two hundred poems, each one composed by one of the Spoon River peoples buried in the cemetery of this small Ohio town and posthumously confessing their frustrations, regrets and stunted dreams. The small-town myth thus gave way to a grim reality of mediocrity and unfulfillment, laying bare the spiritual poverty, cultural void and starved emotional life of the heart of America. What had been portrayed, throughout the 19th century, as the pastoral ideal of the small prairie village and town was now the focus of a critical gaze, mingled with a pervasive nostalgia. Sherwood Anderson and Sinclair Lewis, both sons of the Midwest, had an account to square with the intolerance, repression and sterility epitomized in the Main Street of the American Midlands. "I'm sick to death of this romanticizing of the small town," was Sinclair Lewis' state of mind when he depicted Gopher Prairie in

Main Street; as for Sherwood Anderson, he rendered the pathos of his *Wineburg, Ohio* with all the necessary crudity and ugliness. Despair and hope, distress and humor remained characteristically blended in their ambivalent portrayal of the small American town.

Sherwood Anderson (1876—1914)

Anderson's works looked back to the 19th century United States: his description of the American Midwestern small town on the last frontier of the old pre-factory world read like ambivalent tales of nostalgia, sorrow and pity. Yet the bold experimental style of his fiction influenced 20th century writers in search of new forms and structures.

Anderson, a son of Camden and of Clyde, Ohio, expressed ambivalent feelings about the various Ohio towns where he was brought up and which provided his fiction with a stage. Anderson sought to return to a bygone world that had preceded technology, industry, and urban growth. *Poor White* (1920) portrayed Bidwell, a farming town, and its moral destruction by the encroachment of industrialization at the end of the 19th century. However, disillusion with the world of machines and factories did not bring Anderson back to the cocoon of the rural small town. There too he found frustration and repression. In his best novels, *Windy McPherson's Son* (1916), *Dark Daughter* (1925), and above all, *Winesburg, Ohio* (1919), he attacked the smugness, commercialism, narrow respectability, lack of communication and of love, which, in his eyes, marked Midwestern life.

Hence his interest in maladjusted characters, the victims of violent emotional lesions, crippled by the sterile, dull, stifling society of their time. He analyzed, even psychoanalyzed them with intense pity and sympathy. "If there is anything you do not understand in human life, consult the works of Dr. Freud," he used to say, and indeed, he worked with the subconscious of men and women, probing what went on beneath the surface of everyday life in the America he knew best.

Winesberg, Ohio is a set of connected stories and sketches dealing with the lives of the inhabitants of a fictional Ohio town named Winesberg. In spite of his mosaic-like structure, the novel in unified 1) by its setting (the first edition of the book even contained a map of the small town with the Main Street and the dwellings of the inhabitants); 2) by the central figure and Anderson's alter ego, young George Willard, a reporter on the *Winesberg Eagle*. He is the only character able to communicate with the men and women of the town, and thus able to observe them, comment upon them, and eventually help them. He is the only one to leave Winesberg in the final story, "Departure"; 3) by the concept of the "grotesque" introduced in the first sketch and illustrated by the book's stories. The "grotesques" are the inhabitants of Winesburg, locked into their individual cells and obsessions, wounded by previous traumatic experiences, tottering on the edge of madness because of their inability to communicate. Some of them know short-lived epiphanies, which finally end up in failure, isolation and despair. The book's grim atmosphere is counterbalanced by George Willard's vitality and youth. After all, for George as well for Anderson, the streets of Winesberg, in spite of "their emotional aridity and twisted souls," formed the "background on which to paint the dreams of [their] manhood."

Sinclair Lewis (1885—1951)

① *Biographical Introduction*

Sinclair Lewis was the first American writer to win the Nobel Prize for literature. Born into a middle-class family in Sauk Center, Minnesota, Lewis is well known for his novels which lampooned the American Middle class and satirized bourgeois life in the villages and towns of the Middle West. He began writing when still in college. After graduation from Yale, he knocked about for a number of years, trying to write novels and get them published. From 1912 to 1919 he was able to publish five novels, but it was not until 1920 when his sixth book, *Main Street* (1920), came out that he became a famous man. For the next ten years, he published a series of successful novels, *Babbitt* (1922), *Arrowsmith* (1928), *Elmer Gantry* (1927), and *Dodsworth* (1929), which gained Lewis an international reputation. Thereafter, Lewis continued to write novels, but none of them was successful.

② *His Theme and View*

Against the popular belief of his time that village life was good and city life was sinful, Sinclair Lewis showed the villagers to be narrow-minded, greedy, pretentious and corrupt. He attacked a cherished American idol when he caricatured middle class businessmen, and made them appear coarse, boasting, self-satisfied and ridiculous. He attacked the middle class from every point of view above all for its indifference to art and culture and its immune to criticism. But Lewis also hoped to give positive affirmation of the American values. He wanted to glorify free thought and independence, which he believed had been lost in an age of rising industrialism and wealth.

③ *His Style*

Lewis had an acute power to mimic American speech and a great talent for satiric caricature. His most famous character, George F. Babbitt, becomes an international symbol for the vulgar and philistine business man, and the word "Babbitry" entered the language as a term to describe energetic shallowness and self-satisfaction. Lewis packed his novels with authentic details: descriptions of the clothing, houses, offices, and the booster-club banalities of mid-die-class America. His literary reputation primarily rests today on his sardonic portrayal of his nation's grasping materialism and his mockery of a generation of American buffoons.

④ *His Major Works*

Main Street is the story of Carol Kennicott, a talented girl with a veneer of culture, about which she speaks much and understands little. Carol, as the wife of Dr. Will Kennicott, a beloved physician, tries fruitlessly to reform the town. It was Carol's misfortune that with her slender trimmings of culture she could not reach the crude, rough, honest people who had a deep need for new values. The book is a scathing picture of the dullness, hypocrisy, prejudice and oppression of life in a Middle Western village.

Babbitt is Lewis' best book and is certainly his funniest. It describes a typical businessman in a typical Middle Western small city. Babbitt, the hero, tries briefly to escape from the conformity and smugness of middle class life in order to express his own individuality. But his efforts fail

Arrowsrnith describes the frustrations of altruistic doctor who meets corruption, jealousy, prejudice and meanness from his colleagues, and who struggles to resist the temptations of a fashionable and profitable practice in order to pursue a scientific career.

Elmer Gantry is a cutting satire on the hypocrisy of bigoted religious leaders who prey upon the ignorance of the people to make themselves rich.

Dodsworth is the story of Sam Dodsworth, an automobile magnate of Zenith, self-made millionaire, whose simple devotion to the old fashioned virtues leaves him bewildered but untouched by his trip to Europe.

BABBITT

Chapter 1

The towers of Zenith aspired above the morning mist; austere towers of steel and cement and limestone, sturdy as cliffs and delicate as silver rods. They were neither citadels nor churches, but frankly and beautifully officebuildings,

The mist took pity on the fretted structures of earlier generations: the post office with its shingletortured mansard, the red brick minarets hulking old houses, factories with stingy and sooted windows, wooden tenements colored like mud. The city was full of such grotesqueries, but the clean towers were thrusting them from the business center, and on the farther hills were shining new houses, homes—they seemed—for laughter and tranquility.

Over a concrete bridge fled a limousine of long sleek hood and noiseless engine. These people in evening clothes were returning from an all-night rehearsal of a Little Theater[1] play, an artistic adventure considerably illuminated by champagne. Below the bridge curved a railroad, a maze of green and crimson lights. The New York Flyer[2] boomed past, and twenty lines of polished steel leaped into the glare.

In one of the skyscrapers the wires of the Associated Press[3] were closing down. The telegraph operators wearily raised their celluloid eye-shades after a night of talking with Paris and Peking. Through the building crawled the scrubwomen, yawning, their old shoes slapping. The dawn mist spun away. (Queues) cues of men with lunch-boxes clumped toward the immensity of new factories sheets of glass and hollow tile, glittering shops where five thousand men worked beneath one roof, pouring out the honest wares that would be sold up the Euphrates and across the veldt. The whistles rolled out in greeting a chorus cheerful as the April dawn; the song of labor in a city built—it seemed—for giants.

Chatper 2

There was nothing of the giant the aspect of the man who was beginning to awaken on the sleeping-porch of a Dutch Colonial house in that residential district of Zenith known as Floral Heights.

His name was George F. Babbitt. He was forty-six years old now, in April, 1920, and he made nothing in particular, neither butter nor shoes nor poetry, but he was nimble in the calling of selling house for more than people could afford to pay.

His large head was pink, his brown hair thin and dry. His face was babyish in slumber, despite his wrinkles and the red spectacle-dents on the slops of his nose. He was not fat but he was exceedingly well fed; his checks were pads, and the unroughened hand which lay helpless upon the khaki-colored blanket was slightly puffy. He seemed prosperous, extremely married and unromantic; and altogether unromantic appeared this sleeping-perch, which looked on one sizable elm, two respectable grass-plots, a cement driveway, and a corrugated iron garage. Yet Babbitt was again dreaming of the fairy child, a dream more romantic than scarlet pagodas by a silver sea.

For years the fairy child had come to him. Where others saw but George Babbitt, she discerned gallant youth. She waited for him, in the darkness beyond mysterious groves. When at last he could slip away from the crowded house he darted to her. His wife, his clamoring friends, sought to follow, but he escaped, the girl fleet beside him, and they crouched together on a shadowy hillside. She was so slim, so white, so eager! She cried that he was gay and valiant, that she would wait for him, that they would sail—

Rumble and bang of the milk-truck.

Babbitt moaned, turned over, struggled back toward his dream. He could see only her face now, beyond misty waters. The furnace-man slammed the basement door. A dog barked in the next yard. As Babbitt sank blissfully into a dim warm tide, the paper-carrier went by whistling, and the rolled-up Advocate thumped the front door. Babbitt roused, his stomach constricted with alarm. As he relaxed, he was pierced by the familiar and irritating rattle of some one cranking a Ford: snap-ah-ah, snap-ah-ah.

Himself a pious motorist, Babbitt cranked with the unseen

driver, with him waited through taut hours for the roar of the staring engine, with him agonized as the roar ceased and again he began the infernal patient snap-ah-ah a round, flat sound, a shivering cold-morning sound, a sound infuriating and inescapable. Not till the rising voice of the motor told him that the Ford was moving was he released from the panting tension. He glanced once at his favorite tree, elm twigs against the gold patina of sky, and fumbled for sleep as for a drug. He who had been a boy very credulous of life was no longer greatly interested in the possible and improbable adventures of each new day.

He escaped from reality till the alarm-clock rang, at seven-twenty.

Chatper 3

It was the best of nationally advertised and quantitatively produced alarm-clocks, with all modern attachments, including cathedral chime, intermittent alarm, and a phosphorescent dial. Babbitt was proud of being awakened by such a rich device. Socially it was almost as creditable as buying expensive cord tires.

He sulkily admitted now that there was no more escape, but he lay and detested the grind of the real-estate business, and disliked his family, and disliked himself for disliking them. The evening before, he had played poker at Vergil Gunch's till mid-night, and after such holidays he was irritable before breakfast. It may have been the tremendous home-brewed beer of the prohibition-era[4] and the cigars to which that beer enticed him; it may have been resentment of return from this fine, bold man-world to a restricted region of wives and stenographers, and of suggestions not to smoke so much.

From the bedroom beside the sleeping-porch, his wife's detestably cheerful "Time to get up, George boy," and the itchy sound, the brisk and scratchy sound, of combing hairs out of a stiff brush.

He grunted; he dragged his thick legs in faded baby-blue pajamas, from under the khaki blanker; he sat on the edge of the cot, running his fingers through his wild hair, while his plump feet mechanically felt for his slippers. He looked regretfully at the blanket—forever a suggestion to him of freedom and heroism. He had bought it for a camping trip which had never come off. It symbolized gorgeous loafing, gorgeous cursing, virile flannel shirts.

He creaked to his feet, groaning at the waves of pain which passed behind his eyeballs. Though he waited for their scorching recurrence, he looked blurrily out at the yard. It delighted him, as always; it was the neat yard of a successful business man of Zenith, that is, it was perfection, and made him also perfect. He regarded the corrugated iron garage. For the three-hundred-and-sixty-fifth time in a year he reflected. "No class to that tin shack. Have to build me a frame garage. But by golly it's only thing on the place that isn't up-to-date!" While he stared he thought of a community garage for his acreage development, Glen Oriole. He stopped puffing and jiggling. His arms were akimbo. His petulant, sleep-swellen face was set in harder lines. He suddenly seemed capable, an official, a man to contrive, to direct, to get things done.

On the vigor of his idea he was carried down the hard, clean, unused-looking hall into the bathroom.

Though the house was not large it had, like all houses on Floral Heights, an altogether royal bathroom of porcelain and glazed tile and metal sleek as silver. The towel-rack was a rod of clear glass set in nickel. The tub was long enough for a Prussian Guard, and above the set bowl was a sensational exhibit of tooth-brush holder, shaving-brush holder, soap-dish, sponge-dish, and medicine-cabinet, so glittering and so ingenious that they resembled an electrical instrument-board. But the Babbitt whose god was Modern Appliances was not pleased. The air of the bathroom was thick with the smell of a heathen toothpaste. “Verona been at it again! ‘Stead of sticking to Lilidol[5] like I've repeatedly asked her, she's gone and gotten some confounded stinkum[6] stuff that makes you sick!”

The bath-mat was wrinkled and the floor was wet. (His daughter Verona eccentrically took baths in the morning, now and then). He slipped on the mat, and slid against the tub. He said “Damn!” Furiously he snatched up his tube of shaving-cream, furiously he lathered, with a belligerent slapping of the unctuous brush, furiously he raked his plump checks with a safety-razor. It pulled. The blade was dull. He said, “Damn-oh-oh damn it!”

He hunted through the medicine-cabinet for a packet of new razor-blades (reflecting, as invariable, “Be cheaper to buy one of these dinguses[7] and strop your own blades,”) and when he discovered the packet, behind the round box of bicarbonate of soda, he thought ill of his wife for putting it there and very well of himself for not saying “Damn.” But he did say it, immediately afterward, when with wet and soap-slippery fingers he tried to remove the horrible little envelope and crisp clinging oiled paper from the new blade.

Then there was the problem, oft-pondered, never solved, of what to do with the old blade, which might imperil the fingers of his young. As usual, he tossed it on top of the medicine-cabinet, with a mental note that some day he must remove the fifty or sixty other blades that were also temporarily, piled up there. He finished his shaving in a growing testiness increased by his spinning headache and by the emptiness in his stomach. When he was done, his round face smooth and steamy and his eyes stinging from soapy water, he reached for a towel. The family towels were wet, wet and clammy and vile, all of them wet, he found, as he blindly snatched them—his own face-towel, his wife's, Verona's, Ted's, Tinka's, and the lone bath-towel with the huge welt of initial. Then George F. Babbitt did a dismaying thing. He wiped his face on the guest-towel! It was a pansy embroidered trifle which always hung there to indicate that the Babbitts were in the best Floral Heights society. No one had ever used it. No guest had ever dared to. Guests secretively took a corner of the nearest regular towel.

He was raging, "By golly, here they go and use up all the towels, every doggoneone of,'em, and they use 'em and get 'em all wet and sopping, and never put out a dry one for me—of course, I'm the goat! —and then I want one and—I'm the only person in the doggone house that's got the slightest doggone bit of consideration for other people and thoughtfulness and consider there may be others that want to use the doggone[8] bathroom after me and consider."

He was pitching the chill abominations into the bathtub, pleased by the vindictiveness of that desolate flapping sound; and in the midst his wife serenely trotted in, observed serenely, "Why Georgie dear, what are you doing? Are you going to wash out the towels? Why, you needn't wash out the towels. Oh, Georgie, you didn't go and use the guest towel, did you?"

It is not recorded that he was able to answer.

For the first time in weeks he was sufficiently roused by his wife to look at her.

Notes:

1. Little Theater: theater especially for amateurs.
2. New York Flyer: name of a famous express train.
3. Associated Press: American news agency which gathers and distributes news.
4. prohibition-era: the years from 1920 to 1933, when the 18th Amendment to the U. S. Constitution forbade the manufacture, sale, import and ex-

port of alcoholic drinks. During this time many people made beer, wine, and stronger drinks illegally in their homes. The 21st Amendment ended the Prohibition period.

5. Lilidol: brand name, invented by Lewis, for a variety of toothpaste.
6. stinkum: slang word, formed from "stink" (to emit a strong offensive odor) and the suffix "-um" (used here in place of "-ing").
7. dingus: a thing whose proper name is unknown or momentarily forgotten.
8. doggone: slang word expressing mild frustration or irritation; euphemism for dammed.

Question for Consideration:

Lewis's works are notable for his descriptions of authentic details. Now does this technique of his contribute to his criticism of the smug American philistinism here?

2. Novelists of Lost Generation

Lost Generation is a term used to describe the generation of writers active immediately after World War Ⅰ. Gertrude Stein used the phrase in conversation with Ernest Hemingway, saying "You are a lost generation." The phrase signifies a disillusioned post-war generation characterized by lost values, lost beliefs in the idea of human progress, and a mood of futility and despair leading to hedonism. The mood is described by F. Scott Fitzgerald in *This Side of Paradise* (1920) when he writes of a generation that found all Gods dead, all wars fought, all faiths in man shaken. Lost Generation usually refers specifically to the American expatriate writers associated with 1920s Paris, especially Hemingway and Fitzgerald, and to a lesser extent T. S. Eliot and

Ezra Pound. Hemingway used the phrase "You are a lost generation" as the epigraph to his first novel *The Sun Also Rises* (1926).

Ernest Hemingway (1899—1961)

① *Biographical Introduction*

Born in Oak Park, Illinois in 1899, Hemingway trained as a reporter in Kansas City. Thereafter he began to lead the sort of active and adventurous life that is so often the subject of his fiction. During the First World War he served in France and Italy, suffering serious injuries. In 1922 he returned to Europe as a journalist and mixed in the literary circle in Paris led by Gertrude Stein. This society formed the background of his first major novel *The Sun Also Rises*, published in 1926. For his next important work, *A Farewell to Arms* (1929), he turned to his war experiences in Italy. During this period he also wrote a number of short stories. In 1937 he took part in the Spanish Civil War. This provided material for one of his best novels, *For Whom the Bell Tolls* (1940). The decade following this novel was one of silence. Then in 1952 his last successful work of fiction, *The Old Man and the Sea* appeared. In 1954 Hemingway was awarded the Nobel Prize. He committed suicide in 1961.

② *His Theme and View*

Hemingway's point of view was shaped by his experience as a young man in the First World War, and his near death on the battle field. Many of his stories dealt with war or injury, and nearly all of them examined the nature of courage. His exploration of courage took many forms. He wrote about courage as "an instinctive movement toward or away from the center of violence, with self-preservation and self-respect, the mixed motives." He denied the romantic idea that courage was a noble emotion which could govern a man's action or prepare him to perform a brave act. He also wrote about the courage with which men face the tragedies of life that can never be remedied. His typical hero is one who, wounded but strong, enjoys the pleasures of life (sex, alcohol, sport) in face of ruin and death and maintains, through some notion of a code, an ideal of himself. His short story "In Another Country" deals with the courage of an old soldier who must face permanent injury and the death of his young wife.

③ *His Literary Style*

Under the influence of Mark Twain and with the help of Gertrude Stein, and Ezra Pound, Hemingway developed a new colloquial style characterized by directness, freshness, simplicity, and apparent naturalness. Hemingway always managed to choose words concrete, specific, common, casual and conversational, and employ them often in a syntax of short, simple sentence, which are orderly and patterned, conversational, and sometimes ungrammatical. But his style is deliberate and polished and never natural as it seems to be, and its simplicity can be disastrously deceptive, as it is highly suggestive and connotative and capable of offering layers of under-currents of meaning.

④ *His Major Works*

The Sun Also Rises is about the disillusionment of the "lost generation"—young British and American expatriates in France and Spain—in the aftermath of World War Ⅰ. There is Lady Brett Ashley, who is waiting for her divorce to marry Michael Campbell; Jake Barnes, American correspondent, emasculated by a war injury, whom Brett loves but will not marry because she needs the physical relationship of marriage; Robert Cohn, American novelist and Frances Clyne, his mistress whom he no longer loves; and Pedro Romero, the bullfighter with whom Brett has a brief affair. These oddly assorted people, restless, dissolute, corrupt, are held together by their love for bullfighting, which appeals to them because they have lived so long with violence and because to them the ritual and precision of the sport is beauty. With economy of phrase Hemingway relates the obvious frustrations and the bitter, subtle pain of these representatives of the Lost Generation.

A Farewell to Arms tells of the love of Frederic Henry, American lieutenant in the Italian Ambulance Service, and Catherine Barckley, English nurse, in the First World War. Love flowers during an idyllic period when Henry is hospitalized in Milan. He returns to the front in time for the fateful retreat from Caporetto. Caught in the horror, he loses all sense of responsibility to the army and escapes to Switzerland with Catherine, where they await the birth of their child. When Catherine and their baby die, Henry has nothing left but his own courage to rely on.

For Whom the Bell Tolls expresses Hemingway's growing conviction that man cannot withdraw from society, that he cannot make his separate peace. His thesis is embodied in the life and death of Robert Jordan, a volunteer American guerrilla in

Spain, who blows up a strategic bridge as part of an attack which he knows is doomed to failure. In the end, he is left to die, yet he does his best for his comrades-in-arms and for the cause which he believes in.

The Old Man and the Sea is a short simple novel that has been hailed as a classic. It tells about an old Cuban fisherman, Santiago, who struggles for three days for a great marlin found only in the deep where few men venture and who finally catches it only to see it devoured by sharks. Santiago's deep loneliness, his venture into the unknown, forbidden sea, and his struggle with the great marlin is the symbol of man's loneliness, pride, and struggle against nature. This book capped Hemingway's career, and led to his receipt of the Nobel Prize.

A FAREWELL TO ARMS

Chapter 36[1]

That night there was a storm and I woke to hear the rain lashing the window-panes. It was coming in the open window. Someone had knocked on the door. I went to the door very softly, not to disturb Catherine, and opened it. The barman stood there. He wore his overcoat and carried his wet hat.

"Can I speak to you, Tenente?"[2]

"What's the matter?"

"It's a very serious matter."

I looked around. The room was dark. I saw the water on the floor from the window. "Come in," I said. I took him by the arm into the bathroom; locked the door and put on the light. I sat down on the edge of the bathtub.

"What's the matter, Emilio? [3] Are you in trouble?"

"No, you are, Tenente."

"Yes ?"

"They are going to arrest you in the morning."

"Yes ?"

"I came to tell you. I was out in the town and I heard them talking in a cafe."

"I See."

He stood there, his coat wet, holding his wet hat and said nothing.

"Why are they going to arrest me?"

"For something about the war."

"Do you know what?"

"No, But I know that they know you were here before as an officer and now you are here out of uniform. After this retreat they arrest everybody."

I thought a minute.

"What time do they come to arrest me?"

"In the morning. I don't know the time."

"What do you say to do?"

He put his hat in the washbowl. It was very wet and had been dripping on the floor.

"If you have nothing to fear an arrest is nothing. But it is always bad to be arrested—specially now."

"I don't want to be arrested."

"Then go to Switzerland."

"How?"

"In my boat."

"There is a storm," I said.

"The storm is over. It is rough but you will be all right."

"When should we go?"

"Right away. They might come to arrest you early in the morning."

"What about our bags?"

"Get them packed. Get your lady dressed. I will take care of them."

"Where will you be?"

"I will wait here. I don't want any one to see me outside in the hall."

I opened the door, closed it, and went into the bedroom. Catherine was awake.

"What is it, darling?"

"It's all right, Cat," I said. "Would you like to get dressed right away and go in a boat to Switzerland?"

"Would you?"

"No," I said. "I'd like to go back to bed."

"What is it about?"

"The barman says they are going to arrest me in the morning."

"Is the barman crazy?"

"No."

"Then please hurry, darling, and get dressed so we can start." She sat up on the side of the bed. She was still sleepy. "Is that the barman in the bathroom?"

"Yes."

"Then I won't wash. Please look the other way, darling, and I'll be dressed in just a minute."

I saw her white back as she took off her nightgown and then I looked away because she wanted me to. She was beginning to be a little big with the child and she did not want me to see her. I dressed hearing the rain on the windows. I did not have much to put in my bag.

“There’s plenty of room in my bag, Cat, if you need any.”

“I’m almost packed,” she said. “Darling, I’m awfully stupid, but why is the barman in the bathroom?”

“She—he’s waiting to take our bags down.”

“He’s awfully nice.”

“He’s an old friend,” I said. “I nearly sent him some pipe-tobacco once.”

I looked out the open window at the dark night. I could not see the lake, only the dark and the rain but the wind was quieter.

“I’m ready, darling,” Catherine said.

“All right.” I went to the bathroom door. “Here are the bags, Emilio,” I said. The barman took the two bags.

“You’re very good to help us,” Catherine said.

“That’s nothing, lady,” the barman said. “I’m glad to help you just so I don’t get in trouble myself. Listen,” he said to me. “I’ll take these out the servants-stairs and to the boat. You just go out as though you were going for a walk.”

“it’s a lovely night for a walk,” Catherine said.

“It’s a bad night all right.”

“I’m glad I’ve an umbrella,” Catherine said.

We walked down the hall and down the wide thickly carpeted stairs. At the foot of the stairs by the door the porter sat behind his desk.

He looked surprised at seeing us.

“You’re not going out, sir?” he said.

“Yes,” I said. “We’re going to see the storm along the lake.”

“Haven’t you got an umbrella, sir?” “No,” I said. “This coat sheds water.”

He Looks at it doubtfully. “I’ll get you an umbrella, sir,” he said. He went away and came back with a big umbrella. “It is a little big, sir,” he said. I gave him a ten-lire note. “Oh you are too good, sir. Thank you very much,” he said. He held the door open and we went out into the rain. He smiled at Catherine and she smiled at him. "Don't stay out in the storm," he said. "You will get wet, sir and lady." He was only the second porter, and

his English was still literally translated.

"We'll be back," I said. We walked down the path under the giant umbrella and out through the dark wet gardens to the road and across the road to the trellised pathway along the lake. The wind was blowing offshore now. It was a cold, wet November wind and I knew it was snowing in the mountains. We came along past the chained boats in the slips along the quay to where the barman's boat should be. The water was dark against the stone. The barman stepped out from beside the row of trees.

"The bags are in the boat," he said.

"I want to pay you for the boat," I said.

"Now much money have you?"

"Not so much."

"You send me the money later. That will be all right."

"How much?"

"What you want."

"Tell me how much."

"If you get through send me five hundred francs. You won't mind that if you get through."

"All right."

"Here are sandwiches." He handed me a package. "Everything there was in the bar. It's all here. This is a bottle of brandy and a bottle of wine." I put them in my bag. "Let me pay you for those."

"All right, give me fifty lire."

I gave it to him. "The brandy is good," he said. "You don't need to be afraid to give it to your lady. She better get in the boat." He held the boat, it rising and falling against the stone wall and I helped Catherine in. She sat in the stern and pulled her cape around her.

"You know where to go?"

"Up the lake."

"You know how far?"

"Past Luino."

"Past Luino, Canner, Cannobio, Tranzano. You aren't in Switzerland until you come to Brissago. You have to pass Monter Tamara."

"What time is it?" Catherine asked.

"It's only eleven o'clock," I said.

"If you row all the time you ought to be there by seven o'clock in the morning."

"Is it that far?"

"It's thirty-five kilometers."

"How should we go? in this rain we need a compass."

"No. Row to Isola Belin. Then on the other side of Isola Madre go with the wind. The wind will take you to Pallanza. You will see the lights. Then go up the shore."

"Maybe the wind will change."

"No," he said. "This wind will blow like this for three days. It comes straight down from the Uattarone. There is a can to bail with."

"Let me pay you something for the boat now."

"No, I'd rather take a chance. If you get through you pay me all you can."

"All right."

"I don't think you'll get drowned."

"That's good."

"Go with the wind up the lake."

"All right." I stepped in the boat.

"Did you leave the money for the hotel?"

"Yes. In an envelope in the room,"

"All right, Good luck, Tenente,"

"Good luck. We thank you many times."

"You won't thank me if you get drowned."

"What does he say?" Catherine asked.

"He says good luck."

"Good luck," Catherine said. "Thank you very much."

"Are you ready?"

"Yes."

He bent down and shoved us off. I dug at the water with the oars, then waved one hand, The barman waved back deprecatingly. I saw the lights of the hotel and rowed out, rowing straight out until they were out of sight. There was quite a sea running but we were going with the wind.

Notes:

1. This chapter describes how the loves, through the help of friendly barman, flee to Switzerland by rowing a small boat up a border lake during the night.
2. Tenente: Lieutenant.
3. Emilio: Name of the barman.

Question for Consideration:

How do you like Hemingway's style? Can you find something subtle and suggestive beneath its simplicity?

F. Scott Fitzgerald (1896—1940)

① *Biographical Introduction*

Fitzgerald was the most representative novelist of the 1920s. He was both a leading participant in the typically frivolous, carefree, moneymaking life of the decade and, at the same time, a detached observer of it. Born in Saint Paul, Minnesota, Fitzgerald was the only son of a socially prominent and genteelly poor family. With the financial aid of relatives he entered Princeton University in 1913. In 1917 he left before graduating to serve in the U. S. Army in Alabama, where he became engaged to Zelda Sayre an embodiment of all his romantic notions of a southern Belle. After his discharge from the army in 1919, he took a job with an advertising agency and worked on short stories and a novel at night. Eventually his first novel, *This Side of Paradise* was accepted for publication and appeared in March 1920. It was an instant success and brought Fitzgerald fame and wealth. In the same year Fitzgerald and Zelda Sayre were married. The couple plunged into the gaudy, wealthy society of their generation. They lived so extravagantly that they frequently spent more money than Fitzgerald earned. In order to earn more money, Fitzgerald continued to write. In 1922 he published his second novel. *The Beautiful and Damned*, and a collection of short stories, *Tales of the Jazz Age*. In 1925, Fitzgerald managed to complete *The Great Gatsby*. It was a critical success but a commercial failure. His next novel, *Tender Is the Night* (1934) was received coldly mainly because America was deep in the Great Depression and nobody wanted to read about expatriates in France. Battered by the failure of the book and Zelda's mental breakdowns, he drank to excess and grew seriously ill. He died in 1940, with his last novel, *The Last Tycoon*, unfinished.

② *His Theme and View*

In his first books and stories, Fitzgerald saw life through "a haze of youth", where tragedy consisted only of growing older. He expressed what very young people believed in 1920: that they could wipe out the past and rebuilt the world into something much better, free from the ideas of the older generation. He wrote about himself and his friends. At first he presented the charm and glamour of the new generation, but within a few short years he turned from its spokesman into its most incisive judge. In his finest works, he revealed, as no other American writers had, the stridency of an age of glittering innocence, and portrayed the hollowness of the American worship of riches and the unending American dreams of love, splendor, and gratified desires.

③ *His Style*

Fitzgerald's style is closely related to his theme. It relies on an accumulation of well-chosen and ironic detail, carefully observed from life. He exactly reproduces the language and conversation of the time. In his chapters, he moves rapidly from one brightly presented scene to the next, leaving the tedious process of transition to the reader's imagination.

④ *His Major Works*

This Side of Paradise, like all of his other works, is autobiographical. In it he drew on his own experience, putting in actual episodes of his life or of others. Its hero, Amory Blaine, like Fitzgerald himself, goes to prep school and then to Princeton, where he becomes a member of the literary coterie. He serves in World War Ⅰ and then works in advertising. He has several romantic affairs, none of them lasting. His only unselfish love is

Rosalie, who marries another man because she believes she cannot be happy without money. *This Side of Paradise* developed out of disharmony of Fitzgerald's own nature. Romantic and moralistic, Fitzgerald wanted both to entertain and preach. What he succeeded in doing was to catch the spirit of part of a generation caught between two wars and give it life in the particular, glamorous characters.

The Beautiful and Damned is also in a sense autobiographical. Anthony and Gloria are Scott and Zelda. They pet, drink, and throw wild parties to show their freedom from hypocrisy. They claim wealth, romance, and thrills and achieve unhappiness. Anthony Patch is an alcoholic whose goal in life is to inherit and spend his grandfather's money. Though he is eventually successful in contesting the will that has disinherited him, by the end of the novel he and his wife Gloria have declined both physically and spiritually because of their dissolute, alcoholic lifestyle.

The Great Gatsby is another story of passion and wealth of Scott and Zelda, and is considered by many to be Fitzgerald's best novel. The young Mid-Westerner Jay Gatsby loves the beautiful Daisy, who has married Tom Buchanan, a brute of a man, for his wealth. In later years Gatsby, possessed of legendary wealth from his various criminal activities, including bootlegging, seeks out Daisy and Tom. Drawn by his wealth and his devotion, Daisy becomes his mistress. When as a hit-and-run driver she kills Myrtle, wife of a garage man and Tom's mistress, Gatsby tries to protect her. He is shot when Tom in a fit of jealousy betrays him falsely to Myrtle's husband. At his death, all of his so-called friends abandon him. The book is a severe criticism of the whole society.

Tender Is the Night is a novel about the squandering of creative promise. It is the story of Dick Diver, a young American psychiatrist, who marries Nieole Warren, a beautiful and wealthy patient. Dick sacrifices all his talent and energy to maintain an illusion of love with a wife who abandons him anyway. The book passes a harsh judgment on the false values of the 1920s.

THE GREAT GATSBY

Chapter 3

There was music from my neighbor's house through the summer nights. In his blue gardens men and girls came and went like moths among the whisperings and the champagne and the stars. At high tide in the afternoon I watched his guests diving from the tower of his raft, or taking the sun on the hot sand of his beach while his two motor-boats slit the waters of the Sound,[1] drawing aquaplanes over cataracts of foam. On week-ends his Rolls-Royce[2] became an omnibus, bearing parties to and from the city between nine in the morning and long past midnight, while his station wagon scampered like a brisk yellow bug to meet all trains. And on Mondays eight servants, including an extra gardener, toiled all day with mops and scrubbing-brushes and hammers and garden-shears, repairing the ravages of the night before.

Every Friday five crates of oranges and lemons arrived from a fruiter in New York—every Monday these same oranges and lemons left his back door in a pyramid of pulpless halves. There was a machine in the kitchen which could extract the juice of two hundred oranges in half an hour if a little button was pressed two hundred times by a butler's thumb.

At least once a fortnight a corps of caterers came down with several hundred feet of canvas an enough colored lights to make a Christmas tree of Gatsby's enormous garden. On buffet tables, garnished with glistening hors-d'soeuvre, spiced baked hams crowded against salads of harlequin designs and pastry pigs and turkeys bewitched to a dark gold. In the main hall a bar with a real brass rail was set up, and stocked with gins and liquors and with cordials so long forgotten that most of his female guests were too young to know one from another.

By seven o'clock the orchestra has arrived, no thin five piece affair, but a whole pitful of oboes and trombones and saxophones and viols and cornets and piccolos, and low and high drums. The last swimmers have come in from the beach now and are dressing upstairs; the cars from New York are parked five deep in the drive, and already the halls and salons and verandas are gaudy with primary colors, and hair shorn in strange new ways, and shawls beyond the dreams of Gastile. [3] The bar is in full swing, and floating rounds of cocktails permeate the garden outside, until the air is alive with chatter and laughter, and casual innuendo and introductions forgotten on the spot, and enthusiastic meetings between women who never knew each other's names.

The lights grow bright as the earth lurches away from the sun, and now the orchestra is playing yellow cocktail music, and the opera of voice pitches a key higher. Laughter is easier minute by minute, spilled with prodigality, tipped out at a cheerful word. The groups change more swiftly, swell with new arrivals, dissolve and form in the same breath; already there are wanderers, confident girls who weave here and there among the stouter and more stable, become for a sharp, joyous moment the center of a group, and then, excited with triumph, glide on through the sea-change of faces and voices and color under the constantly changing light.

Suddenly one of these gypsies, in trembling opal, seizes a

cocktail out of the air, dumps it down for courage and, moving her hands like Frisco,[4] dances out alone on the canvas platform. A momentary hush; the orchestra leader varies his rhythm obligingly for her, and there is a burst of chatter as the erroneous news goes around that she is Gilda Gray's understudy from the Follies.[5] The party has begun.

I believe that on the first night I went to Gatsby's house I was one of the few guests who had actually been invited. People were not invited—they went there. They got into automobiles which bore them out to Long Island, and somehow they ended up at Gatsby's door. Once there they were introduced by somebody who knew Gatsby, and after that they conducted themselves according to the rules of behavior associated with an amusement park. Sometimes they came and went without having met Gatsby at all, came for the party with a simplicity of heart that was its own ticket of admission.

I had been actually invited. A chauffeur in a uniform of robin's egg blue crossed my lawn early that Saturday morning with a surprisingly formal note from his employer, the honor would be entirely Gatsby's, it said, if I would attend his "little party" that night. He had seen me several times, and had intended to call on me long before, but a peculiar combination of circumstances had prevented it—signed Jay Gatsby, in a majestic hand.

Dressed up in white flannels[6] he went over to his lawn a little after seven, and wandered around rather ill at ease among swirls and eddies of people I didn't know—though here and there was a face I had noticed on the commuting train. I was immediately struck by the number of young Englishmen dotted about; all well dressed, all looking a little hungry, and all talking in low, earnest voices to solid and prosperous Americans. I was sure that they were selling something: bonds or insurance or automobiles. They were at least agonizingly aware of the easy money in the vicinity and convinced that it was theirs for a few words in the right key.

As soon as I arrived I made an attempt to find my host, but the two or three people of whom I asked his whereabouts stared at me in such an amazed way, and denied so vehemently any knowledge of his movements, that I slunk off in the direction of the cocktail table—the only place in the garden where a single man could linger without looking purposeless and alone.

I was on my way to get roaring drunk from sheer embarrassment when Jordan Baker came out of the house and stood at the head of the marble steps, leaning a little backward and looking with contemptuous interest down into the garden.

Welcome or not, I found it necessary to attach myself to some one before I should begin to address cordial remarks to the passers-by.

"Hello!" I roared, advancing toward her. My voice seemed unnaturally loud across the garden.

"I thought you might be here," she responded absently as I came up. "I remembered you lived next door to—"

She held my hand impersonally, as a promise that she'd take care of me in a minute, and gave ear to two girls in twin yellow dresses, who stopped at the foot of the steps.

"Hello!" they cried together. "Sorry you didn't win."

That was for the golf tournament. She had lost in the finals the week before.

"You don't know who we are," said one of the girls in yellow, "but we met you here about a month ago."

"You've dyed your hair since then," remarked Jordan, and I started, but the girls had moved casually on and her remark was addressed to the premature moon, produced like the supper, no doubt, out of a caterer's basket. With Jordan's slender golden arm resting in mine, we descended the steps and sauntered about the garden. A tray of cocktails floated at us through the twilight, and we sat down at a table with the two girls in yellow and three men, each one introduced to us as Mr. Mumble.

"Do you come to these parties often?" inquired Jordan of the girl beside her.

"The last one was the one I met you at," answered the girl, in an alert confident voice. She turned to her companion. "Wasn't it for you, Lucille?"

It was for Lucille, too.

"I like to come," Lucille said. "I never care what I do, so I always have a good time. When I was here last I tore my gown on a chair, and he asked me my name and address—inside of a week I got a package from Croirier's with a new evening gown in it."

"Did you keep it?" asked Jordan.

"Sure I did. I was going to wear it tonight, but it was too big in the bust and had to be altered. It was gas blue with lavender beads. Two hundred and sixty-five dollars."

"There's something funny about a fellow that do a thing like that," said the other girl eagerly. "He doesn't want any trouble with anybody."

"Who doesn't?" I inquired.

"Gatsby. Somebody told me—"

The two girls and Jordan leaned together confidentially.

"Somebody told me they thought he killed a man once."

A thrill passed over all of us. The three Mr. Mumbles bent forward and listened eagerly,

"I don't think it's so much that," argued Lucille skeptically; "it's more that he was a German spy during the war."

One of the men nodded in confirmation.

"I heard that from a man who knew all about him, grew up with him in Germany," he assured us positively,

"Oh, no," said the first girl, "it couldn't be that, because he was in the American army during the war." As our credulity switched back to her she leaned forward with enthusiasm. "You look at him sometimes when he thinks nobody's looking at him. I'll bet he killed a man."

She narrowed her eyes and shivered. Lucille shivered. We all turned and looked around for Gatsby. It was testimony to the romantic speculation he inspired that there were whispers about him from those who had found little that it was necessary to whisper about in this world.

The first supper-there would be another one after midnight—was now being served, and Jordan invited me to join her own party, who were spread around a table on the other side of the garden. There were three married couples and Jordan's escort, a persistent undergraduate given to violent innuendo, and obviously under the impression that sooner or later Jordan was going to yield him up her person to a greater or lesser degree. Instead of rambling, this party had preserved a dignified homogeneity, and assumed to itself the function of representing the staid nobility of the countryside—East Egg condescending to West Egg, and carefully on guard against its spectroscopic gayety.

"Let's get out," whispered Jordan, after a somehow wasteful and inappropriate half-hour; "this is much too polite for me."

We got up, and she explained that we were going to find the host: I had never seen him, she said, and it was making me uneasy. The undergraduate nodded in a cynical, melancholy way.

The bar, where we glanced first, was crowded, but Gatsby was not there. She couldn't find him from the top of the steps, and he wasn't on the veranda. On a chance we tried an important-looking door, and walked into a high Gothic[7] library, paneled with carved English oak, and probably transported complete from some ruin overseas.

A stout, middle-aged man, with enormous owl-eyed spectacles, was sitting somewhat drunk on the edge of a great table, staring with unsteady concentration at the shelves of books. As we entered he wheeled excitedly around and examined Jordan from head to foot.

"What do you think?" he demanded impetuously.

"About what?"

He waved his hand toward the book-shelves.

"About that. As a matter of fact you needn't bother to ascertain. I ascertained. They're real."

"The books?"

He nodded.

"Absolutely real—have pages and everything. I thought they'd be a nice durable cardboard. Matter of fact, they're absolutely real. Pages and—Here! Lemme show you."

Taking our skepticism for granted, he rushed to the bookcases and returned with Volume One of the"Stoddard Lectures."

"See!"He cried triumphantly. It's a bona-sidepiece of printed matter. It fooled me. This fella's a regular Belasco.[8] It's a triumph. "What thoroughness! What realism! Knew when to stop, too—didn't cut the pages. But what do you want? What do you expect?"

He snatched the book from me and replaced it hastily on its shelf, muttering that if one brick was removed the whole library was liable to collapse.

"Who brought you?" he demanded. "Or did you just come? I was brought. Most people were brought."

Jordan looked at him alertly, cheerfully, without answering.

"I was brought by a woman named Roosevelt, "he continued. "Mrs. Claude Roosevelt. Do you know her? I met her somewhere last night. I've been drunk for about a week now, and I thought it might sober me up to sit in a library."

"Has it?"

"A little bit, I think. I can't tell yet. I've only been here an hour. Did I tell you about the books? They're real. They're —"

"You told us."

We shook hands with him gravely and went back outdoors.

There was dancing now on the canvas in the garden; old men pushing young girls backward in eternal graceless circles, superior couples holding each other tortuously, fashionably, and keeping in the corners-and a great number of single girls dancing individualistically or relieving the orchestra for a moment of the burden of the banjo or the traps.[9] By midnight the hilarity had increased. A celebrated tenor had sung in Italian, and a notorious contralto had sung in jazz, and between the numbers people were doing "stunts" all over the garden, while happy, vacuous bursts of laughter rose toward the summer sky. A pair of stage twins, who turned out to be the girls in yellow, did a baby act in costume, and champagne was served in glasses bigger than finger-bowls. The moon had risen higher, and floating in the Sound was a triangle of silver scales, trembling a little to the stiff, tinny drip of the banjoes on the lawn.

I was still with Jordan Baker. We were sitting at a table with a man of about my age and a rowdy little girl, who gave way upon the slightest provocation to uncontrollable laughter. I was enjoying myself now. I had taken two fingerbowls of champagne, and the scene had changed before my eyes into something significant, elemental, and profound.

At a lull in the entertainment the man looked at me and smiled.

"Your face is familiar," he said, politely. "Weren't you in the Third Division during the war?"

"Why, yes. I was in the ninth machine-gun battalion."

"I was in the Seventh Infantry until June nineteen-eighteen. I know I'd seen you somewhat before."

We talked for a moment about some wet, gray little villages in France. Evidently he lived in this vicinity, for he told me that he had just bought a hydroplane, and was going to try it out in the morning.

"Want to go with me, old sport? Just near the shore along the Sound."

"What time?"

"Any time that suits you best."

It was on the tip of my tongue to ask his name when Jordan looked around and smiled.

"Having a gay time now?" she inquired.

"Much better. I turned again to my new acquaintance. "This is an unusual party for me. I haven't even seen the host. I live over there—I waved my hand at the invisible hedge in the distance, "and this man Gastby sent over his chauffeur with an invitation."

For a moment he looked at me as if he failed to understand.

"I'm Gatsby," he said suddenly.

"What!" I exclaimed. "Oh, I beg your pardon."

"I thought you knew, old sport. I'm afraid I'm not a very good host."

He smiled understandingly—much more than understandingly. It was one of those rare smiles with a quality of eternal reassurance in it, that you may come across four of five times in life. It faced—or seemed to face—the whole external world for an instant, and then concentrated on you with an irresistible prejudice in your favor. It understood you just as far as you wanted to be understood, believed in yourself, and assured you that it had precisely the impression of you that, at your best, you hoped to convey. Precisely at that point it vanished—and I was looking at an elegant young roughneck, a year or two over thirty, whose elaborate formality of speech just missed being absurd. Some time before he introduced himself I'd got a strong impression that he was picking his words with care.

Almost at the moment when Mr. Gatsby identified himself, a

butler hurried toward him with the information that Chicago was calling him on the wire. He excused himself with a small bow that included each of us in turn.

"If you want anything just ask for it, old sport," he urged me. "Excuse me. I will rejoin you later." ...

Notes:

1. the Sound: Long Island Sound, a narrow finger of the Atlantic Ocean between Long Island and the state of Connecticut on the mainland, just east of New York City.
2. Rolls-Royce: a very expensive and luxurious British automobile.
3. Gastile: a region of Spain, once an independent kingdom, renowned for its lace and embroidered shawls.
4. Frisco: short for San Francisco; here, a slang term meaning rapidly, vigorously.
5. the Follies: the Ziegfeld Follies, a musical theatrical revue produced by Florenz Ziegfeld, very popular in the 1920s. Gilda Gray was one of its famous stars.
6. white flannels: casual men's trousers of the 1920s made of wool flannel.
7. Gothic: a style of architecture which originated in France in the 12th century, characterized by great height in the buildings, pointed arches, rib vaulting and large window spaces.
8. Belasco: Davie Belasco (1853—1931), American theatrical producer, manager and writer, known for his minutely detailed. and spectacular stage settings.
9. traps: percussion instruments.

Questions for Consideration:

1. *The Great Gatsby* is regarded as Fitzgerald's summative comment on the Jazz Age: In what ways is this chapter related to

the Jazz Age?

2. Is Gatsby's life the fulfillment of the American dream of wealth?

3. Novelists of Depression

The most severe economic recession in history began in October 1929 with the Wall Street crash. The 1920s had been a boom and for some time before 1929 intense and uncontrolled speculation had driven up share prices to unprecedented and unrealistic levels. The 1929 crash resulted in a severe decline in industrial production and in mass unemployment. By 1933 almost half of the nation's banks had failed and up to 15 million people (almost 30 per cent of the workforce) were unemployed. Farmers, already under pressure, were especially badly hit and many lost their farms. Without any system of social security the unemployed relied on charity and soup kitchens to keep them from starvation. Many became homeless, or migrated to cities, often living on the outskirts in camps known as "Hoovervilles" in mocking reference to the then president. The programmes initiated after 1933 under President Roosevelt's New deal mitigated the Depression's effects, but it was not until later in the 1930s with the European demand for armaments during World War Ⅱ that the Depression began to end, and it was completely over by 1941 when the United States entered the war. During the Depression many writers were assisted by New Deal programmes such as the Federal Theatre Project and the Federal Writers' Project.

The Depression forms an important background to much

writing set in the 1930s by writers such as William Faulkner, John Dos Passos, Richard Wright and Nathanael West (1903—1940), and its effects were powerfully described in much contemporary writing, typically through the technique of social realism and often with a radical edge. Examples include the novels *Somebody in Boots* (1935) by Nelson Algren (1909—1981), *The Grapes of Wrath* (1939) by John Steinbeck , the Studs Lonigan trilogy of J. T . Farrell(1904—1979), and the plays and stories of Clifford Odets (1906—1963) and William Saroyan (1908—1981). During this period in which the failure of capitalism was evident, many writers and intellectuals became aligned with Marxism, and the Depression saw a fresh interest in depicting the American proletariat.

John Dos Passos (1896—1970)

The progressive period (1900—1917) had seen the rise of "political novels" in which social history and ideology served as a basis for the novelists' works. Yet it was with Dos Passos that "the bloody panorama of history" and influence on the lives of individuals and social groups irrupted into the novel as a dynamic force, motivating the narrative and destroying in its wake conventional structural elements. Dos Passos' novels were both sociological and aesthetic experiments which exerted a tremendous influence on young writers in the thirties, both in the United States and in Europe. Dos Passos' specific vision was molded by his early life: the First World War in which he served as an ambulance driver and a private in the medical corps, his investigations and observations as a foreign correspondent and journalist in the 1920s, his social idealism which made him sympathize with the common people and the victims of the "great readjustments of history." By 1930, he was involved in various left-wing activities, and wrote works that criticized capitalism while underlining the alienation and despair of individual destinies, destroyed by an urban, money and power-obsessed, fast-paced, violent society.

The desire to probe some of the sources of American frustration was already perceptible in his first two war-inspired novels, *One Man's Initiation* (1920) and *Three Soldiers* (1921). But it was essentially with the following works, *Manhattan Transfer* (1925) and especially his trilogy *USA* (1938), composed of *The 42nd Parallel* (1930), *1919* (1932), and *The Big Money* (1936); that Dos Passos reached the climax of his art. His later novels reflected the changes in his viewpoint as well as his growing conservatism and disillusion with the ideas of his youth, yet they never recaptured the power and originality of *USA*.

USA follows a large cast of characters—who appear and disappear, and many of whom never know each other—from the dawn of the twentieth century to the beginning of the great Depression. At its literal center are the First World War and the peace negotiations at Versailles—the setting of the middle volume, *1919*. But Dos Passos, drawing upon his own grim memories of the war and its aftermath, suggests that what this history is moving towards is the execution in 1927 of the two non-violent anarchists, Sacco and Vanzetti, after their conviction on the charge of murdering a paymaster in Bridge water country, Massachusetts. This execution, the climatic event in *The Big Mon-*

ey, gives final and desperate significance to the myriad developments over the years, the thrust and counterthrust of social conflict, the various lives and relationships forged by history. But one last perspective that was necessary to bring the entire picture into focus was the stock market crash in 1929 and the spreading misery of the Depression years. Only then did it begin to appear to many Americans that the society had suffered a calamitous division—between rich and poor, the powerful and the powerless. The feeling of a fatal split is very well conveyed toward the end of *USA*: "all right, we are two nations."

What is most obviously striking about *USA* is Dos Passos' experimental method. Influenced by the poetic theory of simultaneity, the cubism of the School of Paris Painters and, especially the cinematographic techniques of Russian film director Eisenstein, Dos Passos invented a new novelistic architecture based on fragmentation, contrast, juxtaposition and "montage." Direct snapshots of life, slogans and songs, snatches of dialogue or newspaper headlines fed his running commentary on history's changes, and were combined into "collages" that kept the tension between the inner voice of the artist and the behavioristic report of the detached observer alive.

John Steinbeck (1902—1968)

① *Biographical Introduction*

John Steinbeck was the foremost novelist of the American Depression of the 1930s. He was born in Salinas, California, the locale of much of his finest fiction. From his childhood, he worked at various unskilled jobs, acquiring the first hand knowledge of the struggles of the migrant workers and the downtrodden, for whom his sympathy was evident in his writing. His literary career began in 1929 with a romantic novel, *Cup of Gold*. But it was the publication of *Tortila Flat* (1935) that brought him sudden fame. In the following years a succession of books appeared, including *In Dubious Battle* (1936), *Of Mice and Men* (1937), *The Long Valley* (1938), and his masterpiece *The Grapes of Wrath* (1939). In the next two decades, he wrote several works, but none of them was as popular with the public as were his earlier works. In 1962, Steinbeck was awarded the Novel Prize for Literature for his life time work, but primarily for the great works in the 1930s.

② His Theme and View

Steinbeck's writing reflected his concern with the rituals of manual labor, the people "doing" rather than "being", and he believed that the writer's first duty was to "set down his time as nearly as he can understand it"and serve as "the watch-dog of society... to satirize its silliness, to attack its injustices, to stigmatize its faults." He wrote sympathetically about the plight of the depressed California farmers, migrants, laborers, and the unemployed, making their lives and sorrows very understandable to his readers. His theme was usually that simple human virtues such as kindness and fair treatment were far superior to official hard-heartedness, or the dehumanizing cruelty of exploiters for their own commercial advantage.

③ His Style

Steinbeck's prose style is noted for poetic quality which

heightens the realism of his naturalistic writing, relieving and brightening the grim subjects which he often wrote about. Steinbeck frequently set a scene, or the mood for a chapter, in short, abrupt passages which were almost like the stage directions for a play, as though the author wanted his reader to see the story clearly in his imagination.

The habit was undoubtedly what encouraged many film producers to turn his novels into films. Steinbeck, like Eugene O'Neill, nearly always wrote the dialogue of his books just as it should sound, using strange spelling to denote the regional accent, and inserting many words of slang and dialect. By reproducing the exact speech patterns of his characters, Steinbeck made his reader feel as though he knew them personally. During the Depression years, his fiction combined warm humor, regionalism, and violence with a realistic technique, which produced a unique kind of social protest.

④ *His Major Works*

In Dubious Battle was Steinbeck's most clearly proletarian novel of class struggle, depicting the lives of migrant workers and their resistance to exploitation by the entrenched forces of society. The protagonist, Jim Nolam, is a young, unemployed communist who, with Mac, an old experienced Party member, sets out to organize the poor migrant fruit-pickers in California in a strike. The workers' union is crushed by the landowners and Jim is killed. But at the end of the book, the farm workers continue their struggle, led on by the old Party member.

Of Mice And Men tells of the friendship of two migrant workers who yearn for a permanent home they will never find.

Lennie Small is an enormously strong, but feeble-minded man, who has an abnormal desire to touch soft objects. His friend George Milton watches over him. They came to a ranch in the Salinas Valley, where Lennie, roused deliberately by the boss's daughter-in-law, a promiscuous young woman, is led to murder her when his hands touch her soft hair. George shoots Lennie to save him from a worse death at the hands of his oppressors.

The Grapes of Wrath was Steinbeck's best known work and the highest point of his career. It is a story of a family fleeing from the dust bowl of Oklahoma to what they hope will be a better life in California, only to find misery, misfortune and maltreatment. Some of the family members die, yet the family survives by helping one another, especially through Ma Joad's selfless love and courage. The novel shows the ability of the common people to endure and prevail in spite of their plight.

THE GRAPES OF WRATH

Chapter 25

The spring is beautiful in California. Valleys in which the fruit blossoms are fragrant pink and white waters in a shallow sea. Then the first tendrils of the grapes, swelling from the old gnarled vines, cascade down to cover the trunks. The full green hills are round and soft as breasts. And on the level vegetable lands are the mile-long rows of pale green lettuce and the spindly little cauliflowers, the gray-green unearthly artichoke plants.

And then the leaves break out on the trees, and the petals drop from the fruit trees and carpet the earth with pink and white.

The centers of the blossoms swell and grow and color:[1] cherries and apples, peaches and pears, figs which close the flower in the fruit. All California quickens with produce, and the fruit grows heavy, and the limbs bend gradually under the fruit so that little crutches must be placed under them to support the weight.

Behind the fruitfulness are men of understanding and knowledge and skill, men who experiment with seed, endlessly developing the techniques for greater crops of plants whose roots will resist the million enemies of the earth: the molds, the insects, the rusts, the blights. These men work carefully and endlessly to perfect the seed, the roots. And there are the men of chemistry who pray trees against pests, who sulphur the grapes, who cut out disease and rots, mildews and sicknesses. Doctors of preventive medicine, men at the borders[2] who look for fruit flies, for Japanese beetle,[3] men who quarantine the sick trees and root them out and burn them, men of knowledge. The men who graft the young trees, the little vines, are the cleverest of all, for theirs is a surgeon's job, as tender and delicate; and these men must have surgeon's hands and surgeons' hearts to slit the bark, to place the grafts, to bind the wounds and cover them from the air. These are great men.

Along the rows, the cultivators move, tearing the spring grass and turning it under to make a fertile earth, breaking the ground to hold the water up near the surface, ridging the ground in little pools for the irrigation, destroying the weed roots that may drink the water away from the trees.

And all the time the fruit swells and the flowers break out in long clusters on the vines. And in the growing year the warmth grows and the leaves turn dark green. The prunes lengthen like little green bird's eggs, and the limbs sag down against the crutches under the weight. And the hard little pears take shape, and the beginning of the fuzz comes out on the peaches. Grape blossoms shed their tiny petals and the hard little beads become green buttons, and the buttons grow heavy. The men who work in the fields, the owners of the little orchards, watch and calculate. The year is heavy with produce. And the men are proud, for of their knowledge they can make the year heavy. They have transformed the world with their knowledge. The short, lean wheat has been made big and productive. Little sour apples have grown large and sweet, and that old grape that grew among the trees and fed the birds its tiny fruit has mothered a thousand varieties,[4] red and black, green and pale pink, purple and yellow; and each variety with its own flavor. The men who work in the experimental farms have made new fruits: nectarines and forty kinds of plums, walnuts with paper shells.[5] And always they work, selecting, grafting, changing, driving themselves,[6] driving the earth to produce.

And first the cherries ripen. Gent and a half a pound. Hell, we can't pick'em[7] for that. Black cherries and red cherries, full and sweet, and the birds eat half of each cherry and the yellow jackets buzz into the holes the birds made. And on the ground the seeds drop and dry with black shreds hanging from them.

The purple prunes soften and sweeten. My God, we can't pick them and dry and suplhur them. We can't pay wages, no matter what wages. And the purple prunes carpet the ground. And first the skins wrinkle a little and swarms of flies come to feast, and the valley is filled with the odor of sweet decay. The meat turns dark and the crop shrivels on the ground.

And the pears grow yellow and soft. Five dollars a ton. Five dollars for forty fifty-pound boxes; trees pruned and sprayed, orchards cultivated—pick the fruit, put it in boxes, load the trucks, deliver the fruit to the cannery—forty boxes for five dollars. We can't do it. And the yellow fruit falls heavily to the ground and splashes on the ground. The yellow jackets dig into the soft meat, and there is a smell of ferment and rot.

Then the grapes—we can't make good wine. People can't buy good wine. Rip the grapes from the vines, good grapes, rotten grapes, wasp-stung grapes. Press stems, press dirt and rot.

But there's mildew and formic acid in the vats.

Add sulphur and tannic acid.

The smell from the ferment is not the rich odor of wine, but the smell of decay and chemicals.

Oh, well. It has alcohol in it, anyway. They can get drunk.

The little farmers watched debt creep up on them like the tide. They sprayed the trees and sold no crop, they pruned and grafted and could not pick the crop. And the men of knowledge have worked, have considered, and the fruit is rotting on the ground, and the decaying mash in the wine vat is poisoning the air. And taste the wine-no grape flavor at all, just sulphur and tannic acid and alcohol.

This little orchard will be a part of a great holding next year,[8] for the debt will have choked the owner.

This vineyard will belong to the bank. Only the great owners can survive, for they own the canneries, too. And four pears peeled and cut in half, cooked and canned, still cost fifteen cents. And the canned pears do not spoil. They will last for years.

The decay spreads over the State,[9] and the sweet smell is a great sorrow on the land. Men who can graft the trees and make the seed fertile and big can find no way to let the hungry people eat their produce. Men who have created new fruits in the world cannot create a system whereby their fruits may be eaten. And the failure hangs over the State like a great sorrow.

The works of the roots of the vines, of the trees, must be destroyed to keep up the price, and this is the saddest, bitterest thing of all. Garloads of oranges dumped on the ground. The people came for miles to take the fruit, but this could not be. How would they buy oranges at twenty cents a dozen if they could drive out and pick them up? And men with hoses squirt kerosene on the oranges, and they are angry at the crime, angry at the people who have come to take the fruit. A million people hungry, needing the fruit—and kerosene sprayed over the golden mountains.

And the smell of rot fills the country.

Burn coffee for fuel in ships. Burn corn to keep warm, it makes a hot fire. Dump potatoes in the rivers and place guards along the banks to keep the hungry people from fishing them out. Slaughter the pigs and bury them, and let the putrescence drip down into the earth.

There is a crime here that goes beyond denunciation. There is a sorrow here that weeping cannot symbolize. There is a failure here that topples all our success. The fertile earth, the straight tree rows, the sturdy trunks, and the ripe fruit. And children dying of pellagra must die because a profit cannot be taken from an orange. And coroners must fill in the certificates—died of malnutrition because the food must rot, must be forced to rot.

The people come with nets to fish for potatoes in the river, and the guards hold them back; they come in rattling cars to get the dumped oranges, but the kerosene is sprayed. And they stand still and watch the potatoes float by, listen to the screaming pigs being killed in a ditch and covered with quicklime, watch the mountains of oranges slop down to a putrefying ooze; and in the eyes of the people there is failure; and in the eyes of the hungry there is a growing wrath. In the souls of the people the grapes of wrath are filling and growing heavy, growing heavy for the vintage.

Notes:

1. color: here, assume a deeper color.
2. the borders: the borders of orchards.
3. Japanese beetle: a shiny, green-and-brown beetle, originally from Japan,

which eats leaves, fruits, and grasses, and is damaging to crops.

4. has mothered a thousand varieties: has been grafted onto and has produced a thousand varieties of grapes.
5. with paper shells: with very thin shells.
6. driving themselves: driving themselves to work hard.
7. 'em: them, i. e. , cherries.
8. This little orchard will be a part of a great holding next year: This little orchard will be sold out to the owner of a large orchard and become a part of it next year.
9. the State: California.

Question for Consideration:

The Grapes of Wrath is one of the classic documents of the Depression. What realities of the Depression are conveyed here? What of Steinbeck's political views?

4. *African American Novelists*

The history of African American literature can be divided into five periods, and in each of these the prominent literature is both shaped by and helps to shape the social situation of blacks at the time. These are the: the time of Slavery(1746—1865); Reconstruction and after (1865—1919); the Harlem Renaissance and Modernism(1919—1960); the Black Arts Movement(1960—1970); and writing after 1971.

Until 1865 writing by African Americans was dominated by the fact of slavery and the dominant genre in the first period of African American writing was the Slave Narrative, which flourished during the 1850s until emancipation. Between 1986 and

1919, African American writing aimed to alter the consciousness of its readership in an attempt to improve or draw attention to the social conditions of blacks. It was the Harlem Renaissance (1923—1940) that African American writing starts to thrive in all genres, with the poets Claude Mckay (1889—1948), Sterling A. Brown (1901—1989), Langston Hughes (1902—1967) and Countee Cullen (1903—1946) and the novelists Zora Neale Hurston, Nella Larson (1893—1964) and Jean Toomer (1894—1967). The renaissance was very much a northern urban movement, associated with modernism. It mainly involved a group of writers and intellectuals associated with Harlem, the center of urbanized blacks. One characteristic of the Harlem Renaissance was a move towards so-called "high art" in black writing, rather than the use of folk idioms, comic writing and vernacular that had often been considered the special realm of African American writing up to that time. The period 1940—1960 after the renaissance was a time of great consolidation and developing diversity of African American writing. Several major writers emerged. In addition to the famous poet Gwendolyn Brooks (1927—2000) there were the novelist and essayists Richard Wright, Ralph Ellison and James Baldwin and the dramatists Lorraine Hansberry (1930—1965), whose *A Raisin in the Sun* (1959) was the first play by a black woman to be produced on Broadway. As ever, social concerns were necessarily evident, exacerbated by an increased expression of black anger and frustration. An intense debate developed between Wright, Ellison and Baldwin over the aesthetic status of the protest novel and the function of the aesthetic for the black writer. It was the Black Arts Movement, however, which sought a fusion between aesthetics and social protest. Sometimes called the "second black renaissance" (the Harlem renaissance being the first), the Black Arts Movement (BAM) began in the mid-1960s and flourished until the mid-1970s. The BAM emphasized the racial distinction of the black, and fostered writing that was specifically black, speech-based, radical, confrontational, anti-assimilationist and dedicated to revolutionary social change, as its leader Imamus Amiri Baraka wrote in his poem : Black Arts (1969), "We want poems that kill'". As well as Baraka, key writers of the period includes the poets Etheridge Knight (1931—1985), Sonia Sanchez (b. 1934) and Nikki Giovanni (b. 1934) and the novelist Alex Haley (1921—1992), whose *Roots* (1976) became an influential best-seller. Since 1970s African American writing has become more diverse that ever before. , and it has notably seen the emergence of two major women, Toni Morrison and Alice Walker. In spite of the rich diversity of contemporary African American writing, many writers are united by an intensive interrogation into American history and share an awareness of the heritage of black writing. Where it was once considered marginal and of minority interest, African American literature has come to be defining force in American writing.

Richard Wright (1908—1960)

Richard Wright, leader of many young black writers, was born on a plantation near Natchez, Mississippi. Too sensitive and too intelligent to submit to the life of the black in the

South, he was unruly as a boy and young man. His answer to the problem, possibly determined by his ambition to become an author after reading H. L. Mencken's Book of Prefaces, led him North to Chicago in 1934. He found that a black had little chance in the Black Belt. Therefore he became interested in Communism and wrote for the New Masses. His *Uncle Tom's Children: Four Novellas* (1938) was enlarged and revised in 1940. The germ of the book was a novelette that won a prize by Story for the best work of any W. P. A. writer. Though the book won him a Guggenheim Fellowship, Wright himself felt that the whites wept over his picture of a black's life but made no effort to help.

Native Son (1940), a best seller, was the story of the horror of black life in America. Bigger Thomas is the product of a dislocated society. In the South he would not submit. In the North his future was uncertain. Since he lived in a world of hate, fear, and violence, he identified himself with the oppressed people of the world and embraced Communism. Though Wright knew the Bigger Thomases of the world and was in part one of them, he waited to publish his novel because he was afraid of what the whites would say, of what the black who are not Bigger Thomases would think, of what the Communists would say and think.

Unconcerned with technique, he mingled the stream of consciousness with his own speaking and with direct narration. He wanted to explain Bigger Thomas's viewpoint, to convey a mood of horror and despair, to limit all by the limitations of Bigger Thomas. The book was prejudiced, bitter, and powerful. Yet the cumulative horror is not so great as that in the more moderate *Black Boy* (1945)—his own story reveals the Bigger Thomas in him.

In Twelve Million Black Voices (1941), a text and picture history of the American black, Wright identified his writings with his race. He had one theme no matter what form it takes: the problem of the black in America. A powerful author, he wrote to free himself from a fear that was a Bigger Thomas fear. Neither white nor black is the villain of his books, but the environment in which he felt trapped.

James (Arthur) Baldwin (1924—1987)

The son of a preacher, Baldwin was born in Harlem, New York City. He left home at 17 and eventually made his way to Paris, where he lived for some years and began to write. His first novel, *Go Tell It on the Mountain* (1953), was based on his experiences in Harlem, and with it he was welcomed as a black writer of unusual promise. It recounts a young boy's coming to terms with the religious beliefs of his father, a storefront preacher incapable of controlling his desires, and of his stoical mother. The boy is desperately in search of some kind of identity; he does not share the fervent belief of others, and this lack obsesses him. His father's lusts and inability to communicate with his children have kept the Lord away from him, for before kneeling to the Lord he must kneel to his father, something he cannot bring himself to do. After a long series of conflicts, he is finally able to reject his father and turn to the Lord at one stroke, and he feels something die in him as well as come alive. He has achieved faith through struggle.

The promise of this first book was borne out in further novels, plays, short stories, and essays, which have shown Baldwin to be a powerful and articulate enemy of racial discrimination. After *Givanni's Room* (1956), which is set in Paris, he returned to black America as a setting for his fiction. *Another Country* (1962) is set in New York City and focuses mainly on Harlem society. The death—perhaps the suicide—of the main character, Rufus Scott, is representative of the treatment individuals receive in an environment which is essentially hostile and which erects barriers to their desire for love. Other works of fiction by Baldwin include *Going to Meet the Man* (1965), *Tell Me How Long the Train's Been Gone* (1968), *If Beale Street Could Talk* (1974), and *Just Above My Head* (i979).

Ralph Ellison (1914—1994)

Unlike so much black fiction, *Invisible Man* is not an autobiography. While his hero is a Southerner, Ellison himself was born and raised in the state of Oklahoma. Between 1933 and 1936 he trained as a musician at the Tuskagee Institute; although he later devoted most of his energies to writing, his interest in music, especially jazz, continued throughout his life.

In 1952 he published *Invisible Man*, a novel he had been working on for five years. The book was instantly and widely acclaimed; it won the National Book Award, an honor rarely given to a first novel. He has also written many short stories, reviews and articles, a number of which are included in the collection *Shadow and Act* (1964).

Invisible Man is a book about the experience of being black in America and, indeed, it is one of the most powerful books yet written on this theme. Many of the people in the novel represent different identities that a black man can adopt, different identities that the hero considers—its characters range from passive blacks like the college students to the rabid black nationalist, Ras the Exhorter.

But, like *Herzog*, the novel transcends the local and ethnic and concentrates on problems shared by modern men of all races. The hero's coal cellar is an apt symbol of the isolation of the individual in an impersonal city. And his search for identity has broad implications; as Irvine Howe observes, Ellison is "deeply concerned with the fate of freedom in a mass society."

Invisible Man has become a classic of modern American fiction because of its intrinsic merit: its author is a superb craftsman. But the book also interests readers for historical and sociological reasons, since Ellison represents one of many possible responses to being a black man, and in particular a black writer, in America today. Earlier black writers often hoped for complete assimilation between the races, and recent novelists like Leroi Jones advocate complete separation of the black and white man. Ellison has occupied a middle position, defining his cultural heritage as a combination of experiences peculiar to the black man and experiences common to all Americans; he argued that it is important for both to be preserved and respected. Similarly, while Ellison's predecessors frequently did not write about their race at all and Ellison's successors have tended to concentrate exclusively on the plight of blacks, Ellison himself was interested in relating his own dilemma to that of all Americans.

Zora Neale Hurston (1901—1960)

Hurston is a novelist and anthropologist who has had a significant influence on the development of African American women's writing. Hurston was born in Alabama, and grew up in the all-black community of Eatonville, Florida. She moved to New York in 1925 and became part of the Harlem Renaissance, working particularly with Langston Hughes, with whom she collaborated on several plays. After graduating from Barnard College in 1928 she studied anthropology at Columbia University. Hurston traveled as a folklorist in the South collecting tales and songs. This resulted in the collections *Mules and Men* (1935) and *Tell My Horse* (1938). In 1934 she published her first novel, *Jonah's Gourd Vine*, and in 1937 her second, *Their Eyes Were Watching God*. She published her autobiography, *Dust Tracks on a Road*, in 1942. Huston's writing was popular but in 1948 she withdrew from public life after a scandal in which a false accusation was made against her. She worked at various jobs and in 1960 she died unrecognized and in financial hardship in Fort Pierce, Florida.

The 1970s saw a significant revival of interest in Hurston, and her work has influenced many later writers. Alice Walker was crucial to the rediscovery of Hurston, and Walker's *I Love Myself When I Am Laughing* (1979) is an excellent selection of Hurston's writing.

Toni Morrison (1931—)

Born in Ohio to working-class parents and educated at Howard and Cornell, Morrison is widely considered to be one of America's leading black novelists. She is the recipient of numerous awards and 1993 she was awarded the Nobel Prize for literature (the first African American to have the honor).

Morrison has written several novels. Although each is distinctive in terms of theme, setting, historical situation and prose style, taken together they form an incisive interrogation of American history and of the relation of African Americans to historical circumstance. Often her focus is particularly on female experience, and she frequently explores the tensions involved in the conflict between "African" and "American." Her first novel, *The Bluest Eye* (1970), is the story of a year in the life of Pecola Breedlove, a young black girl in Ohio who comes to believe that she has blue eyes. In the course of the year Pecola endures a series of degradations, including incest with her father and subsequent pregnancy, until her fixation with the blue eyes of a friend's doll develops into complete insanity. *Sula* (1973), also set in Ohio, focuses on the friendship between two black women, Sula Peace and Nel Wright Greene, as they mature during the 1920s and 1930s. Their friendship is based on a shared sense of alienation from community and family values, and a similar experience of emptiness in their other relationships—especially with men. *Song of Solomon* (1977) is an intricate narrative about Milkman Dead's exploration of his family history, his quest for a place as an individual within a heritage of slavery and violence. *Tar Baby* (1981) is about motherhood and the relationships between black and white cultures in the Caribbean and America.

Morrison has also focused on inescapable tensions within primarily black communities, as in *Jazz* (1992) and *Paradise* (1998). She is also a creative and sophisticated user of existing narratives as in her masterpiece *Beloved* (1987), which utilizes the slave narrative.

Morrison's prose style is complex, intricate and sometimes dense, having affinities with that of Faulkner, though she also makes occasional use of Magic Realism. In 1991 she published *Playing in the Dark: Whiteness and the Literary Imagination*, an important work of criticism in which she eloquently argues for the presence of a potentially destabilizing blackness in white American literature.

Beloved was awarded the 1988 Pulitzer Prize. Set in Ohio during Reconstruction the novel concerns the rehabilitation of Sethe, who as a runaway slave attempts to murder her four children rather than allow them to go into slavery. She succeeds in killing her unnamed elder daughter, referred to as "Beloved", whose ghost 18 years later arrives at Sethe's home, where she lives with her other daughter Denver. Having been ostracized by her community because of the killing, Sethe gradually dedicates herself to Beloved as reparation for the killing, and this further isolates her until Denver initiates contact with the community. In a symbolic repetition of the scene of the original killing, Beloved is expelled and the restoration of Sethe begins. The novel includes references back to slavery at Sweet Home in Kentucky and the experiences of other slaves on the farm, especially Sethe's lover Paul D. and her preacher mother-in-law Baby Suggs. Thematically, the novel's major concern is with finding a livable negotiation between the need to forget or suppress a wounding past in order to function in the present, and the necessity of remembering a past without being paralyzed by it. Although Morrison makes use of the slave narrative and also refers to an actual case of slave infanticide, *Beloved*'s narrative is fragmented and nonlinear, reflecting the problems that the characters must confront in creating order and coherence in their lives.

Alice Walker (1944—)

Novelist and poet, born in Eatonton, Georgia, the eighth child of a family of sharecroppers, educated at Spelman College and Sarah Lawrence College, Alice Walker soon became committed to the civil rights movement. She worked for voter registration in Georgia, welfare rights and Head Start in Mississippi, and the Welfare Department in New York City. She taught for a time in Mississippi, first at Jackson State University (1968—1969) and then at Tougaloo College (1969—1970).

Her first publications were two collections of poetry: *Once: Poems* (1968), which reflects her experience of the civil rights movement and her travel in Africa; *Revolutionary Petunias and Other Poems* (1973), which is a tribute to those who struggle against racism and oppression. Her first novel, *The Third Life of Grange Copeland* (1970), is the story of three generations of black tenant farmers from 1900 to the 1960s. A book of short stories, *In Love and Trouble: Stories of Black Women* (1973), explores the experience and heritage of black women, a theme to which Walker returns in a second collection, *You Can't Keep a Good Woman Down* (1981). The epistolary novel, *The Color Purple* (1982), which won a Pulitzer Prize, centers on the life of Celie, a black woman who has been raped by the man she believed to be her father. She bears his children, and then is forced to marry an older man whom she despises. The novel is made up of Celie's despairing letters to God and to her sister Nettle who has gone to Africa as a missionary, and of Nettie's letters to Celie. Walker's other publications include a biography for children, *Langston Hughes, American Poet* (1974); *Meridian* (1977), a novel about the lives of civil rights workers in the South during the 1960s; and two collections of poems, *Good Night, Willie Lee, I'll See You in the Morning* (1979) and *Horses Make a Landscape Look More Beautiful: Poems* (1984). A volume of essays appeared in 1983 entitled *In Search of My Mothers Garden: Womanist Prose*.

Walker's later novels are *The Temple of My Familiar* (1989), *Possessing the Secret of Joy*, the autobiographical *The Way Forward Is with a Broken Heart* (2001), and *By the Light of My Father's Smile* (2003).

In her early novels and short stories particularly, Walker demonstrates a sophisticated management of narrative technique, especially in the fragmented narrative of *Meridian* and the epistolary style of *The Color Purple*. Thematically her work is united by the project of raising the visibility of black women.

By the Light of My Father's Smile is about a family from

the United States who goes to the remote Sierras in Mexico—the writer-to-be, Susannah, her sister, Magdalena, her father and mother. And there, amid an endangered band of mixed-race Blacks and Indians called the Mundo, they begin an encounter that will change them more than they could ever dream. Moving back and forth in time, and among unforgettable characters and their stories, Walker crosses conventional borders of all kinds as she explores in this magical novel the ways in which a woman's denied sexuality leads to the loss of the much prized and necessary original self; and how she regains that self, even as her family's past of lies and love is transformed. *By the Light of My Father's Smile* presents, as Alice Walker puts it, "a celebration of sexuality, its absolute usefulness in the accessing of one's mature spirituality, and the father's role in assuring joy or sorrow in this arena for his female children." It explores the richness and coherence of alternative culture, experience of sexuality as a celebration of life, of trust in Nature and the Spirit, even as it affirms the belief, as Walker says, "that it is the triumphant heart, not the conquered heart, that forgives. And that love is both timeless and beyond time."

INVISIBLE MAN

Prologue

I am an invisible man. No, I am not a spook like those who haunted Edgar Allan Poe; nor am I one of your Hollywood movie ectoplasms. I am a man of substance, of flesh and bone, fiber and liquids—and I might even be said to possess a mind. I am invisible, understand, simply because people refuse to see me. Like the bodiless heads you see sometimes in circus sideshows, it is as though I have been surrounded by mirrors of hard, distorting glass. When they approach me they see only my surroundings, themselves, or figments of their imagination-indeed, everything and anything except me.

Nor is my invisibility exactly a matter of a biochemical accident to my epidermis, That invisibility to which I refer occurs because of a peculiar disposition of the eyes of those with whom I come in contact. A matter of the construction of their inner eyes, those eyes with which they look through their physical eyes upon reality. I am not complaining, nor am I protesting either. It is sometimes advantageous to be unseen, although it is most often rather wearing on the nerves. Then too, you're constantly being bumped against by those of poor vision. Or again, you often doubt if you really exist. You wonder whether you aren't simply a phantom in other people's minds. Say, a figure in a nightmare, which the sleeper tries with all his strength to destroy. It's when you feel like this that, out of resentment, you begin to bump people back. And, let me confess, you feel that way most of the time. You ache with the need to convince yourself that you do exist in the real world, that you're a part of all the sound and anguish, and you strike out with your fists, you curse and you swear to make them recognize you. And, alas, it's seldom successful.

One night I accidentally bumped into a man, and perhaps because of the near darkness he saw me and called me an insulting name. I sprang at him, seized his coat lapels and demanded that he apologize. He was a tall blond man, and as my face came close to his he looked insolently out of his blue eyes and cursed me, his breath hot in my face as he struggled. I pulled his chin down sharp upon the crown of my head, butting him as I had seen the West Indians do, and I felt his flesh tear and the blood gush out, and I yelled, "Apologize! Apologize!" But he continued to curse and struggle, and I butted him again and again until he went down heavily, on his knees, profusely bleeding. I kicked him repeatedly, in a frenzy because he still uttered insults though his lips were frothy with blood. Oh yes, I kicked Him! And in my outrage I got out my knife and prepared to slit his throat, right there beneath the lamplight in the deserted street, holding him in the collar with one hand, and opening the knife with my teeth—when it occurred to me that the man had not seen me, actually; that he, as far as he knew, was in the midst of a walking nightmare! And I stopped the blade, slicing the air as I pushed him away, letting him fall back to the street. I stared at him hard as the lights of a car stabbed through the darkness. He lay there, moaning on the asphalt; a man almost killed by a phantom. It unnerved me. I was both disgusted and ashamed. I was like a drunken man myself, wavering about on weakened legs. Then I was amused: Something in this man's thick head had sprung out and beaten him within an inch of his life. I began to laugh at this crazy discovery. Would he have awakened at the point of death? Would Death himself have freed him for wakeful living? But I didn't linger. I ran away into the dark, laughing so hard I feared I might rupture myself. The next day I saw his picture in the Daily News, beneath a caption stating that he had been "mugged". Poor fool, poor blind fool, I thought with sincere compassion, mugged by an invisible man!

Most of the time (although I do not choose as I once did to deny the violence of my days by ignoring it) I am not so overtly violent. I remember that I am invisible and walk softly so as not to awaken the sleeping ones. Sometimes it is best not to awaken them; there are few things in the world as dangerous as sleepwalkers. I learned in time though that it is possible to carry on a fight against them without their realizing it.

5. *Jewish Novelists*

A tradition of Jewish writing in Yiddish has survived from the 19th century to the present and has been given high prominence by the fiction of Isaac Bashevis Singer (1904—1991), Tillie Olsen (b. 1913), Bernard Malamud, Saul Bellow, Norman Mailer (b. 1923), Joseph Heller (1923—1999), E. F. Doctorow (b. 1931), Phillip Roth, J. D. Salinger, and so on. Poets and dramatists with a Jewish background have also been prominent. Among them stand out Allen Ginsberg and Arthur Miller. Jewish writers affirm a humanist tradition and demonstrate an ongoing belief in social progress and in the value of learning and scholarship. There is also a use of self-deprecating humor, and an eye for comic incongruity and absurdity, as is evident in the work of Nathanael West (1903—1940), the novels of Heller, Phillip Roth's early fiction and the comic monologues of Woody Allen (b. 1935).

Isaac Bashevis Singer (1904—1988)

Isaac Bashevis Singer was one of the great storytellers of the twentieth century. His writing is a unique blend of religious morality and social awareness combined with an investigation of personal desires. Though his work often took the form of parables or tales based on a 19th century tradition, he was deeply concerned with the events of his time and the future of his people and their culture.

Isaac Bashevis Singer was born on July 24, 1904 in Radzymin, Poland. His parents were religious Jews and pushed him towards a career as a religious scholar. In 1921 he enrolled in Rabbinical School, but left only two years later to work for a Yiddish literary magazine. Though his rabbinical studies would remain a strong influence on him, he longed to be a part of a literary community. Working as a journalist, translator, and proofreader, Singer began to write short stories on the side. By 1935 he had published his first book, *Satan in Goray* (1935).

That same year, Singer followed his brother, Isaac Joshua Singer to America. Isaac Joshua Singer is considered one of the major Yiddish writers of the twentieth century, and was the first and greatest literary influence on his younger brother Isaac. In New York, Isaac Bashevis Singer began working for *The Jewish Daily Forward*, a Yiddish newspaper dedicated to issues of interest to its newly immigrated readership.

Throughout the 1940s, Singer's reputation began to grow among the many Yiddish-speaking immigrants. After World War Ⅱ and the near destruction of the Yiddish-speaking peoples, Yiddish seemed a dead language. Though Singer had moved to the United States, he believed in the power of his native language and knew that there was still a large audience that longed for new work, work that would address the lives and issues of theirs. In 1950 Singer produced his first major work, *The Family Moskat*—the story of a twentieth century Polish Jewish family before the war. He followed this novel with a series of well-received short stories, including his most famous, "Gimpel, the Fool."

Though not primarily nostalgic, Singer's work hearkened

back to a former time. The setting for much of the work was his native Poland, and the writing addressed existential and spiritual questions through folk tales and parables. These works caught the attention of a number of American writers including Saul Bellow and Irving Howe, who were greatly responsible for not only translating Singer's work, but championing it as well. Throughout the 1960s Singer continued to write on questions of personal morality. One of his most famous novels was *Enemies: A Love Story*, in which a Holocaust survivor deals with his own desires, complex family relationships, and the loss of faith. Singer also wrote two novels about nineteenth century Polish-Jewish history before returning to more modern topics in the 1970s.

By the 1970s, he had become a major international writer. After World War Ⅱ there were few Yiddish writers remaining and Singer was not only a vocal proponent of Yiddish writing, but the major figure in Yiddish letters. Throughout the 1970s he wrote dozens of stories that were eventually collected into books, and published in Yiddish and English as well as many other languages. He branched out, writing memoirs and children's books as well as two other major novels set in the twentieth century, *The Penitent* (1974) and *Shosha* (1978). The same year as his publication of *Shosha*, Singer won the Nobel Prize in literature. For many, this award was bittersweet in that it brought worldwide attention to an important language at the same time it seemed to signal the language's demise.

After being awarded the Nobel Prize, Singer gained a monumental status among writers throughout the world. He continued to write during the last years of his life, often returning to Polish history which so entranced him throughout his early life. In 1988 he published *The King of the Fields* and three years later, *Scums*. That same year, Isaac Bashevis Singer died at the age of eighty-seven in Surfside, Florida. Incredibly prolific, Singer created an insightful and deep body of work that will forever remain an important part of literary history.

J.D. Salinger (1919—)

J. D. Salinger held a central place in American letters for about fifteen years in the post-war period. His fairly small literary output in the 1950s and 1960s was the subject of enthusiastic critical acclaim and extreme admiration among university students and young intellectuals after the Second World War. He wrote in the authentic voice of disillusioned, alienated American youth, and for this reason he holds a significant position in the modern literature.

Jerome David Salinger was born in New York City in 1919. His father was Jewish and his mother was Christian. He grew up in the city, first attending public schools and then a military academy, on the insistence of his parents. However, he had no interest in a military career: He attended New York University and Columbia University, but did not stay to graduate because he wanted to devote all his time to writing. He spent four years in the U. S. Army during the Second World War, on the European Front, and then he returned to his writing in America.

In 1951, he published his first and only novel, *The Catcher in the Rye*. It is the story of a 16-year-old boy who runs away from his upper-class private school and spends four days roaming around New York, searching for truth and goodness, but finding only hypocrites and liars. The story is told in the first person, using typical teenage idioms and colloquial expressions which convey a strong mood of suffering and loneliness, as well as humor. The book quickly became an best seller, bought and avidly read by young people.

Saul Bellow (1915—2005)

Saul Bellow, Nobel prize winner in 1976, introduces a gallery of characters at odds with society and with themselves. His fiction is set in a modern world of chaos, noise and junk, which destroys the vulnerable spaces of individual freedom. Centering on the conflict between force and spirit—the man of will and the man of love—his novels weave together social, psychological and metaphysical treads, and work as parables of the writer's personal search for achievement and expression.

Born in Canada of Russian Jewish parents, Saul Bellow spent most of his youth in Chicago—a city whose atmosphere permeates much of his fiction. After briefly enrolling at the University of Chicago Bellow became dissatisfied with its traditional syllabus, and went on to take a degree in sociology and anthropology at Northwestern University. Like many contemporary American writers, he has held a variety of academic posts.

In Tradition and Dream (1964) the critic Walter Allen suggests that Bellow's early fiction shows a marked dichotomy: he "sometimes seems to be two writers, one introvert, the other extrovert." *Dangling Man* (1944) and *The Victim* (1947) are both introverted novels; in a claustrophobic and sometimes surreal manner, they deal with the private anxieties of modern urban man. In the first novel the hero lives in limbo while awaiting induction into the Army, while in the second he is the victim of antisemitism. *Seize the Day* (1956) returns to this mode, but in *The Adventures of Augie March* (1953) and *Henderson, the Rain King* (1959) Bellow reveals a new dimension to his talents. Both are loose and freewheeling, abundant in movement and picaresque comedy; Henderson, in particular, moves into a realm of extravagant comic fantasy.

These works established Bellow as the most important of that generation of postwar Jewish novelists who were becoming increasingly prominent in the American literary scene. After the appearance of *Seize the Day* the influential critic Leslie Fiedler pronounced: "Saul Bellow has become not merely a writer with whom it is possible to come to terms, but one with whom it is necessary to come to terms—perhaps of all our novelists the one we need most to understand, if we are to understand what the novel is doing at the moment." This judgment was handsomely confirmed with the publication of *Herzog* in 1964. The novel was greeted with a hailstorm of superlatives from the reviewers; more than a decade later it still looks like one of the most substantial achievements of modern fiction.

The essence of Bellow's success lies in his reconciliation of his two earlier modes, the introverted and the extroverted. The story of Moses E. Herzog—the failed, confused, half-crazy academic—combines rich comic invention with a deep understanding of the dilemma of the modern intellectual. The result is a tragicomedy that lies close to the nerve-center of modern anxieties. Taken by itself, it goes a long way towards justifying Tony Tanner's description of Bellow as "perhaps, the most sheer intelligent of postwar novelists."

Humboldt's Gift (1975) was awarded the Pulitzer Prize. Both *Herzog* and *Mr. Sammler's Planet* were awarded the National Book Award for fiction. Mr. Bellow's first non-fiction work, *To Jerusalem and Back: A Personal Account*, published on October 25, 1976, is his personal and literary record of his sojourn in Israel during several months in 1975. Bellow's later works include *The Dean's December* (1983), *A Theft* (1989), *Ravelstein* (2000), etc.

Norman Mailer (1923—)

American author, innovator of the nonfiction novel. Norman Mailer developed in the 1960s and 1970s a form of journalism, that combines actual events, autobiography, and political commentary with the richness of the novel. Mailer's works have aroused controversy—because of both their stylish nonconformity and his controversial views of American life.

Brought up in Brooklyn and educated at Harvard, Norman Mailer served with the American Army in the Pacific during the Second World War. This experience provided the basis for his first (and still most famous) novel, *The Naked and the Dead* (1948). The book's frank sexual descriptions and its use of obscene language earned it a temporary success of scandal; but it has also gained a lasting reputation as the most important novel to emerge from the last war. It was a hard novel for a young writer to follow up, and it may have been inevitable that his next two novels, *Barbary Shore* (1951) and *The Deer Park* (1955), should have been found disappointing by critics and reviewers. Perhaps because of these reverses Mailer temporarily abandoned fiction, returning to the genre to write *An American Dream* (1965) and *Why Are We in Vietnam?* (1967). His main energies have been devoted to non-fictional essays and journalism, and in this area he has produced at least two master-pieces: *The Presidential Paper of Norman Mailer* (1963), a collection of essays nominally addressed to President Kennedy, and *The Armies of the Night* (1968), an account of the 1967 pentagon march in protest against the Vietnam War. Mailer is now America's prime example of the artist as ebullient and rebellious public figure, and his writing gives the reader a vivid impression of the turbulence and vitality of contemporary America.

More recently, *Harlot's Ghost* (1992) was a 1,300 pages long chronicle of the CIA—the author himself considered it one of his best books. While gathering material for it, Mailer also found not previously known Russian documents for *Oswald's Tale* (1995), his exhaustive biography of Lee Harvey Oswald. *The Time of Our Time* (1998) was an anthology of Norman Mailer's fiction and non-fiction writings. (Michiko Kakutani in *The New York*) Mailer celebrated his 80th birthday in New York and published *The Spooky Art* (2003), a collection of writings about writing.

Bernard Malamud (1914—1986)

Malamud is most renowned for his short stories, oblique allegories often set in a dreamlike urban ghetto of immigrant Jews. His prose, like his settings, is an artful pastiche of Yiddish-English locutions, punctuated by sudden lyricism. On Malamud's death, Philip Roth wrote: "A man of stern morality, [Malamud was driven by] a need to consider long and seriously every last demand of an overtaxed, overtaxing conscience torturously exacerbated by the pathos of human need unabated." His best-known novel, *The Fixer*, won the National Book Award in 1966, and also the Pulitzer Prize for Fiction. Malamud's novel *The Natural* was made into a movie starring Robert Redford.

Born and educated in New York City, the son of immigrant Russian parents, Malamud was one of the foremost contemporary Jewish-American writers. His first novel, *The Natural* (1962), deals with baseball as a realm of American heroism and myth. *The Assistant* (1957) is about a poor New York Jewish shopkeeper who takes on a delinquent Italian-American youth as a helper; the young man comes to look on his employer as a father, but the powerful emotional bonds between them are complicated by cultural barriers. Malamud's interest in the Jewish experience as a metaphor for the human condition has become one of the permanent features of his work. His next novels *A New Life* (1961), *The Fixer* (1966), and *Pictures of Fidelman* (1969), all explore aspects of the personal struggle involved in the Jewish experience. *The Fixer* is about the story of a Russian Jew falsely accused of murder. Later novels are *The Tenants* (1971), *Dubin's Lives* (1979), and *God's Grace* (1982). Malamud's short stories are collected in *The Magic Barrel* (1958), *Idiots First* (1963), and *Rembrandt's Hat* (1973). *The Stories of Bernard Malamud* is a selection of the author's own favorites.

Philip Roth (1933—)

Roth grew up in the Weequahic neighborhood of Newark, New Jersey, as the oldest child of first generation American parents, Jews of Galician descent. After graduating from high school at the age of 16, Roth went on to attend Bucknell University, earning a degree in English. He then pursued graduate studies at the University of Chicago, receiving a M. A. in English literature and then working briefly as an instructor in the university's writing program.

Between the end of his studies and the publication of his first book in 1959, Roth served two years in the army and then wrote short fiction and criticism for various magazines, including movie reviews for *The New Republic*. His first book, *Goodbye Columbus*, a novella and five short stories, won the prestigious National Book Award in 1960, and afterward he published two long, bleak novels, *Letting Go* and *When She Was Good*; it was not until the publication of his third novel, *Portnoy's Complain*t in 1969 that Roth enjoyed widespread commercial and critical success.

During the 1970s Roth experimented in various modes, from the political satire *Our Gang* to the Kafkaesque fantasy *The*

Breast. By the end of the decade, though, Roth had created his Nathan Zuckerman alter-ego. In a series of highly self-referential novels that have followed since, Zuckerman almost always appears as either the main character or at least as an interlocutor. The number of books published during this period as well as the prestigious awards several of them have won lead many to consider it the most productive in Roth's career.

In 1995's comic masterpiece *Sabbath's Theater*, Roth presented his most lecherous protagonist yet in Mickey Sabbath, a disgraced aging former puppeteer. In complete contrast, the first volume of Roth's late trilogy, 1997's *American Pastoral*, focuses on the life of the virtuous Newark athletics star Swede Levov and the tragedy that befalls him when his daughter becomes a terrorist.

Philip Roth is unarguably the most decorated writer of his era: two of his works of fiction have won the National Book Award; two others were finalists. Two have won National Book Critics Circle awards; again, another two were finalists. He has also won two PEN/Faulkner Awards and a Pulitzer Prize for Fiction—for *American Pastoral*. In 2002, he was awarded the National Book Foundation's Award for Distinguished Contribution to American Letters. Most remarkably, four of his last six novels have either won or been named finalists for one or more of America's four most prestigious literary awards, a phenomenal achievement for a writer now entering his seventh decade. Literary critic Harold Bloom has named him as one of the four major American novelists still at work, along with Thomas Pynchon, Don DeLillo, and Cormac McCarthy.

In early 2004, the Philip Roth Society announced publication of the Philip Roth Studies journal. The inaugural issue was released in the fall of 2004. His latest novel, *The Plot Against America*, was released in the summer of 2004 and won the Sidewise Award for Alternate History in 2005.

THE CATCHER IN THE RYE

Chapter 23

We danced about four numbers. In between numbers she's funny as hell. She stays right in position. She won't even talk or anything. You both have to stay right in position and wait for the orchestra to start playing again, That kills me. You're not supposed to laugh or anything, either.

Anyway, we danced about four numbers, and then I turned off the radio. Old Phoebe lumped back in bed and got under the covers. "I'm improving, aren't I?" she asked me.

"And how", I said. I sat down next to her on the bed again. I was sort of out of breath. I was smoking so damn much, I had hardly any wind. She wasn't even out of breath.

"Feel my forehead," she said all of a sudden.

"Why?"

"Feel it. Just feel it once."

I felt it. I didn't feel anything, though.

"Does it feel very feverish?" she said.

"No. Is it supposed to?"

"Yes—I'm making it. Feel it again."

I felt it again, and I still didn't feel anything, but I said, "I think it's starting to, now." I didn't want her to get a goddam inferiority complex.

She nodded. "I can make it go up to over the thermometer."

"Thermometer. Who said so?"

"Alice Homberg showed me how. You cross your legs and hold your breath and think of something very, very hot. A radiator or something. Then your whole forehead gets so hot you can burn somebody's hand."

That killed me. I pulled my hand away from her forehead, like I was in terrific danger. "Thanks for telling me," I said.

"Oh, I wouldn't ve burned your hand. I'd've stopped before it got too—Shhh!" Then, quick as hell, she sat way the hell up in bed.

She soared hell out of me when she did that. "What's the matter?" I said.

"The front door!" she said in this loud whisper. "It's them!"

I quickly jumped up and ran over and turned off the light over the desk. Then I jammed out my cigarette on my shoe and put it in my pocket. Then I fanned hell out of the air, to get the smoke out—I shouldn't even have been smoking, for God's sake. Then I grabbed my shoes and got in the closet and shut the door. Boy, my heart was beating like a bastard.

I heard my mother come in the room.

"Phoebe?" she said, "Now, stop that. I saw the light, young lady."

"Hello!" I heard old Phoebe say. "I couldn't sleep. Did you have a good time?"

"Marvelous", my mother said, but you could tell she didn't mean it. She doesn't enjoy herself much when she goes out. "Why are you awake, may I ask? Were you warm enough?"

"I was warm enough, I just couldn't sleep."

"Phoebe, have you been smoking a cigarette in here? Tell me the truth, please, young lady."

"What?" old Phoebe said.

"You heard me."

"I just lit one for a second. I just took one puff. Then I threw it out of the window."

"Why, may I ask?"

"I couldn't sleep."

"I don't like that, Phoebe. I don't like that at all," my mother said. "Do you want another blanket?"

"No, thanks. G'night!" old Phoebe said. She was trying to get rid of her, you could tell.

"How was the movie?" my mother said.

"Excellent. Except Alice's mother. She kept leaning over and asking her if she felt grippy during the whole entire movie, We took a taxi home."

"let me feel your forehead."

"I didn't catch anything. She didn't have anything. It was just her mother."

"Well. Go to sleep now. How was your dinner?"

"Lousy," Phoebe said.

"You heard what your father said about using that word. What was lousy about it? You had a lovely lamb chop. I walked all over Lexington Avenue just to —"

"The lamb chop was all right, but Charlene always breathes on me whenever she puts something down. She breathes all over the food and everything. She breathes on every thing."

"Well. Go to sleep. Give mother a kiss. Did you say your prayers?"

"I said them in the bathroom. G'night!"

"Good night. Go right to sleep now. I have a splitting headache", my mother said. She gets headaches quite frequently. She really does.

"Take a few aspirins", old Phoebe said. "Holden'll be home on Wednesday, won't he?"

"So far as I know. Get under there, now Way down."

I heard my mother go out and close the door. I waited a couple of minutes. Then I came out of the closet. I bumped smack into old Phoebe when I did it, because it was so dark and she was out of bed and coming to tell me. "I hurt you?" I said. You had to whisper now, because they were both home. "I gotta get a move on," I said. I found the edge of the bed in the dark and sat down on it and started putting on my shoes. I was pretty nervous. I admit it.

"Don't go now," Phoebe whispered. "Wait'll they're asleep!"

"No. Now. Now's the best time," I said. "She'll be in the bathroom and Daddy'll turn on the news or something. Now's the best time." I could hardly tie by shoelaces, I was so damn nervous. Not that they would've killed me or anything if they'd caught me home, but it would've been very unpleasant and all. "Where the hell are ya?" I said to old Phoebe. It was so dark, I couldn't see her.

"Here." She was standing right next to me. I didn't even see her.

"I got my damn bags at the station," I said. "Listen. You got any dough, Phoebe? I'm practically broke."

"Just my Christmas dough. For presents and, all. I haven't done any shopping at all ye."

"Oh." I didn't want to take her Christmas dough.

"You want some?" she said.

"I don't want to take your Christmas dough."

"I can lend you some," she said. Then I heard her over at D. B.'S desk, opening a million drawers and feeling around with her hand. It was pitch—black, it was so dark in the room. "If you go away, you won't see me in the play", she said. Her voice sounded funny when she said it.

"Yes, I will. I won't go away before that. You think I wanna miss the play?" I said. "What I'll do, I'll probably stay at Mr. Antolini's house till maybe Tuesday, night. Then I'll come home. If I get a chance, I'll phone ya."

"Here," old Phoebe said. She was trying to give me the dough, but she couldn't find my hand.

"Where?"

She put the dough in my hand.

"Hey, I don't need all this," I said. "Just give me two bucks, is all. No kidding—here." I tried to give it back to her, but she wouldn't take it.

"You can take it all. You can pay me back. Bring it to the play."

"How much is it; for God's sake?"

"Eight dollars and eighty-five cents. Sixty-five cents. I spent some."

Then, all of a sudden, I started to cry. I couldn't help it. I did it so nobody Could hear me, but I did it. It scared hell out of old Phoebe when I started doing it, and she came over and tried to make me stop, but once you get started, you can't just stop on a goddam dime. I was still sitting on the edge of the bed when I did it, and she put her old arm around my neck, and I put my arm around her, too, but I still couldn't stop for a long time. I thought I was going to choke to death or something. Boy, I scared hell out of poor old Phoebe. The damn window was open and everything, and I could feel her shivering and all, because all she had on was her pajamas: I tried to make her get back in bed, but she wouldn't go. Finally I stopped, but it certainly took me a long, long time. Then I finished buttoning my coat and all. I told her I'd keep in touch with her. She told me I could sleep with her if I wanted to, but I said no, that I'd better beat it, that Mr. Antolini was waiting for me: and all. Then I took my hunting hat out of my coat pocket and gave it to her. She likes those crazy hats. She didn't want to take it, but I made her. I'll bet she slept with it on. She really likes those kind of hats. Then I told her again I'd give her a buzz if I got a chance, and then I left.

It was a helluza lot easier getting out of the house than it was getting in, for some reason. For one thing, I didn't give much of a damn any more if they caught me. I really didn't. I figured if they caught me, they caught me. I almost wished they did, in a way.

I walked all the way downstairs, instead of taking the elevators. I went down the back stairs. I nearly broke my neck on about ten million garbage pails; but I got out all right.

6. *Southern Novelists*

There is a notable lack of imaginative literature produced in the South before 1800. It has been argued that oratory, historiography and politics rather fiction, drama and poetry engaged the creative and intellectual energies of Southerners. However, increasing attacks on the South over the issue of slavery galvanized Southern writing at the start of the 19th century. The plantation novels by writers such as Sarah J. Hale (1788—1879), John Pendleton Kennedy (1795—1870) and William Gilmore Simms (1806—1870) placed emphasis on the South as a different kind of society than that of the North, and laid the basis for the nostalgia of post-war plantation literature. Theirs is the version of the "Old South" that becomes familiar in the 20th century, a South of leisure, grace and aristocratic chivalry.

After the Civil War there was a notable hiatus in Southern literature, until it revived and flourished during the period 1929—1955, which is described as Southern Renaissance. The renaissance developed particularly with the work William Faulkner. Faulkner is both the major writer of the renaissance and the writer who did most to articulate distinctively Southern themes in the 20th century. To a large extent he defines modern Southern literature, with its preoccupation with the lurid, the grotesque, with forms of Romantic and, above all, with the tragic sense of a Southern past that is simultaneously legacy, burden and curse. Faulkner was deeply ambivalent towards the South: he understood its faults and self-delusion from within, yet never lived elsewhere for any length of time, and the South and its history constantly formed the focus for his finest fiction. Faulkner's sense of a fractured past also is evident in the work of writers such as Flannery O'Connor, Eudora Welty (1909—2001) and Carson McCullers (1917—1967). Confronting it led also to the fullest restoration of the myth of the Old South in *Gone With the Wind* (1936) by Margaret Mitchell (1900—1949). Much of the appeal of this myth, even in the hands of sophisticated writers such as Allen Tate (1899—1979) and Robert Penn Warren (1905—1989), had to do with a sense that the modern South was becoming or was in danger of becoming an industrial, mechanized pastless society indistinguishable from the North. Since the 1960s, What was often considered the theme of Southern literature, the relation between past and present, has become less prominent, and notably less tragic.

Margaret Mitchell (1900—1949)

Margaret Mitchell was the author of the enormously popular

novel *Gone with the Wind* (1936), a story about the Civil War and Reconstruction as seen from the Southern point of view. The book was adapted into a highly popular film in 1939, starring Clark Gable and Vivien Leigh. At the novel's opening in 1861, Scarlett O'Hara is a young girl. During the story she experiences Secession, the Civil War, Reconstruction, as well as three marriages and motherhood.

Margaret Mitchell was born in Atlanta. Her mother was a suffragist and father a prominent lawyer and president of the Atlanta Historical Society. Mitchell grew up listening to stories about old Atlanta and the battles the Confederate Army had fought there during the American Civil War. Mitchell graduated from the local Washington Seminary and started in 1918 to study medicine at Smith College. In her youth Mitchell adopted her mother's feminist leanings which clashed with her father's conservatism—but she lived fully the Jazz age and wrote about it in nonfiction, like in her article 'Dancers Now Drown Out Even the Cowbell' in the Atlanta Journal *Sunday Magazine*.

When Mitchell's mother died in 1919, she returned home to keep house for her father and brother. In 1922 she married Berrien Kinnard Upshaw. The disastrous marriage was climaxed by spousal rape and was annulled in1924. Mitchell started her career as a journalist in 1922 under the name Peggy Mitchell, writing articles, interviews, sketches, and book reviews for the Atlanta Journal. Four years later she resigned after an ankle injury. Her second husband, John Robert Marsh, an advertising manager, encouraged Mitchell in her writing aspirations. From 1926 to 1929 she wrote *Gone with the Wind*. The outcome, a thousand page novel, which was later compared with Tolstoy's *War and Peace*, was published by the Macmillan Publishing Company in 1936.

Mitchell's book broke sales records, the New Yorker praised it, and the poet and critic John Crowe Ransom admired "the architectural persistence behind the big work" but criticized the book as overly Southern, particularly in its treatment of Reconstruction. In 1937, *Gone with the Wind* was awarded the Pulitzer Prize.

The protagonist of the novel is Scarlett O'Hara, who loves Ashley Wilkes. However, the reader is soon assured that the most important man in her life will be the strong and shrewd Rhett Butler. Ashley marries Melanie Hamilton and Scarlett marries Melanie's brother Charles, but she is soon widowed. Then she marries Frank Kennedy, her sister's fiancé, to save Tara, the family plantation, her home. Frank is also killed, and Scarlett finally marries Rhett, who walks out on her with the famous words "My dear, I don't give a damn."

During World War Ⅱ Mitchell was a volunteer selling war bonds and volunteer for the American Red Cross. She was named honorary citizen of volunteers France, in 1949, for helping the city obtain American aid after World War Ⅱ. Mitchell died in Atlanta on August 16, 1949—she was accidentally struck by a speeding car while crossing Peachtree Street.

Flannery O'Connor (1925—1964)

Born in Savannah, Georgia, O'Connor was educated at

Georgia State College for Women and also studied at the Writers' Workshop at the University of Lowa. She suffered from a terminal illness, lupus, for much of her adult life and was frequently hospitalized and in great pain until her death at the age of 39.

Despite the brevity of her career, however, she made a strong impression on the American literary scene, and exerted considerable influence on the development of the American short story. Her own Southern origins and devout Roman Catholic faith are evident throughout her fiction, in which she often uses poor, disabled, or socially marginal characters involved in absurd and violent situations to convey the spiritual poverty and crippled intellect of the modern world. Her vision of violent spiritual struggle in the rural South is marked by a grotesque humor and unnerving irony. Her first novel, *Wise Blood* (1952), tells the story of Hazel Motes, the lonely prophet of a "church without Christ, where the blind stay blind, the lame stay lame, and them that's dead stays that way." Another novel, *The Violent Bear It Away*, was published in 1960. Her short stories are collected in *A Good Man Is Hard to Find* (1955, published in England in 1959 as *The Artificial Nigger and Other Stories*) and the posthumously published *Everything That Rises Must Converge* (1965). *Mystery and Manners: Occasional Prose* appeared in 1969, her *Complete Stories* in 1971, and a collection of her letters, *The Habit of Being*, in 1979.

Katherine Anne Porter (1890—1980)

Born in Indian Creek, Texas, Porter worked on a newspaper

in Denver, Colorado, and then lived in Mexico and Europe for a number of years. Her first collection of stories, *Flowering Judas, and Other Stories*, was published in 1930. *Hacienda: A Story of Mexico* appeared in 1934. She received widespread critical acclaim for the volume *Pale Horse, Pale Rider* (1939), which consists of three short novels: "Old Mortality"; "Noon Wine," which is set on a Texan ranch and had previously been published as a volume in 1937; and the title piece, which tells of a short-lived love affair between a soldier and a young Southern newspaper woman during the influenza epidemic of World War I.

Porter published two further collections of stories, *The Leaning Tower, and Other Stories* (1944) and *The Old Order: Stories of the South* (1944), as well as two volumes of essays, *The Days Before* (1952) and *A Defense of Circe* (1954). Her best-known work, *Ship of Fools*, appeared in 1962 after 20 years in the writing. A bitterly ironic novel, it is set on a German passenger ship sailing from Mexico to Germany in 1931, and explores the origin and potential of human evil through the allegorical use of characters as almost one-dimensional representatives of various national and moral types. *The Collected Stories of Katherine Anne Porter* (1965) received both the Pulitzer Prize and the National Book Award. *Collected Essays and Occasional Writings* appeared in 1970. *The Never-Ending Wrong* (1977) is an account of the infamous Sacco-Vanzetti trial and execution. Her other works include *The Itching Parrot* (1942), *Holiday* (1962), and *A Christmas Story* (1967).

William Faulkner (1897—1962)

① *Biographical Introduction*

Faulkner was born in New Albany, Mississippi, into a family which had played a prominent role in the history of the south. The strict family code of honor, its sense of white social status, and its often violent exploits would provide a good deal of material for Faulkner's fiction. When he was five the family moved to Oxford, which became his permanent home and the prototype of his imaginary Yoknapatawpha county (the setting of most of his works). After briefly attending the University of Mississippi, Faulkner worked as a bookshop assistant in New York and a journalist in New Orleans, where he became a close friend of the writer Sherwood Anderson. He then returned to Oxford and began to write poems. As his poetry was undistinguished, he turned to the writing of prose in 1925. With the publication of *Sartoris* in 1929, Faulkner's most productive period began. He created the novels for which he is now best known: *The Sound and the Fury* (1929), *As I lay Dying* (1930), *Sanctuary* (1931), *Light in August* (1932), *Absalom, Absalom!* (1936), and *Go Down, Moses* (1942). At the time of their publication, these books were received with indifference or hostility. However, in the early 1940s, the tide of opinion began to turn, and in 1950, Faulkner received recognition with the award of the Nobel Prize for literature. Today he is regarded as the most important American novelist of the twentieth century, ranking with Ernest Hemingway.

② *His Theme and View*

Faulkner generally shows a grim picture of human society, where violence and cruelty are frequently included. His intention was to show the evil, harsh events in contrast to such eternal virtues as love, honor, pity, compassion and self-sacrifice. He felt that it was a writer's duty to remind his readers constantly of true values and virtues. Faulkner's major theme was the glorious past and the sterile present of the south. He wrote about the southern society by inventing families of different social forces: the old, decaying upper class, the rising, ambitious, unscrupulous class of "poor whites", and the Negroes who labored for both of them. Through the portrayal of the southern people, Faulkner presented his universal theme: "the problems of the human heart in conflict with itself."

③ *His Style*

Faulkner's stylistic innovations were often adapted from the experiment of other modern writers, which he then used in his own way. His books are sometimes difficult to read, and need close study by the reader. His works are distinguished by complex plots, sometimes extending over several novels in which the same characters appear. The hero of one story may appear as a minor character in another. He successfully advanced two modern literary techniques: stream of consciousness, and multiple point of view. Stream of consciousness, first used by James Joyce, the Irish novelist, tells a story by recording the thoughts of one character. Action and plot are less important than the reactions and inner musings of the narrator. Time sequences are often dislocated. Faulkner became a master as presenting multiple points of view, showing within the same story how the characters reacted differently to the same person or the same situation. This technique makes the reader recognize the difficulty of arriving at a true judgment.

④ *His Major Works*

Sartoris is principally concerned with the decline of the Sartoris family, representative of the Old South. The family is followed from the old slave society before the Civil War until the present. Here the old Colonel and the young Colonel reflect Faulkner's great grandfather and grandfather. The Sartorises and the Faulkners, though not identical, have an organic relationship.

The Sound and the Fury, the story of the ruin of a great plantation and the decay of a once great family, the Compsons, is a brilliant, intense, difficult novel, unfolding slowly, moving from the obscure first section, the babblings of the idiot, Benjy, through the second section, the stream of consciousness of the neurotic, sensitive, proud, romantic boy Quentin, contemplating suicide because in his mind he has committed incest with his sister Candace, who is bearing a stranger's child, to the objective narration of the third section, related by the hard, mean brother, Jason, who by birth one of the old aristocracy, becomes by virtue of viciousness a leader of the new south. The fourth section is presented by an outside observer. Here is a family living out its doom in the greater frame work of a disintegrating society.

Absalom Absalom ! is the story of the Sutphen family, a tale of violence and morbid passions, of the founding of dynasty and the building of a great house, and of the destruction of both. Sutphen's eldest son, disowned by his father because the mother had Negro blood, unknowingly falls in love with his half-sister and is killed by his half-brother who dies in a fire that destroys the house. Sutphen himself is killed by the grandfather of a girl he has seduced in the hope of producing another son and heir.

The Hamlet (1940), *The Town* (1957), and *The Mansion* (1959) form a trilogy on the saga of the unscrupulous Snopes family. Energetic and ambitious, the low class whites took the place of the Negroes who migrated to the North after the First World War, and rose to power in Yoknapatawpha county by using modern methods and modern ideas to oust the traditional class of white leaders, symbolized by the Sartoris family.

SARTORIS

(*Exerpt*)

Later they returned for the jug in Bayard's car, Bayard and Hub and a third young man, freight agent at the railway station, with three Negroes and a bull fiddle[1] in the rear seat. But they drove no farther than the edge of the field above the house and stopped there while Hub went on afoot down the sandy road toward the barn. The moon stood pale and cold overhead, and on all sides insects shrilled in the dusty undergrowth. In the rear seat the Negroes murmured among themselves.

"Fine night," Mitch, the freight agent, suggested. Bayard make no reply. He smoked moodily, his head closely helmeted in its white bandage. Moon and insects were one, audible and visible, dimensionless and without source.

After a while Hub materialized against the dissolving vagueness of the road, crowned by the silver slant of his hat, and he came up and swung the jug on to the door and removed the stopper. Mitch passed it to Bayard.

"Drink," Bayard said, and Mitch did so. The others drank.

"We ain't got nothing for the niggers to drink out of," Hub said.

"That's so," Mitch agreed. He turned in his seat, "Ain't one of you boys got a cup or something?" The Negroes murmured again, questioning one another in mellow consternation.

"Wait," Bayard said. He got out and lifted the hood and removed the cap from the breather-pipe. "It'll taste a little like oil for a drink or two. But you boys won't notice it after that."

"Naw, suh," Negroes agreed in chorus. One took the cup and wiped it out with the corner of his coat, and they too drank in turn, with smacking expulsions of breath. Bayard replaced the cap and got in the car.

"Anybody want another right now?" Hub asked, poising the corn cob.[2]

"Give Mitch another," Bayard directed. "He'll have to catch up."

Mitch drank again. Then Bayard took the jug and tilted it. The others watched him respectfully.

"Dam'f he don't drink it," Mitch murmured. "I'd be afraid to hit it so often, if I was you."

"It's my damned head." Bayard lowered the jug and passed it to Hub. "I keep thinking another drink will ease it off some."

"Don't put that bandage on too tight," Hub said. "Want it loosened some?"

"I don't know." Bayard lit another cigarette and threw the match away. "I believe I'll take it off. It's been on there long enough." He raised his hands and fumbled at the bandage.

"You better let it alone," Mitch warned him. But he continued to fumble at the fastening; then he slid his fingers beneath a turn of the cloth and tugged at it savagely. One of the Negroes leaned forward with a pocket knife and severed it, and they watched him as he stripped it off and flung it away.

"You ought not to done that," Mitch told him.

"Ah, let him take it off if he wants." Hub said. "He's all right". He got in and stowed the jug away between his knees, and Bayard turned the car about. The sandy road hissed beneath the broad tires of it and rose shaling[3] into the woods again where the dappled moonlight was intermittent, treacherous with dissolving vistas. Invisible and sourceless among the shifting patterns of light and shade, whippoorwills were like flutes tongued liquidly. The road passed out of the woods and descended, with sand in shifting and silent lurches, and they turned on to the valley road and away from town.

The car went on, on the dry hissing of the closed muffler. The Negroes murmured among themselves with mellow snatches of laughter whipped like scraps of torn paper away behind. They passed the iron gates and Bayard's home serenely in the moonlight among its trees, and the silent, box-like flag station and the metal-roofed cotton gin on the railroad siding.

The road rose at last into hills. It was smooth and empty and winding, and the Negroes fell silent as Bayard increased speed. But still it was not anything like what they had anticipated of him. Twice more they stopped and drank, and then from an ultimate hilltop they looked down upon another cluster of lights like a clotting of beads upon the pale gash where the railroad ran. Hub produced the breather-cap and they drank again.

Through streets identical with those at home they moved slowly, toward an identical square. People on the square turned and looked curiously after them. They crossed the square and followed another street and went on between broad laws and shaded windows, and presently beyond an iron fence and well back among black andsliver trees, lighted windows hung in ordered tiers like rectangular lanterns strung among the branches.

They stopped here, in shadow. The Negroes descended and lifted the bass viol out, and a guitar. The third one held a slender tube frosted over with keys upon which the intermittent moon glinted in pale points, and they stood with their heads together, murmuring among themselves and touching plaintive muted chords from the strings. Then the one with the clarinet raised it to his lips.

The turns were old tunes. Some of them were sophisticated tunes and formally intricate, but in the rendition this was lost, and all of them were imbued instead with a plaintive similarity, a slurred and rhythmic simplicity; and they drifted in rich, plaintive chords upon the silver air, fading, dying in minor reiterations along the treacherous vistas of the moon. They played again, an old waltz. The college Gerberus[4] came across the dappled lawn to the fence and leaned his arms upon it, a lumped listening shadow among other shadows. Across the street, in the shadows there, other listeners stood. A car approached and slowed to the curb and shut off engine and lights, and in the tiered windows heads leaned, aureoled against the lighted rooms behind, without individuality, feminine, distant, delicately and divinely young.

They played "Home, Sweet Home," and when the rich minor died away, across to them came a soft clapping of slender palms. Then Mitch sang "Good Night, Ladies" in his true, over-sweet tenor, and the young hands were more importunate, and as they drove away the slender heads leaned aureoled with bright hair in the lighted windows and the soft clapping drifted after them for a long while, fainter and fainter in the silver silence and the moon's infinitude...

The moon stood well down the sky. Its light was now a cold silver on things, spent and a little wearied, and the world was empty as they rolled without lights along a street lifeless and fixed in black and silver as any street in the moon itself. Beneath stippled intermittent shadows they went, passed quiet intersections dissolving away, occasionally a car motionless at the curb before a house. A dog crossed the street ahead of them trotting, and went on across a lawn and so from sight, but saving this there was no movement anywhere.

The square opened spaciously about the absinthe cloudy mass of elms that surrounded the courthouse. Among them the round spaced globes were more like huge, pallid grapes than ever. Above the exposed vault in each bank burned a single bulb; inside the hotel lobby, before which a row of cars was aligned, another burned. Other lights there were none.

They circled the courthouse, and a shadow moved near the hotel door and detached itself from shadow and came to the curb, a white shirt glinting within a spread coat; and as the car swung slowly toward another street, the man hailed them. Bayard stopped and the man came through the blanched dust and laid his hand on the door.

"Hi, Burk," Mitch said. "You're up pretty late, ain't you?"

The man had a sober, good-natured horse's face. He wore a metal star on his unbuttoned waistcoat. His coat humped slightly over his hip. What you boys doing?" he asked. "Been to a dance?"

"Serenading," Bayard answered. "Want a drink, Buck?"

"No, much obliged." He stood with his hand on the door, gravely and good-naturedly serious. "Ain' t you fellers out kind of late, yo' selves?"

"It is getting' on[5]," Mitch agreed. The marshal lifted his foot to the running-board. Beneath his hat his eyes were in shadow. "We're going home now," Mitch said. The other pondered quietly, and Bayard added:

"Sure; we're on our way home now."

The marshal moved his head slightly and spoke to the Negroes. "I reckon you boys are about ready to turn in[6], ain't you?"

"Yes, suh," the Negroes answered, and they got out and lifted the viol out. Bayard gave Reno a bill and they thanked him and said good night and picked up the viol and departed quietly down a side street. The marshal turned his head again.

"Ain't that yo' car in front of Rogers' cafe, Mitch?" he asked.

"Reckon so. That's where I left it."

"Well, suppose you run Hub out home, lessen[7] He's goingto stay in town tonight. Bayard better come with me."

"Aw, hell, Buck," Mitch protested.

"What for?" Bayard demanded.

"His folks are worried about him," the other answered.

"They ain't seen hide nor hair of him since that stallion throwed him. "Where's yo' bandage, Bayard?"

"Took it off," he answered shortly. "See here, Buck, we're going to put Mitch out and then Hub and me are going straight home."

"You been on yo' way home ever since fo' o'clock, Bayard," the marshal replied soberly, "but you don't seem to git no nearer there. I reckon you better come with me tonight, like yo' aunt said."

"Did Aunt Jenny tell you to arrest me?"

"They was worried about you, son. Miss Jenny just phoned and asked me to kind of see if you was all right until mawning'. So I reckon we better. You boys go on, and Bayard better come with me."

Mitch and Hub got out and Hub lifted out his jug and they said good night and went on to where Mitch's car stood before the restaurant. The marshal got in beside Bayard. The jail was not far. It loomed presently about its walled court, square and implacable, its silted upper windows brutal as saber-blows. They turned into an alley, and the marshal descended and opened a gate, and Bayard drove into the grassless and littered compound and stopped while the other went on ahead to a small garage in which stood a Ford. He backed this out and motioned Bayard forward. The garage was built to the Ford's dimensions and about a third of Bayard's car stuck out the door of it.

"Better'n nothin's, though," the marshal said. "Come on." They entered through the kitchen, into the jailkeeper's living-quarters, and Bayard waited in a dark passage until the other found a light. Then he entered a bleak, neat room, containing spare conglomerate furnishings and a few scattered articles of masculine apparel.

"Say," Bayard objected, "aren't you giving me your bed?"

"Won't need it befo' mawnin'", the other answered. "You'll be gone, then. Want me to help you off with yo' clothes?"

"No. I'm all right." Then, more graciously: "Good night, Buck. And much obliged."

"Good night," the marshal answered.

He closed the door behind him and Bayard removed his coat and shoes and his tie and snapped the light off and lay on the bed. Moonlight seeped into the room impalpably, refracted and sourceless; the night was without any sound. Beyond the window a cornice rose in a succession of shallow steps against the opaline and dimensionless sky. His head was clear and cold; the whisky he had drunk was completely dead. Or rather, it was as though his head were one Bayard who lay on a strange bed and whose alcohol-dulled nerves radiated like threads of ice through that body which he must drag forever about a bleak and barren world with him. "Hell," he said, lying on his back, staring out the window where nothing was to be seen, waiting for sleep, not knowing if it would come or not, not caring a particular damn either way. Nothing to be seen, and the long, long span of a man's natural life.

Three score and ten years to drag a stubborn body about the world and cozen its insistent demands. Three score and ten, the Bible said. Seventy years. And he was only twenty-six. Not much more than a third through it. Hell. . .

Notes:

1. bull fiddle: slang for bass viol.
2. corn cob: here, the stopper of a jug.
3. shaling: unevenly.
4. Gerberus: in Greek mythology, the three-headed dog guarding the gate of Hades; here, a watchman.
5. getting' on: (*colloq.*) getting on, becoming late.
6. turn in: go to bed.
7. lessen: (*dialect*) unless.

7. War Novelists

Many American writers served in two world wars and wrote novels based on their wartime experiences. Novels dealing directly with the first world war and its aftermath include *Three Soldiers* (1921) by Dos Passos, Cummings' *The Enormous Room* (1922), Hemingway's *In Our Time* (1925) and *A Farewell to Arms* (1926), and Faulkner's *Soldier's Pay* (1926) and *A Fable* (1954). Novels directly concerned with the second world war are notably Norman Mailer's *The Naked and the Dead* (1948); James Jones (1921—1977)'s *From Here to Eternity* (1951), *Pistol* (1959) and *The Thin Red Line* (1962); Kurt Vonnegut's *Slaughterhouse-Five* (1969); Joseph Heller's *Catch-22* (1961); and Herman Wouk's *The Winds of War* (1971) and *War and Remembrance* (1978).

Herman Wouk (1915—)

Herman Wouk is an American bestseller writer who has dealt in his work with moral dilemmas and the Jewish experience. Wouk's epic war novels have been tremendously popular. Several of them have been filmed, including *The Caine Mutiny* (1951). Wouk's two-volume historical novel set in World War Ⅱ, *The Winds of War* (1971) and *War and Remembrance* (1978), was also very successful as a television mini-series. This large novel has been be called an American *War and Peace*, which set individual values, actions, and fates against a panoramic, all-embracing picture of the world.

Herman Wouk was born in New York into a family of Jewish immigrants from Russia. He entered Columbia University, New York where he edited the college humor magazine. After completing a BA degree at Columbia University, he became a radio scriptwriter, working with Fred Allen from 1936. In 1941 he briefly served in the U. S. government, producing radio broadcasts to sell war bonds. He then joined the United States Navy and served in the Pacific. This period he credited later as a major part of his education. "I learned about machinery, I learned how men behaved under pressure, and I learned about Americans." Wouk began his first novel during off-duty hours at sea.

Since 1946 Wouk worked as a full-time writer. Wouk made his debut as a novelist with *Aurora Dawn* (1947). The satire about the New York advertising business was inspired by a wave of post-war experimentation. *City Boy* (1948) was a partly autobiographical story of a Bronx boy. *The Caine Mutiny* was awarded the 1952 Pulitzer Prize for fiction. The book was made into a hit Broadway play, starring Henry Fonda, and a film, starring Humphrey Bogart.

The Winds of War (1971) was a large canvas of the relationship between the actions of individuals and the events leading up to the Japanese attack on Pearl Harbor. Wouk focuses on the various members of the Henry family, famous for its naval heroes. The patriarch is Captain Victor "Pug" Henry, military man, scholar, translator, and advisor to Franklin Roosevelt and other statesmen. *War and Remembrance* (1978) concluded the story and attempted to explain the causes and implications of the war.

Wouk's books have been translated into some 30 languages. His novels display narrative skill, satire, and humor. They are meticulously researched and have won admiration for historical accuracy. Wouk has received several awards, including the Pulitzer Prize (1952), Columbia University Medal of Excellence (1952) Hamilton medal (1980); American Academy of Achievement Golden Plate award (1986), Washingtonian award (1986), U. S. Navy Memorial Foundation award (1987), Kazetnik award (1990). He also has several honorary degrees from American and Israeli universities.

Kurt Vonnegut (1922—)

Vonnegut was the most popular and widely read author among university students, young intellectuals and cultural protesters of all kinds during the 1960s. He held the same position at the center of "disaffected literature" that Salinger had occupied during the 1950s. A satirist and black-humorist, sometimes also classified as a science fiction writer, Vonnegut's primary concern has been for morality and compassion in a savage, wartorn world. He envisions a better human society, which he symbolizes as an imaginary distant planet named Tralfamadore, inhabited by virtuous, intelligent creatures. His satires on the stupidity and cruelty of the human race have sometimes been compared with Mark Twain's on the same subject.

Vonnegut was born and grew up in the Middle West, in a family which originally came from Germany. He studied at Cornell University in New York State, and then joined the U. S. Air Force in World War Ⅱ. He was captured by the Germans and, as a prisoner-of-war, he lived through the American fire-bombing of Dresden in 1945. Vonnegut considered the destruction of that beautiful, unarmed city a senseless outrage. Almost twice as many people died in the one-night fire-bombing of Dresden as were killed by the atomic bomb in Hiroshima, Japan, two months later, but for no military advantage.

From this experience, Vonnegut wrote his best book, *Slaughterhouse Five*, in 1969, at the height of the anti-Vietnam War protests. This partly autobiographical book spoke out forcefully against the insane conduct of all modern warfare. It contained a sincere note of truth and gave a sharp warning of what future wars might be like. At the same time, Vonnegút hoped that people might reform their barbaric attitudes before it was too late.

Joseph Heller (1923—1999)

The humor of Joseph Heller is more savage and bitter than Thurber's and Nash's satires on the middle class or Roth's Jewish satires. Heller attacks the whole institutional structure of society and, like the others, his hero in the novel is the victim.

Heller was born in Brooklyn and grew up in New York. The Second World War began when he was eighteen, so he was taken into the army. He was sent to the European front, where he became an Air Force bombardier and flew on many bombing missions. After the war, he finished his university studies, took an M. A. in literature from Columbia University and spent a year at Oxford in England. During the 1950s, he taught English at Pennsylvania State University but soon left that job to work in the advertising sections of various national magazines, including *Time*. Throughout this time, however, he was writing a novel in his spare time.

Heller's sardonic novel, *Catch-22*, was published in 1961, and it is considered to be one of the most significant works of "protest literature" to appear since the Second World War. The action of the novel takes place in the Air Force during the war, but the real subject is the dehumanization of all contemporary institutions and the corruption of individuals who gain power in institutions. In Heller's view, the armed forces were the most outrageous example of these two evils. This novel scorns the tradition of naturalistic war novels like Mailer's *The Naked and The Dead* and it mocks the idealistic notion of patriotic heroism. The book is full of incongruous details and misplaced events. It combines comic absurdity with the horrors of war in order to criticize bureaucratic authority and people who attain power over the lives of others.

CATCH-22

(*Excerpt*)

They gave Yossarian total anesthesia and knocked him out. He woke up thirsty in a private room, drowning in ether fumes. Colonel Kern was there at his bedside, waiting calmly in a chair in his baggy, wool, olive-drab shirt and trousers. A bland, phlegmatic smile hung on his brown face with its heavybearded cheeks, and he was buffing the facets of his bald head gently with the palms of both hands. He bent forward chuckling when Yossarian awoke, and assured him in the friendliest tones that the deal they had made was still on if Yossarian didn't die. Yossarian vomited, and Colonel Kern shot to his feet at the first cough and fled in disgust, so it seemed indeed that there was a silver lining to every cloud, Yossarian reflected, as he drifted back into a suffocating daze. A hand with sharp fingers shook him awake roughly. He turned and opened his eyes and saw a strange man with a mean face.

Yossarian shut his eyes to make him go away. When he opened them, Aarfy was gone and the chaplain was there. Yossarian broke into laughter when he spied the chaplain's cheerful grin and asked him what in the hell he was so happy about.

"I'm happy about you," the chaplain replied with excited candor and joy. "I heard at Group that you were very seriously injured and that you would have to be sent home if you lived. Colonel Kern said your condition was critical. But I've just learned from one of the doctors that your wound is really a very slight one and that you'll probably be able to leave in a day or two. You're in no danger. It isn't bad at all."

Yossarian listened to the chaplain's news with enormous relief. "That's good."

"Yes," said the chaplain; a pink flush of impish pleasure creeping into his cheeks. "Yes, that is good."

Yossarian laughed, recalling his first conversation with the chaplain. "You know, the first time I met you was in the hospital. And now I'm in the hospital again. Just about the only time I see you lately is in the hospital. Where've you been keeping yourself?"

The chaplain shrugged. "I've been praying a lot," he confessed. "I try to stay in my tent as much as I can, and I pray every time Sergeant Whitcomb leaves the area, so that he won't catch me."

"Does it do any good?"

"It takes my mind off my troubles," the chaplain answered with another shrug. "And it gives me something to do."

"Well, that's good, then, isn't it?"

"Yes," agreed the chaplain enthusiastically, as though the idea had not occurred to him before. "Yes, I guess that is good." He bent forward impulsively with awkward solicitude. "Yossarian, is there anything I can do for you while you're here, anything I can get you?"

Yossarian teased him jovially. "Like toys, or candy, or chewing gum?"

The chaplain blushed again, grinning self-consciously, and then turned very respectful. "Like books, perhaps, or anything at all. I wish there was something I could do to make you happy. You know, Yossarian, we're all very proud of you."

"Proud?"

"Yes, of course. For risking your life to stop that Nazi assassin. It was a very noble thing to do."

"What Nazi assassin?"

"The one that came here to murder Colonel Cathcart and Colonel Korn. And you saved them. He might have stabbed you to death as you grappled with him on the balcony. It's a lucky thing you're alive."

Yossarian snickered sardonically when he understood. "That was no Nazi assassin."

"That was Nately's girl friend. And she was after me, not Colonel Cathcart and Colonel Korn. She's been trying to kill me ever since I broke the news to her that Nately was dead."

"But how could that be?"the chaplain protested in livid and resentful confusion. "Colonel Cathcart and Colonel Korn both saw him as he ran away. The official report says you stopped a Nazi assassin from killing them."

"Don't believe the official report," Yossarian advised dryly. "It's part of the deal."

"What deal?"

"The deal I made with Colonel Cathcart and Colonel Korn. They'll let me go home a big hero if I say nice things about them to everybody and never criticize them to anyone for making the rest of the men fly more missions."

The chaplain was appalled and rose halfway out of his chair. He bristled with bellicose dismay. "But that's terrible! That's a shameful, scandalous deal, isn't it?"

"Odious'" Yossarian answered, staring up woodenly at the ceiling with just the back of his head resting on the pillow. "I think odious is the word we decided on."

"Then how could you agree to it?"

"It's that or a court-martial, Chaplain."

"Oh," the chaplain exclaimed with a look of stark remorse, the back of his hand covering his mouth. He lowered himself into his chair uneasily. "I shouldn't have said anything. "Question for

Consideration: Is there anything absurd revealed in this passage? If so, give an account of it.

8. Asian American Novelists

The history of Asian American literature began around the 1940's or before. Books about Asia or Asian Americans were written by non-members such as Pearl Buck. There were many Japanese Americans who wrote autobiographies about their experiences in the concentration camps in the United States. The first Chinese author to achieve financial success and was a mentor to many other Asian writers was C. Y. Lee who wrote *The Flower Drum Song* in 1955 which was made into a Broadway play and a motion picture . Notable Chinese works include: *Fifth Chinese Daughter* (1945) by Jade Snow Wong (b. 1922); *Eat a Bowl of Tea* (1961) by Louis Chu (1915—1970) and *The Joy Luck Club* (1989) by Amy Tan (b. 1952). *The Woman Warrior* (1976) by Maxine Hong Kingston has been considered a key text of Asian American literature, Not only was it acclaimed and accepted into mainstream American literature, but it also articulated the duality of identity confronted by Asian Americans while demonstrating the potential for intercultural fusion and enrichment.

Pearl Buck(1892—1973)

Pear Buck was one of the most popular American authors of her day, humanitarian, crusader for women's rights, editor of Asia magazine, philanthropist, noted for her novels of life in China. Pearl S. Buck was awarded the Nobel Prize for Literature in

1938, the third American to win the Nobel Prize in Literature, following Sinclair Lewis and Eugene O'Neill.

Pearl S. Buck was born in Hillsboro, West Virginia. She spent her youth in China, in Chinkiang on the Yangtse River. She learned to speak Chinese before she could speak English. Her parents were missionaries. Buck's father was a humorless, scholarly man who spent years translating the Bible from Greek to Chinese. Her mother had traveled widely in her youth and had a fondness for literature.

After being educated by her mother and by a Chinese tutor, who was a Confucian scholar, Buck was sent to a boarding school in Shanghai (1907—1909), Buck continued her education in the United States at Randolph—Macon Woman's College in Virginia, where she studied psychology. After graduating in 1914, she returned to China as a teacher for the Presbyterian Board of Missions. Buck married Dr. John Lossing Buck, an agricultural expert. They settled in a village in the North China. Buck worked as a teacher and interpreter for her husband and traveled through the countryside. In the 1920s the Bucks moved to Nanking, where she taught English and American literature at the university. In 1924 she returned to the United States to seek medical care for her first daughter, who was mentally retarded. In 1926 she received her M. A. in literature from Cornell University.

As a writer Buck started with the novel *East Wind: West Wind* (1930), which received critical recognition. She had earlier published autobiographical writings in magazines and a story entitled 'A Chinese Woman Speaks' in the *Asia Magazine*. Her breakthrough novel, *The Good Earth*, appeared in 1931. Its style, a combination of biblical prose and the Chinese narrative saga, increased the dignity of its characters. The book gained a wide audience, and was made into a motion picture.

The Good Earth (1931) has been translated into more than thirty languages and was awarded the Pulitzer Prize for fiction in 1932. The story follows the life of Wang Lung, from his beginnings as an impoverished peasant to his eventual position as a prosperous landowner. Wang Lung collects a slave, O-lan, from the prosperous house of Hwang. O-lan's parents sold her to Hwang because they were poor and needed money. According to an old Chinese custom, Wang Lung's and O-lan's marriage is prearranged. The fiancée is not beautiful, she is humble but shares with him the devotion to land, to duty, and to survival. First year is happy: the crop is good and they have two sons. Then the crops fail, and O-lan gives birth to a girl. The family moves to south, and the man abandons the plan to sell the child. Revolution breaks out, houses are plundered, and Wang Lung gets in his possession a silver treasure. The family returns to their home region. Wang Lung buys land and soon owns also the house of now impoverished Hwang. The only problem is their retarded child, a girl, who don't speak. O-lan gives birth to twins, a boy and a girl. The elder boys go to school. Wang Lung buys another wife, Lotus. O-lan is not well after the birth of the twins, and she dies after the wedding of her sons. In his old days, Wang Lung gives his love to a young slave girl, who also takes care of the retarded girl. His youngest son moves from the house to become a soldier because he also loves the young slave girl. Old Wang Lung witnesses for his sorrow that his children do not share his unyielding devotion to the land. The novel was followed by two sequels, *Sons* (1932), which focused on the youngest son, Wang the Tiger, and *A House Divided* (1935), which was Yuan's story. The three novels were published in 1935 in one volume as *The House of Earth*. At her death Buck was working on *The Red Earth*, a further sequel to *The Good Earth*, presenting the modern-day descendants of that novel's characters.

Maxine Hong Kingston (1940—)

Kingston's parents were Chinese immigrants. They operated a gambling house in Stockton, California, when Maxine was born in 1940. (She was named after a gambler who always won.) Shortly after her birth, the family opened a laundry where she and her five brothers and sisters joined their parents in working long, arduous hours. Kingston attended public schools, where she was an excellent student. After graduation, with the help of eleven scholarships, she enrolled in the University of California at Berkeley, one of the finest public colleges in the country. She at first intended to study engineering, but changed her major to English literature. Kingston graduated with a bachelor's degree in 1962. In November of that year, she married Earl Kingston, whom she had met in an English course. She earned a teaching certificate from the state of California and in 1965 taught high school for a year in Hayward. In 1967, the Kingstons moved to Hawaii, where Kingston took various teaching posts. From 1970 to 1977, she taught at the Mid-Pacific Institute, a private boarding school.

Maxine Hong Kingston is a highly acclaimed writer of both fiction and nonfiction and one of the first Asian Americans to make Asian American literature to the top of the literary world in America. Her first book, a memoir published in 1976 called *The Woman Warrior: Memoirs of a Girlhood Among Ghosts*, won the National Book Critic's Circle Award and made her a literary celebrity at the age of 36. Kingston has since written two other critically hailed books. *China Men*, a sequel to *The Woman Warrior*, was published in 1980 and also received the National Book Critic's Circle Award; and in 1989 Kingston published her third book, *Tripmaster Monkey: His Fake Book*. Kingston's writing is often cited for its melodiousness and poetry. The New York Times Book Review commented, "*The Woman Warrior* is about being Chinese in the way that (the James Joyce novel) *Portrait of the Artist (as a Young Man)* is about being Irish. It is an investigation of soul, not landscape. Its sources are dream and memory, myth and desire. Its crises are the crises of a heart in exile from roots that bind and terrorize it.

The Woman Warrior was an immediate success. In the memoir, Kingston writes of the conflicting cultural messages she received as the daughter of Chinese immigrants growing up in the America of the 1950s. The book also tells the story of the generations of Chinese women that preceded her and the weight she felt as an American trying to emerge from their sometimes stifling presence. The subtitle of the book, *Memoirs of a Girlhood Among Ghosts*, suggests the book's almost fantastic tone, but also refers specifically to the ghosts of Kingston's female relatives and the tragedy of many of their lives, lives lived in the extremely male-dominated society of China. She writes of Chinese folk sayings such as, "When fishing for treasures in the flood, be careful not to pull in girls" and "There's no profit in raising girls. Better to raise geese than girls."

Amy Tan (1952—)

Amy Tan is a second generation Chinese who lived in California. Her original degree and career was in linguistics. She received her degrees from San Jose City College. In 1985, she joined the Writer Workshop at University of California and began to sell stories. Her stories were offered to be published, and she collected them to form the *Joy Luck Club* (1989) which received the ALA Notable Books Award 1990, and other national awards. The second book *The Kitchen God's Wife* (1991) was based on her mother's life in China. Her mother never told Amy her life story until Amy convinced her it was worth telling. Amy Tan then published some children's stories such as *The Moon Lady* (1992). In 1995, she published *The Hundred Secret Senses*, and in 2001 *The Bonesetter's Daughte*r. Her essays (autobiography pieces) were collected in *The Opposite of Fate* (2003).

Joy Luck Club is the story of eight Chinese women. Four are mothers each of whom has different hardships, that forced them to leave China. Four are the daughters each of whom face their own struggles in their everyday living. Each chapter is a vignette of each women viewpoint of events. The first main character is the daughter Jing Mei "June" Woo whose mother passed away and is asked to join the Joy Luck Club and play Mah Jong with her adoptive aunts. Her mother started the Joy Luck Club and selected the players from people at church. Also June's mother struggled to find the lost twins she had to leave behind in China. Upon its publication in 1989, Tan's book won enthusiastic reviews and spent eight months on the *New York Times* bestseller list. The book has been translated in 17 languages, including Chinese.

9. *Women Novelists*

With the rapid development of the women's liberation movement in the United States in the 1960s, a new literary critical approach—feminism—came into being. The emergence of "gynocritics" in the 1970s (Elaine Showalter, Patricia Meyer Spacks, Judith Gardiner and Adrienne Rich), marked the beginning of new ways of looking at texts written by women, by taking into account of the existence of a female culture which necessarily implied alternative modes of expression. Gynocriticism seeks to rediscover, revise and rehabilitate literary works by women. Central to its action was the desire to inform women readers by offering modes on interpretation and new perspectives on literary history. Gynocritic s like Ellen Moers uncovered various traditions in the history of the women's novel: the epic tradition, characterized by a violence and anger invested in great causes (such as slavery in *Uncle Tom's Cabin*); the realistic tradition underlining the economic dependency of women and upholding a feminist work ethic(such as Louisa May Alcott's *Little Women*, 1868 and Ann Petry's *The Street*, 1946); the gothic tradition starting with

Mary Shelley and blossoming with the works of Sylvia Plath (*The Bell Jar*, 1971), Flannery O'Connor, Carson McCullers and Toni Morrison; and the heroinistic tradition which placed women characters at the center of the action, giving them the power of action and language to define their identity and freedom (as evidenced in the works of Willa Cather, Gertrude Stein, Grace Paley, and the great living women novelist Jane Smiley). At the heart of the feminine novel, there exists a specific mythos based on the attempt of these "mad women" to "get out of their attics" and find individual and collective definitions — a motif which provides the structure to black novelist Gloria Naylor's novel, *Linden Hills* (1985). Indeed the accomplishment of black women (Alice Walker, Toni Morrison and so on) and other ethic women novelists (Buck Pearl, Amy Tan, etc.) has formed a crucial chapter in this collective literary venture.

Carson McCullers (1917—1967)

Carson McCullers's original name was Lula Carson Smith. McCullers examined the psychology of lonely, isolated people, and published only eight books. Her best known novels are *The Heart Is a Lonely Hunter* (1940), written at the age of twenty-two, and *Reflections in a Golden Eye* (1942), set in a military base. Both of the books have been filmed. Although McCullers depicted homosexual characters and she has female lover, the theme of homosexuality is placed in a wider context of alienation and dislocation.

"The late autumn sun laid a radiant haze over the new sodded winter grass of the lawn, and even in the woods the sun shone through places where the leaves were not so dense, to make fiery golden patterns on the ground. Then suddenly the sun was gone. There was a chill in the air and a light, pure wind. It was time for retreat. From far away came the sound of the bugle, clarified by distance and echoing in the woods with a lost hollow tone. The night was near at hand." (from *Reflections in a Golden Eye*)

Carson McCullers was born in Columbus, Georgia, as the daughter of a well-to-do watchmaker and jeweler of French Hugenot extraction. At the age of 17 she moved to New York to study piano at Juilliard School of Music, but never attended the school McCullers worked in menial jobs and devoted herself to writing. In 1937 she married Reeves McCullers, a failed author. They moved to North Caroline, living there for two years. During this time she wrote *The Heart Is a Lonely Hunter*, a novel in the Southern Gothic tradition.

Set in the 1930s in a small Georgian mill town, *The Heart Is a Lonely Hunter* tells about an adolescent girl with a passion to study music, an unsuccessful socialist agitator, a black physician struggling to maintain his personal dignity, a widower who owns a caf, and John Singer, the deaf-mute protagonist. He is confidante of people who talk to him about loneliness and misery. When Singer's Greek mute friend goes insane, Singer is left alone. He takes a room with the Kelly family, where he is visited by the town's misfits. After discovering that his mute friend has died, Singer shoots himself—there is no one left to communicate with him. The novel was well-received when it came out, and it was interpreted as an anti-fascist book.

Joyce Carol Oates (1938—)

A novelist, poet, short-story writer, and critic, Oates was born in Lockport, New York, in the "Eden County" of many of her novels. She received a BA from Syracuse University in 1960 and an MA from the University of Wisconsin in 1961. She has taught English at the University of Detroit, the University of Windsor, Ontario, and at Princeton.

Her intense, often violent vision is perhaps most powerfully expressed in the novel *Wonderland* (1971), which is structured around Lewis Carroll's Alice stories, and in the loosely arranged trilogy, *A Garden of Earthly Delights* (1967), *Expensive People* (1968), and *Them* (1969, National Book Award). Her other novels are *With Shuddering Fall* (1964), *The Assassins: A Book of Hours* (1975), *Bellefieur* (1980), *Angel of Light* (1981), *A Bloodsmoor Romance* (1982), *Mysteries of Winterthurn* (1984), and *Solstice* (1985). Her short-story collections are *By the North Gate* (1963); *The Wheel of Love* (1970), which includes the often anthologized "Where Are You Going, Where Have You Been" and "The Region of Ice"; *The Goddess and Other Women* (1974); *The Seduction and Other Stories* (1975); and *Last Days* (1984). Her essays and criticism have appeared in several volumes, including *The Edge of Impossibility: Tragic Forms in Literature* (1972), *The Hostile Sun: The Poetry of D. H. Lawrence* (1973), and *Contraries: Essays* (1981). Her volumes of poetry include *Women in Love and Other Poems* (1968) and *Anonymous Sins, and Other poems* (1969). Oates's recent works include the novels — *What I Lived For*

(1994); *My Heart Laid Bare* (1998); *Blonde* (2000), a fictional work based on the life of Marilyn Monroe; and *The Falls* (2004), and her short stories are collected in *Heat* (1991), *Will You Always Love Me?* (1996), *Faithless* (2001), and *I Am No One You Know* (2004).

Oates writes about contemporary American life, which she sees as often defined by violence. She is particularly concerned with the connection between violence and love. Her characters are mainly ordinary, inarticulate people who sublimate the terrible things that happen to them. Although some of her novels have been labeled gothic, the violence in them is neither mysterious nor necessarily dramatic; it occurs randomly as in everyday life.

Mary McCarthy(1912—1989)

Mary McCarthy noted for her satirical commentaries on marriage, intellectuals, and the role of women. McCarthy's novels were often drawn from autobiographical sources; she put friends, enemies, ex-husbands, thinly disguised, into her fiction. Her best-selling novel, *The Group* (1963), was about her classmates at Vassar and their subsequent lives. McCarthy's seven novels appeared between the years 1942 and 1979. Most of her fiction and nonfiction explored the response of intellectuals to political and moral problems. McCarthy's attraction to Communism ended in 1936—1937, but in the mid-1960s she re-emerged as a political essayist, writing against the Vietnam War.

Mary McCarthy was born in Seattle, WA. Orphaned at the age of six, when both her parents died in the great flu epidemic of 1918, she was brought up by two sets of rich but austere grandparents—both in a strict Catholic environment and in a Protestant one. McCarthy was educated at the Annie Wright Seminary, Tacoma, Washington and Vassar College, New York, where she studied literature and met Elizabeth Bishop and Muriel Rukeyser. After graduating with honors aged 21, she married the first of her husbands and moved to New York.

In 1938 McCarthy married her second husband, the critic Edmund Wilson (1895—1972). McCarthy's first book, *The Companys She Keeps* (1972), was a collection of loosely linked stories. The satire about New York intellectuals depicted the failure of a marriage, and the search for personal identity through psychoanalysis. *The Oasis* (1949) was a short novel about artists and intellectuals living in a utopian society. *The Group* (1963) was a sexually outspoken depiction of eight Vassar graduates in the 1930s. It followed the group of friends through their first sexual experiences, marriage, and domestic duties. Intended to be a partial parody, it portrays women as they embrace or oppose ideas of political and social progress fashionable in the 1930s and 1940s. The book was made into a movie in 1966. Comically titled *Birds of America* (1971) focused on a boy whose mother refuses to accept modern conveniences; gradually the boy understands his mother's views of "progress."

Among McCarthy's other publications are critical works, travel books, and the autobiographical *Memoirs of a Catholic Girlhood* (1957). As important as her fiction are criticism and political reporting, such as *The Mask of State Watergate Portraits* (1971). *Cannibals and Missionaries* (1979) was a topical novel about the psychology of terrorism.

From 1962 McCarthy spent half of her time in Paris. She died of cancer in New York on October 25, 1989. McCarthy was a member of the American Academy, National Institute of Arts and Letters. Her several awards include Edward MacDowell Medal (1982), National Medal of Literature (1984), and the first Rochester Literary Award (1985). She had honorary degrees from six universities.

Jane Smiley (1951—)

Jane Smiley turned fifty just in time for the new millennium. She lives in California with her three children, three dogs, and her sixteen horses. Born in Los Angeles, California, Jane moved to the suburbs of St. Louis, Missouri, as an infant, and lived there through grammar school and high school (The John Burroughs School). After getting her BA at Vassar College in 1971, she traveled in Europe for a year, working on an archeological dig and sight-seeing, then returned to Iowa for graduate school at the University of Iowa.

MFA and Ph. D. in hand, she went to work in 1981 at Iowa State University, in Ames, where she taught until 1996. She has been married three times. Jane is the author of ten works of fiction, including *The Age of Grief*, *The Greenlanders*, *Ordinary Love and Good Will*, *A Thousand Acres*, which won the Pulitzer Prize in 1992 and *Moo*, as well as many essays for magazines. She has written on politics, farming, horse training, child-rearing, literature, impulse buying, getting dressed, marriage, and many other topics. Her new novel *Horse Heaven* was being published in April 2000, and *Good Faith* in April 2003.

Smiley's novel, *A Thousand Acres* (*King Lear*), portrays the enduring violence of incest to body and spirit. The narrative voice describes her family—a wealthy farmer and his three daughters. Family relationships are explored, especially the hidden roots that shape and define behaviors and conflicts, some lasting a lifetime. The disclosure of a horribly dark secret explains the personalities of the three daughters and, for two, their metaphoric afflictions (infertility and breast cancer). The novel is layered with rich complexities, but none more powerful and astonishing than the core event, the sexual victimization of two vulnerable teenage girls who, as the story unfolds, are permanently scarred. Through a reinterpretation of Lear, Smiley demonstrates the cost of this hideous form of male domination and female victimization.

Nell Freudenberger(? —)

Nell Freudenberger has taught English in Bangkok and New Delhi, and currently lives in New York City. *Lucky Girls* is her first book.

Lucky Girls is the debut collection by an author who first came to national attention with the 2001 publication of the title story in The New Yorker fiction issue. Here are five stories, set in Southeast Asia and on the Indian subcontinent-each on bearing the weight and substance of a short novella—narrated by young women who find themselves, often as expatriates, face to face with the compelling circumstances of adult love. Living in unfamiliar places, according to new and often frightening rules, these characters become vulnerable in unexpected ways—and learn, as a result, to articulate the romantic attraction to landscapes and cultures that are strange to them. In *Lucky Girls*, an American woman who has been involved in a five-year affair with a married Indian man feels bound, following his untimely death, to her memories of him, and to her adopted country. The protagonist of "Outside the Eastern Gate" returns to her childhood home in Delhi to discover a house still inhabited by the desperate and impulsive spirit of her mother who, years before, abandoned her family for a wild, dangerous journey across the Kyber Pass to Afghanistan. And, in "Letter from the Last Bastion," a teenage girl begins a correspondence with a middle-aged male novelist, who, having built his reputation writing about his experiences as a soldier in Vietnam, confides in her the secret truth of those experiences, and the lie that has defined his life as a man.

Lucky Girls marks the arrival of a writer of exceptional talents, one whose generosity of spirit, clarity of intellect and emotion, and skill in storytelling set her among today's most gifted and exciting young voices.

10. Other Contemporary Novelists

John Updike (1932—)

John Updike is a novelist, short story writer and poet, internationally known for his novels *Rabbit, Run* (1960), *Rabbit Redux* (1971), *Rabbit Is Rich* (1981), and *Rabbit at Rest* (1990). They follow the life of Harry "Rabbit" Angstrom, a star athlete, from his youth through the social and sexual upheavals of the 1960s, to later periods of his life, and to final decline. Updike's oeuvre has been large, consisting of novels, collections of poems, short stories, and essays. He has written a great deal of literary criticism. Among the writers whose works he has reviewed are such names as Philip Roth, Saul Bellow, Kurt Vonnegut, Joyce Carol Oates, Iris Murdoch, Michael Tournier, Raymond Queneau, Umberto Eco, Milan Kundera, Evgenii Evtushenko, Gabriel Garc a Mrquez, Mario Vargas Llosa, and Isabel Allende.

John Updike was born in Reading in Pennsylvania, but until he was 13 he lived in Shillington, a smaller city near Reading, and then he moved away to Plowville, PA. Updike's childhood was shadowed by psoriasis and stammering, but his mother encouraged him to write. After high school in Shillington, where his father worked as a science teacher, Updike attended Harvard. Updike majored in English in 1954, and contributed to and later edited the Harvard Lampoon. He started as a cartoonist, but then shifted to poetry and prose.

From the age of 23, Updike supported himself by writing. In 1958 Updike made his debut as a poet with the volume *The Carpentered Hen and Other Tame Creatures*. Updike's first novel, *The Poorhouse Fair* (1959), was about the residents of an old people's home. *The Centaur* (1963) used a mythological framework to explore the relationship of a schoolmaster father and his son. *The Coup* (1979) was an exotic first-person narration by an ex-dictator of a fictitious African state. In 2000 appeared Updike's prequel to *Hamlet*, in which the moody prince is not the central character but the story focuses on his mother Queen Gertrude, her husband, and Claudius, her husband's younger brother.

The first book about Updike's famous hero, Harry Angstrom, the natural athlete, a sexually magnetic, blue-eyed

Swede, ended with the verb "Runs." Updike wrote the book in the present tense, giving it a sort of cinematic quality. In *Rabbit, Redux* (Redux is Latin meaning "brought back") Harry is a middle-aged bourgeois, who finds his life shattered by the infidelity of his wife. Updike leaves the reader with a question—O. K.? The last word in *Rabbit Is Rich* was 'His.' *Rabbit at Rest*, set in the late 1980s, paralleled the decay of society, AIDS-plagued America, and Rabbit's swollen body, his chest pains, and his feeling that there is "nothing under you but black space....". After leaving Rabbit in 1990, Updike published in 2000 a 182-page novella called "Rabbit Remembered" in *Licks of Love*, a collection of short stories. 'Rabbit Remembered' ends with the word 'Gladly.'

John Barth (1930—)

John Simmons Barth is a novelist and short-story writer, known for the postmodernist and meta-fictive quality of his work.

John Barth was born in Cambridge, Maryland, on the Eastern Shore of the Chesapeake Bay. Music was Barth's first vocation. He was a student of orchestration for a year at the Juilliard School before he enrolled as a journalism major on a scholarship at John Hopkins University.

Barth's early fiction is conventional in form and language, but *The Sot-Weed Factor* (1960) and *Giles Goat-Boy* (1966) are very long, experimental comic novels, indebted to the fiction of Jorge Luis Borges and Vladimir Nabokov. Reviewers praised both of these novels for their display of erudition and bawdy wit.

Other publications include *The Literature of Exhaustion* (1982), Barth's analysis of postmodernist literary aesthetics, and the novels *Tidewater Tales* (1987) and *Last Voyage of Somebody the Sailor* (1991).

The Sot-Weed Factor was a literary quantum leap, an 800-page mock epic of the colonization of Maryland based on an actual poet, Ebenezer Cook, who wrote a poem of that name. *The Sot-Weed Factor* was what Northrop Frye called an anatomy—a large, loosely structured work, with digressions, distractions, stories within stories, and lists (such as a lengthy exchange of insulting terms by two prostitutes). The fictional Ebenezer Cooke (repeatedly described as "poet and virgin") is a Candide-like innocent who sets out to write a heroic epic and is disillusioned enough that the final poem is a biting satire.

Giles Goat-Boy, of comparable size, was a speculative fiction based on the conceit of the university as universe. It could be described as a fictional gospel about a half-man half-goat who discovers his humanity and becomes a savior in a university that allegorically represents the universe, presented as a computer tape given to John Barth, who denies that it is his work, preceded by an alleged note from the publisher to the effect that Barth really did write it. In the course of the book, Giles carries out all the tasks prescribed by Joseph Campbell in *The Hero with a Thousand Faces*. Barth kept a list of the tasks taped to his wall while he was writing the book.

The short story collection *Lost in the Funhouse* and the novella collection *Chimera*, were even more meta-fictional than their two predecessors, foregrounding the writing process and presenting achievements such as seven nested quotations. Letters was yet another tour de force, in which Barth and the characters of his first six books interacted.

While writing those books, Barth was also pondering and discussing the theoretical problems of fiction writing, most notably in an essay, "The Literature of Exhaustion"(first printed in the Atlantic, 1967), which was widely considered to be a statement of "the death of the novel." Barth has since insisted that he was merely making clear that a particular stage in history was passing, and pointing to possible directions from there. He later (1979) wrote a follow-up essay, "The Literature of Replenishment," to clarify the point.

John Hawkes, Jr. (1925—1998)

Hawkes is considered one of the most original American writers of the 20th century. His highly experimental works—complex, ambiguous, and grimly humorous—blend everyday reality with menacing hallucinations.

Hawkes was born in Connecticut and educated at Harvard; he has taught at Brown University since 1958. His first novel, *The Cannibal* (1949), is a bleak and formally complex work about the horrors of World War Ⅱ. Subsequent novels, such as *The Beetle Leg* (1951), *The Goose on the Grave* (1954), *The Lime Twig* (1961), and *Second Skin* (1964), continued to evoke the extremes of violence he saw as characteristic of the modern world. His more recent work has become more popular, but it remains macabre. He is, with John Barth, a leading figure of what has come to be called postmodernist fiction, a position evidenced by the collection of stories, *Lunar Landscapes* (1969), and by the novels *Death, Sleep and the Traveller* (1974), *Travesty*(1976), *The Owl* (1977), *The Passion Artist* (1979), *Virginie: Her Two Lives* (1981), *Innocence in Extremis* (1985), *Adventures in the Alaskan Skin Trade* (1985), and *An Irish Eye* (1997)

Thomas Pynchon (1937—)

Thomas Pynchon is best known for *V.*, *The Crying of Lot 49*, and *Gravity's Rainbow*, *Vineland*, and *Mason & Dixon*, complex fictions noted for their encyclopedic erudition and parodistic, labyrinthine plots.

Pynchon was born in Glen Cove, New York. and graduated from Cornell in 1958. He worked for a time at the Boeing Aircraft Corporation in Seattle, but little else is known about his life—he avoids interviews. His first novel *V.* (1963, Faulkner Award) is a long, dark-toned fantasy—his preferred medium for depicting American life in the latter half of the 20th century. In *The Crying of Lot 49* (1966, Rosenthal Memorial Award), he explores the attempts of the modern mind to organize an apparently chaotic universe, and juxtaposes various systems and ideologies that exist in contemporary society. His third novel *Gravity's Rainbow*, appeared in 1973, and received the National Book Award. He has also published a collection of his early short stories, *Show Learner* (1984), which includes "Lowlands" and "Entropy."

In *The Crying of Lot 49*, Pynchon combines the themes of decay and conspiracy developed in *V.* with observations on communication theory. The main character, Oedipa Maas, has been given the job of administering the estate of her deceased lover, Pierce Inverarity, who in addition to being a real estate tycoon, is also a stamp collector. In the course of investigating Inverarity's holdings, Oedipa uncovers a conspiracy in opposition to the postal system which dates back to the sixteenth century. The conspiracy, called Tristero, manifests itself in certain small ways such as counterfeit stamps.

Don DeLillo (1936—)

Don DeLillo was born on Nov. 20, 1936, in New York City's borough of the Bronx, to Italian immigrants. DeLillo had little contact with literature until he was 18, when he describes being carried away by the power and beauty of language. He attended Fordham University in New York, but found the city a far more exciting playground, citing its access to experimental art, jazz, and movies (he describes French filmmaker Jean-Luc Godard as the primary influence over his early work). He had a brief stint in the advertising world, and though he claims it was an uninteresting time of his life, his obsession with media and American culture may find its roots there, as well as in his immigrant background.

DeLillo's first novel, *Americana* (1971), traces these issues of media and culture through the travels of a television executive who tries to rediscover America through a film project. DeLillo delves into deeper questions of death, celebrity, cults, and consumerism in *End Zone* (1972), about a football player, and *Great Jones Street* (1973), about a reclusive rock star. His next series of books—*Ratner's Star* (1976), *Players* (1977), *Running Dog*

(1978), and *Amazons* (1980, written under the pen name Cleo Birdwell)—all deal with highly specific fictional worlds. *Ratner's Star*, for instance, is about astronomy, and *Amazons* tells a woman's "true" memoirs of playing in the National Hockey League.

DeLillo moved to Greece for several years and wrote *The Names* (1982), largely set in Greece. When he returned to the U. S. and wrote *White Noise* in 1985, his work broke through to the mainstream, winning the National Book Award. Thereafter, DeLillo focused more intently on conspiracy and cults in *Libra* (1988) and *Mao II* (1991). His *magnum opus*, *Underworld* (1998), spans the latter half of the 20th-century and explores celebrity, consumerism, and waste. DeLillo has also written two plays—*The Day Room* (1986) and *Valparaiso* (1999), and he recently published the novellas *The Body Artist* (2001) and *Pafko at the Wall* (2001), released on the 50th-anniversary of New York Giant baseball player Bobby Thomson's pennant-winning home run against the Dodgers. The novella is an adaptation of the opening pages of *Underworld*, which tracks several people, famous and not, on that historic day.

DeLillo shows no signs of slowing in production or award-collecting, nor does his preference to remain reclusive seem to be as overpowering as it is for his major postmodern literary counterpart, Thomas Pynchon. Though some readers find his writing cold and abstract, DeLillo blends intellectualism with human characters and a dark sense of humor in ways few writers can, living or dead.

Starting with a 1951 baseball game and ending with the Internet, *Underworld* is not a book for the faint-hearted. Elegiac in tone and described variously as DeLillo's *magnum opus* and his attempt to write the Great American Novel, the book weighs in at a hefty 827 pages and zips back and forwards in time, moving in and out of the lives of a plethora of different characters.

Following three main themes—the fate of a baseball from the winning game of the 1951 world series, the threat of atomic warfare and the mountains of garbage created by modern society—DeLillo moves forwards and backwards through the decades, introducing characters and situations and gradually showing the way their lives are interconnected.

The book focuses on Nick Shay, a former hoodlum who now works in the burgeoning waste management industry and owns the baseball from the 1951 game, "the shot heard around the world". In addition to Nick we hear from Frank Sinatra, J. Edgar Hoover, Lenny Bruce and the various people who move in and out of Nick's life: lovers, family, friends and colleagues. Through these seemingly disconnected narratives DeLillo paints a picture of Cold War paranoia at its peak—the baseball game happened the same day as the USSR's first nuclear test—and the changes affecting his characters as a microcosm of American society as a whole.

Chapter Ⅳ Modern Playwrights

1. *Eugene O'Neill (1888—1953)*

① *Biographical Introduction*

Eugene O'Neill is America's greatest playwright, and the

only one ever to receive the Nobel Prize. He was the first American play-wright to regard drama as serious literature and the first one to write tragedies consistently. Before his time, Americans saw only imported plays from Europe. Born in New York City, O'Neill was the younger son of James O'Neill, a popular actor. As a child he toured with his father, and attended university for one year, then held a series of jobs, observing and learning about the life of rough and uneducated workers. He then spent time in a tuberculosis sanatorium, and his early one-act plays date from this period of confinement. His involvement with the Provincetown players brought him to the attention of the public with a sequence of short plays. In 1920 his first full-length play, *The Emperor Jones*, was produced on Broadway. During the next fifteen years he wrote 20 plays and many short ones, for which he was awarded the Nobel Prize in 1936.

② *His Theme and View*

O'Neill held a tragic vision. He, like many of the modern writers, believed that modern man, separated from the Gods of his fathers, stands rootless and alone. His protagonists are aware of their alienation from a meaningful universe, and yet try to seek meaning and purpose in their lives, some through love, some through religion, others through revenge, but all meet disappointment. O'Neill's great purpose was to try and discover the roots of human desires and frustrations. Most of his plays were very pessimistic, leaving the characters without illusions or hope.

③ *His Style*

O'Neill wrote plays which were highly experimental in form

and style, combining literary theories of realism, naturalism, symbolism and expressionism. Starting with realistic writing in such plays as *Beyond the Horizon* and *Anna Christie*, he shifted to expressionistic writing in *The Emperor Jones*, wherein the inner mind and primitive fear of the hero are expressed by symbolic scenes and sound effect. O'Neill wrote in a wide variety of styles. His plays ranged from one act long with a single actor alone on the stage to eleven acts long having to be presented throughout a whole afternoon and evening. O'Neill wrote very long introductions and directions for every scene, explaining the mood, the effects and the atmosphere which should be evoked on the stage.

④ His Major Works

About 20 O'Neill's plays are considered as major works. The following are among the very best known.

The Emperor Jones (1920) tells about the disintegration of an American black railway porter who becomes the dictator of a tropical island. He is the victim of his own fears as he struggles to escape from danger. His attempts are in vain, yet he emerges as a heroic figure.

The Hairy Ape (1922) tells about the strong, proud, brutish coal-stoker in the engine-room of a passenger ship. He is insulted and hurt when an upper-class girl is frightened of him and calls him a hairy ape. Seeking revenge, the man loses his pride, his unity with his comrades, and finally his sanity. Feeling that he is akin to animals, he goes by night to a zoo and sets free a large ape which kills him.

Desire Under the Elms (1924) uses ancient Greek themes of murder and fateful retribution. Set on a lonely, stony farm, it tells of the tangled relationships between a lustful father, a weak son and an unfaithful wife who kills her own baby. Written in a very sparse style, without melodrama, its honesty of emotion makes it one of O'Neill's greatest plays.

Mourning Becomes Electra (1931), in eleven acts, uses ancient Greek forms, themes and characters. However, O'Neill sets the play in New England at the time of the Civil War. A heroic soldier returns home after the war, only to be murdered by his unfaithful wife. The jealous, revengeful daughter compels her weak brother to kill their mother, but he then commits suicide as well.

The Iceman Cometh (1946) was written in 1939, but it was not performed or published until seven years later. It is one of the finest and most complex of O'Neill's tragedies. It tells about a group of poor men who cling to a belief in their own worth and continue to hope for a better life. They are gradually stripped of their illusions about themselves, and thereby they lose all hope.

Long Day's Journey into Night (1956) was written between 1939 and 1941, but it was not produced until three years after O'Neill's death. This long autobiographical play describes one day in the life of his own family, his father, his mother, his older brother and himself. It depicts their agonized relationships in a straightforward style. Little by little, the play strips away the pretenses and defenses of the four characters, revealing the mother to be a defeated drug addict, the father a frustrated failure, the older brother a bitter alcoholic, and the younger son (O'Neill himself as a young man) a disillusioned, ill youth with little chance for happiness in his life.

2. Three Dominant Playwright

At the time after World War Ⅱ when Eugene O'Neill was writing his last great plays, two young playwrights, totally unlike one another, rose up to take his place. Arthur Miller wrote plays on broad social themes while Tennessee Williams looked deeply, even morbidly, into the psychology of social misfits. During the 1940s and 1950s, these two were pre-eminent. They were followed by Edward Albee, who held the central position in American drama until present times. Strongly influenced by O'Neill and Europe's "Theatre of the Absurd" movement, his plays explore modern man's capacity for self delusion and self-destruction.

Arthur Miller (1915—2005)

Miller is a playwright of social philosophy, concerned with the inner thoughts of individuals and their conflicts with the morality of their society. He took different points of view on this question. Two of his plays *All My Sons* (1947) and *A View from the Bridge* (1955) show the society's morality as correct, causing only suffering to those who oppose it. However, four of his plays, including the best ones, show that the morality of American society is false, and that following it will destroy honest individuals. These plays are *Death of a Salesman* (1949), *The Crucible* (1953), *Incident at Vichy* (1964) and *The Price* (1968).

Death of a Salesman was a great success and is considered Miller's masterpiece. It is the story of a traveling salesman—a metaphor for American society—who chooses popularity and getting rich as the false goals for his life and is finally driven to suicide. Miller believes that the common man is the tragic hero of modern times.

In the 1990s Miller wrote such plays as *The Ride down Mount Morgan* (1991) and *The Last Yankee* (1993), but in an interview he stated that "It happens to be a very bad historical moment for playwriting, because the theater is getting more and more difficult to find actors for, since television pays so much and the movies even more than that. If you're young, you'll probably be writing about young people, and that's easier—you can find young actors—but you can't readily find mature actors." In 2002, Miller was honored with Spain's prestigious Principe de Asturias Prize for Literature, making him the first U. S. recipient of the award. Miller died of heart failure at home in Roxbury, Connecticut, on February 10, 2005.

Tennessee Williams (1911—1983)

Written in a totally different vein from Arthur Miller, Williams's plays portray the loneliness and isolation of modern man, revealing depths of frustration, sex and violence underneath a veil of romantic politeness. His style is a combination of coarseness and poetry.

Williams's first full-length play infuriated conservative critics because it mixed sex and religion, so Williams had to take whatever jobs he could find—as a theatre usher and a film script writer. However, his next play was a great success. *The Glass Menagerie* (1944) is a pessimistic, even morbid, play about a fallen Southern family living in a slum. The domineering mother lives in romantic delusions about her elegant past life. She and her cynical son try, but fail, to find a husband for the shy, crippled daughter who withdraws from reality, and stays alone with her collection of glass animals, imagining a better life.

In 1947, he won even greater success with another pessimistic play *A Steetcar Named Desire*. Again the heroine was an aging Southern beauty who was full of delusions. She finally had to confront reality when she went to live with her pregnant sister and brutal brother-in-law, who drove her to insanity.

In the 1980s Williams gained a huge fame in the Soviet Union—he was called "the biggest success since Chekhov"—with *Cat on a Hot Tin Roof*, *Rose Tattoo*, and other classics. Williams's frank memoirs appeared in 1975. From the late 1940s Key West became one of Williams's favorite places. He loved swimming and while he painted—he was a gifted amateur painter—he listened Billie Holliday's records. His final play, *A House Noty Meant to Stand*, had its premiere at the Goodman Theater of Chicago in 1982. Williams died from choking after a heavy night of drinking on February 25, 1983. According to some speculations, he was assassinated.

Edward Albee (1928—)

Albee, the youngest of the three playwrights, took over the foremost position in American drama after Miller and Williams were no longer producing their best work. A native of Washington, D. C. who was educated in the best East coast schools and colleges, Albee has written serious criticisms of American society; several of his plays are studies of families where a strong-willed wife dominates a weak husband. Such a play is *Who's Afraid of Virginia Woolf*? (1962) which brought him fame and critical recognition. Other plays are *Tiny Alics* (1965), A *Delicate Balance* (1966), *All Over* (1971) and *Seascape* (1975), and

Three Tall Women (1994).

Albee's early plays were influenced by European experimental movements of the 1950s such as "Theatre of the Absurd" and "Theatre of Cruelty", but he developed his own powerful style, neither as sociological as Miller nor as individualistically psychological as Williams. He made several stage adaptations from the books of other authors.

Albee's plays may seem at first glance to be realistic, but the surreal nature of them is never far from the surface. In *A Delicate Balance* (1966), for example, Harry and Edna carry a mysterious psychic plague into their best friends' living room, and George and Martha's child in *Who's Afraid of Virginia Woolf?* (1962) turns out to be nothing more than a figment of their combined imagination, a pawn invented for use in their twisted, psychological games. In *Three Tall Women* (1994), separate characters on stage in the first act turn out to be, in the second act, the same character at different stages of her life.

DEATH OF A SALESMAN

Biff: No! Nobody's hanging himself, Willy! I ran down eleven flights with a pen in my hand today. And suddenly I stopped, you hear me? And in the middle of that office building, do you hear this? I stopped in the middle of that building and I saw the sky. I saw the things that I love in this world. The work and the food and time to sit and smoke. And I looked at the pen and said to myself, what the hell I am grabbing for this? Why am I trying to become what I don't want to be? What am I doing in an office, making a contemptuous begging fool of myself, when all I want is out there, waiting for me the minute I say I know who I am! Why can't I say that, Willy? (He tries to make Willy face him, but Willy pulls away and moves to the left.)

WILLY (with hatred, threateningly): The door of your life is wide open!

BIFF: Pop! I'm a dime a dozen, and so are you!

WILLY (turning on him now un an uncontrolled outburst): I am not a dime a dozen! I am Willy Loman, and you are Biff Loman!

(Biff starts for Willy, but is blocked by Happy. In his fury, Biff seems on the verge of attacking his father.)

BIFF: I am not a leader of men, Willy, and neither are you. You were never anything but a hard-working drummer who landed in the ash can like all the rest of them! I'm one dollar an hour, Willy! I tried seven states and couldn't raise it. A buck an hour! Do you gather my meaning? I'm not bringing home any prizes any more, and you're going to stop waiting for me to bring them home!

WILLY (directly to Biff): You vengeful, spiteful nut! (Biff breaks from Happy. Willy, in fright, starts up the stairs. Biff grabs him.)

Biff (at the peak of his fury): Pop, I'm nothing! I'm nothing, Pop. Can't you understand that? There's no spite in it any more. I'm just what I am, that's all.

(Biff's fury has spent itself, and he breaks down, sobbing, holding on Willy, who dumbly fumbles for Biff's face.)

WILLY (astonished): What're you doing? What're you doing? (To Linda)

Why is he crying?

BIFF (crying, broken): Will you let me go, for Christ's sake? Will you take that phony dream and burn it before something happens? (Struggling to contain himself, he pulls away and moves to the stairs). I'll go in the morning. Put him—put him to bed. (Exhausted, Biff moves up the stairs to his room.)

WILLY (after a long pause, astonished, elevated): Isn't that-isn't that remarkable? Biff-he likes me!

LINDA: He loves you, Willy!

HAPPY, (deeply moved): Always did, Pop.

WILLY: Oh, Biff! (Staring wildly): He cried! Cried to me. (He is choking with his love, and now cries out his promise): That boy-that boy is going to be magnificent! (Ben appears in the light just outside the kitchen.)

BEN: Yes, outstanding, with twenty thousand behind him.

LINDA: (sensing the racing of his mind, fearfully, carefully): Now come to bed, Willy. It's all settled now.

WILLY (finding it difficult not to rush out of the house): Yes, we'll sleep. Come on. Go to sleep, Hap.

BEN: And it does take a great kind of a man to crack the jungle.

(In accents of dread, Ben's idyllic music starts up.)

HAPPY (his arm around Linda): I'm getting married, Pop, don't forget it. I'm changing everything. I'm gonna run that department before the year is up. You'll see, Mom. (He kisses her.)

BEN: The jungle is dark but full of diamonds, Willy. (Willy turns, moves, listening to Ben.)

LINDA: Be good. Youre both good boys, just act that way, that's all.

HAPPY: Night, Pop. (He goes upstairs).

LINDA (to Willy): Come, dear.

BEN (with greater force): One must go in to fetch a diamond out.

WILLY (to Linda, as he moves slowly along the edge of the kitchen, toward the door): I just want to get settled down, Linda. Let me sit alone for a little.

LINDA (almost uttering her fear): I want you upstairs.

WILLY (taking her in his arms): In a few minutes, Linda. I couldn't sleep right now. Go on, you look awful tired. (He kisses her.)

BEN: Not like an appointment at all. A diamond is rough and hard to the touch.

WILLY: Go on now. I'll be right up.

LINDA: I think this is the only way, Willy.

WILLY: Sure, it's the best thing.

Ben: Best thing.

WILLY: The only way. Everything is gonna be-go on, kid, get to bed. You look so tired.

LINDA: Come right up.

WILLY: Two minutes.

(Linda goes into the living-room, then reappears in her bedroom. Willy moves just outside the kitchen door.')

WILLY: Loves me. (Wonderingly): Always loves me. Isn't that a remarkable thing? Ben, he'll worship me for it!

BEN (with promise): It's dark there, but full of diamonds.

WILLY: (Can you imagine that magnificence with twenty thousand dollars in his pocket!

LINDA (calling from her room): Willy! Come up!

WILLY (calling into the kitchen): Yes! Yes. Coming! It's very smart, you realize that, don't you, sweetheart? Even Ben sees it. I gotta go, baby. By! By! (Going over to Ben, almost dancing): Imagine? When the mail comes he'll be ahead of Bernard again!

BEN: A perfect proposition all around.

WILLY: Did you see how he cried to me? Oh, if I could kiss him, Ben!

BEN: Time, William, time!

WILLY: Oh, Ben, I always knew one way or another we were gonna make it, Biff and I!

BEN (looking at his watch): The boat. We'll be late. (He moves slowly off into the darkness.)

WILLY (elegiacally, turning to the house): How when you

kick off, boy, I want a seventy-yard boot, and get right down the field under the ball, and when you hit, hit low and hit hard, because it's important, boy. (He swings around and faces the audience.) There's all kinds of important people in the stands, and the first thing you know... (Suddenly realizing he is alone): Ben! Ben, where de I...? (He makes a sudden movement of search): Ben, how do I...?

LINDA (calling): Willy, you coming up?

WILLY (uttering a gasp of fear, whirling about as if to quiet her): Sh! (He turns around as if to find his way; sounds, faces, voices, seem to be swarming in upon him and he flicks at them, crying): Sh! Sh! (Suddenly music, faint and high, stops him. It rises in intensity, almost to an unbearable scream. He goes up and down on his toes, and rushes off around the house): Shhh!

LINDA: Willy?

(There is no answer. Linda waits. Biff gets up off his bed. He is still in his clothes. Happy sits up. Biff stands listening.)

LINDA (with real fear): Willy, answer me Willy! (There is the sound of a car starting and moving away at full speed.)

LINDA: No!

BIFF (rushing down the stairs): Pop!

(As the car speeds off, the music crashes down in a frenzy of sound, which becomes the soft pulsation of a single cello string. Biff slowly returns to his bedroom. He and Happy gravely don their jackets. Linda slowly walks out of her room. The music has developed into a dead march. The leaves of day are appearing over everything. Charley and Bernard, somberly dressed, appear and knock on the kitchen door. Biff and Happy slowly descend the stairs to the kitchen as Charley and Bernard enter. All stop a moment when Linda, in clothes of mourning, bearing a little bunch of roses, comes through the draped doorway into the kitchen. She goes to Charley and takes his arm. Now all move toward the audience, through the wall-line of the kitchen. At the limit of the apron, Linda lays down the flowers, kneels, and sits back on her heels. All stare down at the grave.)

Requiem

CHARLEY: It's getting dark, Linda.

(Linda doesn't react. She stares at the grave.)

BIFF: How about it, Mom? Better get some rest, heh? They'll be closing the gate soon.

(Linda makes no move. Pause.)

HAPPY (deeply angered): He had no right to do that. There was no necessity for it. We would've helped him.

CHARLEY (grunting): Humm.

BIFF: Come along, Mom.

LINDA; Why didn't anybody come?

CHARLEY: It was a very nice funeral.

LINDA: But where are all the people he knew? Maybe they blame him.

CHARLEY: Naa. It's a rough world, Linda. They wouldn't blame him.

LINDA: I can't understand it. At this time especially. First time in thirty-five years we were just about free and clear. He only needed a little salary. He was even finished with the dentist.

CHARLEY: No man only needs a little salary.

LINDA: I can't understand it.

BIFF: There were a lot of nice days. When he'd come home from a trip; or on Sundays, making the stoop; finishing the cellar; putting on the new porch; when he built the extra bathroom; and put up the garage. You know something, Charley, there's more of him in that front stoop than in all the sales he ever made.

CHARLEY: Yeah. He was a happy man with a batch of cement.

LINDA: He was so wonderful with his hands.

BIFF: He had the wrong dreams. All, all, wrong.

HAPPY (almost ready to fight Biff); Don't say that!

BIFF: He never knew who he was.

CHARLEY (stopping Happy's movement and reply. To Biff): Nobody dast blame this man. You don't understand. Willy was a salesman. And for a salesman, there is no rock bottom to the life. He don't put a bolt to a nut, he don't tell you the law or give you medicine. He's a man way out there in the blue, riding on a smile and a shoeshine. And when they start not smiling back-that's an earthquake. And then you get your self a couple of spots on your hat, and you're finished. Nobody dast blame this man. A salesman is got to dream, boy. It comes with the territory.

BIFF: Charley, the man didn't know who he was.

HAPPY (infuriated): Don't say that!

BIFF: Why don't you come with me, Happy?

HAPPY: I'm not licked that easily. I'm staying right in this city, and I'm gonna beat this racket! (He looks at Biff, his chin set): The Loman Brothers!

BIFF: I know who I am, kid.

HAPPY: All right, boy. I'm gonna show you and everybody else that Willy Loman did not die in vain. He had a good dream. It's the only dream you can have-to come out number-one man. He fought it out here, and this is where I'm gonna win it for him.

BIFF (with a hopeless glance at Happy, bends toward his mother): Let's go, Mom.

LINDA: I'll be with you in a minute. Go on, Charley. (He hesitates). I want to, just for a minute. I never had a chance to say good-by.

(Charley moves away, followed by Happy. Biff remains a slight distance up and left of Linda. She sits there, summoning herself. The flute begins, not far away, playing behind her speech.)

LINDA: Forgive me, dear. I can't cry. I don't know what it is, but I can't cry. I don't understand it. Why did you ever do that? Help me, Willy, I can't cry. It seems to me that you're just on another trip. I keep expecting you. Willy, dear, I can't cry. Why did you do it? I search and search and I search, and I can't understand it, Willy. I made the last payment on the house today. Today, dear. And there'll be nobody home. (A sob rises in her throat.) We're free and clear. (Sobbing more fully, released): We're free. Biff comes slowly toward her. We're free... We're free...

(Biff lifts her to her feet and moves out up right with her in his arms. Linda sobs quietly. Bernard and Charley come together and follow them, followed by Happy. Only the music of the flute is left on the darkening stage as over the house the hard towers of the apartment buildings rise into sharp focus, and the curtain falls.)

Questions for Consideration:

1. How well do you think Miller has succeeded in making a tragic hero out of Willy Loman?
2. How are social comment and family tensions interwoven within the play?

3. Contemporary Playwrights

David Alan Mamet (1947—)

David Alan Mamet was born in Flossmoor, Illinois on November 30, 1947, and often incorporates overtones of his hometown in his plays. He studied at Goddard College in Vermont and at the Neighborhood Playhouse School of Theater in New York.

He has taught at New York University, Goddard College, and the Yale Drama School, and he regularly lectures at the Atlantic Theater Company, of which he is a founding member.

David Alan Mamet made his name with *Sexual Perversity in Chicago*.(1974), *The Duck Variations* (1976) and *American Buffalo* (1977). These dark dramas have strong male characters with highly charged dialogue that build dramatic tension within the confines of the play. He often portrays the plight of small-time drifters, salesmen, and hoods and the con games they play. *The Woods* (1977) and *Edmond* (1982) were followed by two successful plays; *Glengarry Glen Ross* (1984) for which he won his Pulitzer prize, is a damning representation of the American business practices, and *Speed-the-Plow* (1988), which gives a savage view of the underside of the film industry. *Glengarry Glen Ross* was later made into a film version in 1992 using Mamets' own script.

Sam Shepard (1943—)

Sam Shepard has been a major force in contemporary American theatre since his earliest work. Shepard's plays are not easy to categorize, but in general they blend images of the Old West, fascination with pop culture—rock and roll, drugs and television—and bizarre family problems. Before he was thirty, Shepard had over thirty plays produced in New York. Shepard has repeatedly examined the moral anomie and spiritual starvation that label the world of his drama.

Sam Shepard was born Samuel Shepard Rogers Ⅲ in Fort Sheridan, Illinois, where the family had deep roots. At high school, he took little interest in his classes, but read poetry and played drums in a garage band. Samuel Beckett's play *Waiting for Godot*, which he read as a teenager, was a revelation for him. Especially Shepard's early plays show absurdist influence.

Shepard studied agriculture at San Antonio Junior College, but after a year he joined a touring company of actors. Later he was appointed playwright-in-residence at the Magic Theatre in San Francisco. At the age of 19 he settled in New York, where he changed his name from Steve Rogers to Sam Shepard. He supported himself by serving tables at the Village Gate, and pursued his theatrical interests. His first complete play, *Cowboys*, was autobiographical, and received good review in *The Village Voice*. Shepard's reputation was built with a series of one act-plays, produced in off-off Broadway theatres. After receiving a Rockefeller Foundation grant and a Guggenheim grant, Shepard became a full-time writer.

In the 1965—1966 season, Shepard won *Village Voice* newspaper's Obie awards for his plays *Chicago*, *Icarus's Mother*, and *Red Across*. The works were written hastily. His bizarre comedy, *La Turista*, was produced in 1967 in New York and two years later in London. In the *New York Review of Books*, Shepard was called "one of the three or four most gifted playwrights alive."

With the rock singer Patti Smith he collaborated on the rock opera *Cowboy Mouth* (1971), which was premiered in Edinburgh, Scotland. Despite the critical acclaim of *Mad Dog Blues* (1971), Shepard left New York, its drug scene, and moved with his wife and son to England, where he lived until 1974. He wrote several medium-length plays, that were successful on both sides of the Atlantic, among others *The Tooth of Crime* (1972), a musical-fantasy about an outlaw-rock star which was staged at the Open Space Theatre in New York, and *Geography of a Horse Dreamer* (1974), a mystery about a young cowboy, produced at the Royal Court and directed by Shepard.

In the mid-1970s Shepard wrote in California the plays that secured his reputation—*Curse of the Starving Class* (1976), and the Pulitzer Prize-winning *Buried Child* (1979), a story of incest and murder. On one level the story deals with the passing of the family farm from Dodge, representing the older generation, to Vince, his grandson. On the other level the play is a mythical story of a family curse. Dodge dies unnoticed after saying: "When the blaze is at its highest, preferably on a cold, windless night, my body is to be pitched into the middle of it and burned till nothing remains but ash." He apparently has committed infanticide and his son Tilde brings the buried child out of his grave.

Shepard's characters are often deprived of their dreams and sense of continuity. His plays express a sense of loss, nostalgia for the original rural world and the national myths, destroyed by pragmatism, money and power. In the modern world, the connection between myth, land, community, and a feeling of purpose in life had been broken. All we have, Shepard has said, is "ideas that don't speak to our inner self at all... ." Among his works from the 1990s are *Simpatico* (1994) and *Cruising Paradise* (1996), which contains 40 short stories exploring the themes of solitude and loss of angry and anguished men.

Tony Kushner (1956—)

Born in Manhattan in July of 1956, Tony Kushner grew up in Lake Charles, Louisiana, where his family moved after inheriting a lumber business. He earned a bachelor's degree from Columbia University and later did postgraduate work at New York University. In the early 1980s, he founded a theater group and began writing and producing plays. In the early 1990s, he scored a monster hit with the epic, seven-hour, two-part, Broadway blockbuster *Angels in America: A Gay Fantasia on National Themes*, which earned for Kushner a Pulitzer Prize and many other awards. This groundbreaking play focuses on three households in turmoil: a gay couple, one of whom has AIDS; a Morman man coming to terms with his sexuality; and the infamous lawyer Roy Cohn, a historical figure who died of AIDS in 1986, denying his homosexuality all the way to his deathbed. The play, originally written in 1990, is a sweeping indictment of the Reagan era that follows the story of Prior, an AIDS sufferer caught between an ex-boyfriend and a married lover with a mentally disabled wife.

Kushner has also written *A Bright Room Called Day* (1985) and *Slavs*! (1994) as well as several adaptations including Goethe's *Stella*, Brecht's *The Good Person of Setzuan*, Corneille's *The Illusion*, and S. Ansky's *The Dybbuk*. Kushner's other plays include *Home Body/Kabul*, an eerily prescient play written pre-9/11 that links the modern worlds of London and New York to the fanatical politics of the Taliban, and the forthcoming *Caroline or Change*, a work set in Civil Rights-era Louisiana. He is also the author of the recently published call to arms, *Save Your Democratic Citizen Soul! Rants, Screeds and Other Public Utterances for Midnight in the Republic*, a book targeted at young activists.

Kushner's work has been produced at the Mark Taper Forum, the New York Shakespeare Festival, New York Theatre Workshop, Hartford Stage Company, Berkeley Repertory Theatre and the Los Angeles Theatre Center as well as theatres in over 30 countries across the globe. He is the recipient of a 1990 Whiting Foundation Writers Award and playwriting and directing fellowships from the New York Foundation for the Arts, the New York State Council on the Arts and the National Endowment for the Arts. Mr. Kushner is currently an adjunct faculty member of New York University's Dramatic Writing program.

Glossary of Literary Terms

allegory	a story (etc.) in which the characters and events represent good and bad qualities; *adj.* allegorical
antagonist	the adversary of the protagonist
aphorism	a concise saying that illustrates or defines a general principle or statement
assonance	imperfect rhyme in which the stressed vowels correspond
ballad	short story told in the form of a poem
black humor	being funny about cruelty, unpleasant or dangerous people or situations
blank verse	poetry (*verse*) without rhymes
canto	one of the main divisions of a long poem
classicism	a form of literary criticism that emphasized the classic qualities of form, reason, restraint and is based on distinguished artistic models of the past
comedy	a play, often amusing, always with a happy ending
consonance	a rhyme scheme in which only consonant sounds correspond
couplet	two lines (of poetry) together, ending in the same sound (*rhyme*)

criticism	judging the good and bad points of writing etc.
drama	serious (writing of) plays for the theatre
epic	long poem telling a story of great deeds or history
episode	one event or happening in a book
epithet	a word or short phrase that aptly describes and labels a person or thing
essay	short piece of writing on a single subject
existentialism	a philosophy that asserts that existence precedes essence (It denies the existence of absolute principles or objective meanings and insists that man is responsible for himself and acts with free will. The themes of existential literary work stress man's isolation, his lonelines, his sense of futility, and the irrevocability of his actions.)
expressionism	a literary school that stresses the internal, or subjective, rather than the eternal, or objective, reality
fable	a short tale that relates a moral
flat character	usually, a minor character in a story who is a stereotype or a ploy for the major characters
fiction	stories from a writer's imagination
folklore	stories (*folk tales*), customs and beliefs of a racial or national group
foot	the basic unit of rhythm in verse
free verse	poetry in a form that does not follow, any regular pattern
genre	particular kind of writing

Gothic novel eighteenth-century story of mystery and horror set in lonely places

hedonism a philosophical belief that pleasure constitutes man's highest good

humanism a philosophical doctrine that emphasizes the perfectibility of man (It originated during the Renaissance period and held that man was not inherently wicked or fallen from grace, as the medieval view had proclaimed, but that human values are good and should be the center of the study of man himself.)

hyperbole the use of extravagance for emphasis

iambic pentameter a metrical line consisting of five iambic feet

image a picture brought into the mind by words

irony a use of words which are clearly opposite to one's meaning, often laughingly (as when one says "What beautiful weather!" on a day of very bad weather)(*adj. ironic*, *ironical*)

journalism writing for newspapers

legend old story passed down (possibly based on actual events)

light verse poetry without a (very) serious purpose

lyric(al) expressing strong feelings, usually in song-like form melodrama play which is very exciting but unlike real life

metaphor a way of expressing one idea by naming another thing to which it can be compared (not using "as" or "like"), example: the roses in her cheeks

metaphysical poetrytury — a term applied to the poetry of a group of 17th cenpoetry poets who emphasized the intellectual and psychological aspects of emotion and religion

meter — arrangement of words in regular groups of strong and weak beats in poetry

metonymy — the use of one name for something closely associated with it

montage — a piece of writing made from separate parts combined together

motif — a narrative element that serves as the basis for an expanded poem, tale, or song

Muckraker — one who collects the shameful facts (*muck* = dirt) about people

myth — ancient story with magic elements (*mythical*: of or like myths; *mythology*: collection of myths)

narrator — person who tells (*narrates*) the story (*narrative*)

naturalism — the idea that art and literature should present the world and people just as science shows they really are

neoclassical — new (*neo-*) or modern style based on ancient Greek or Roman writing

new criticism — the name given to a modem school of literary critics concerned primarily with analyzing a work of art as an object in and of itself

novel — book-length story (*novelist*: a writer of novels

	novelette: a work of prose fiction that is longer then the short story and shorter than the novel
pamphlet	short book of a few pages
pantheism	a religious-philosophic attitude that asserts that God exists in everything (finite objects) and finite objects are what make up the glory of God, so that nature reveals God and, at the same time, is God
parable	a short, fictional story that teaches a moral lesson, usually in the form of an extended metaphor or allegory
paradox	a statement that seemingly is self-contradictory or silly, but in fact is true
parallelism	a structural arrangement of syntactical, similar words, phrases, or clauses so that one element is developed equally with another
pastoral verse	poems dealing with rustic life, particularly that of shepherds, and elegies in which a death is lamented in pastoral imagery
personality	character
phase	stage of development
playwright	writer of plays for the theatre
plot	set of events that make up a story
preface	the writer's introduction to his or her book
prologue	an introduction to a play or literary work that prepares the reader for what is to follow
prose	written language which is not-poetry
protagonist	the chief character in a narrative play or story
prototype	the original or first form of a thing or species

quatrain	group of lines of poetry in fixed form
realism	showing things as they really are
review	critical essay on new books etc. (*to review*: to consider or reconsider the value of)
rhythm	expected beat or movement
romanticism	admiring wild beauty and feelings (emotions), not thought
satire	making the reader laugh at the faults in people or ideas
sentimental	expressing (too much of) tender feelings (*sentimentalism*: too great an interest in such feelings)
sermon	religious address
sonnet	14-line poem with definite rhyme patterns
stanza	one of the groups of lines that make up a poem
stock character	a conventional, stereotyped character
stream-of-consciousness novel	the type of psychological novel in which the consciousness of one or more characters is explored
surrealism	a modern literary and artistic movement that attempts to depict objects "beyond reality" (surreal)—man's imagination, dreams, visions, etc.
symbol	something that represents an idea (*adj. symbolic*; *symbolism*: a use in literature of symbols to represent real things, feelings etc.)
synecdoche	the use of a part of one thing to signify the whole
tall tale	an early American folk tale recounting the fan-

	tastically exaggerated heroic exploits of frontier heroes
theme	subject (of a piece of writing etc.)
tragedy	serious play for the theatre, with a sad ending; any very sad event
transcendentalist	one who believes that man can find truth through his own feelings
trilogy	a group of three related works in subject but each complete in itself, esp. three novels or operas
trochaic	using trochees, feet of two sounds, stressed followed by unstressed
utopia	a perfect country (as described in Sir Thomas More's *Utopia*)

References

Abrams, M. H. *A Glossary of literary Terms*. Harcourt Brace College Publishers, London, 1999.

Battle, Kemp P. *Great American Folklore*. Doubleday & Company, Inc. , New York, 1986.

Bilton, Alan. *An Introduction to Contemporary American Fiction*. Edinburgh university press, Edinburgh, 2002.

Booz, Elisabeth B. *A Brief Introduction to Modern American Literature*. Shanghai Foreign Language Education Press, Shanghai, 1982.

Brooks, Cleanth R. *American Literature: The Makers and the Making*. St. Martin's Press, New York, 1973.

Budd, Louis J. *On Mark Twain*. Duke University Press, Durham, 1987.

Burtis, Mary Elizabeth. *Recent American Literature*. Littlefield Adams & Co. Paterson, 1961.

Christol, Héléne. *An Introduction to American Novel*. Longman France, Paris, 1991.

Conn, Peter. *Literature in American*. Cambridge University Press, Cambridge, 1989.

Daker, Philip. *Colonization to the American Renaissance*. Gale Research Press, Gale, 1988.

Daker, Philip. *Realism, Naturalism, and Local Color*. Gale Research Inc. , Gale, 1988.

Day, S. Martin. *History of American Literature*. Doubleday & Company, Inc. , New York, 1971.

Elkins, William R. *Literary Reflections*. McGraw-Hill Book Company, New York, 1976.

Elliot, Emory. *Columbia Literary History of the United States*. Columbia University Press, Columbia, 1988.

Hart, D. James. *The Oxford Companion to American Literature*. Oxford University Press, New York, 1965.

Hilfer, Tony. *American Fiction Since* 1940. Longman Group UK Limited, Harlow, 1992.

Holman, Hugh C. *A Handbook to Literature*. Macmillan Publishing Company, New York, 1986.

Howe, Irving. *The Literature of America*. McGraw-Hill Book Company, New York, 1971.

Kaplan, Charles, & Anderson, William. *Criticism Major Statements*. St. Martin's Press, New York, 1991.

Kennedy, J. Gerald. *Poe, Death, and the Life of Writing*. Yale University Press, New Haven and London, 1987.

Landy, Alice S. *The Heath Introduction to Literature*. D. C. Heath and Company, Lexington, Massachusetts, 1980.

Litz, A. Walton. *Modern American Fiction*. Oxford University Press, Oxford, 1967.

Lodge, David. 20th *Century Literary Criticism*. Longman, London & New York, 1983.

Ludwig, M. Richard & Nault, Clifford A. Jr. *Annals of American Literature*. Oxford University Press, Oxford, 1986.

O'connor, William Van. *Modern American Novelists*. WashingtonSquare Press, New York, 1973.

Matterson, Stephen. *The Essential Glossary of American Liter-*

ature. Oxford University Press, London, 2003.

McMichael George. *Anthology of American Literature*. New York, 1974.

Ousby Lan. Fifty *American Novels*. Heinemann, London, 1979.

Parler, T. H. *Approach to Modern Poetry*. Pergamon Press, Oxford, 1966.

Perkins, George. *The American Tradition in Literature*. Random House, New York, 1985.

Prescott, S. Peter. *American Short Stories*. W. W. Norton & Company, New York, 1988.

Przybylowicz, Donna. *Esire and Repression*. The University of Alabama Press, Alabama, 1986.

Rubinstein, Annette T. *American Literature: Root and Flower*. Foreign Language Teaching and Research Press, Beijing, 1988.

Salzman, Jack. *The Cambridge Handbook of American Literature*. Cambridge University Press, Cambridge, 1990.

Sanders, Nelson, & Rosenthal. *Chief Modern Poets of Britain and America*. Macmillan Publishing Co., Inc., New York, 1970.

Shaw, Harry, *Concise Dictionary of Literary Terms*. McGraw-Hill Book Company, New York, 1976.

Warren, French. *20th Century American Literature*. Macmillan Press Limited, London, 1980.

Weimer, R. David. *Modern American Classics*. Random House, New York, 1969.

Wellek, Rene. *A History of Modern Criticism*. Yale University Press, New Haven and London, 1986.

Wiener, S. Harvey. *American Literature*. McCormick-Mathers Publishing Company, Kansas, 1966.

Wimsatt, William K. Jr. & Brooks, Cleanth. *Literary Criticism*. Routledge & Kegan Paul, London, 1970.

Wu Weiren. *History and Anthology of American Literature*. Foreign Language Teaching and Research Press, Beijing, 1990.

Zhang Yaoxin. *A Survey of American Literature*. Nankai University Press, Tianjin, 1993.